North Wales
Intended as a Guide to Future Tourists

'We have no hesitation in declaring that these Volumes deserve to be ranked among the best performances of the kind; nor will any one hereafter act wisely, who should visit North Wales without making them his companion'
British Critic, 1800

'after reading Bingley's description & that ascending Dinas Bran might be a substitute to those who had not ascended Snowdon I was disappointed we could not see near to the end of the Vale of Llangollen'
Anne Lister, diary entry, 1822

'When Bingley set out deliberately to guide the "tourist" he did not realise that his work would have the result of turning the Welsh mountains in the 1850s and 60s into symbols of patriotism for the Welsh themselves. He could never have foreseen, either, the astonishing growth of mountain tourism in north Wales during the twentieth century, and which continues unabated into our own time'
Professor Prys Morgan, 2022

MONICA KENDALL was born in north London. She gained a Master's degree at St Hugh's College, Oxford University in Arabic and went into publishing, sorting through the slush pile at Victor Gollancz in Covent Garden. After a second Master's degree at University College London in Medieval Studies (with distinction) she focused on editing academic books, latterly for Oxford University Press. There were also periods as an actress, as a Hansard reporter in the House of Lords and as an editor of books on archaeology. She has travelled widely, from the hippy trail to Nepal through Afghanistan in the 1970s, to walking the Owain Glyndŵr trail and her son's Snowdonia Way in the 2010s. She climbed Snowdon up the Pyg Track and moved to North Wales, inspired by her great-great-grandfather's *hiraeth am Gymru*. Her article on her ancestor Rev. Evan Jenkins is in the *Dictionary of Welsh Biography*. He went to Ystrad Meurig school in Cardiganshire in the early 1800s under John Williams, who was taught by Edward Richard. Richard also taught the scholar and poet Evan Evans (Ieuan Fardd) and corresponded with Lewis Morris, whose children were at the school.

Other books by Monica Kendall:

https://monicakendall.com

John Webster, *The Duchess of Malfi*, ed. (2004)
Miss Cavell Was Shot: The Diaries of Amy Hodson, 1914–1920, ed. (2015)
Lies and the Brontës: The Quest for the Jenkins Family (2021)

NORTH WALES

Intended as a Guide to Future Tourists

WILLIAM BINGLEY
(1804)

Abridged and edited by Monica Kendall

Foreword by Jim Perrin

SilverWood

Published in 2023 by SilverWood Books

SilverWood Books Ltd
14 Small Street, Bristol, BS1 1DE, United Kingdom
www.silverwoodbooks.co.uk

© Monica Eve Kendall 2023

The right of Monica Eve Kendall to be identified as the author of this work
has been asserted in accordance with the Copyright, Designs
and Patents Act 1988 Sections 77 and 78.

All rights reserved. No part of this publication may be reproduced,
stored in a retrieval system, or transmitted in any form or by any means,
electronic, mechanical, photocopying, recording or otherwise,
without prior permission of the copyright holder.

ISBN 978-1-80042-243-8 (paperback)

British Library Cataloguing in Publication Data

A CIP catalogue record for this book is
available from the British Library

To my splendid father
who loved Tryfan and first took me to Aber Falls
Peter Helmut Kendall né Kowalski
1924–2017

> I admire –
> None more admires – the painter's magic skill,
> Who shews me that which I shall never see,
> Conveys a distant country into mine,
> And throws Italian light on English walls:
> But imitative strokes can do no more
> Than please the eye – sweet Nature ev'ry sense.
>
> – William Cowper, *The Task* (1785)

> Proud of her ancient Race, Britannia shows
> Where, in her Wales, another Eden glows,
> And all her Sons, to Truth, and Honor dear,
> Prove they deserve the Paradise they share.
>
> – Anna Seward, 'Verses on Wrexham' (1796)

Contents

List of illustrations	*ix*
Foreword by Jim Perrin	*xi*
Preface and acknowledgements	*xvi*
Note on the text	*xviii*

Introduction	1
Biographical sketch	1
The route: transport, accommodation and advice	15
Previous 'tours'	18
Taste: the Picturesque, the Sublime and poetry	23
Industry and improvement	30
Religion, superstition and the Welsh	34
Flora and fauna: botanical treats and pickled puffins	38
Notes	39
Bingley's guide to Welsh pronunciation	43
Bingley's map of North Wales	44–7

North Wales	49
Preface to the 1800 edition	51
Preface to the 1804 edition	56
1 Chester to Flint	59
2 Flint to Holywell	64
3 Holywell to St. Asaph	73
4 Excursion from St. Asaph to Rhyddlan	77
5 Excursion from St. Asaph to Denbigh	81
6 St. Asaph to Conwy	85
7 Excursion from Conwy round the Creiddin	92
8 Excursion from Conwy to Caer Rhun	97
9 Conwy to Bangor	100
10 Excursion from Bangor Ferry through Nant Frangon	115
11 Bangor to Caernarvon	123
12 Excursion from Caernarvon to Llanberis	131
13 Excursion from Caernarvon to the Summit of Snowdon	146
14 Excursion from Llanberis to the Summit of Snowdon and Ascent of Snowdon from Llyn Cwellyn	153

15	Excursion from Caernarvon to the Summits of the Mountains Glyder and Trivaen	157
16	Excursion from Caernarvon into Anglesea	163
17	Voyage from Caernarvon to Priestholme	187
18	Excursion from Caernarvon to Beddgelert; and thence to Pont Aberglasllyn, into Nant Hwynan, and to the Summit of Snowdon	193
19	Excursion from Caernarvon to the Nantlle Pools	214
20	Excursion from Caernarvon into the Promontory of Llŷn	218
21	Voyage from Caernarvon to the Isle of Bardsey, and thence to Pwllheli	225
22	Excursion from Caernarvon, by Capel Curig, to Llanrwst; and from thence, by the Vale of Ffestiniog, and Tanybwlch again to Caernarvon	236
23	Caernarvon, through Beddgelert, to Harlech	249
24	Excursion from Harlech to Cwm Bychan	255
25	Harlech to Barmouth	259
26	Barmouth to Dolgelle	262
27	Excursion from Dolgelle to Kemmer Abbey and the Waterfalls	265
28	Dolgelle to Machynlleth	269
29	Machynlleth to Llanydloes	275
30	Llanydloes to Newtown	278
31	Newtown to Montgomery	282
32	Montgomery to Welsh Pool	288
33	Welsh Pool to Oswestry	290
34	Oswestry to Ruabon	298
35	Excursion from Ruabon to Bangor Iscoed	302
36	Ruabon to Wrexham	307
37	Excursion from Wrexham to Holt	311
38	Wrexham to Mold	314
39	Mold to Ruthin	319
40	Ruthin to Llangollen	323
41	Llangollen to Corwen	332
42	Corwen to Bala	336
43	Bala to Shrewsbury	346

Explanatory notes	*353*
Further reading	*382*
Index by Bingley	*385*
Index of people	*394*

List of illustrations

Cover

Dolbadarn Castle, by J. M. W. Turner, oil on panel (1799–1800). By permission of Llyfrgell Cymru / National Library of Wales. Bingley may have seen Turner sketching the castle.

Map of North Wales showing Bingley's route (1804). By permission of Llyfrgell Cymru / National Library of Wales   44–7

Pont y Pair, near Betws-y-Coed, drawing by Edward Dayes, engraved by John Roffe, frontispiece to vol. I (1804). By permission of Llyfrgell Cymru / National Library of Wales   48

Title-page to Bingley's vol. I (1804). By permission of Llyfrgell Cymru / National Library of Wales   49

1. *Peter Bailey Williams* (c.1790)   2
2. *James Edward Smith*, by William Ridley, with 'The Pursuit of the Ship containing the Linnaean Collection' (1800). © National Portrait Gallery, London   5
3. The first road built by Richard Pennant, Lord Penrhyn, along Nant Ffrancon (2016). Photo: Monica Kendall   16
4. *The Last Bard*, engraving after Philippe de Loutherbourg, in Edward Jones, *Musical and Poetical Relicks of the Welsh Bards* (1784, 1794)   29
5. *Paris Mines in the Year 1800*, engraving by I. Havell after Edward Pugh, in Pugh, *Cambria Depicta: A Tour through North Wales, Illustrated with Picturesque Views*, published by Evan Williams (1816)   31
6. *Richard Pennant, Lord Penrhyn*, by Henry Thomson, pointing at a map showing his new road (c.1800). Photo credit: National Trust, 'Penrhyn Castle', Image No. 205065   32
7. *Conwy Castle*, drawing by William Bingley, engraved by Samuel Alken (1800)   88
8. *Nant Mill cascade*, drawing by William Bingley, engraved by Samuel Alken (1800)   195
9. *Harlech Castle*, drawing by William Bingley, engraved by Samuel Alken (1800)   252
10. *Valle Crucis Abbey*, drawing by William Bingley, engraved by Samuel Alken (1800)   325
11. *Pistyll Rhaiadr*, drawing by Edward Dayes, engraved by James Sargant Storer (1804)   348

Figs 1, 4–5, 7–11 are by permission of Llyfrgell Cymru / National Library of Wales.

Foreword by Jim Perrin

In the summer of 1798 the coach from Chester conveyed along the 'great Irish road' and deposited at Caernarfon a plump, affable, endlessly curious and physically indefatigable Cambridge student by the name of William Bingley. At 24 he was quite old to be counted thus, and was soon to be ordained. He was an enthusiastic botanist and a reversion in many ways to the earlier exploratory and scientific tradition of Johnson, Ray and Lhuyd. In his *North Wales; including its Scenery, Antiquities, Customs, and some sketches of its Natural History; Delineated from Two Excursions*[1] of 1804, which included an appendix termed by its author a 'Flora Cambrica', he provides an indispensable pedestrian record of Regency Wales. Along with those of Pennant and George Borrow, his is the most abidingly useful, sympathetic, and certainly the most impressively energetic of all the classic early Welsh tours. It's also one that's quite different in tone to those of his peers. Bingley is gossipy, light-hearted. His itinerary has been out of print for far too long, and we can be grateful to Monica Kendall for remedying that omission so well. Over little short of two centuries it has only been available in library collections, or rarely and expensively from second-hand booksellers with good Welsh topographical sections. Yet Bingley belongs in a select peer group that includes Pennant, Borrow, Condry. He's one of the most companionable of writers on the Welsh landscape, and certainly one of the most enterprising. With a companion, the Reverend Peter Bailey Williams, Vicar of Llanrug, he recorded what is generally accepted as the first significant ascent in the annals of Welsh rock-climbing:

---

[1] William Bingley, *North Wales ... Delineated from Two Excursions* (Longman and Rees, 1804) – an earlier edition had appeared in 1800, but the greatly expanded one of 1804, written after a second tour undertaken in the summer of 1801, is much the more useful and comprehensive.

Foreword

> In my first journey I went from [Dolbadarn] castle to Cwm Brwynog, but, instead of following the above route, I wandered to *Clogwyn du'r Arddu*, to search that rock for some plants which Lhwyd and Ray have described as growing there. The Reverend Mr. Williams accompanied me, and he started the wild idea of attempting to climb up the precipice.

These two botanists were seeking to ascend a line right up the centre of the most architectonic, impressive and forbidding cliff-face in Wales. They were, to use the lexis of the early Romantics, venturing into the darkest heart of horrible sublimity. What they were tackling is known as the Eastern Terrace of Clogwyn Du'r Arddu ('the black cliff of Satan' is one possible translation of the name). Nowadays the feature is most usually employed as a descent route by climbers who have completed routes of extreme severity pioneered on the steepest faces hereabouts in modern times. But that should not be allowed to detract from the scale and atmosphere of this magnificent cliff-feature. A presiding principle of the cliff's unique geological structure, it slants up at a steep diagonal from right to left below the huge, leaning mass of the slabby West Buttress. Its lower part runs above a subsidiary 200-foot buttress known as the Middle Rock, with steep ground beneath it (Bingley is scarcely exaggerated in his estimates – looked at from above, from the steepness of the slope beneath this would certainly seem to be 300 feet or more). It is, I think, likely that they traversed in along ledges below the great central wall of the East Buttress to join the terrace above and left of the Middle Rock, by way of an open gully with steep, wet, rock-steps of loose material where Bingley's grabbing for a tuft of rushes to save himself from falling most likely took place. The rushes still grow there, the gully taking all the drainage from the terrace above, and its rock is notably fissile. All of this lends authenticity to Bingley's account. At the top of the gully, they arrived at a slabby, ascending ramp where 'the increasing size of the masses of rock above' must have become very obvious as the ramp narrowed and slipped beneath a huge, bulging buttress now known to climbers as 'The Boulder'. A belt of smooth slabs comes in here from the left and abuts this, making a short rock-pitch, smooth but not steep, twelve or fifteen feet high at most, which cuts off access to the easier scree-slopes of the basin-like upper terrace (down which, incidentally, it is most likely that Thomas Johnson in 1639 descended some distance to secure specimens that still grow across the base-rich rocks at the back of the terrace). We take up Bingley's narrative again at this point:

It happened fortunately that the steep immediately above us was the only one that presented any material danger. Mr. Williams having on a pair of strong shoes with nails in them, which would hold their footing better than mine, requested to make the first attempt, and after some difficulty he succeeded. We had along with us a small basket to contain our provisions, and hold the roots of such plants as we wished to transfer to his garden; this he carried behind him by means of a leathern belt fastened round his waist. When, therefore, he had fixed himself securely to a part of the rock, he took off his belt, and holding firmly by one end, gave the other to me: I laid hold, and, with a little aid from the stones, fairly pulled myself up by it.

This is all admirably sensible, uninflated and sharply observed – yet it was a remarkable departure from precedent. People at this time just did not choose to ascend places of such grim and terrifying aspect. Its claim to being the first *recorded* rock-climb in Eryri seems to me a reasonable one, given the appearance of the line of ascent, the sections where it is necessary to use both hands and feet, the exposure at several points above sheer and considerable drops, problems of route-finding, and the ground through which it leads. It's a feat that grows in stature the more consideration you give to it, and it certainly makes me want to know more about the two characters who achieved it. Bingley's companion, Peter Bailey Williams, was a Carmarthenshire man who, after study at Edward Lhuyd's old and neglectful Oxford college of Jesus, had been Rector of Llanberis and Llanrug since 1792 and was to remain thus until his death in 1836. His prowess among the mountains can be judged from Bingley's account of him in his hob-nailed boots casually making the fearsomely exposed leap between the two natural obelisks known as Adam and Eve that form the summit of Tryfan, rockiest of Welsh hills. (I once had to make this leap several times to and fro in tandem with a cameraman who was filming it for an HTV series some years ago – it may only be a long stride but it's not to be taken lightly.) A prickly conservative and an anti-Jacobin, Williams became through the long years of his ministry under Snowdon an eminent botanist in correspondence with many leading figures of his day, a very worthy local educator and historian, and a crucial figure in the Welsh cultural life in the region – one of a group of clergyman-scholars who did much to preserve the poetry, traditions and purity of Welsh language in the region around Snowdon, and who were known as 'yr offeiriaid llengar' – the learned priests.

It is well worth noting Bingley's other explorations on Snowdon after the Eastern Terrace ascent. On the same day, he and Williams went on to seek for plants on the gully-seamed and decaying cliff of Clogwyn y Garnedd right under Yr Wyddfa itself, where there 'is at all times some difficulty in searching ... but when the rocks are rendered slippery from heavy mists or rain, this becomes, from the insecurity of the footing, greatly increased'. Bingley then made a vigorous circuit of the botanical sites across the north-eastern face of the mountain around Cwm Glas and Cwm Glas Mawr, crossing into them by way of Bwlch Coch, between Crib Goch and Crib y Ddysgl, and finishing his day by descending an arduous route the embarking on which he came much to regret directly down to Nant Peris through the broken crags of Clogwyn Llwyd. Nothing daunted, the next day he rode round to Bron y Fedw Uchaf, hired a guide, stayed on horseback as far as Llyn Ffynnon-y-gwas, and from there traversed the ridge above the cliff he and Williams had ascended the previous day and climbed back towards the summit. As with Pennant twenty-odd years before, a clear morning was not to last, and gave way to rough weather. There was a brief spat between Bingley and his guide when the latter urged the necessity of immediate descent, but the severity of the storm that arrived, the battering by huge hailstones and the soaking they received on the way down convinced Bingley and they retreated to sit, with clothes steaming, round Bron y Fedw's hospitable fire.

As his next objective, and in order to complete his plan of ascending Snowdon by all three main routes in use at the time, the indomitably energetic Bingley next repaired to Beddgelert. There he secured the services of a waiter, William Lloyd, at what is now the Royal Goat and was then the Beddgelert Hotel to guide him up Snowdon. Lloyd was also the village schoolmaster, though like a present-day Cuban doctor he found tourist tips in the brief season more lucrative than his pedagogic stipend. The route by which Lloyd led Bingley to the summit starts from the prominent glacial erratic of Pitt's Head near to Ffridd Uchaf farmhouse two miles north of Beddgelert village. It joins the path from Rhyd Ddu at Pen ar Lon, where a quarry-path clattery with slates leads off east to Bwlch Cwm Llan, and climbs by way of Rhos Boeth on to the ridge above the cliffs of Llechog, before curving round east and north to reach the foot of Clawdd Coch, Snowdon's south-east ridge, at Bwlch Main. This was probably the most spectacular section on all the Snowdon paths in common use at the time, and Bingley describes it thus:

> This narrow pass, not more than ten or twelve feet across, and two or three hundred yards in length, was so steep, that the eye reached on each side, down the whole extent of the mountain ... in some parts of it, if a person held a large stone in each hand, and let them both fall at once, each might roll above a quarter of a mile, and thus, when they stopped, they might be more than half a mile asunder.[2]

It might sound dramatic, but this is a reasonably accurate appraisal, from a time when other writers delighted in fearful exaggerations, of the actual topography. The ridge above Bwlch Main *is* quite narrow and exposed in places, with considerable drops at either hand into Cwm Clogwyn and Cwm Tregalan, and only the petty-minded would quibble with Bingley's description. He himself was obviously not affrighted by it, and when, in order to spice up his narrative, he presents us with horrifying tales stemming no doubt from Lloyd of how people who had been guided across it in the hours of darkness, on returning in daylight would often baulk entirely or resort to crawling on hands and knees, there is the hint of a suspicion that the ascensionist of Clogwyn Du'r Arddu is mildly entertaining himself at the expense of other people's credulity. That seems to fit with his character too. If he is making amiable fun of his readers, he's also giving them the fun and entertainment his more serious peers often fail to provide. Here he is, then, in all his benign guises, to entertain you once again. May you enjoy him!

Jim Perrin, Llandrindod Wells, 2023

---

[2] Ibid. pp. 385–6.

Preface and acknowledgements

Jim Perrin's book on Snowdon first got me curious about Yorkshire-born William Bingley, who died prematurely in 1823. After moving to North Wales in 2018, I researched for two years at Aberystwyth University as I delved into guidebooks to Wales in the Romantic and early Victorian periods, which no one had studied before. Captivated by Bingley, I escaped to work on this edition.

Apart from a few mountaineering aficionados, Bingley has been neglected, unlike the later travel writer George Borrow. Bingley is quoted often, but seldom with any biographical information. I wanted to remedy that, and to prepare a portable book, which he might have appreciated, to guide people through the North Wales of over two hundred years ago, before the Snowdon Mountain Railway, before the bridge over the Menai Strait, before Bethesda, Porthmadog or the seaside towns on the north coast existed, before the river Vyrnwy became a reservoir, before deep time was discovered, as the antiquarians, botanists and geologists hunted for new knowledge. And before the rampaging motorcars, off-roaders and motorbikes. The accommodation is better now, with no bed fleas; the climbing and walking equipment vastly improved, and we now understand the impact of glaciers, but I envy him. I also hope, through his text and my notes, to convey a sense of North Wales at this period and of those who loved it, whether Welsh or English.

My particular thanks go to Jim Perrin, for promptly and kindly agreeing to write the Foreword. I am also honoured that Emeritus Professor Prys Morgan read the text and was so positive about it and Bingley.

Also to my son Alexander. I wouldn't be living in North Wales if it wasn't for him, and he kindly checked Bingley's routes up Snowdon for me.

Preface and acknowledgements

I thank the following people for kindly answering my emails and/or giving help: Judith Curthoys, Archivist, Christ Church, Oxford; Nicolas Davalan, Welsh *tiwtor extraordinaire*; Michael Freeman, Early Tourists in Wales, https://sublimewales.wordpress.com; Dr Timothy Heimlich; Joanna Hulin, Emma Farmer and other staff at The Museum of English Rural Life and University of Reading Special Collections; Emeritus Professor Dafydd Johnston; Adam Jones, Archives, Hampshire Record Office, Winchester; Glyn Roberts, Lead Custodian, Caernarfon Castle; Dr Carl Thompson; and Marcia Watson.

I am also grateful to the staff at Bangor University Archives and the Borthwick Institute for Archives, York; and to the Linnean Society of London for digitalizing their archives and making them freely available online.

I thank the University of South Wales for inviting me to read a paper on poetry in Romantic-period Welsh guides in 2021; and the University of Wales Trinity Saint David, Lampeter, where I delivered a paper on Lord Penrhyn, William Bingley et al. at their conference on 'Wales and the World' in 2022.

Diolch o galon to my Welsh–Yorkshire neighbours, Jan and Mark, for being there and coming round with the odd gorgeous snack, and to the fantastic team at SilverWood, above all Helen Hart.

Thanks to the following for providing images: to the staff at Llyfrgell Cymru / National Library of Wales, Aberystwyth, in particular Emyr Evans, for supplying scans from Bingley's books, the images of Peter Bailey Williams, of *The Last Bard* and *Paris Mines*, and the cover image of Turner's *Dolbadarn Castle*; to the National Portrait Gallery, London for the engraving of James Edward Smith; and to the National Trust for the painting of Richard Pennant, Lord Penrhyn.

Dolgellau, Gwynedd, North Wales / Gogledd Cymru
March 2023

Note on the text

Yorkshire-born William Bingley's first tour of North Wales, as an undergraduate at Cambridge, was in 1798. It resulted in his first book, *A Tour Round North Wales Performed during the Summer of 1798 ... intended as a guide to future Tourists*. It was published in 1800 by the London Welsh publisher Evan Williams and the Cambridge publisher John Deighton. However, this modern edition uses William Bingley's second, expanded and often rephrased and restructured edition of 1804, which had the title *North Wales; including its scenery, antiquities, customs, and some sketches of its natural history; delineated from two excursions through all the interesting parts of that country, during the summers of 1798 and 1801*. I have given my modern edition the title of *North Wales: Intended as a Guide to Future Tourists*. It is likely that his publishers in 1804, Thomas Norton Longman and South Walian Owen Rees, advised that it should be a different title from his first edition, perhaps to avoid copyright issues. But Bingley clearly wanted to emphasize that his was a useful guidebook and not a rambling or 'novelistic' travel account, since his one-volume edition of 1814 used that subtitle again.

In 1839, sixteen years after Bingley's death, his son used the subtitle 'Intended as a Guide to Tourists' for the fourth and final edition, called *Excursions in North Wales* (published by Longman, Orme, and Co.). It was updated, restructured and sadly depersonalized, apart from retaining Bingley's chapter on Tryfan and the Glyders (which his son didn't climb) and his ascent up Penmaen Mawr. Bingley's personal narrative, which gives his account such value, has almost entirely disappeared to leave an impressively thorough but impersonal (modern) guidebook. His climb up Clogwyn Du'r Arddu with Peter Williams was deleted and may not have been climbed again for a hundred years. But it is touching that his son, who had lost his father at the age of nine, set off to discover Wales also in his mid-twenties. I have a sneaking

Note on the text

suspicion that William Richard Bingley *did* climb Tryfan but pretended he didn't so that his father's voice could remain somewhere in the book.

In order to reduce Bingley's two volumes of 1804 into one portable guide, I have omitted his chapters on the English towns of Chester (where he started his tour) and Shrewsbury (where he ended it), and deleted his history of the Welsh Marches. However, I have retained his section on Oswestry in Shropshire. This means that my chapter numbers are different from Bingley's, especially as he started again from I in his Volume II.

I have also left out the chapters at the end of his Volume II on manners and customs of the Welsh, on the Welsh language, and on the Welsh bards and music, which includes several Welsh airs. I have omitted his catalogue of *Flora Cambrica*, a few smaller lists of plants within the text, a list of cromlechs and marine creatures, several overlong pages on copper, puffins and bow-staves (although displaying Bingley's wide interests), and most of his lengthy 'Memoranda' and 'Anecdotes'. These are biographical sketches, mainly of Welshmen, such as the travel writer and naturalist Thomas Pennant, the hero Owain Glyndŵr, the poets Dafydd ap Gwilym and Goronwy Owen, and the sixth-century bard Taliesin, who is muddled with the later, legendary Taliesin. I have also deleted some of his sections on castles that he labels 'History of'. This is either because it is difficult to visit because it is on private land (Hawarden Castle), or because modern guidebooks are available on site (Edward I's castles of Rhuddlan, Conwy, Caernarfon, Beaumaris and Harlech; and those of Denbigh, Powis and Chirk). Some of Bingley's histories are trimmed when they get a bit dull (Cathedrals of St Asaph and Bangor).

Also gone is his lengthy section on 'Caernarvonshire Feuds', the pedigree of the Wynne family and Arthur Aikin's description of the Devil's Bridge in Ceredigion, which Bingley didn't visit: he resolved to stay in North Wales. Minor deletions include his summary descriptions at the start of each chapter, which was a standard feature at the time, and his footnotes, which contain his sources or sometimes erudite digressions. However, I have placed some in my 'Explanatory notes'. At one point after his description of 'Jumpers', new Anglican clergyman Bingley writes at length about the 'problem' with Methodists in Britain, who were then

Note on the text

still part of the established church: that has been omitted. I mark the place of deleted sections with ***. (His full text is available in facsimile reprints and online.)

I have replaced double inverted commas with single, but I have incorporated his few errata, retained his italics, spellings (unless there is an obvious mistake) and punctuation – other than replacing em dashes with spaced en dashes and deleting the full stop after the names of kings, as in 'Edward I.'. I have not corrected Bingley's apparent errors in copying poetry.

Occasionally I have divided his text into shorter paragraphs. I have put the modern spelling of a place (following Ordnance Survey) in the Index by Bingley, and I have added an Index of people largely not mentioned by him.

I have included the Preface to his first edition of 1800 because it is much more frank and interesting than his later polished Preface of 1804, which follows it here.

In selecting what to explain or expand in my 'Explanatory notes' at the end of this book, other than adding a few of Bingley's footnotes there, I have echoed the words in the Preface to his 1800 edition, that his rule was 'to put down for the information of others, every thing that I wished to have known when I was myself making the tour' – and thus everything I wished to have known as I began researching his life and studying his guidebook.

Introduction

Biographical sketch

Young botanist William Bingley is tentatively climbing up a rock face with his partner:

> It happened fortunately that the steep immediately above us was the only one that presented any material danger. Mr. Williams having on a pair of strong shoes with nails in them, which would hold their footing better than mine, requested to make the first attempt, and after some difficulty he succeeded. … When, therefore, he had fixed himself securely to a part of the rock, he took off his belt, and holding firmly by one end, gave the other to me: I laid hold, and, with a little aid from the stones, fairly pulled myself up by it. After this we got on pretty well, and in about an hour and a quarter from the commencement of our labour, found ourselves on the brow of this dreadful precipice, and in possession of all the plants we expected to find. (p. 147)

Bingley's climb on Snowdon in 1798, as he searched for rare plants with his new friend, the Welsh Anglican clergyman Peter Bailey Williams, is well known to mountaineers, who celebrate this first recorded climb of Clogwyn Du'r Arddu on the north flank of Snowdon. It is described by the mountain photographer Nick Livesey as 'an unnerving, architectonic wall of rock'.[1] The outdoor writer and rock climber Jim Perrin is enthusiastic about Bingley:

> he provided one of the indispensable records in the history of our mountain [Snowdon]. It is also, along with that of Pennant and the later one by George Borrow, one of the most abidingly useful, sympathetic, and certainly the most impressively energetic of all the classic Welsh tours.[2]

Three years later, the pair also made the first recorded climb of the iconic mountain Tryfan. Although Bingley probably acquired letters of introduction to Welsh botanists, his meeting with Peter Williams, ten years older and a graduate of Jesus College, Oxford, seems to have been a lucky chance, as he wrote to Dr James Edward Smith:

> I however was fortunate enough in meeting with a Clergyman, a Gentleman of much information who resides at a small village betwixt Caernarvon and Llanberris[,] this Gentleman tho not much of a Botanist himself, was so civil as to attend me in most of my Excursions amongst the mountains, and his knowledge of every place we went to I found of the greatest use.[3]

Fig. 1. *Rev. Peter Bailey Williams* (c.1790).

Introduction

Bingley's book, *A Tour round North Wales Performed during the Summer of 1798 ... intended as a guide to future tourists*, was first published in two volumes octavo in 1800.[4] After another trip to Wales in 1801 he published a second edition in 1804 with a slightly different title and with a different publisher. My book uses that edition, which is expanded, slightly restructured, often rephrased and with a pruning of references.

Bingley's book is quoted from often, whether by botanists, experts on slate quarries or copper mines, writers on pedestrian travel and the Picturesque in the Romantic period, on Welsh roads or Methodism, but sometimes with errors, sometimes oddly hostile, and seldom with any biographical context, except to call him 'Rev.', as if he was a stereotypical Oxford- or Cambridge-educated clergyman of a certain age. Yet his first tour of North Wales in 1798 was made when he was an undergraduate, in his mid-twenties, about to start his final terms of examinations. It is also treated as just another 'tour', but it is a guidebook, which involved much more work and research than a description of one's holidays or one's geological findings. It is the first guidebook to North Wales, which then comprised the historic counties of Flint, Denbigh, Caernarvon, Anglesey, Merioneth and Montgomery.

Bingley was baptized on 7 June 1774 in the parish church in Doncaster, South Yorkshire. His father, also William (1732–86), was a saddler and kept an establishment near the Angel Inn in Frenchgate, Doncaster, and was a member of the corporation. An advertisement for the sale of the stock after his father's death in October 1786 (seven years after Bingley's mother died) notes that 'for these Sixty Years last past has had a regular and profitable Trade'.[5] Although his father died when he was twelve, Bingley would have remembered the busy activity, the apprentices, and the strong leather and tanning smells in his father's workshop, even after the guardianship of a well-off uncle who was a 'gentleman',[6] and his years at Doncaster Grammar School, legal training, which he disliked, and then Cambridge. He matriculated at Peterhouse (also called St Peter's College) in 1795 at the mature age of twenty-one: most students started at eighteen. I have found no image of Bingley, but there is a pen portrait of him wearing spectacles and carrying a rucksack as he walked through a Welsh hamlet on his own (p. 64), and although he had a head for heights and was fit enough to climb Snowdon many times, he was terrified by the daredevil antics of his new friend. He was enthusiastically fond of music (his words in a letter to Dr Smith) and an indefatigable researcher, annoyed with fabrications and shoddy scholarship. Why Wales?

Bingley notes that 'Long before I had conceived the thought of making a tour through Wales, I had been told much in praise of the ride from Bangor to Caernarvon' (p. 123). Cambridge University is the key to both Bingley's interest in botany and his decision to tour Wales. Joseph Hucks's *A Pedestrian Tour through North Wales* (accompanied by Samuel Taylor Coleridge) was published in the autumn of 1795, when Bingley started his first term, and was on sale at three Cambridge booksellers, including his later publisher Deighton. Although Bingley does not mention this short epistolary tour, he would surely have been aware of it. Hucks was born in North Yorkshire and claimed Welsh ancestors. After gaining his BA at St Catharine's College he was elected a Fellow in 1795, dying five years later. Perhaps he was an acquaintance – he was just two years older than Bingley; if not, there would have been several students who had visited Wales while the Continent was closed to them during the French Wars and who talked about their travels.

We can date Bingley's decision to travel to Wales precisely to the spring of 1798. On 12 March, Bingley wrote his first letter, from Peterhouse, to Dr James Edward Smith (1759–1828), founder and president of the Linnean Society of London. The renowned botanist, then in his late thirties, had retired from London to his home town of Norwich, taking with him the entire Linnaean collection that he had acquired after the death of the celebrated Carl Linnaeus. Dr Smith's replies to Bingley in a correspondence lasting from 1798 to 1817 do not survive, but he obviously provided encouragement and advice for the younger man and helped him in his election as Fellow of the Linnean Society of London in 1799.

In Bingley's first letter he mentions that he is acquainted with Dr Smith's brother in Wakefield and that he has discovered some rare plants in Yorkshire and Cambridge. He adds that 'I shall be in Yorkshire again the next summer ... or in Cumberland where I shall most probably reside great part of the summer', that is, the summer of 1798. He adds that he is 'yet not very learned in Botany having begun only about two years ago'. We do not know what Dr Smith replied two weeks later (the methodical Smith noted the date of his reply on the letters he received), but it was obviously a letter of encouragement. Bingley replied on 26 June. Dr Smith's letter had enthused him; one might say that the reply changed the direction of his life:

Fig. 2. *Dr James Edward Smith*, by William Ridley, with 'The Pursuit of the Ship containing the Linnaean Collection' (1800).

my expedition into the north has been put an end to by an event entirely unexpected. – Your extremely obliging letter in answer to mine has I believe been the cause of my being much more attentive to the study of Botany than I sho^d otherwise have been – and I now find it a study that so much accords with my own taste that I am about to set off <u>alone</u> on <u>Tuesday or Wednesday next</u>, tho an entire stranger to the country, to Caernarvon, in or near which place it is my Intention to reside 'till the latter end of October. – I am particularly induced to do this now as I may not perhaps for some years have a summer so completely at my command as the present.

That is, Bingley hopes to be ordained by next summer and has no idea what duties his curacy, if he can find one, will involve. He then asks Dr Smith how to procure and preserve lichens:

as that is a branch of the study I have very little attended to yet, but which I shall have in Wales the best opportunity possible of cultivating. –

I also wish to ask you as I have had but little time upon my hands since the resolution was formed of going into Wales of procuring many Letters of Introduction to families there; whether you suppose my calling upon and asking Information of any Botanist I may hear of in my Journey wo^d be looked upon as an improper Intrusion, or whether it generally happens that Botanists like to part with Information to Strangers. – I mention this particularly, as I sho^d like to call on Mr. Griffith of Garn near Denbigh whose knowledge of Welsh Botany might be of great use to me, but of whom I have not yet been able to meet with an acquaintance. –

These are questions which I undoubtedly sho^d not have troubled you with had it not been for the encouragement you gave me by so obligingly answering those I asked of you before.

Bingley set out for Wales, on a coach to Chester, possibly on 4 July. Unable to go to Yorkshire or the Lake District in the summer vacation, his mind had turned to botanizing in Wales, and during the spring he presumably thoroughly read Thomas Pennant's *A Tour in Wales* (the second edition of 1784) as well as books on botany that he lists in his appendix on rare Welsh plants. Many were available in the Cambridge University Library thanks to two Professors of Botany: John Martyn (1699–1768) and his son Thomas, who was an early proponent of Linnaean views. A specialist library for botany was founded based on the books presented by John Martyn in 1765, who had also written a book for undergraduates attending his lectures, largely based on the work of the seventeenth-century botanist John Ray.[7] His son, Thomas Martyn (1735–1825), lectured annually for most years from 1762, but in the midsummer term of 1796 (at the end of Bingley's first year) he gave his last course because of his state of health and, his *Memoirs* recall, 'in truth, there was so little zeal for the study in the University, that it was scarcely possible to form a Class!' The 'elegant science' of botany at that time 'met with little favour at Cambridge'.[8]

It is likely that Bingley was one of the few at those last lectures, and it probably explains why, when Thomas Martyn departed, Bingley's initial enthusiasm began to wane until reignited by Dr Smith. What may also be of relevance to Bingley's trip to Wales was that Thomas Martyn had written guidebooks to Italy and Switzerland after a tour of the Continent in the late 1770s. The beginning of Martyn's Preface in *The Gentleman's Guide in his Tour through Italy* is so apposite that it seems likely that Bingley glanced at it: 'It will naturally be asked, why we have more travels into Italy, when we have had too many already? The answer I shall make to the question is this: Most of our travelling books have been evidently written with a view to be read by the fire side at home, rather than to accompany a man abroad; to amuse the indolent, rather than to instruct the active. And of those few whose aim it has been to inform the traveller on the spot, their works have been either very partial and defective, or else too voluminous to be carried about with tolerable convenience.'[9] Contrast this with Bingley's Preface to his first edition:

> To Mr. Pennant's accurate and learned work on this country, I have in various instances, as will be hereafter seen, been much indebted.
>
> It may indeed, and not improperly, be asked, what need there was for any other account, when one so accurate as the above was already extant? In answer to this, I have to observe, that the present is more commodious for carriage; the former being in two volumes quarto, is extremely heavy and inconvenient for persons to carry along with them. (p. 53)

What Bingley disregarded was Martyn's next phrase recommending his '*one* volume of a portable size'. However portable Bingley's octavo volume is, two are less so, unless the travelling botanist went by carriage rather than Bingley's recommendation of walking, or sent luggage on ahead. But perhaps that is how the idea of a botanical guidebook came into Bingley's mind, rather than yet another travel account with its digressions and anecdotes (and novelistic fabrications). But also a guidebook fits the character that we can glean of a young man who enjoyed the discipline of the Linnaean system of identifying and categorizing plants. His later writing career also shows that he had a talent for synthesizing a lot of information and making it clear. His forte was not for entertaining, egotistical ramblings, though his delight in the landscape and light of Wales (if not always the rain) led to many lyrical passages. But he also knew about cattle hides: he observes some cattle bellowing in agony who are being attacked by gadflies; he catches one of the flies and explains (surely from his childhood experience) that hides with 'bot-holes' are esteemed by dealers as the best (p. 217).

What also may have influenced him was Thomas West's popular *A Guide to the Lakes* (first published 1778), or rather his antipathy to it. Bingley writes in the Preface to his first (1800) edition:

> In the description of the country, I have invariably endeavoured to let the scenes form themselves, and to paint nature simply as I found her. The tourist, who is desirous of forming reflections for himself, will, I doubt not, at all events thank me for my intentions in this respect. I shall ever remember, in a tour that I made some years ago to the Lakes of the north of England, how much I found myself deceived and disappointed, by the turgid and high-flown descriptions which fill almost every page of Mr. West's Guide through that country, a book, in other respects certainly of merit. This circumstance alone led me to a determination, if possible, to avoid that error. When the scenery exceeds the description, it will be viewed with pleasure; but when it falls short of it, no one but a traveller can tell the disappointment that is felt. (p. 53)

This is similar to Wordsworth, some years later, explaining why he had not written a 'tour' (that is, a guidebook) to the Lake District describing the 'different scenes in the most favourable order': 'if well executed, it would lessen the pleasure of the Traveller by anticipation, and, if the contrary, it would mislead him'.[10]

In his book, Scottish-born Thomas West (a Catholic priest; c.1720–79) told his readers where to station themselves for the best view for their sketchpads. For example at Windermere: 'STATION I. Near the isthmus of the ferry point, observe two small oak trees ... ascend to the top of the nearest rock ... The trees are of singular use in answering the purposes of fore-ground.'[11] What Bingley may also have found irritating were the

Introduction

orders: 'Set out for KESWICK, seventeen miles good road. Having seen the wonders of KESWICK, and the environs, depart for AMBLESIDE,' which infantilizes the traveller, if not the tourist.[12] West also recommends the Claude glass, which he calls the 'landscape mirror' (a convex glass for sketching purposes in which you viewed the landscape by turning your back to it).[13] Despite being an amateur artist, Bingley never mentions it; it was probably regarded as passé twenty years later.

Bingley sums up in his Preface what he wanted to achieve in his guidebook:

> in these volumes, I have, as far as lay in my power, made it my rule to put down for the information of others, every thing that I wished to have known when I was myself making the tour. This, allowing for all the differences of taste and opinion, seemed to me the best criterion by which to judge of the wishes of the public; in what manner I have succeeded, the volumes themselves must shew. (p. 52)

In autumn 1798, Bingley prepared hard for his exams and worked on his guidebook. The publishers for his first edition were Evan Williams of the Strand, London, and John Deighton in Cambridge. Deighton (c.1747–1828) was a long-established bookseller and publisher, and a heavyweight at the university. Deighton's premises were central to student life on Trinity Street, which Bingley would know well: class lists were even posted there. One can conjecture that on Bingley's return to Cambridge from Wales in October 1798, with his journal written over three months, that he first approached Deighton with his plan for a book. Most publishers combined to share the financial risk and the expense, especially when a book involved illustrations and music, as Bingley's did, so perhaps Deighton then contacted Williams and they bought the copyright from Bingley.

Evan Williams (1749–1835) was one of the notable sons of a Calvinistic Methodist exhorter and blacksmith in Ceredigion. He was educated at the renowned Ystrad Meurig school, six miles north of Tregaron, under its founder Edward Richard, who also taught the bard Ieuan Fardd (Rev. Evan Evans). His elder brother, Rev. John Williams, 'Yr Hen Syr', another former pupil, took over the school after Richard's death in 1777.[14] Evan Williams went to London and became a member of the Gwyneddigion Society, establishing a bookselling business in the Strand at first with his brother Thomas, publishing many important books of Welsh interest. It was presumably Evan Williams who contracted the printers since they were both London based and he knew that they had Welsh type for letters, especially those with long vowel signs. It was normal to have a different printer to typeset a different volume in order to save time and avoid piracy, which didn't always work. (One Welsh printer pirated several of Bingley's chapters, including his footnotes and Itinerary, and published them without mentioning Bingley's name.[15]) The Errata lists at the end of each volume show the errors that Bingley found, including those in some classes of plants that were numbered wrongly. The Preface, however, is much more interesting than his second, shorter version, with its criticism of fellow authors, why it was difficult to carry around Thomas Pennant's two hefty quarto volumes (which were out of print anyway), his first thoughts on why he wrote the guidebook and who for, and his acknowledgement 'for the kind and liberal assistance of several gentlemen in Wales', whom he names (p. 55).

After graduating from Cambridge in January 1799, Bingley was ordained deacon to the West Yorkshire parish of Mirfield in October at the low stipend of £25 a year. Earlier in September, writing from Wakefield to the archbishop's secretary, he persuaded him to accept that small sum for a curate because of the ill health of the vicar (bishops were on the look out for fraudulent offers of curacies), and the letter reads as if Bingley had failed once already. The other documents in his deacon's bundle suggest that he had a fraught time, right up to a few days before the ordination, waiting for confirmation that the curacy was acceptable. The length of time from graduating, and the miserly amount, suggest that he had no family or college connections to ease him into a curacy and that he grabbed at Mirfield, nine miles to the west of Wakefield, as the first step into the church, as many desperate graduates had to do.[16] (A man had to be offered a job before being ordained, called a 'title for orders'.) He was a member of his college until the end of 1800, probably coming down to Cambridge to use the libraries.

On 14 June 1800 he wrote to Dr Smith about the dedication in his book:

> I have taken a liberty which may not altogether be justifiable in dedicating to you the two volumes of my Tour through North Wales. – I fear they are scarcely worth your acceptance. – I have in a measure trodden close in the steps of Mr. Pennant, but I think I have given to the future tourist a book that may aid him in his visits to this country.

Bingley returned to Wales in 1801 and approached a new publisher about a second edition. This derived from dissatisfaction with his first, possibly lack of interest from Deighton and Williams, combined with an unexpected free summer (he had probably resigned his curacy at Mirfield) and a desire to see more of North Wales with Peter Williams, with more walks and climbs. A further motivation could have been the favourable mention in the *Critical Review*. Having picked on several 'little inelegancies', such as his (Yorkshire?) use of 'lay' for 'lie', the reviewer wrote: 'So great is the general merit of this work, however, that we doubt not a second edition will in process of time be called for.'[17] On 10 May 1801 Bingley wrote to Dr Smith:

> In the course of two months I intend again to visit North Wales previously to the publication of a 2^d Edition of the Tour. Here I mean to pick up as much Zoological information as possible; and I think I can obtain some assistance from Mr. Davies of Aber, who greatly aided Mr. Pennant. I wish I could by any means get a sight into the papers that this Gentleman has left behind him, both for the Tour, and the Synopsis.

Bingley set off for Wales not long after this letter, as there is a testimonial from Reverends Peter Williams and William Griffith, Vicar of Caernarfon, in Bingley's priest ordination bundle stating that Bingley was in Wales from May to September 1801. Later that year, on 30 December, Bingley was working on a natural history book in London, and he remarked to Dr Smith:

> I hope a second Edition of the Welsh Tour will prove a much more respectable work than the first. I have been in the country four months this Summer, and have collected sufficient of new matter to allow an omission of all the most dry details of history; and to suffer it to be somewhat more closely printed.

Bingley moved to Hampshire in 1802 or early 1803, appointed curate to Christchurch on the south coast, for the slightly better sum of £60 per annum. On 16 February 1803, he wrote to the Bishop of Winchester, Brownlow North, asking to be excused from the examination for priest ordination (he offered to write a sermon instead): 'I am at present in the middle of the second volume of a new edition of my Tour in North Wales, which if not finished before the first of April will throw me out of the receipt of about £300 for upwards of two years.' That is a good amount from selling the copyright of his new edition to Longman and Rees. What is also significant is that Bingley states that 'my own small fortune and the emoluments of my curacy are such as in the present times not even to afford me a subsistence'. There had been enough money to pay full fees (that is, as a pensioner) at Cambridge University, but whatever money Bingley received now from his deceased father's legacy was 'small': he would have to live largely on the sales of his books during a period of wartime inflation.

On 3 December 1803, he wrote to Dr Smith from Christchurch:

> In the course of six weeks I shall have in the world what I hope will prove a tolerably perfect account of <u>North Wales</u>. In the year 1801 I made a second journey of four months into this romantic country, and was very fortunate in collecting matter for the present work. This will be in two volumes, and will contain all the essential materials of the <u>Tour</u>. I shall of course take the liberty to place your name at its head.
>
> <u>Animal Biography</u> has been sufficiently fortunate to run through one edition already.

Bingley also mentions the war for the first time: 'I hope you are in no consternation respecting your collections and library becoming the property of the Corsican's banditti. ... – I am upon the coast but have no fears nor any other unpleasant sensations respecting them. They are yet in their own harbours, when they venture out, if they ever do venture out, it will be to inevitable destruction.' Two weeks later, Bingley was ordained priest in Winchester, though that had been another fraught process as he couldn't get acceptable testimonials and it was delayed from the spring. However, five months later, in May 1804, the new version of his North Wales guidebook was published by Longman and Rees.

The house of Longman was founded in 1724 and became the longest-lasting family dynasty of publishers in the UK into the mid-twentieth century. In 1797, Thomas Norton Longman succeeded his father, and was to remain head of the firm for over forty years. His first partner was a Welshman, Owen Rees, who arrived from bookselling experience in Bristol, where the Longman family had originally resided. In 1799 they bought the business of Joseph Cottle of Bristol, who had published Wordsworth and Coleridge's *Lyrical Ballads* the year before, which was of 'nil' monetary value having sold few copies and the copyright was returned to Wordsworth. Wordsworth published his second edition with Longman in 1800, having removed Coleridge's poems, but that was not financially successful either.[18]

Owen Rees (1770–1837) 'brought Welsh vitality, coming from a good mixture of Presbyterian and Unitarian stock in Carmarthenshire'.[19] A more recent view agrees: 'The partnership between Thomas III and Rees ... has rightly been identified as a landmark event in the history of the publishing house.'[20] It was probably Rees who wanted Bingley's book, and not coincidental that in 1804 he also published Benjamin Heath Malkin's topographical and antiquarian volume, in expensive quarto, *The Scenery, Antiquities, and Biography of South Wales*, perhaps as a companion piece to Bingley's.

Much of the early Longman archives was lost in a fire in 1861, and more was destroyed during the Blitz in 1940, but a few draft letters from Longman survive from 1813 when Bingley's next (third) edition, condensed to one volume, was discussed along with one of his other books. The most obvious change in Bingley's 1804 edition for Longman had been that to the title, especially the deletion of 'intended as a guide'. This may have been for copyright reasons – to make it appear as a different book. But Bingley perhaps was not happy with that. Whatever he wrote to Longman, the reply on 15 May 1813 (whether drafted by Rees is not known) was: 'We will thank you to inform us with the terms on which you would be disposed to agree with us for a reduction of your "Tour in North Wales" into one Volume agreeable to your letter of Oct. 24 last to be called a Guide through North Wales or some such Title.'[21]

There are fewer illustrations in the 1804 edition and none of Bingley's sketches were used. It is a more professional production; there are more words to a page since the excessive leading has been reduced. Some of the unnecessary appendices have disappeared. The running heads are now more useful, giving the route for each chapter, for example: 'Flint to Holywell' on both verso and recto, or 'Excursion from' on a verso and 'Caernarvon into Anglesea' on the recto. Even more helpful to the tourist on the road are the subheadings, centralized in caps, such as: WATERFALLS OF BEN GLOG ... Y TRIVAEN. This may well be thanks to the one printer for both volumes. Design was left to the discretion of the printer, who knew the Longman house style, but Bingley might have offered suggestions.

Meanwhile he had been writing other books. At the end of volume II of his 1800 edition is an advertisement for *A General History of Music* in three volumes octavo. Bingley also mentions it in a letter to Dr Smith on 3 August 1800, but I have found no trace of it. It might have eventually been published in 1814 by a different publisher as *Musical Biography*. However, his first publisher, Evan Williams, did publish Bingley's *Sixty of the Most Admired Welsh Airs collected principally during his excursions into Wales* in 1803, the same year that Richard Phillips published Bingley's popular *Animal Biography*, in three volumes, which was in its seventh edition in 1829 and translated into German. The first edition sold out within a year, as Bingley told Dr Smith on 3 December.

In February that year, Bingley reported that he had been asked to write a county history of Hampshire by the MP for Christchurch, the wealthy, Scottish-born George Rose, a close ally of William Pitt, who opposed ending the slave trade. Bingley prepared a voluminous questionnaire which shows how thorough and methodical he was, and his notes broke new ground in their concern for the working lives of ordinary people, but the history was never completed, because of a worsening relationship with Rose.[22] However, it reinforces the impression of the hard work Bingley put into his guidebook to Wales and also highlights his wide sympathies.

Bingley produced works for various publishers. In 1805 appeared an outlier, three volumes of *Correspondence between Frances, Countess of Hartford (Afterwards Duchess of Somerset,) and Henrietta Louisa, Countess of Pomfret, between the years 1738 and 1741*. It is probable that his publisher Richard Phillips paid him to research and write the 'Prefatory Memoirs' and notes (Bingley's name doesn't appear). This was followed by Bingley's usual territory of *Memoirs of British Quadrupeds* in 1809, *Animated Nature*, for the use of schools (and delicate females), in 1814, *Useful Knowledge: or, a familiar and explanatory account of the various productions of nature, mineral, vegetable, and animal* in 1816, and *A Practical Introduction to Botany* in 1817.

From 1818 there appeared a series of *Biographical Conversations* on British characters, eminent voyagers and travellers 'for the use of young persons', and a year later he began his series on travel writers, also for 'young persons', starting with *Travels in Africa, from modern writers*. These were not anthologies; instead Bingley followed the practice of summarizing, editing and making comments, a style established around the 1750s.[23] This may have originally been to avoid copyright infringement, and of course the cost of paying the original authors, but they took a lot of work. In them Bingley displays the mainspring of his life: a desire to educate. They were popular and thus could potentially be lucrative.

In 1822 came *The Economy of a Christian Life*, which is a compilation of maxims from the Bible under headings such as 'Benevolence and

Introduction

Charity'. His last work was published posthumously in 1824, intended for young persons, *Biography of Celebrated Roman Characters*, which contains a memoir by his editor. The early twentieth-century historian of Bingley's college, Peterhouse, remarks that the alumni in the second half of the eighteenth century were unimpressive – merely reputable schoolmasters or a respectable parochial divine and a variety of minor poets – but Bingley does get a mention: he 'established a considerable reputation as a popular writer on Natural History', though the historian was more impressed by the naturalist John Hogg, who was 'moved to higher flights' and whose brother 'was an intimate associate of P. B. Shelley'.[24] I detect a Cambridge sniffiness about writing popular books.

In his late thirties, on 25 June 1812, Bingley married a wealthy widow, Susanna Morgan née Iliff, in Bloomsbury, London; she was a few years older. They had one son, William Richard Bingley, born in July 1813 in Christchurch, who became a barrister. Susanna's stepson, Sir Thomas Morgan, married in January 1812 the famous Irish novelist now known as Lady Morgan. The Bingleys moved from Hampshire to London in 1816 when Bingley was offered his first living, the incumbency of Fitzroy Chapel in what became Maple Street, near Tottenham Court Road; it was destroyed by air raids in 1945. Bingley died at his home at 2 Charlotte Street, Bloomsbury, on 11 March 1823 at the age of about forty-eight.[25]

The route: transport, accommodation and advice

In 1798, Bingley travelled, largely on foot, anticlockwise around North Wales, from Chester via Caernarfon (his main residence) to Shrewsbury:

> [Travelling on foot], notwithstanding all the objections that have been made against it, will, I am confident, upon the whole, be found the most useful, if health and strength are not wanting. To a naturalist, it is evidently so, since, by this means, he is enabled to examine the country as he goes along, and when he sees occasion, he can also strike out of the road, amongst the mountains or morasses, in a manner completely independent of all those obstacles that inevitably attend the bringing of carriages or horses. (p. 51)

Bingley states that people can use carriages only along the great roads, but post chaises can be hired at inns in a town; however, 'owing to the great numbers who now make this fashionable tour, delays are at times unavoidably occasioned by these being all employed' (p. 52). Bingley recommends buying John Evans's smaller map of North Wales, which costs eighteen shillings, from his publisher Evan Williams in the Strand. But in his 1804 edition, Longman and Rees provided a fold-out map showing Bingley's route. Among the mountains, a small pocket compass is necessary, he advises, as is learning to pronounce and understand Welsh names, using his book.

Over twenty years before the building of bridges over the Afon Conwy and the Menai Strait, Bingley describes the ferries, and vents his anger about the ferrymen across the Conwy, describing 'the wilful delays, and the gross and bare-faced impositions of the ferry-men'. He lists the ferries to Anglesey and the various disasters, the latest being in 1785, which perhaps some travellers preferred not to know: 'all the passengers perished except one', he says, and he recounts the grisly details given to him by that one survivor (pp. 85, 164).

There are new roads since his first visit, much appreciated by Bingley, who noted in his first edition his painful struggle along what he called one of the most tiresome footpaths that even North Wales could boast –

Fig. 3. The road built by Richard Pennant, Lord Penrhyn, in the late eighteenth century along Nant Ffrancon, looking south towards Glyder Fawr and Tryfan. The quarry lies to the right (2016).

from Pont Aberglaslyn, south of Beddgelert, alongside Traeth Mawr to Penmorfa, over the rocks. He delights in the new road that has been built from Beddgelert to Tanybwlch: it is 'exceedingly good' (p. 249), and he admires the road built by Richard Pennant, the first Baron Penrhyn of Louth, along the west side of Nant Ffrancon, from Capel Curig to Bangor Ferry on the Menai Strait. Penrhyn's later turnpike road is on the eastern side of the Afon Ogwen, now below Thomas Telford's road and the modern A5. (See below for more on Lord Penrhyn.)

For his second edition, Bingley visited new places, such as Great Orme's Head (Pen-y-Gogarth), the headland that towers above the Victorian seaside resort of Llandudno, but which was then a site of 'desolation and barrenness' (p. 95). Perhaps the 'intimate friend' who was with him was Peter Williams, who clambered down the rock high above the sea for some yards, to Bingley's horror, and who also enticed Bingley up Tryfan, where Williams jumped from what are now called Adam and Eve (Siôn a Siân), the two upright stones 'twelve or fourteen feet in height' on the summit (pp. 92, 160).

The climb of Tryfan, Bingley says, was part of a long day: 'I rose early one morning to undertake, in company with my friend Williams, by far the most laborious walk that I ever ventured upon in the course of one day. This was no less than to ascend the summits of three mountains, Trivaen, Glyder Bach, and Glyder Vawr, none of them very much inferior to Snowdon' (p. 157). Bingley had climbed Glyder Fawr on his previous visit and it is hard to be certain, from his use of his earlier description, whether he did climb it again. But I don't believe that Bingley would fabricate; I am convinced that his 'fourteen hour's [sic] ramble, among crags and precipices' was genuine and that after only a fifteen-minute rest he strolled to the end of the lake that evening and breathed in the sunset, described in a glorious passage of nature writing (p. 161).

Bingley's solo adventures (without Williams) seem to have been on the cutter he hired to sail from Caernarfon to Priestholm (Ynys Seiriol / Puffin Island), where he dragged a few puffins out of their burrows (in a scientific experiment), and for several days in the opposite direction, in a failed attempt to land on Bardsey Island (Ynys Enlli). Also new on his tour in 1801 was visiting Caer Rhûn, the site of Roman Conovium south of Conwy, climbing Penmaen Mawr, walking to Nantlle Pools (one of the lakes no longer exists because of quarrying), and a longer visit to Lord Penrhyn's estate and his quarry near Bangor.

Although Bingley assumes that you have a human guide with you, he strives to be meticulous about guiding; sometimes he can be seen as an ancestor of the authors of Cicerone books as he guides the tourist up Snowdon from Dolbadarn Castle, parallel to the Llanberis Path and the modern route of the Snowdon Mountain Railway. He provides descriptions of three other routes up Snowdon for the tourist, including the Rhyd Ddu Path from Beddgelert (descending down to Nantgwynant), when Bingley was accompanied by a female climber. He describes 'a tremendous ridge of rock, called Clawdd Coch ... The lady who accompanied us, to my great surprize, passed this ridge without the least apparent signs of fear or trepidation,' in contrast to the tales he had heard of terrified men, one of whom had crawled over it (p. 211). His adventurous rock climb, while searching for plants, with Peter Williams up Clogwyn Du'r Arddu, is not a recommended route for the tourist up Snowdon in his Index.

He gives advice about climbing Snowdon: 'Welsh tourists have been much in the habit of over-rating the difficulties that are to be encountered in the journey to the summit of this mountain,' but people don't need a stick with a spike or nails on their boots. They may be useful but all you need is 'good health and spirits' and to take sufficient time, leaving at dawn, and stopping to rest frequently to admire the view. It is also necessary to take 'eatables' (pp. 151–2).

Bingley's comments about accommodation are often entertaining for the modern reader, if not for the proprietor, but they were certainly useful to forewarn tourists. I can only speculate that the wide circulation of Bingley's guidebook brought about changes; indeed the vast improvement in accommodation at Beddgelert could well have been inspired by his anecdote about the fleas he suffered from in 1798. When Bingley returned three years later he found a new hotel was being built (now known as the Royal Goat Hotel). Bingley gives praise when an inn was comfortable or the hosts were civil, hospitable or kind, such as Mrs Lewis in Barmouth, with whom the 'Ladies of Llangollen' had stayed in 1797.

Previous 'tours'

When Bingley first went to Wales in 1798 the only book on Wales he knew were the two substantial quartos of *A Tour in Wales* by Thomas Pennant, whom he admired but occasionally corrected. In homage to Pennant he quoted or referenced him around 130 times, at one point preferring Pennant's account of climbing Snowdon to his own. But this changed in his next edition and many of the references and quotations were cut. Bingley had found his own voice. Pennant (1726–98), squire of

Downing in Flintshire, was a pioneering Welsh antiquarian, naturalist and travel writer. In 1769 and 1772 he toured Scotland, later publishing his discoveries. His first edition of *A Tour in Wales* appeared in 1778, followed by *A Journey to Snowdon* (1781) and *A Continuation of the Journey* (1783).[26] These were combined in the 1784 edition that Bingley read.

In his 1800 edition, Bingley is particularly scathing about the errors (and, he suggests, fabrications) of one tour writer, Rev. Richard Warner, who wrote *A Walk through Wales, in August 1797* (1798). Bingley deleted his criticisms in his next edition, apart from a passing mention in his Preface. Perhaps he may have seen that Warner's walking tour had reached a fourth edition in 1801 after only three years (if the publisher is to be believed) and that Warner had published *A Second Walk through Wales* in 1799: it might be politic for a new author not to be so publicly critical about what seemed to be popular. Warner's confusion about the two Bangors inspired an appalled footnote by Bingley (p. 363). One can almost feel the scornful, emphatic pen strokes of Bingley's exclamation marks.

He also poured scorn on Warner's anecdote that drinking brandy on mountains can intoxicate and cause accidents: 'the writer of the account has very much mistaken the fact. By the advice of the clergyman [Peter Williams], who attended me in this and my other mountain excursions, we always took along with us a pint of brandy.' Bingley then rubs it in by saying that he had talked with the guide, William Lloyd, whom Warner had employed, who had indeed told Warner that it was dangerous to be 'intoxicated', but some brandy was useful, and the same guide later encouraged Bingley to take a bottle of rum on a climbing trip. There is an element of *schadenfreude* in detailing the errors in a competitor's book, especially since the indefatigable Bingley climbed Snowdon seven times by different routes in preparation for his guidebook, while Warner climbed it but once on 21 August 1797, walking 25 miles that day, from Beddgelert to Caernarfon.[27]

Bingley also enjoyed Warner's error about a bizarre route supposedly taken by a farmer up and down Snowdon to get to Caernarfon: 'the poor fellow,' Bingley wrote of the route Warner describes, 'in order *to avoid* a circuitous route, used to cross over the highest peak of the mountain, and go by Dolbadarn Castle', which added six miles to the road. Bingley remarks witheringly that it was 'certainly not an English method of avoiding a circuitous route'.[28]

London-born Warner (1763–1857) was for a few years William Gilpin's curate in the New Forest, keen on antiquities, and on acquiring fame and money by his writing. He moved to a curacy in Bath in 1794. He says that he conceived the idea of his Welsh walking trip (from Bath to Caernarfon and back again) on the way to Bristol to see the great Polish/Lithuanian patriot General Tadeusz Kościuszko.[29] His intention for the trip was 'to breathe the inspiring air where liberty made her last stand in these kingdoms, against the strides of Roman power'.[30] However, Warner's two-volume *Literary Recollections* of 1830 reveal him (admittedly thirty years later) as a pious, patriotic, collector of people, and thus his meeting with Kościuszko – who had tragically failed to prevent the disintegration of Poland as a nation – and praise for the 'last stand' of Wales may be less radical regarding Wales, and for the increasingly repressive situation in wartime 1798, and more a nostalgic sigh.

It has been argued that Wordsworth took some of his description of the Wye in 'Tintern Abbey' from Warner's walking account.[31] But Wordsworth saw far more of the Wye than Warner ever did. On Wordsworth's visit in 1798 with Dorothy, they rambled for about five days in the area, whereas Warner averaged a daily twenty-six miles. In Warner's *Literary Recollections* he mentions Wordsworth so briefly ('our call at the peaceful retreat of Wordsworth'), whilst giving his rambles with Coleridge a much longer entry, that it hardly gives an impression that Wordsworth was fascinated by the man or his travel account and vice versa.[32]

Bingley is also withering about the equally 'novelistic' tour of Samuel Jackson Pratt in his *Gleanings through Wales, Holland and Westphalia*, published by Longman in 1795. Pratt was a defrocked clergyman and a failed actor. He may have been a couple of times to Wales but what he writes is often fabricated, or taken from other books, such as his remark about eternal snow on Cadair Idris (at 893m, there is just occasional snow in the winter). Pratt only once mentions that the Welsh speak Welsh; he never claims to know any Welsh himself yet he has long conversations, seemingly in fluent English, with fishermen and peasants, and with a landlady at Ffestiniog, who apparently remembered Lord Lyttelton of forty years before (it seems that Pratt didn't know that Lyttelton's account was written in 1756).

The Welsh answered back: 'Cymro's' article in the *Cambrian Register* (1799) about travel writers on Wales, including Pratt and Warner, is scornfully and amusingly dismissive about 'travelling authors [who] sacrifice truth to novelty'.[33] 'Cymro' has been identified as Theophilus Jones (1759–1812), Welsh lawyer, author of *A History of the County of*

Brecknock and grandson of Theophilus Evans, who wrote a popular account of the mythical early history of Wales, *Drych y Prif Oesoedd* ('The Mirror of Past Ages'; 1716), with whom he was close. Jones remarks on Pratt: 'from the perusal of this author, I am almost persuaded that he has adopted the too fashionable mode of introducing the novelist into the company of the traveller' and 'when a writer, who seems to think himself entitled to credit, (and, in general, perhaps, not without reason) in relating his real adventures, condescends to embellish his account with fiction, however I may admire his abilities, I cannot help reprobating his practice'. He also discussed Warner's tour: 'He too has the happy knack of embellishing his tour a la Pratt.'[34] Bingley read the article and copied Jones's comments about Pratt in his first book. Yet Pratt's book went into several editions. Bingley removed his complaint about 'novelistic' in 1804, possibly because he was now also being published by Longman. But Jones's article would have made him careful not to arouse Welsh censure and to use their voices when he could.

But Bingley trusted other writers, whom he names and quotes. The earliest was the anonymous author of *Letters from Snowdon: Descriptive of a Tour through the Northern Counties of Wales* (1770), which is often oddly and mistakenly assigned to a later tour writer, Joseph Cradock (d. 1826), an amateur actor, friend of David Garrick and Oliver Goldsmith, who had an estate in Leicestershire. Cradock made a tour of Wales in 1776 and published *An Account of Some of the Most Romantic Parts of North Wales* a year later. But it is clear from the second edition of the *Letters* (also in 1777) that the anonymous author has died: his editor in the Preface writes: 'The Author of these Letters resided some years of the latter part of his life in Wales ... A few copies of these Letters were published in the Author's life-time.' Whether the 'years' in Wales is true is impossible to say. The author himself says that he sought a place of retirement, wearied with the artificial life of the city, and stayed for several months in a village near Snowdon with a clergyman 'on the eve of threescore'. There is a mystical account of their climb up Snowdon: 'As our situation was exalted above the globe, so were our ideas. And the nearer we were to the etherial regions, the more our souls seemed to partake of their purity.'[35] The letters are largely philosophical reflections with a little bit of travel. He was clearly learned: he knew the work of the naturalist and philologist Edward Lhuyd (see note to p. 146) and was particularly interested in law and history. The mystery of who he was will perhaps never be solved, but he certainly wasn't simultaneously living in retirement near Snowdon and helping Garrick with the Shakespeare jubilee in Stratford.

Another early tour writer whom Bingley mentions is Henry Penruddocke Wyndham (1736–1819), from an old county family in Wiltshire, who published his tour of the whole of Wales on horseback, from Chepstow to Monmouth, via Caernarfon, in 1775. His short, portable book, published by Thomas Evans of the Strand, was entitled *A Gentleman's Tour through Monmouthshire and Wales, in the Months of June and July, 1774*. There was an expanded, illustrated edition after a second tour (published 1781). His itinerary of 717 miles is listed in the endmatter, with asterisks for where he stayed. He was a friend of Sir Richard Colt Hoare (1758–1838), wealthy English baronet, traveller, amateur artist, art collector and patron, archaeologist and antiquarian, owner of magnificent Stourhead in Wiltshire and of a lakeside bungalow near Bala (from 1796). Hoare also translated Gerald of Wales (1806) and provided the illustrations for William Coxe's *Historical Tour of Monmouthshire* (1801). Wyndham states in his book that on his six-week tour he met no one else travelling and got only 'trifling assistance' from the Welsh; he remarks on Cadair Idris: 'I never saw an object more awfully sublime.' Annotated copies in the National Library of Wales show that people used it to plan their own tours. One could say that tourism to Wales took off in 1775.

Bingley pointedly comments that Arthur Aikin's book was the only one he could trust to describe Devil's Bridge in Ceredigion (p. 355). Natural scientist Aikin (1773–1854), also in his mid-twenties, published his *Journal of a Tour through North Wales* in 1797. He was more interested in geology but he also made botanical observations, though he failed to acquire a guide up Snowdon because it was Sunday. 'Cymro' (Theophilus Jones) was fairly impressed by his account: 'his journey was professedly, and principally, if not wholly, made with a view to improvement, or, at least, amusement in mineralogy ... he writes with considerable abilities'. And he was pleased that 'the Welsh names are more properly spelt than by most other travellers'.[36] Bingley was noticeably careful with his Welsh spellings, and usually gave Welsh place names before English translations.

The word 'guidebook' is today often used imprecisely when writing about travel books at this period. Above all there must be an author's intention to guide the reader on the ground from place to place (which implies also a route); it must be portable (smaller than a quarto); and it should offer some practical advice, such as on where to stay, what to see and how to travel around.[37] Bingley's intention is clear that his book is a guide and he compiled a detailed itinerary for the tourist (not included here). Guidebooks were published in the eighteenth century for the Grand Tourists, and domestic travel writers published their journals or letters, hoping that they might be used as a companion by the tourist, but Bingley broke new ground for Wales with his methodical approach (even if he uses the first person and sometimes digresses). Some twenty years later, the Yorkshire landowner Anne Lister borrowed his first edition from the library in Halifax for her trip to Wales in 1822, and bought George Nicholson's *The Cambrian Traveller's Guide*,[38] an alphabetical 'pocket companion' for the whole of Wales (first published in 1808) that quoted Bingley extensively along with eleven other travel writers.

Taste: the Picturesque, the Sublime and poetry

Professor Cesare de Seta remarks about the eighteenth century: 'the notion of the "picturesque" gradually emerged as a way of looking at nature informed by the hindsight of art: Claude, Poussin and Salvator Rosa provided a new framework for the appreciation of landscape'.[39] Wealthy English Grand Tourists snapped up the works of these seventeenth-century artists to decorate their mansions, though Poussin was often confused with his brother-in-law. James Thomson, in his poem 'The Castle of Indolence' (1748; see note to p. 346), managed to combine the three in just two lines: 'now rude mountains frown amid the skies; / Whate'er Lorrain [Claude] light-touched with softening hue, / Or savage Rosa dashed, or learnèd Poussin drew'. Bingley also names all three, invoking the pencil of a Claude or Salvator Rosa, which by then was a cliché. J. M. W. Turner was influenced by Claude and made one of his extended visits to North Wales in 1798; both he and Bingley visited many of the same places that summer, so Bingley may have seen the slightly younger Londoner intently sketching.

Bingley does not mention the amateur artist and theorist Rev. William Gilpin (1724–1804), one of the popularizers of the Picturesque movement, but he probably knew his writing. Gilpin wrote a series of books (not guidebooks; he called his first one a 'hasty sketch'; they consist of notes he made) describing picturesque views around Britain, beginning with *Observations on the River Wye, and Several Parts of South Wales, &c: Relative chiefly to picturesque beauty, made in the summer of the year 1770* (1782), which taught other amateurs how to make better sketches by moving a boulder or introducing a tree, while learning that smoke added grandeur and cattle variety. It was prefaced by a letter to the poet William Mason (see note to p. 113). He wrote to Sir Joshua

Reynolds in 1791 that 'picturesque' meant 'such objects, as are proper subjects for painting'. He distinguishes between the beautiful and the picturesque: the latter must have variety and roughness. He comments: 'among all the objects of art, the picturesque eye is perhaps most inquisitive after the elegant relics of ancient architecture; the ruined tower, the Gothic arch, the remains of castles, and abbeys. These are the richest legacies of art. They are consecrated by time.'[40] Above all, composition was the foundation of picturesque beauty, which nature was defective in, and had to be assisted. Only some scenes in nature were 'correctly picturesque'.[41]

Claims for his influence are sometimes exaggerated, though his books did try to teach his readers how to see nature and it gave them another reason for trips. The famous art historian Kenneth Clark (1903–83) was not impressed:

> In the works of Gilpin the craze [for the picturesque] reached its height. To the usual ecstasies he added a technical jargon of landscape painting by which his readers could impress the uninitiated; and his works were widely read. Ultimately the fashion died of its own popularity. Exquisite and awful sensations cannot be shared with the vulgar, and the appearance of *Dr. Syntax* showed that picturesque beauty was no longer a subject for the polite.[42]

The very popular *Tour of Doctor Syntax in Search of the Picturesque, a Poem* (1812) is an utterly delightful verse narrative by the extraordinary William Combe. Dr Syntax is a learned, kind and impoverished curate-schoolmaster who decides he can make a fortune by publishing a tour of the Lake District. He sets off with sketchpad and wig on his mare Grizzle: 'I'll ride and write, and sketch and print, / And thus create a real mint; / I'll prose it here, I'll verse it there, / and picturesque it everywhere.' It originated as verses attached to caricatures by Thomas Rowlandson in a magazine. Eton-educated Combe was seventy and on day release from a debtors' prison, with a wife (another man's cast-off mistress) in a madhouse, and having eloped with another woman.

Perhaps the last word on the Picturesque should go to Jane Austen in *Northanger Abbey* (written 1798–9). Henry Tilney gives a lecture on the Picturesque to Catherine Morland:

> He talked of fore-grounds, distances, and second distances – side-screens and perspectives – lights and shades; – and Catherine was so hopeful a scholar,

that when they gained the top of Beechen Cliff, she voluntarily rejected the whole city of Bath, as unworthy to make part of a landscape.

Julian Mitchell comments, gloriously, that Gilpin's rules were a godsend for tourists 'who needed help first to look in the right direction, then to know how and what to feel, and finally to talk with authority about the beauty of sheep, the picturesqueness of goats, the sublimity of bulls, and the disagreeable glare of white houses'.[43]

Bingley certainly disliked white buildings and knew the jargon of middle distance and foreground, such as when he walks to Nantlle Pools and looks back:

> The steep black rocks of Mynydd Mawr, on the left, and the craggy summits of the elegant and varied range of the Drws y Coed mountains, on the right of the vale, on whose side I stood, and appearing even still darker than usual, from the light on the mountain beyond them, formed a truly elegant middle distance. … The rude trunks, and weather-beaten limbs of the old oaks around, not only added beauty to the foreground, but varied, by their intervention, the otherwise too uniform appearance of the meadows of the vale, and of some parts of the mountains' sides.

But thankfully he doesn't mention Gilpin's 'side-screens' and he ends with an emotional response: 'This landscape is not exceeded in beauty by any in North Wales' (p. 215). He sees beyond the rigid rules, such as when he describes with awe a view from the banks of the Dee or on a moonlit stroll to Pont Aberglaslyn. He displays a response to light and colour, just as his contemporary Turner did. Bingley's description when becalmed, trying to sail around the Llŷn peninsula at sunset, evokes Turner's paintings:

> As the orb became immersed, the horizontal rays of light gleamed along the water, and tinged it with colours uncommonly brilliant. A vessel of some burthen passed, almost along the line of the horizon, before the sun at this moment. Its distance was very considerable, but its situation rendered the whole of its rigging perfectly visible to us: Almost every rope became black and distinct. (p. 228)

Bingley wanted variety in a landscape, and especially trees, thus he disliked Anglesey and moorland and was fierce, for aesthetic reasons, about trees being cut down. He had a connoisseur's eye for waterfalls, with some getting poor reviews, and he was amused about a painting at Chirk Castle of a waterfall falling into the sea, giving a splendid anecdote of how that might have come about (p. 298).

In his Preface he remarks on those who would find Wales attractive: 'The traveller of taste (in search of grand and stupendous scenery), the naturalist, and the antiquary, have all, in this romantic country, full scope for their respective pursuits' (pp. 56–7). He is appalled at modern interference in the landscape, for example at Lord Bulkeley's seat, Baron Hill on Anglesey, where he spots an ugly new *white* building. He was also not impressed by the terraced gardens at Powis Castle since they were laid out in the 'wretched French taste', but maybe worse were the modern sash windows. Lord and Lady Penrhyn's small villa, Ogwen Bank, near the quarry, doesn't get his approval either since the grounds were 'laid out in too *gay* a stile to accord with the bleakness of the surrounding mountain scenery' (p. 118).

Other than the Picturesque, the experience of the Sublime was fashionable. Bingley was possibly familiar with Edmund Burke's *A Philosophical Enquiry into the Origin of Our Ideas of the Sublime and Beautiful* (1757), in which Burke, then in his twenties, summarized:

> Whatever is fitted in any sort to excite the ideas of pain, and danger, that is to say, whatever is in any sort terrible, or is conversant about terrible objects, or operates in a manner analogous to terror, is a source of the *sublime*; that is, it is productive of the strongest emotion which the mind is capable of feeling.[44]

Bingley doesn't use the word often, except when describing a mountain view, or when he climbs down to Cwm Idwal from Glyder Fawr and looks back up at the precipice of Twll Du he has just descended: 'A more grand, or more sublime scene, the pencil even of Salvator Rosa could not have traced' (p. 159).

The modern writer Robert Macfarlane explored the 'pleasure to be found in fear' in his *Mountains of the Mind* and agreed with Burke that delight occurs when the terror 'does not press too close': 'So it would be impossible to appreciate the Sublime if one were, say, hanging by a handhold from a cliff-face. But if you came just near enough to a waterfall or a cliff-edge to suggest to your imagination the possibility of self-destruction, then you would feel a sublime rush.'[45] Bingley recognizes this edge of the Sublime. At the top of the perpendicular rocks of Great

Orme's Head, high above 'the roaring of the water' below, 'we each pulled off our boots, and crept with the utmost caution to the very verge of the precipice. A slight trip of the foot might have sent either of us headlong into a corvorant's nest, or amongst the fishermen who were employed with their boats below. The view had enough of sublimity in it' (p. 94). Like other tourists, Bingley also experienced the Sublime at the Parys copper mine (see below).

Bingley used verse and play extracts to enhance and vary his descriptions of the landscape and abbey or castle ruins, and sometimes to convey the mood his reader should feel. The origins of what has been called the 'literary guidebook' date back at least to Joseph Addison and his travel account, *Remarks on Several Parts of Italy* (1705). It elicited some criticism for his numerous quotations from classical poets but was used as a guidebook into the twentieth century. Bingley joined a party of tourists to climb Snowdon via the Rhyd Ddu Path, led by the schoolmaster/guide William Lloyd:

> The steep rock of *Clogwyn y Garnedd*, whose dreadful precipices are, some of them, above two hundred yards in perpendicular height, and the whole rock, a series of precipices, was an object which first struck one of my companions with terror, and he exclaimed, almost involuntarily:
>
> > How fearful
> > And dizzy 'tis to cast one's eyes so low!
> > The crows and choughs that wing the midway air
> > Shew scarce so gross as beetles. (p. 212)

It is not the only quotation from Shakespeare and other poets that Bingley weaves through his guidebook, but it is the only one uttered by someone in situ, and he expects his reader to recognize most of the quotations and authors, whom he seldom names. At one point he quotes six words without naming the source – 'On the gentle Severn's sedgy bank' (p. 278). He assumes his readers will know they are from Hotspur's speech in *Henry IV, part I*. But he invariably names the sixteenth-century poet Thomas Churchyard when he quotes lines from *The Worthines of Wales* at the appropriate place, which few might recognize. That someone could exclaim 'involuntarily' four lines of Shakespeare on the summit of Snowdon underlines how central poetry was to the educated classes.[46]

There is a power in poetry, and in fiction, that can make one see, and feel, a place more deeply, certainly differently. Edmund Burke wrote that 'It is one thing to make an idea clear, and another to make it *affecting* to the imagination,'[47] words which Bingley may well have read. If, in 1800, a tourist had explored the ruins of Valle Crucis, Bingley's book in hand, only the antiquarian with his tape measure might have appreciated Bingley's prosaic description of 'a grand and majestic ruin, affording some elegant specimens of the ancient gothic architecture', while the Romantic might have sighed with pleasure at hearing Anna Seward's lines that Bingley inserted into the text and that might be read aloud on the spot (p. 324).

Seward took part in domestic poetry competitions, as did the friends of William Madocks, who later transferred his energies to embankment building on the borders of Caernarfonshire and Meirionydd. He bought land at Dolmelynllyn in his twenties, and built a cottage there by the waterfalls just north of Dolgellau not long before Bingley's first tour in 1798. Madocks's biographer describes his guests sketching and fishing in the day, while in the evenings they wrote verse: 'When a contribution was completed, it was thrown into an old wooden salt-box, chosen with the intention that its contents should have the wit of Attic salt; after dinner ... these literary efforts would be read aloud as they sat around the fire.'[48] One of these compositions was sent to Bingley and incorporated in his second edition. The author was the Hon. William Robert Spencer, an Oxford friend of Madocks, one-time pupil of William Gilpin.[49] His verses were about the faithful dog Gelert killed in error by Llywelyn the Great, which was to become the most famous legend in Wales. The poem was inspired, Spencer said, by Bingley's account in his 1800 edition.

There was also poetry while walking. In April 1798, on his twentieth birthday, William Hazlitt walked along the Dee valley to Llangollen, 'repeating' lines from Coleridge's poetry (perhaps out loud; whether with book in hand or from memory he does not say).[50] Three months later, Wordsworth famously composed 'Tintern Abbey' while walking along the Wye valley with his sister Dorothy. Desperation for water on the summit of Penmaen Mawr four years earlier may have inspired some of Coleridge's *Ancient Mariner*. His companion, Joseph Hucks, carried a volume of Churchyard's poem on Wales in his pocket and thought of Milton's lines from *Paradise Lost* at the top of Cadair Idris. These tourists were Bingley's university contemporaries.

The most personal use of poetry is at an inn at Bangor Ferry. It is

Introduction

On a rock, whose haughty brow
Frowns o'er old Conway's foaming flood,
Robed in the sable garb of woe,
With haggard eyes the Poet stood;
(Loose his beard, and hoary hair
Stream'd, like a meteor, to the troubled air)
And with a Master's hand, and Prophet's fire,
Struck the deep sorrows of his lyre.

Gray's *Bard*

Fig. 4. *The Last Bard* (after Thomas Gray's poem), engraving after Philippe de Loutherbourg, frontispiece to Edward Jones, *Musical and Poetical Relicks of the Welsh Bards* (1784, 1794).

sunset, a harpist is playing, and Bingley sits by a window gazing across the water to Anglesey, 'the isle of the Druids'. As he ponders on the past in a 'pleasing melancholy' he remembers Thomas Gray's lines in 'The Bard': 'Ruin seize thee, ruthless king! ...' (p. 113). He had probably seen prints or paintings depicting Gray's ode, of which there were many, such as by Paul Sandby and the Welsh artist Thomas Jones, and he would certainly have seen the engraved frontispiece of the Bard in Edward Jones's *The Musical and Poetical Relicks of the Welsh Bards*. Bingley's reflective musings on the Welsh past, which leads into anger at the alleged massacre of the bards, show how Wales had got fiercely under his skin.

Industry and improvement

Bingley was especially curious about mines and quarries, which is not surprising in a young man from Yorkshire in the early years of the Industrial Revolution, but perhaps it is a surprise to some who think of North Wales at this period as a land of backward farmers, waterfalls and mountains, but many parts of Wales were at the forefront of technological development. On his first tour he explored the famous Parys copper mine on Anglesey. Bingley may have seen paintings of it by Julius Caesar Ibbetson and his friend John Warwick Smith of the 1780s and 1790s. Standing 'on the verge of a vast and tremendous chasm', Bingley recalls, 'excited the most sublime ideas, intermixed, however, with sensations of terror' (pp. 175–6). But, like Thomas Pennant, he was alarmed by the pollution. He also describes being at the bottom of the chasm during gunpowder blasts when he crept into a shelter and stopped his ears because of the noise, which amused the workmen. The mines were part-owned by the Welsh 'copper king', Thomas Williams, who had smelting and manufacturing works in Holywell, also described by Bingley. Metal objects for the African slave trade were made here, but although Bingley is clear that he abhors the slave trade (see below), he doesn't make the obvious link, or doesn't want to in a guidebook.

Another man with links to the slave trade was Richard Pennant, the first Baron Penrhyn of Louth (c.1737–1808), who owned plantations in Jamaica. Bingley made an excursion to see Lord Penrhyn's new port and the quarries after visiting his estate. Penrhyn's house was later partly incorporated in the neo-Norman castle built by his successor, but Bingley saw the original house as it was being altered and was largely appreciative of the elegant 'military gothic' style of the redesigned medieval manor house, the stables, the rebuilt Gothic chapel and the baths on the beach.

Fig. 5. *Paris Mines in the Year 1800*, engraving after Edward Pugh in his *Cambria Depicta: A Tour through North Wales, Illustrated with Picturesque Views* (1816).

Richard Pennant was born either on a ship between Jamaica and England, or in London, and went to Cambridge University in the 1750s. His father had Welsh ancestry (he was a distant cousin of Thomas Pennant), as did the woman he married in 1765, Ann Susanna Warburton, by whom he acquired part of the Penrhyn estate in Caernarfonshire, later buying the rest of it. Penrhyn was an ancient Welsh seat in the parish of Llandegai, near Bangor, traced back to a palace belonging to prince Rhodri Molwynog in the eighth century.[51] Ann Susanna was a descendant of the warrior Ednyfed Fychan (d. 1246), steward (*cynghellor*) to prince Llywelyn ab Iorwerth. He and his two sons, from both of whom she was descended, were granted large tracts of land in North Wales.[52] King Charles III is also descended from Ednyfed Fychan, via Henry VII, the first monarch of the House of Tudor.

Richard Pennant inherited extensive plantations in Jamaica on his father's death in 1782, which had been owned by the family for over a hundred years. He was then in his mid-forties. He had been elected an MP, as a Whig, in 1760, later representing Liverpool. He was recommended for an Irish peerage in 1783 during the short-lived coalition government of Charles James Fox and Lord North at a time of constitutional crisis. It is

Fig. 6. *Richard Pennant, Lord Penrhyn*, by Henry Thomson, with his dog Crab (c.1800). Penrhyn is pointing at a map showing his new road through Nant Ffrancon. Behind him is the inn he built at Capel Curig which Bingley visited in 1801. The inn is now Plas y Brenin outdoor centre.

plausible that Pennant obtained the title via a large 'donation', but Fox has been considered as unswerving in his distaste for slavery, so this is a conundrum. The campaign for its abolition, led in Parliament by William Wilberforce, was set in motion four years later. It was opposed by the new Lord Penrhyn, who used the profits from his Jamaican plantations to expand the slate quarry in Caernarfonshire, create a port, build roads, an iron tramway and two hotels, and make agricultural improvements, including planting hundreds of thousands of trees.

Penrhyn died owing £150,000: perhaps 15 million in today's money. The French Wars – until the temporary Treaty of Amiens in 1802 – had depressed the trade for non-war-essential items such as roofing slates, and Pitt's government had introduced a war tax. His wife's family home in Cheshire was sold, as was property in Jamaica, to pay off the debt. Penrhyn had no children, the title became extinct, and the Jamaican and Welsh estates were inherited by his second cousin, George Hay Dawkins, who added Pennant to his surname.

Bingley had probably read 80-year-old William Hutton's travel book, *Remarks upon North Wales* (1803) – he quotes some verses from it – and maybe Hutton's fulsome dedication to Lord Penrhyn motivated Bingley to add more about Penrhyn and his works. Bingley was impressed at Capel Curig:

> Those tourists who, like myself, have visited this vale a few years ago, when the only place of public accommodation was a mean pot-house … will be able with some justice to appreciate the spirited conduct, and truly patriotic exertions of the noble proprietor, who has not only constructed for them an inn, but who was the first to make this part of the country passable in carriages. (p. 236)

Yet there was a moment of doubt at the quarry when Bingley approached the whitewashed cottages built for the workers, where he saw broken windows and ragged children.

Bingley doesn't mention slaves in the context of Lord Penrhyn, but in his chapter on 'manners and customs' (not included here) he comments on the inhuman practice: Welsh princes and other lords 'had the power of offering [slaves] to sale in the same manner they would their cattle. This inhuman custom prevailed in Wales for many years after the death of the last prince of Wales. There is yet extant a deed of sale, dated even so late as the year 1448, by which seven slaves and their families became transferred from one person to another.'[53] In a later book, *Travels in North America*, he unequivocally states:

> What a foul stain is it upon the American republic, professing, as they do, the principles of liberty and of equal rights, that, out of twenty states, there should be eleven in which slavery is an avowed part of the political constitution.[54]

Lord Penrhyn brought huge employment and opportunities to an impoverished area of North Wales. Bingley had strong feelings against slavery, yet he applauded Penrhyn's achievements, as did many of his contemporaries. Perhaps the kind of man that Penrhyn was can be gleaned from a letter to his agent in Jamaica in 1782:

> The life & health of the negroes is of the utmost importance. Humanity, as well as the interest of the proprietor, demand that they should be taken care of – that they should not be overworked, and that they should be treated with tenderness – when they are ill, and with humanity & [?] attention, at all times. That the women be treated with indulgence at those times especially, when their situations call for it.[55]

What a man did with his money was important, and Bingley recommends the slate quarry as an attraction.

There is a vivid description of a visit to a copper mine at Llanberis where he climbs into a waggon with other tourists and enters a narrow, damp, dark cavern. It was a terrifying, unforgettable adventure (p. 138). On his second trip in 1801 Bingley had heard about William Madocks and his first embankment of 1800, which enclosed areas of marsh north up the estuary on his new Penmorfa estate. The embankment was an interesting enough event for Bingley to call attention to it in his chapter summary: '*Traeth Mawr – Embankment of Land from the Sea*'. Madocks 'has, within the last four years, recovered above 1500 acres by embanking out the sea. The land is found exceedingly good, and has already produced excellent wheat, barley, and oats' (p. 205). The future town of Tremadog, begun in 1805, and the port at Porthmadog were then just seeds in Madocks's fertile imagination.

Religion, superstition and the Welsh

Bingley has long chapters on the 'manners and customs of the Welsh' and on the Welsh language, which I have not included in this edition, apart from his guide to pronunciation. He followed the contemporary practice of using the adjective 'British' for the 'Welsh' of the Dark Ages and early medieval period, such as when he refers to the 'British court' at Aberffraw on Anglesey in the fourth century, but he is not always precise. At the beginning of the twelfth century, Welsh writers of Latin stopped calling the Welsh 'Britons' and followed the example of English writers since the Norman conquest in calling the country 'Wales'

(*Wallia*) and the inhabitants 'Welsh'.[56] He shows respect for the Welsh: 'that hardy race of warlike characters which were with so much difficulty subdued by the English monarchs'.[57] But he can get annoyed whether by ferrymen or by being overcharged: 'I have good authority for asserting that at some of the inferior inns, if an Englishman sits down at table with Welshmen, the charge for his eating will be at least one third more than that of each of the rest of the company. This is a provoking imposition.'[58] But he is also reflective:

> What has been repeatedly asserted of the Welsh people, that they are naturally inquisitive and curious respecting strangers is certainly true, but it is a circumstance by no means peculiar to this country. In all wild and unfrequented parts of the world it is the same, and it is in such parts of Wales that this disposition is chiefly observable. It is easily accounted for when we consider their manners of life, and general ignorance. Surprize on the appearance of strangers, where in their limited ideas there could seem no inducement to repay the trouble or expence of a journey, would naturally excite their wonder, and this as naturally leads to the questions 'Where do you come from?' – 'Why do you come here?' – and, 'Where do you go to from hence?' – Unsatisfied with my answers, that I was an Englishman come to visit the mountains and waterfalls, I have often and often been asked with the utmost simplicity, 'Are there then no rocks nor rivers in England?' In all accounts of travels through unfrequented countries we find this disposition to curiosity very common, and a slight acquaintance with the nature of the human mind is sufficient to allay any surprize that may be excited in discovering that it is prevalent in Wales.[59]

However, it is the glimpses of particular people whom he encounters that are most interesting. Rev. Peter Williams showed him the cottage of a small farmer in Cwm y Clo, near Llanberis, as typical of Caernarfonshire. There was a 'wretched hovel' for the old farmer's cattle that afforded them little shelter. The door of the cottage was so low that Bingley had to stoop and couldn't at first see what was in the hut because it was so dark. As a typical clergyman of his time, he doesn't display a radical response about poverty, but instead quotes from Oliver Goldsmith's 'The Traveller' on the poor not needing material goods to make them content, which doesn't acknowledge Goldsmith's line that 'Laws grind the poor, and rich men rule the law'. Bingley also relates an anecdote about a woman who often climbed down her chimney when she had misplaced her key. He does not comment why, in rural North Wales, she needed to lock her door.

On his first tour he met Peter Williams's curate in a mean-looking cottage, but whose smiles 'were such as would render even misery cheerful'. Poignantly, three years later, the man has died, and Bingley rephrases his description to the past tense, and inserts a new ending: 'This person, after sustaining a severe illness with the utmost resignation and fortitude, died in the beginning of the year 1801, leaving a widow and one daughter to survive him' (p. 142). Williams rode with him over the mountains to the funeral of a little girl. Bingley gives a vivid and moving description as more and more mountain people followed the 'cavalcade', which to him had 'the air of romantic times'. The coffin was lowered into its grave by female mourners and Bingley was deeply struck: 'A more solemn office I had never witnessed ... I shall never forget the stifled shriek that was uttered, when, in Welsh, the solemn words, "we commit her body to the ground," &c. were read' (p. 143).

Some Welsh women could look after themselves. Bingley gives a sympathetic description of one of Williams's parishioners, Caddy of Cwm Glâs, an athletic female with a masculine voice. She is taunted in Caernarfon, but at home she chases after a burglar and thwacks him with her cudgel. As for guides, there is a touch of Cambridge-graduate mockery regarding schoolmaster and inn-keeper Edward Jones of the Blue Lion near Tal-y-Llyn, who guided him up Cadair Idris, and whom Bingley 'found somewhat too talkative, particularly on the subject of his own qualifications. ... I smiled several times at his efforts to shew off his learning and talents, these, however, in so obscure a situation, were perhaps excusable' (p. 271). But sometimes Bingley is impressed by his guides, such as John Richards in Harlech: 'a man who speaks English fluently, is well acquainted with the neighbourhood, and, for his situation, has a very superior understanding' (p. 254). Richards may have returned home after working in England; he was probably inundated afterwards with tourists wanting to see cromlechs.

As an enlightened new clergyman, Bingley rebukes superstitious practices, such as on Anglesey: 'But when we consider, that superstition and enthusiasm have generally little to do with reason, we must not wonder at this addition to the heap of incongruities that all ages have afforded us' (p. 180). He doesn't mention Nonconformism, but he is exercised by the practice of 'Jumpers' that he witnesses, who were part of the Methodist movement. He attended some meetings in Caernarfon and was concerned at their 'enthusiastic extravagancies' (p. 130). He is careful to give Welsh opinions on this movement: he quotes from a letter by 'one of their own countrymen', perhaps Peter Williams, whose father had been a Methodist exhorter; and from another by someone (presumably Welsh) in Denbigh (pp. 130, 364). He also read Theophilus Jones's criticism of 'Jumpers' in the *Cambrian Register*: 'The extravagant ravings of methodism, which the author [Pratt] very truly and very properly represents as exceeding every thing which can be seen or heard in any civilized country, are certainly a reproach to the good sense and understanding of the inhabitants.'[60] I have omitted Bingley's further discussion of Methodism (which separated from the established church in 1811), but in it he gives a glimpse of what kind of clergyman he was: 'the clergy are too often contented with *reading* dry and tedious essays on morality. The grand subject of human redemption, and the interesting doctrines of revelation, seem kept entirely in the back ground. ... They should, in the place of moral essays, preach the gospel of peace.'[61]

He deleted one passage for his 1804 edition which gives more of an insight into his feelings for the religion of the past. He is at the ruins of the Cistercian abbey of Valle Crucis and quotes from John Webster's Jacobean revenge tragedy *The Duchess of Malfi* (1613/14). The play was rarely performed in the eighteenth century and Bingley probably found Antonio's speech ('I doe love these aunciant ruynes ...'; p. 325) in Francis Grose's epigraph to one volume of his *Antiquities of England and Wales* (1772; see note to p. 326). In his 1800 edition, Bingley followed the quotation with his musings:

> In this solemn and peaceable retreat, how grand must have been the deep toned organ's swell, the loud anthem of a hundred voices rolling through these roofs, and penetrating the hallowed grove! What devotion would not rise upon Enthusiasm's wings, when it heard the toll of a vesper bell undulating with the breeze. Even now, when all these heaven-inspiring sounds have ceased, does memory recur to them; and fancy peoples the gloom with all it's former inhabitants.[62]

Did his first years as a clergyman teach him that this nostalgia for Roman Catholicism was inappropriate? But his passage would be later used by others: 'we cannot reconcile our ideas in language more descriptive and sublime than what Mr. Bingley has expressed himself in on this occasion', wrote George Alexander Cooke some years later as he quoted Bingley's words.[63]

Flora and fauna: botanical treats and pickled puffins

At Diganwy, Bingley comments: 'The ruins are now almost covered with earth and shrubs, and in different parts of them the young botanist may meet with much amusement' (p. 92; 'amusement' = thoughtful reflection). Most of his discoveries of plants are reserved for his long catalogue or the occasional list in the main text (not included here). His main reference work in his 1804 edition were the first two volumes of Dr James Edward Smith's *Flora Britannica*, which was to appear in three volumes (1800–4). Bingley referred to Dr Smith's ongoing work in a letter to him of 18 August 1799:

> Will you be so obliging as to inform me when you suppose the first volume of your Flora will be out – I wish very much to see it previous to the publication of my Welsh Tour as it is my intention to insert at the end of that work a list of the habitats of rare Cambrian plants of which I have already got upwards of 300 and am in expectations of more … When I was in Wales I wished for such an assistant & I think such will be of use to every young botanist who is making the tour. I wish to see your work to affix to them their proper names.

Dr Smith's two volumes appeared too late to be used in Bingley's 1800 edition, which is perhaps why Bingley was so keen to make another trip to Wales in 1801.

Botanical pursuits can be dangerous: he warns botanists to be careful hunting for alpine plants on Snowdon: 'There is at all times some difficulty in searching them, but when the rocks are rendered slippery from heavy mists or rain, this becomes, from the insecurity of the footing, greatly increased' (p. 149). He has several tumbles as he climbs to the summit of Penmaen Mawr in search of a shrub 'of which I had heard many nonsensical accounts, called by the Welsh Pren Lemwn, *Lemon-tree*'. He discovered it was 'nothing more than *Crataegus aria* of Linnaeus, which does not often occur among the Welsh mountains' (p. 103).

Bingley records the loss of beavers, which were reintroduced into Wales only in 2021 near Machynlleth. He states that 'Snowdon was formerly a *royal forest* that abounded with deer; but the last of these were destroyed early in the seventeenth century' (p. 149). He enjoys seeing the goats, but they are all now private property, he says. He hears stories about one-eyed trout, and reports from the vicar of Aberdaron that the small sheep on the Island of Bardsey squall like hares and are good swimmers. He is enthralled by the salmon leap near Pont Aberglaslyn but is censorious about the way some are killed with harpoons.

But Bingley seems less concerned about puffins. He was able to land on uninhabited Ynys Seiriol / Priestholm after a member of the crew fired a 'swivel gun' (presumably a flintlock) to see the effect on the thousands of birds perched on the rocks: 'such a scream of puffins, gulls, and other sea birds, was heard, as beyond all conception astonished me' (p. 191). On the other side of the island Bingley encountered fifty thousand Puffins which he found 'either so tame or so stupid, as to suffer me to approach near enough to have knocked one or two of them down with a stick' (p. 191). Wearing a glove, he takes a few puffins from their burrows to test Thomas Pennant's assertion that puffins will bite themselves if seized, which Bingley disproves. The man with him shot a few to take to the boat and Bingley describes the pickling process. He makes no comment; he is the naturalist observing foreign customs, and he is as fascinated when he observes a species of 'medusae, *sea-blubber*' – jellyfish – while 'carelessly leaning over the side of the vessel' (p. 189). Explaining nature was to become a large part of his life's work, and without his two tours of North Wales and the encouragement of Dr Smith that might never have happened.

But by writing the first guidebook to North Wales he also informed the English about Wales's 'rich and copious' language, history and culture.[64] Tourists would learn about the poet Dafydd ap Gwilym, about Llywelyn 'the Great' ab Iorwerth and Owain Glyndŵr, and about Welsh scholars David Powel and Edward Lhuyd. His initial intention had been to write a guide for botanists, but as his love for Wales grew, so did his book. Without it, we would never know that a Welsh–Yorkshire duo had been such pioneering climbers (though I wish we had the journal of the Welshwoman who beat them up Tryfan).

Notes

Bangor University Archives: PENRH/The Jamaica Estates/Richard, Lord Penrhyn:
    Penrhyn 1248, Richard Pennant, letter to his agent in Jamaica, 1782
Borthwick Institute for Archives, York
    Ordination papers: William Bingley BA, deacon (1799), BIA17186305
Hampshire Record Office, Winchester
    Ordination papers: William Bingley BA, priest (1803), 21M65/E1/4/2054
Linnean Society of London, Correspondence of Sir James Edward Smith
    Letters from William Bingley:
    GB-110/JES/COR/20/84, 85–102 [online; 12 March 1798 to 2 November 1813]
The National Archives
    Will of Reverend William Bingley, Clerk of Bloomsbury, Middlesex, PROB 11/1668/315

The National Library of Wales / Llyfrgell Genedlaethol Cymru
    Letter from William Bingley to John Wynne Griffith, 22 July 1798: Garn Estate, FPG 3/1
University of Reading, Special Collections: Longman Archives
    Draft letters to Revd. W. Bingley:
    MS 1393 1 98 53, London May 15/13
    MS 1393 1 98 56, London June 12 1813
    MS 1393 1 98 62, London September 3 1813
    Ledgers: William Bingley's *North Wales*:
    MS 1393 1 A1 p. 170 (1804)
    MS 1393 1 B6 pp. 70 (1841), 74 (1839–40)
    MS 1393 1 H5 p. 103 (1804)
    MS 1393 1 H8 p. 144 (1814–15, 1818)

1. Nick Livesey, *Photographing the Snowdonia Mountains* (2018), p. 147.
2. Jim Perrin, *Snowdon* (2018), p. 133.
3. Bingley to Dr James Edward Smith, undated, before 13 Feb. 1799.
4. An octavo resulted from a sheet of paper folded three times; the larger quarto was folded twice. Bingley's 1804 octavo books are 22cm high. Paper sizes varied.
5. *Leeds Intelligencer*, 31 Oct. 1786, p. 2.
6. Joseph Johnson, Esq., possibly second husband of his father's sister Ann Sheppard née Bingley; see *Northern Star*, vol. 1, issue 1 (July 1817), p. 48.
7. David McKitterick, *Cambridge University Library: A History: The Eighteenth and Nineteenth Centuries* (1986), pp. 14, 41.
8. George Cornelius Gorham, *Memoirs of John Martyn, F.R.S., and of Thomas Martyn, B.D., F.R.S., F.L.S., Professors of Botany in the University of Cambridge* (1830), pp. 217–18.
9. [Thomas Martyn], *The Gentleman's Guide in his Tour through Italy. With a correct map, and directions for travelling in that country* (1787), p. iii.
10. William Wordsworth, 'Excursions to the top of Scawfell and on the banks of Ullswater', in Ernest de Sélincourt (ed.), *Wordsworth's Guide to the Lakes*, 5th edn (1835) (Oxford, paperback edn 1977), p. 112.
11. [Thomas West], *A Guide to the Lakes: dedicated to the lovers of landscape studies...* (1778), pp. 59–60.
12. Ibid. p. 12.
13. Ibid. pp. 15–16.
14. See Monica Kendall, *Lies and the Brontës: The Quest for the Jenkins Family* (2021), ch. 3.
15. *A Short Account of Caernarvon, and Bedd-Kill-Hart; or, Beddgelart, &c.* (Caernarvon: printed by T. Roberts, 1806).
16. See Frances Knight, *The Nineteenth-Century Church and English Society* (1998) for the difficulty of getting a title for orders.
17. Review of *A Tour round North Wales, performed during the Summer of 1798. By the Rev. W. Bingley, B.A. &c. Illustrated with Views in Aqua-tinta, by Alken. 2 Vols. 8vo. 1l. 1s. Boards.* Williams. 1800, *The Critical Review*, vol. 30 (Sept. 1800), p. 70.
18. Harold Cox and John E. Chandler, *The House of Longman: With a Record of their Bicentenary Celebrations, 1724–1924* (1925), p. 16; Philip Wallis, *At the Sign of the Ship: Notes on the House of Longman 1724–1974* (1974), pp. 15–16.
19. Wallis, *Sign of the Ship*, p. 15.
20. Michael F. Suarez and Michael L. Turner (eds), *The Cambridge History of the Book in Britain*, vol. 5: *1695–1830* (2014), p. 409.

21. Reading University: Longman Archives: Reading MS 1393-1-98-53.
22. Jill Clayton, 'William Bingley's history of Hampshire', *Proceedings of the Hampshire Field Club and Archaeological Society* 64 (2009), 223–43. The article is admirably researched but contains errors about his books (though these are minor compared to the poor *ODNB* article revised in 2020 which hasn't even got the date of his baptism correct). Bingley's notes, which he made between 1803 and 1814 (when Rose cancelled the project), are at the Hampshire Record Office.
23. See Percy G. Adams, *Travelers and Travel Liars 1660–1800* (1962), p. 88.
24. Thomas Alfred Walker, *Peterhouse* (1906), p. 182.
25. Obituary, Rev. William Bingley, *Gentleman's Magazine*, vol. 133 (May 1823), p. 472.
26. Mary-Ann Constantine and Nigel Leask (eds), *Enlightenment Travel and British Identities: Thomas Pennant's Tours in Scotland and Wales* (2019), pp. 245–8.
27. William Bingley, *A Tour round North Wales* (1800), vol. I, pp. 237–8; Richard Warner, *A Walk through Wales, in August 1797* (1798), pp. vii, 121–34.
28. Bingley, *A Tour*, vol. I, pp. 239–41; Warner, *A Walk through Wales*, pp. 124–5.
29. Richard Warner, *Literary Recollections* (1830), vol. II, pp. 132–5.
30. Warner, *A Walk through Wales*, p. 2.
31. Damian Walford Davies, *Presences that Disturb: Models of Romantic Identity in the Literature and Culture of the 1790s* (2002), pp. 126–8.
32. Warner, *Literary Recollections*, vol. II, p. 154.
33. 'Cymro', 'Cursory remarks on Welsh tours or travels', *Cambrian Register* (1799), p. 423.
34. Ibid. pp. 426–7, 452.
35. Anon., *Letters from Snowdon: Descriptive of a Tour through the Northern Counties of Wales* (2nd edn, 1777), pp. iii, iv; (1st edn, 1770), pp. 53, 58.
36. 'Cymro', 'Cursory remarks', p. 453.
37. Useful studies of the genre of the guidebook are John Vaughan, *The English Guide Book c 1780–1870: An Illustrated History* (1974) and Giles Barber 'The English-language guide book to Europe up to 1870', in Robin Myers and Michael Harris (eds), *Journeys through the Market: Travel, Travellers and the Book Trade* (1999). See also Carl Thompson, *Travel Writing* (2011).
38. 'Anne Lister's diary, tour of North Wales 11–27 July 1822', transcribed by Kirsty McHugh, ed. Elizabeth Edwards, editions.curioustravellers.ac.uk/doc/0023.
39. Cesare de Seta, 'Grand Tour', in Andrew Wilton and Ilaria Bignamini (eds), *Grand Tour: The Lure of Italy in the Eighteenth Century*, Tate exhibition catalogue (1996), pp. 15–16.
40. William Gilpin, *Three Essays on Picturesque Beauty* (2nd edn, 1794), pp. 36, 20, 46.
41. William Gilpin, *Observations on the River Wye* (1782), p. 18.
42. Kenneth Clark, *The Gothic Revival: An Essay in the History of Taste* (3rd edn, 1975), p. 68.
43. Julian Mitchell, *The Wye Tour and its Artists* (2010), p. 11.
44. Edmund Burke, *A Philosophical Enquiry … into the Sublime and Beautiful*, ed. Paul Guyer (2015), pp. 33–4.
45. Robert Macfarlane, *Mountains of the Mind: A History of a Fascination* (2004), p. 75.
46. See William St Clair, *The Reading Nation in the Romantic Period* (2007), pp. 133–4, 225.
47. Burke, *A Philosophical Enquiry*, p. 49.
48. Elizabeth Beazley, *Madocks and the Wonder of Wales* (1967), p. 41.

49. Anon., 'Biographical memoir', in *Poems by the Late Hon. William R. Spencer* (1835), pp. 2–3.
50. William Hazlitt, 'On going a journey', in *Selected Writings*, ed. Ronald Blythe (1987), p. 143.
51. William Williams, *Observations on the Snowdon Mountains* (1802), p. 164. Williams 'of Llandygai' (1738–1817) was born in poverty in Anglesey and apprenticed as a saddler, but he became a clerk on the Penrhyn estate and learnt surveying, and was in charge of the production of slates from 1782 to 1802. On his resignation he was given an annual salary for life and focused on his Welsh literary studies.
52. The National Trust, *Penrhyn Castle, Gwynedd* (1991), p. 5 and family tree.
53. William Bingley, *North Wales* (1804), vol. II, p. 256.
54. William Bingley, *Travels in North America, from Modern Writers* (1821), p. 169.
55. Bangor University Archives: Richard Pennant, letter to his agent in Jamaica, 1782.
56. A. Huw Pryce, 'Frontier Wales c.1063–1282', in Prys Morgan (ed.), *The Tempus History of Wales* (2001), p. 103.
57. Bingley, *North Wales*, vol. II, p. 264.
58. Ibid. p. 265.
59. Ibid. p. 268.
60. 'Cymro', 'Cursory remarks', p. 432.
61. Bingley, *North Wales*, vol. I, p. 213.
62. Bingley, *A Tour*, vol. II, p. 122.
63. George Alexander Cooke, *Topographical and Statistical Description of the Principality of Wales* (1817?), p. 109.
64. Bingley, *North Wales*, vol. II, p. 290.

Bingley's guide to Welsh pronunciation*

The following is an account of those letters that, in their powers, differ from similar ones in the English language:

A has only the sound of our open *a* in the word *bard*: as *castell*, a castle.

C, invariably, is hard, as the English *k*: thus *cader*, a fort, is pronounced *kader*. C joined with w, and having a vowel succeeding, supplies the place of our Qu.

Ch (marked ç in Mr. Owen's Welsh Dictionary*) is a guttural, of the same power as the Greek χ.

Dd, or, as it is sometimes written, *dh*, is an aspirated *d*. It has nearly the sound of *th* in the word *this*: *dda*, good, is pronounced *tha*.

F has the sound of our *v*: thus *felen*, yellow, is pronounced *velen*.

Ff supplies the place of our single *f*.

G is invariably hard, as the *g* in *gain*.

I has the same sound as it has in the Italian language, of *ee*, as in our word *seen*: thus *cil*, a retreat, is pronounced *keel*.

Ll is an aspirated *l*, having much the sound of *thl*: thus *llan*, a church or village, is pronounced much like *thlan*.

R, when it begins a word, is always aspirated.

U has the sound of *i* in the word *sin*: thus *pump*, five, is pronounced *pimp*.

W is a vowel, and has the power of our *oo* in soon: thus *rhiw*, an ascent, is pronounced *rhioo*.

Y, in some words, has the sound of the English *i* in *sin*: thus *ffynnon*, a well, is pronounced *finnon*. It has also sometimes the sound of *o* in the word *honey*; and sometimes of *u* in *mud*.

HOLYHEAD ISLAND
I N G L E S E A
LLANERCH Y MEDD
BEAUMARIS
BANGOR
CAERNARVON
CAERNARVON BAY
S H I R E
Beddgelert
NEVIN
PWLLHELI
HARLECH
C A R D I G A N
B A Y
Sarn Badrwyg or Causway of St Patrick
Bardsey I.
Dutch Bank
Penbool Bank
Newborough
Aberffraw
Llanidan
Llangefni
Dulas
Llangybi
Abererch
Llanarmon
Pen Cilan Point
Llangelynin
TOWYN

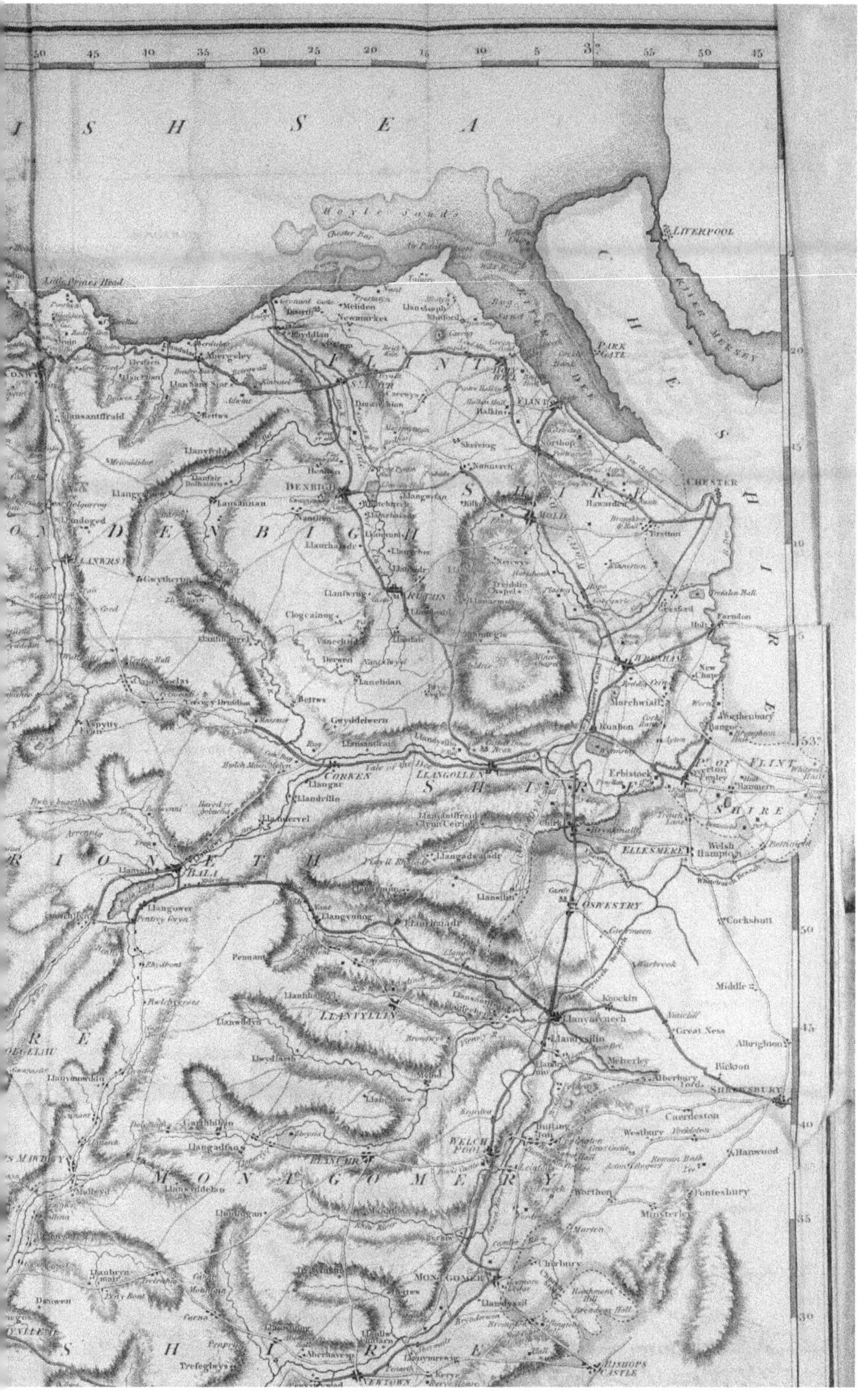

S H S E A
LIVERPOOL
PARK GATE
CHESTER
FLINT
MOLD
DENBIGH
RUTHIN
Hawarden
Llanrwst
Gwytherin
Bettws
Gwyddelwern
Llansantffraid
LLANGOLLEN
CORWEN
Llandrillo
Llandervel
BALA
Llangower
Llangynnog
Erbistock
Marchwiail
Ruabon
Bangor
Hanmer
ELLESMERE
Welsh Hampton
OSWESTRY
Cockshutt
Middle
Knockin
Great Ness
Llanymynech
LLANVYLLIN
Melverley
Alberbury
SHREWSBURY
Caerdeston
Westbury
Hanwood
WELCH POOL
Pontesbury
Worthen
Minsterley
Marton
Chirbury
MONTGOMERY
Llangadfan
Llanbrynmair
Trefeglwys
NEWTOWN
BISHOPS CASTLE
Llanidloes
Mallwyd
Llanymowddwy
Pennant
Llandinam
M O N T G O M E R Y
S H I R E

BEAUMARIS
BANGOR
CAERNARVON
C A E R N A R V O N
B A Y
S H I R E
NEVIN
PWLLHELI
Llanbedrog
Pwllheli Bay
Porth dinlleyn
Voyage to Bardsey and Pwllheli
Bardsey I.
Bardsey Sound
St. Tudwals Road
St. Tudwals Isle
Dutch Bank
C A R D I G A N
B A Y
Sarn Badrwyg or Causway of St. Patrick
HARLECH
Llanbedr
Barmouth
Barmouth Bar
Llangelynin
TOWYN
Penall
Birds Point
Capel Cynvelyn
Sarn Gynfelyn
The Patches
ABERYSTWITH
Llanfihangel Croithon
Llanilar
Scale of Miles
53°
5°
4°

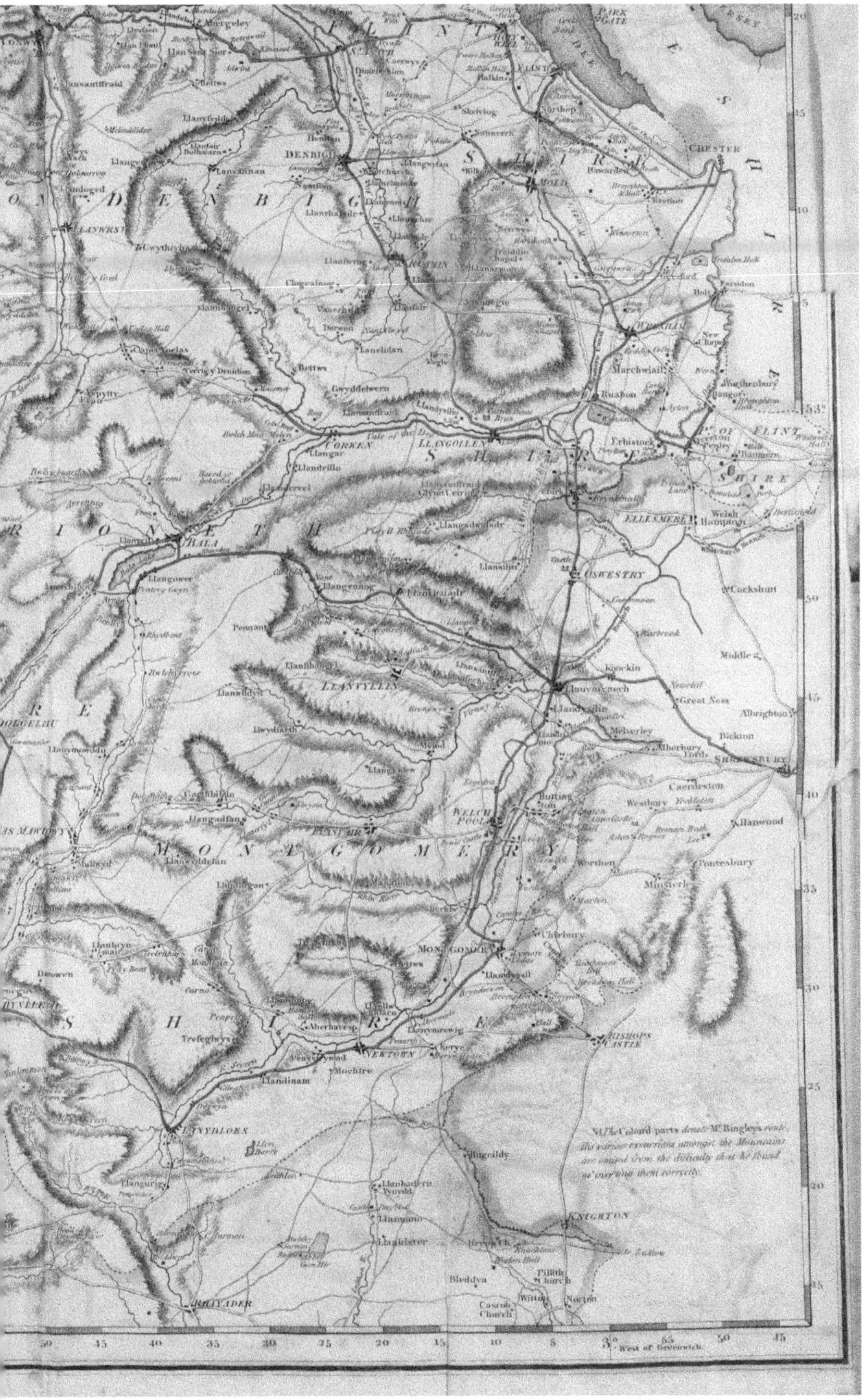

Abergeley
Llan Sant Sior
Llansantffraid
Llanfydd
DENBIGH
Llansannan
Whitchurch
Llangwyfan
LLANRWST
Cwytheyin
Llanrhaiadr
Llanfwrog
RUTHIN
Clocainog
Llanfair
Derwen
Llanelidan
Bettws
Gwyddelwern
Llansaintfraid
CORWEN
Llangar
Llandrillo
Vale of the Dee
LLANGOLLEN
Llansantfraid Glynt Ceiriog
Llangadwaladr
BALA
Llangower
Llangynog
Llanrhaiadr
Pennant
Llanfihangel
LLANFYLLIN
Llanwddyn
Llanymowddu
DOLGELHU
Llangadfan
Llanfair
Llanerfyl
Llanbrynmair
Darowen
Trefeglwys
Aberhavesp
NEWTOWN
Llandinam
Mochtre
LLANYDLOES
Llangurig
RHAYADER
Llanbadarn Fynydd
Llananno
Llanbister
Bleddva
Cascob Church
Pilleth Church
Norton
KNIGHTON
Beguildy
BISHOPS CASTLE
MONTGOMERY
Chirbury
Llandyssil
Kerry
WELCH POOL
Guilsfield
Meifod
Llandrinio
Llanymynech
Llansantffraid
Knockin
Great Ness
Albrighton
Bicton
Alberbury
Ford
SHREWSBURY
Caerdeston
Westbury
Yockleton
Hanwood
Pontesbury
Minsterley
Worthen
OSWESTRY
Llansilin
Chirk
Whittington
ELLESMERE
Cockshutt
Middle
Welsh Hampton
Erbistock
Overton
Penley
Bettisfield
Ruabon
Marchwiail
WREXHAM
Gresford
Holt
Bangor
Worthenbury
Hanmer
MOLD
Hawarden
CHESTER
FLINT
Northop
HOLY WELL
CAERWYS
Halkin
Skeiviog
Dee
PARK GATE
M O N T G O M E R Y
S H I R E
D E N B I G H
F L I N T S H I R E
C H E S H I R E
N.B. The Colourd parts denote Mr. Bingleys route. His various excursions amongst the Mountains are omited from the difficulty that he found in tracing them correctly.
West of Greenwich.

FRONTISPIECE.

Pont-y-Pair near Llanrwst.

NORTH WALES;

INCLUDING ITS

SCENERY, ANTIQUITIES, CUSTOMS,

AND SOME SKETCHES OF ITS

NATURAL HISTORY;

DELINEATED FROM

TWO EXCURSIONS THROUGH ALL THE INTERESTING
PARTS OF THAT COUNTRY,

During the Summers of 1798 and 1801.

By THE REV. W. BINGLEY, A.M.
FELLOW OF THE LINNEAN SOCIETY,
AND LATE OF PETERHOUSE, CAMBRIDGE.

Illustrated with a Map, Frontispieces, and Music.

IN TWO VOLUMES.

VOL. I.

London:

PRINTED FOR T. N. LONGMAN AND O. REES,
PATERNOSTER-ROW.

1804.

TO

JAMES EDWARD SMITH, M.D. F.R.S.*

PRESIDENT OF THE LINNEAN SOCIETY,

THESE VOLUMES,

DESCRIPTIVE OF

A HIGHLY ROMANTIC AND INTERESTING

PART OF THE

BRITISH EMPIRE,

ARE INSCRIBED,

AS A TESTIMONY OF THE SINCERE ESTEEM,

OF HIS VERY AFFECTIONATE,

AND OBEDIENT SERVANT,

WILLIAM BINGLEY.

Preface to the 1800 edition

The accounts that I had at different times received of the stupendous and picturesque scenery of some of the counties of North Wales, induced me, in the summer of 1798, to spend three months that I had to spare from my College avocations, in that romantic part of Great Britain. These I justly conceived, would be so amply sufficient, that they would allow me time *leisurely* to examine all the most material places.

I can here truly say, that every expectation I had been taught to raise, was more than fulfilled. The traveller of taste, who is in search of the grandest scenes that nature has formed in these islands; the naturalist, and the antiquary, may all rest assured that they will find here ample entertainment in their respective pursuits.

My mode of travelling was chiefly on foot, but sometimes I took horses, and at other times proceeded in carriages, as I found it convenient. The former, notwithstanding all the objections that have been made against it, will, I am confident, upon the whole, be found the most useful, if health and strength are not wanting. To a naturalist, it is evidently so, since, by this means, he is enabled to examine the country as he goes along, and when he sees occasion, he can also strike out of the road, amongst the mountains or morasses, in a manner completely independent of all those obstacles that inevitably attend the bringing of carriages or horses.

Next to being on foot, the tourist will find a horse the most useful, but in this case, if he intends to ramble much amongst the mountains, it will be necessary for him to take a Welsh poney, which, used to the stony paths, will carry him, without danger, over places where no English horse, accustomed to even roads and smooth turf, could stand with him.

In carriages, no persons will, of course, expect to travel, except along the great roads, (which indeed extend quite round the country), but at all the inns, horses may be procured to penetrate into the mountainous and more romantic parts.

There is an inn at almost every respectable town, where post chaises are kept; but owing to the great numbers who now make this fashionable tour, delays are at times unavoidably occasioned by these being all employed. This, however, is a circumstance that seems to me of but little consequence to the tourist, since, at almost every place where he has occasion to stop, amusements may be found more than sufficient to occupy the two or three hours of delay.

Evans's smaller map of North Wales,* which is the correctest map I ever travelled by, will be found a most useful companion. The roads have in this been laid down with so much accuracy, that, wherever the traveller may have occasion to find fault, it will be more than probable that some change has taken place since the survey was taken. A small pocket compass, amongst the mountains, will be almost as necessary as the map.

The tourist, who happens to take along with him these volumes, will, in pronouncing and understanding the Welsh names, be somewhat assisted, by examining carefully the former part of the chapter on the language,* where he will find the force of the letters, and the explanation of such words as commonly occur in the composition of the names of places, &c.

The expences of travelling in Wales, notwithstanding what Mr. Pratt,* and some other writers have said upon the subject, I found in general, but little less than those on the roads in the central parts of England. Provisions are here very little cheaper than with us; and the expences of house-keeping have, within the few last years, been considerably increased.

Having put down these previous hints for the future tourist, it is now proper that I should say somewhat of the present work.

Throughout the whole of my journey, I endeavoured to make my pursuits and my observations as general as possible: and in these volumes, I have, as far as lay in my power, made it my rule to put down for the information of others, every thing that I wished to have known when I was myself making the tour. This, allowing for all the differences of taste and opinion, seemed to me the best criterion by which to judge of the wishes of the public; in what manner I have succeeded, the volumes themselves must shew.

I have, as will be found upon perusal, interspersed them but little, either with reflections or incidental stories: indeed of the latter, I ought candidly to confess, that I met with very few which I thought worth recording. Two late tourists, Mr. Pratt and Mr. Warner,* if they have not introduced the novelist too often in their works, (which, by the way, I shrewdly suspect they have) were infinitely more fortunate in meeting with adventures than I was.

In the description of the country, I have invariably endeavoured to let the scenes form themselves, and to paint nature simply as I found her. The tourist, who is desirous of forming reflections for himself, will, I doubt not, at all events thank me for my intentions in this respect. I shall ever remember, in a tour that I made some years ago to the Lakes of the north of England, how much I found myself deceived and disappointed, by the turgid and high-flown descriptions which fill almost every page of Mr. West's Guide* through that country, a book, in other respects certainly of merit. This circumstance alone led me to a determination, if possible, to avoid that error. When the scenery exceeds the description, it will be viewed with pleasure; but when it falls short of it, no one but a traveller can tell the disappointment that is felt.

As the present work was intended chiefly for the use of the tourist, I judged also that I should be rendering myself of more service, in not permitting it to lay claim entirely to originality: but in return for this, I have, I believe, (except in the first and last chapters of the *Tour*) always inserted marks of reference to the authors from whence my information is extracted. To Mr. Pennant's accurate and learned work on this country, I have in various instances, as will be hereafter seen, been much indebted.*

It may indeed, and not improperly, be asked, what need there was for any other account, when one so accurate as the above was already extant? In answer to this, I have to observe, that the present is more commodious for carriage; the former being in two volumes quarto, is extremely heavy and inconvenient for persons to carry along with them. Mr. Pennant has taken no general rout. He begins near his own house in Flintshire, proceeds through that country, part of Cheshire, Shropshire, and Denbighshire, and returns to Downing; from whence he again sets out, and takes not a regular rout over the remainder of North Wales. I by no means mention this circumstance as a derogation from the intrinsic merits of his work, it is only done to shew it's inconvenience as a guide to the tourist. It contains much matter, and many long dissertations on subjects of antiquity, (particularly an excellent life of the Welsh hero, Owen Glyndwr, which alone occupies about 70 pages) these, though well calculated both to instruct and amuse in the closet, are too long and uninteresting for the generality of persons when upon their journey. And to conclude the whole, it has been *out of print* for some time.

The literary world has been much indebted to the industry and abilities of Mr. Pennant, for his accurate examinations and descriptions of Wales, Scotland, and several parts of England, in which he has evinced a depth of knowledge that does not fall to every man's lot. He was the first who made the taste for home travels so prevalent in this country; and it would be uncandid not to declare, that this gentleman has given us some of the earliest descriptions that are worth preserving. In his tour in North Wales, from being a native of the country, and having access to all the principal libraries there, he possessed many advantages that in his other journies he did not, which of course must tend to render this his most correct work.

In the present volumes, from my being resident in Cambridge, and having had access to several libraries there, I may perhaps be permitted to flatter myself that I have been able to insert some curious information, and many historical facts, which even Mr. Pennant has omitted.

When I made the journey, I very strangely took but short descriptions of the towns of Chester and Shrewsbury, intending to confine my observations entirely to Wales: but afterwards, upon considering the matter, these places seemed so materially connected with the others, that rather than omit them, I determined to add to my own the most useful observations of Mr. Pennant and Dr. Aikin;* and since the references for these would, if inserted, have occurred very often, I thought it better to leave them out.

In the *History of the Bards*, I have been much indebted to several parts of Mr. Jones's excellent work, entitled 'Musical and Poetical Relics of the Welsh Bards.'* In the more antient part of the history, I have taken the liberty to prefer the authorities of the Roman writers to that of Mr. William Owen, who has lately, in the introduction to his translation of the elegies of Llywarch Hên, given us a history of bardism,* very different from any we ever heard of before, for in what manner soever new opinions may have sprung up, it appears to me difficult, if not impossible, to overthrow the accounts of contemporary writers, whose authority no one seems before to have doubted, and who were certainly themselves present in some of the scenes they describe.

The *Itinerary* I have attempted to make as useful as possible. When I made the tour, I took with me one, somewhat similar, extracted from the accounts of former writers. The distances are marked, I believe, pretty accurately; and all the villages, and some other places, are here inserted, many of which, from their insignificance, have not been noticed in the body of the work.

Preface to the 1800 edition

In the Appendix, I have placed, chiefly at the desire of some of my Welsh friends, Lord Lyttleton's two interesting Letters on this Country,* and a few other detached things, that I thought might be of use.

Very little of *Botany* will be found to occur in the interior of the volumes; this I have confined almost entirely to the catalogue at the end, where I have given the habitats of the plants with as great a degree of exactness as I possibly could.

In the *Index,* which is pretty full, I believe I have inserted every minute place whose name occurs, in order to render that, to naturalists in particular, of as much use as possible. They frequently want to know the situations of very small and obscure places, which, without some such guide, it would be difficult to find. The indexes to Mr. Pennant's Tour, I found by no means sufficient for this purpose; for in many cases, where the places were not described at length in the body of the work, they were omitted there.

I have now, in conclusion, to acknowledge my obligations for the kind and liberal assistance of several gentlemen in Wales, but in a most particular manner to the Reverend Peter Williams, late of Jesus College, Oxford, Rector of Llanrûg, near Caernarvon, who was my companion in many of the scenes here described;* to John Wynne Griffith, Esq. F.L.S. of Garn, near Denbigh;* the Reverend Hugh Davies, F.L.S. of Aber, near Bangor;* the Reverend Evan Lloyd, of Maes y Porth, near Newborough;* and to Mr. David Thomas, of Red Wharf, near Beaumaris, Anglesea.

W. B.

Preface to the 1804 edition

In the summer of the year 1798, I was induced, from the various accounts that had reached me respecting the grandeur of the mountain scenery of North Wales, to appropriate three months to a ramble through all its most interesting parts. I accordingly set out from Cambridge, (where I was then resident,) soon after the commencement of the long vacation, and proceeded, in the cross-country coaches, immediately to Chester. From Chester I leisurely skirted the north coast of Wales, along the great Irish road,* through St. Asaph and Conwy, to Bangor. At Caernarvon I remained for a considerable time, making excursions in all directions among the mountains, and through the principal parts of the island of Anglesea. When I had examined all the places that I could learn were worth notice, I continued my route, entirely *round* the country, visiting, in my course, Harlech, Barmouth, Dolgelle, Machynlleth, Llanydloes, Newtown, Montgomery, Welsh Pool, Oswestry, Wrexham, and Mold. From Mold I crossed over (towards the interior) to Ruthin, and proceeded through Llangollen, Corwen, and Bala, to Shrewsbury, whence, in the month of September, I returned to Cambridge.

Not satisfied with this single journey, I returned into North Wales in the year 1801, and resided there four months more; during June, July, August, and September. In this latter excursion my time was chiefly occupied in examining the counties of Caernarvon and Merioneth, and the island of Anglesea, visiting again, in these counties, all the places that I had before seen, ascending most of the principal mountains, and searching about for other, new and interesting, objects.

Previously to my first journey, I had made several tours through nearly all the romantic parts of the North of England. I can, however, with truth declare, that, taken in the whole, I have not found these by any means so interesting as four of the six counties of North Wales, namely, Denbighshire, Caernarvonshire, Merionethshire, and Anglesea. The traveller of taste (in search of grand and stupendous scenery), the naturalist, and the antiquary, have all, in this romantic country, full scope for their respective pursuits.

My mode of travelling was principally as a pedestrian, but sometimes I took horses, and at other times proceeded in carriages, as I found it convenient. A traveller on foot, if he has health and spirits, has, in my opinion, many advantages over all others: of these, the most essential is that complete independence on every thing but his own exertions, which will enable him, without difficulty, to visit and examine various places that are altogether inaccessible to persons either in carriages or on horseback.

From my first entrance into the country I had formed a determination, if I found my observations sufficiently interesting, to lay the result of them before the public. This I did in my *Tour round North Wales*, published about four years ago. Till that journey was nearly completed, no tour of any importance, later than that of Mr. Pennant, (originally published in 1778,) had come to my knowledge. I had not then heard of those either of Mr. Aikin,* Mr. Warner, or Mr. Skrine,* and therefore, not without reason, considered myself as filling an unoccupied place in British topography. The work, notwithstanding there were no fewer than half a dozen others, of a nearly similar nature, published about the same time, was so well received by the public, as to afford reasonable hopes of success to fresh exertions. The present volumes are the offspring of these exertions. How they will be received, remains yet to be decided.

To this work is attached a *Map of North Wales*, compiled from the most authentic sources, to which I could have access, and corrected by my own observations. I fear that, in many instances, it may be found inaccurate, but as Mr. Evans's 'Map of North Wales,' which contains by far the fewest errors of any that has been yet published, now sells at the enormous price of a guinea, I was, from this circumstance, induced to attempt the compilation of a new one to illustrate my own journey. If it only tends to reduce the price of Evans's map, I shall consider the labour and expence that have been bestowed upon it as sufficiently repaid.

The *Itinerary*,* inserted in the second volume, will be found of considerable use to the traveller, as it contains a notice of almost every object worth visiting throughout the whole of North Wales. It contains also an account of the distances, and a character (as I found them) of most of the inns.

Since, in a periodical work of deservedly high celebrity, it was remarked of my 'Tour round North Wales,' that I had quoted many books* as authority for my historical data, the references to which appeared rather to be taken through the medium of other books, than from the writers themselves; I think it necessary here to declare, that, of all the following authors, I have perused the originals, and every reference to them is made on my own examination. Various other writers are quoted from my own perusal, but of the titles of their works I have preserved no memorandum.

***

Christchurch, Hants,
  April 1, 1804.

1

Chester to Flint

It was early in the morning of the sixth of July that I commenced my route from Chester into Wales, in a direction towards St. Asaph and Conwy. The day had not dawned more than two hours, the dew then sparkled upon the leaves and grass, and the sun shot his red beams through the undispersed fog. The birds on every side were pouring forth their melodious notes, and the cheering coolness of the air corresponding with my own disposition at the time, to enjoy in the full all these beauties of nature, rendered the outset of this journey infinitely more pleasing than that of any of my rambles through the romantic parts of England. The fog soon cleared away, and the now unclouded sky seemed to indicate a continuance of the most delightful weather. I wandered so slowly along, that it was near seven o'clock before I arrived at

HAWARDEN.

This is a small clean-looking town in Flintshire, celebrated only for its *castle*, which has been an extensive building, and was formerly of considerable importance to the interests both of the Welsh and English people. This building, of which at present little more than the fragments of the walls and keep are left, stood on a considerable eminence, near the road, at the east end of the town, within the grounds of Sir Richard Stephen Glynne, Bart. It commands an extensive prospect towards the river Dee and the county of Chester.

The late Sir John Glynne was at the expence of having much of the rubbish removed from the ruins: and in one place there was discovered a long flight of steps, at the bottom of which was a door, and formerly a draw-bridge. This crossed a deep long chasm, to another door leading to two or three small rooms, probably places of confinement, where prisoners, after pulling up the bridge over the chasm, might be lodged in the utmost security.

The circular keep, which is more elevated and perfect than the other parts of the building, has, within these few years, had a room fitted up in it in the modern stile. This addition, however, and the painted statues interspersed in the grounds, but ill accord with the wild and shattered ruins around them.

***

Having finished my examination of Hawarden and its castle, I continued my route towards Northop. A little beyond the ninth mile-stone from Chester, I turned, on the right, over some meadows, in search of a small fortress called

EULOE CASTLE.

It stands about a quarter of a mile from the road, and from its situation on the edge of a glen, and being surrounded with wood, I had no little difficulty in finding it. It formerly consisted of two parts; the larger of which was an oblong tower, rounded at one end, and about fourteen yards long, and ten or twelve in width, guarded on the accessible side by a strong wall. The other part consists of an oblong court, at the extremity of which are the remains of a circular tower. This fortress has been well defended, on one side by a trench, and on the other by the deep valley that runs beneath it. Leland* says that Euloe Castle was the property of a gentleman of Flintshire, of the name of Howell, who, by ancient custom, a privilege he inherited from his ancestors, used to give the badge of a silver harp to the best harper in North Wales. In his own time it was, he informs us, 'a ruinous castelet or pile.'

It was in the wood adjoining to this place, called

COED EULOE,

that king Henry II in an expedition against Owen Gwynedd,* prince of North Wales, received a severe and most memorable repulse from David and Conan, the two sons of that hero. The army of Owen was encamped, and seemed ready for engagement, and some slight skirmishes were commenced. These, however, were but artifices to draw the English into a narrow and dangerous pass between the hills, where a numerous ambuscade was secretly placed under the command of his sons. Henry, too confident in the strength of his men, and not relying sufficiently on the opinion of those who had a more perfect knowledge of the country than himself, fell into the snare, and paid dearly for his rashness; for when he and his vanguard, following the

Welsh into the valley, were engaged in fight, another party, with horrible outcries, arose on a sudden from under the cover of the woods, which hung over the steep, and assaulted them with stones, arrows, and other missile weapons. The disadvantageous situation of the English army, and the confusion into which they were thrown, totally disabled them from resisting this unexpected attack; and they were routed with dreadful slaughter.

NORTHOP

When I arrived at Northop, a small village, containing a handsome and somewhat ancient church, I turned out of the usual road to Holywell, and went towards Flint.* About two miles from this place, and from the slope of a hill, at the bottom of which stands the town, the scenery opened in a most pleasing manner. It was high water; and the estuary of the Dee, which runs up towards Chester, enlivened by the vessels 'lightly floating on its surface,' the towns of Park-Gate, and some others on the opposite shore, appeared to peculiar advantage. At the ebb of the tide this wide arm of the sea dwindles into a narrow stream, inclosed on each side by long and dreary banks of sand.

FLINT

is a market town, small, irregularly built, and by no means pleasant. It has once been surrounded by a ditch and ramparts, but these are now nearly destroyed. Being situated near the sea, it is resorted to by a few from the neighbouring country, as a bathing-place; but the marshy coast which extends from the edge of the water almost to the town, must render it, in this respect, extremely disagreeable. The *church*, or rather chapel, for it is but a chapel of ease to Northop, is a dirty ill-looking building, with a boarded turret. – From this place there are packets which sail every tide, when the wind permits, for Chester and Park-Gate. This is from hence a charming, and, as far as relates to Park-Gate, certainly an expeditious mode of travelling.

Though the great sessions for the county are held at Mold, the *county gaol* is at Flint, situated in the castle-yard, in a fine healthy situation. It is a good building, and constructed on a plan similar to the gaol of Ruthin. Over the front door of this prison, on a black and white marble slab, is an elegant inscription, the composition of Mr. Pennant, which informs us of the benevolent purposes for which it was erected.

***

The *castle* stands upon a rock in the marsh, and so near the river, that sometimes at high-water the walls are washed by the tide. It has been a square building, with a tower at each angle, some remains of every one of which are yet left. The tower at the south-east corner, which is called the Double Tower, is much larger than the others. In its outward diameter it measures forty feet: it is formed by two concentric walls, each six feet thick, having a gallery eight feet wide included between them, and leaving a circular area of about twenty feet in diameter, into which there was an entry from the gallery by four doors. This appears to have been the keep. The interior of the castle is a square court, containing about an acre of ground. In the curtain on the west side there are yet left several windows with pointed arches.

HISTORY OF FLINT CASTLE

The founder of this castle has not yet been decidedly ascertained. Camden* and Lord Lyttleton attribute it to Henry II after his defeat at Coed Euloe, and concur in the opinion that it was finished by Edward I: whilst Fabian,* Stowe,* and many others, say that it was built by Edward only, about the year 1275, not mentioning a word of its being begun by Henry, though in the same sentence they each tell us that Edward strengthened Rhyddlan Castle; which plainly evinces that they distinguished betwixt building and repairing.

On Palm Sunday, 1281, the Welsh, wearied of their subjection to the English, as a signal of general insurrection seized this and other castles, plundering at the same time all who refused to join their party. In the year following, therefore, Edward, repairing to Wales, took Caergwrle castle, and marched on immediately afterwards to this place, from whence Llewelyn and his brother David* fled in precipitation, leaving it undefended.

In the year 1332 Edward III granted this and other castles, with all his lands here, to the Black Prince, to hold to him and his heirs, kings of England: and in 1385 it was bestowed by Richard II with the chief-justiceship of Chester, upon Robert Vere, Earl of Oxford.

It was surrendered fourteen years after to Percy Earl of Northumberland, who betrayed into it the unfortunate Richard II under the insidious pretence that Bolingbroke, who was waiting for him here, desired only to have his property restored, and that the kingdom should have a parliament. Northumberland met the king at Conwy, where he had gone after his return from Ireland; and they were proceeding together towards this place, when, among the recesses of the mountains near Penmaen Rhôs, the latter observed a band of soldiers. Alarmed for his safety, and now fearful of the snare that was laid for him, he attempted to return; but Percy springing forward, caught his horse's bridle, and forcibly directed his course. They dined at Rhyddlan, and arrived in the same evening at Flint. The next day, 'after dinner, (says Stowe,) the Duke of Lancaster entered the castle all armed, his basenet excepted. King Richard came down to meet him; and the duke, as soon as he saw the king, fell down on his knees, and coming near unto him, he kneeled a second time with his hat in his hand: and the king then put off his hoode and spoke first: 'Fair cousin of Lancaster, you are right wellcome.' The duke, bowing low to the ground, answered, 'My lord, I am come before you sent for me; the reason why I will shewe you. The common fame among your people is such, that ye have for the space of twenty or two and twenty years, ruled them very rigorously: but, if it please our lord, I will helpe you to govern better!' The king answered, 'Faire cousin of Lancaster, sith it pleaseth you, it pleaseth me well!' The duke then with a high sharpe voyce, bad bring forth the king's horses, and two little nagges, not worth fourtie franks were brought forthe: the king was set on the one, and the earl of Salisbury on the other: and thus the duke brought them from Flint to Chester;' from whence, after a night's rest, they were taken to London.

From this period I have been able to meet with no documents relative to the castle of Flint, till the civil wars of the reign of Charles I when it appears to have been garrisoned for the king, after having been repaired at the expence of Sir Roger Mostyn, who was appointed governor. In 1643 it was besieged by sir William Brereton and sir Thomas Middleton, and was defended till all the provisions, even to horses, failing, the governor surrendered it upon honourable terms. It must afterwards have been retaken by the royalists; for in August 1646 it appears to have been surrendered to major-general Mytton. In December of the same year it was, with Hawarden, and three other castles, ordered by the parliament to be so far destroyed as to render it untenable.

In the year 1283 Flint was made a free borough, and received its charter, which was afterwards confirmed in the reign of Philip and Mary, and again in the twelfth of William III.

This place, in conjunction with Caerwys, Rhyddlan, Caergwrle and Overton, sends a member to parliament. The election is made by such of the inhabitants as pay parochial taxes; and the returning officers are the two bailiffs appointed by the mayor.

2

Flint to Holywell

Nothing very interesting occurred in the road betwixt Flint and Holywell; and had it not been for the shortness of the journey, scarcely six miles, it would have seemed somewhat tedious. – I soon became in a great measure separated as it were from the country, by a range of hills on the left of the road, which did not allow me one pleasing prospect: and on the opposite side a long and dreary marsh, with an extant of sand in the bed of the river not less than two miles in any direction beyond it, presented such a dull uniformity of objects, that I was glad to be indebted even to a few straggling gulls, which at intervals came whirling over my head, uttering their harsh screams, for sources of reflection and amusement.

About mid-way I passed a little hamlet, where the dingy countenances of the inhabitants plainly indicated their employment to be in some of the many lead works with which this neighbourhood abounds. My appearance seemed to afford them considerable diversion; and the broad grin and vacant stare met my eyes whichever way I turned them. The ideas of a pair of spectacles and a wallet, were what they had never been accustomed to associate in the same person: and though either of them, separately, would have strongly excited their curiosity, yet, when connected, the phenomenon appeared entirely unaccountable by any of the data their experience had afforded them. About three hundred yards beyond the place, I turned round, and beheld a group consisting of about twenty men, women, and children, collected in the middle of the road, (in earnest consultation), which did not disperse so long as I continued in sight.

HOLYWELL

I know no town in North Wales that in a commercial view is of more importance than Holywell. The numerous manufactures in its vicinity, and its easy access to the sea, have rendered it the great mart of this part of the kingdom. The town is spacious, but irregular; pleasantly situated on the slope of a mountain which extends nearly to the water. Many of the houses are good, and give to it an air of considerable opulence.

The parish church is a building of no beauty whatever, situated near

St. Wenefred's Well. It is so much below the rest of the town, that the bell is scarcely audible at a little distance. When the inhabitants are to be called to prayers, they are therefore under the necessity of adopting the following singular remedy for this defect: – a person hired for the purpose, fastens a leathern strap round his neck, to the end of which a bell of tolerable weight is suspended, and over one of his knees he buckles a cushion; thus accoutred he sets out a certain time before the service commences, and walks through the principal parts of the town, jingling the bell every time his cushioned knee comes forward.

WENEFRED'S WELL,

From which the name of Holywell was given to this place, springs with vast impetuosity from a rock at the foot of a steep hill near the bottom of the town. It is covered by a small Gothic building, said to have been erected by Margaret the mother of Henry the VII, but Mr. Grose* was of opinion, that the frieze of the outside cornice, which is ornamented with monkies, and other grotesque figures, indicates it to be of more ancient date. Nothing, observes this accurate writer, can exceed the delicacy and elegance of the Gothic work on the inside of this building, which forms a canopy over the well, having in the centre, and serving as origin to the gothic arches, a circular shield on which was once carved a coat of arms. Above this was the chapel; at present converted into a charity school. The water passes from the small well, under an arch, into a larger one, which was intended for the bath.

THE LEGEND

The legendary origin of this well is singular. Wenefred,* who is supposed to have lived in the early part of the seventh century, is reported to have been a beautiful and devout virgin, of noble descent. She was placed under the protection of her relation Beuno, a descendant from the kings of Powys, who had founded a church here. A young prince of the name of Cradoc, struck with the elegance of her person, resolved to attempt her virtue; and, seizing an opportunity when all except herself were at prayers, he declared to her his passion. She made some excuse to escape from the room, and then fled from the house to the church, which appears to have been situated at the foot of the hill. Before she could reach this sanctuary he overtook her, and with his sword, in an extacy of rage and disappointment, struck off her head. This, like an elastic ball, bounded down the side of the hill, through the door of the church, and up one of the aisles directly to the altar where her friends were assembled at prayer: resting here, a clear and copious fountain immediately gushed out. St. Beuno snatched up the head, and again joining it to the body, it was, to the surprize and admiration of all present, immediately re-united, the place of separation being only marked by a white line encircling the neck. Cradoc dropped down on the spot where he had committed the atrocious act; and the legend informs us that it was not known whether the earth opened to receive his impious corpse, or whether his master, the devil, carried it off, but that it was certainly never seen afterwards. The sides of the well were covered with a sweet-scented moss, and the stones at the bottom became tinctured with her blood!

> The liveless tears shee shed into a fountaine turne,
> And, that for her alone, the water should not mourne,
> The pure vermillion blood that issued from her veines
> Unto this very day the pearly gravel staines;
> As erst the white and red were mixed in her cheeke,
> And that one part of her might be the other like,
> Her haire was turned to mosse, whose sweetness doth declare
> In liveliness of youth the natural sweets she bare.*

Wenefred survived her decapitation about fifteen years, and having, towards the latter end of that time, received the veil from St. Elerius at Gwytherin, in Denbighshire, died abbess of that monastery. There her body rested in quiet for near *five hundred years*, till the reign of king Stephen, when a miracle having been wrought, by her intercession, on a monk at Shrewsbury, the abbot of the convent there determined on a translation of her remains to their monastery, which, after much difficulty and many pretended visions from heaven, was at last effected, about the year 1138.

The well, after her death, was endowed with many miraculous properties: it healed the diseases of all who plunged into its water, and Drayton* says that no animal whatever could be drowned in it.

The following is one of the numerous wonders that have been recorded of its powerful influence: a party of depredators stole a cow from a pasture not far distant, and that their footsteps might not be traced, dragged her along some neighbouring rocks. But how were the impious wretches deceived: not one step was set without leaving an impression on the stones, as if they had been passing over soft clay; nay, the learned editor of the life of St. Wenefred says that the original describes them as at every step *sinking up to the very knees!* The owner was, by this means enabled to recover his beast; and the terrified wretches, coming in penitence to the altar, confessed their crime, and were, no doubt by the intercession of the saint, forgiven.

The sweet-scented moss, growing plentifully on the sides of this well, is nothing more than *jungermannia asplenoides* of Linnaeus;* it is found in many other springs in the kingdom, and is also occasionally to be met with in moist places, by road sides, and in woods. The supposed tincture of the blood is likewise a vegetable production, *byssus jolithus*. I have some doubt whether the moss, as it is called, does not entirely derive its smell from that of the byssus, which is very powerful, and which I have known it to retain on a stone in a cabinet for a great length of time, even though itself was almost dried away and become invisible.

The day of the commemoration of St. Wenefred is the 3d of November, and it is yet observed by the Roman Catholics of this part of the country.

Dr. Powel* has ascribed the invention of this well to the monks of Basingwerk, an abbey about a mile distant, from the circumstance of its not being mentioned by any person who wrote previous to the foundation of that monastery. Giraldus Cambrensis,* a man ever ready to relate any wonderful story, though he lodged there a night, in his journey through Wales, in the year 1187, does not once speak of it. – Dr. Fuller, in his peculiar manner of writing, remarks of the legend of St. Wenefred, 'that if the tip of his tongue who first told, and the top of his fingers who first wrote this damnable lie, had been cut off, and they had both been sent to attend their cure at the shrine of St. Beuno, they would certainly have been more wary afterwards how they reported or recorded such improbable untruths.'*

The devotees of the saint were formerly very numerous, and in the last age the well was so noted, that, according to Mr. Pennant, a crowned head dignified the place with a visit. 'The prince who lost three kingdoms for a mass, payed his respects on the 29th of August, 1686, to our saint, and received as a reward a present of the very shift in which his great grandmother, Mary Queen of Scots, lost her head.'* Of late years the visitors have much fallen off: however, if I may judge from seven crutches and two hand-barrows stuck among the gothic ornaments of the roof, I should suppose that the well was not yet entirely forsaken. Indeed the sanative properties of this water, in common with those of cold baths in

Flint to Holywell

general, are not to be disputed; but to attribute to the intercession of a saint those things which from the common course of nature are to be accounted for, seems only worthy the ages of superstition and ignorance.

The quantity of water thrown up here has been found, on an accurate calculation, not less than *eighty-four hogsheads* in a minute. The well has never been known to be frozen, and it scarcely ever varies in quantity, either in droughts, or after the greatest rains. These circumstances render it of inestimable value: for, although the water has only a mile and a hundred and twenty-four yards to run, before it arrives at the sea, it turned, a few years ago, the machinery to eleven different extensive

MILLS AND MANUFACTORIES.

1. *A Corn Mill*, a large building that stands near the head of the stream.
2. *The Upper Cotton Mill*, erected in the autumn of the year 1783, and finished in the short space of six weeks from the laying of the foundation. It is six stories high, and forty yards long. – This and all the other cotton works on the stream belong to a partnership concern, under the firm of the 'Cotton and Twist Company'.
3. *The Old Cotton Mill*, erected in the spring of 1777. This is only three stories high: it is thirty-three yards long, and eight wide.
4. *The Crescent Cotton Mill*, erected in the spring of 1790. It is six stories high; twenty-six yards long, and ten wide.
5. *The Brass Battery Mills*, built in the year 1765. These works are at present in the hands of Thomas Williams, Esq. and Co. under the firm of 'The Greenfield Copper and Brass Company.'* Goods are here prepared for Africa, America, and other parts of the globe. For Africa, large brass pans, called *Neptunes*, in which the negroes make salt: pans for getting the gold out of the beds of the rivers, that has been washed from the mountains by the violence of the torrents: bright and black *manillas*; the latter are the current coin of some parts of the African coast, and the first are rings to ornament the arms and the legs of the negroes.* Brass vessels are also made here for various other purposes; and brass and copper rods.
6. *A Copper Rolling Mill*, erected in 1787. This is the largest and most commodious building of the kind in the kingdom, being eighty-six feet long, sixty-nine wide, and near thirty high in the centre. It is the property of the Greenfield Copper and Brass Company.
7. *The Lower Cotton Mill*, was built in the summer of 1785. It is six stories high; thirty-six yards long, and ten wide.
8. *A Copper Wire Mill*, belonging to the Parys Mine Company,* situated

on the east side of the stream. This is a manufactory for brass wire of every denomination. Square materials are also drawn at this place for making copper nails, in the common way of beating and heading.

9. *A Copper Rolling Mill* of the Parys Mine Company.

10. *Brass Melting Houses* belonging to the Greenfield Copper and Brass Company. At these works the proprietors make plate-brass for the purpose of being manufactured at their Battery Mills; plate-brass for wire for the pin manufacturers, and ingot brass for the founders, &c. They have a mill, conveniences to calcine, buddle, and grind calamine, &c. and a copper forge. The latter is now out of use.

11. *A Copper Forge*. This is the property of the Parys Mine Company, and stands on the lower part of the stream, next the sea. These buildings were finished in the year 1780. Here is a great forge for heating the cakes of copper previously to their being beat into pans, or rolled into sheathings, &c. From hence our navy is in part supplied with sheathing, bolts, and nails. Some of the bolts are twenty feet long, and so hardened by rolling and battering as, when facilitated, by boring with an auger two-thirds of their length, to be capable of being driven almost to their heads, into places where the beds of timber are extremely thick. Rudder bands and braces are manufactured here; and nails, from a foot long to the size of a sadler's tack. Braziers are furnished from hence with all kinds of copper vessels. – These, and all the other works on the stream of this description, are furnished with copper from the Anglesea mines.

The Mine Companies employ near forty vessels of from thirty to fifty tons burthen each, to convey the several manufactures, or the materials, to and from Liverpool, and other places where they have connections.

In this stream it is remarked that the waterwheels are very soon destroyed: so much so that an oak wheel, which in most other waters ought to have lasted at least thirty years, has been known to become unfit for use in twelve. A species of moss, the *hypnum riparium*, vegetates on the wood, and harbours the larvae of some species of insect in such immense quantities, that they soon eat even into the heart of the wood. On this account, the Greenfield Company's Copper and Brass Rolling Mill, has its water wheels formed of cast-iron in the place of timber.

By the road side, near the larger well is a *small spring* that was once famous for the cure of weak eyes. An offering was made to the tutelar saint (for most of the springs in this country are dedicated to some imaginary saint) of a crooked pin, and at the time of laving the eyes, an ejaculation, by way of addition to the charm, was uttered by the patient. In the present age the waters have lost nearly all their efficacy.

BASINGWERK ABBEY

In search of Basingwerk Abbey, I proceeded along the road by the side of the stream, for about a mile, till I came to the marsh, and then crossing it to the right, I found myself within sight of the ruin, which stands on an eminence just above. These shattered time-worn remains, with the surrounding sycamores, are from some points of view highly picturesque and beautiful.

> The ivy now in rude luxuriance bends
>   Its tangled foliage through the cloistered space,
> O'er the green window's mould'ring height ascends,
>   And fondly clasps it in a last embrace.*

The little at present left is scarcely sufficient to indicate to us what this Abbey was when in its flourishing state. The church, which lay on the east side, is totally destroyed. The refectory is the most entire part of the building, and has on one side a large recess with a couple of circular arches. The pillars that support these are somewhat singular, being formed of stones that at present, according to the remark of a friend who attended this part of my ramble, bear an appearance not unlike that of cheeses piled on each other. Above the refectory was the dormitory where the monks had their cells. The chapel of the Knights Templars, founded here by Henry II, is spacious and elegant. The brick building striped with timber, that joins the Abbey, and certainly adds nothing to its beauty, is conjectured by Mr. Grose to have been the granary. The situation is delightful, commanding an extensive prospect of the river Dee, Chester, Park-Gate, and the Lancastrian hills. The architecture is mixed, the round arches and short massy columns exhibiting the Saxon, and the narrow pointed windows the Gothic style.

Tanner* and Dugdale* say that Basingwerk Abbey was founded by Ranulph Earl of Chester, about the year 1131, and that this foundation was afterwards confirmed by Henry II and Llewelyn prince of North Wales.* Many of the old writers ascribe the original foundation to Henry, but Mr. Pennant is of opinion that it ought to be referred to a period considerably anterior to either of these.

At the dissolution of abbeys in the reign of Henry VIII its revenues appear to have amounted to somewhat more than a hundred and fifty pounds *per annum*.

BASINGWERK CASTLE

Vestiges of this fortress are yet visible in the foundation of a wall on the edge of Watt's Dyke, and by the road side near the turnpike gate, at a little distance from the Abbey: but these are very trifling. It is supposed to have been indebted for its erection to Richard the son of Hugh Lupus earl of Chester. In the year 1119, after his return from Normandy, where he had been educated, he attempted a pilgrimage to Wenefred's well; but either in his journey thither, or on his return, he was attacked by a party of Welsh, and obliged to seek for shelter in Basingwerk Abbey. Thus situated, he implored protection from Wenefred, who, tradition says, raised certain sands betwixt Flintshire and the opposite coast, to permit his constable and men to pass over to his relief, which, from that circumstance, were called *Constable's Sands!* If any reliance whatever is to be had as to the origin of this tradition, it tends to prove that the foundation of the Abbey was prior to the date generally assigned to it, and that the well was accounted miraculous before the journey of Giraldus Cambrensis, notwithstanding his being entirely silent respecting it. I must confess myself inclined to the former opinion, but I have inserted the story, that the matter may be decided by heads wiser than my own.

The castle is well known to have been rebuilt in the year 1157, by Henry II after his escape in the battle near Euloe; he, however, first cleared all the passes and cut down the woods around it, which at that time were impenetrable forests, affording shelter, as he had keenly experienced, to powerful enemies. The Welsh ever looked upon this fortress as a disagreeable check upon their proceedings and liberty, and therefore about eight years afterwards, Owen Gwynedd, after many unsuccessful attempts, at last took it by storm, and immediately levelled it with the ground. From this time it does not appear to have been the cause of any further contentions.

WATT'S DYKE

This barrier begins at Maesbury near Oswestry, passes by that town, through the grounds at Wynnstay, near Wrexham, Hope, and Northop, and terminates in the Dee at this place. Churchyard is almost the only writer that has not confounded this with Offa's Dyke. He assigns as the object of its formation that the space betwixt the two, for they run to a considerable distance nearly parallel with each other, was to be free ground, where the Britons and Danes might meet for all commercial purposes.

> There is a famous thing,
> Call'd Offa's Dyke, that reacheth farre in length.
> All kind of ware the Danes might thither bring,
> It was free ground and call'd the Briton's strength.
> Wat's Dyke, likewise, about the same was set,
> Between which two the Danes and Britons met,
> And traffic still, but passing bounds by sleight,
> The one did take the other pris'ner streight.*

3

Holywell to St. Asaph

The road from Holywell to St. Asaph is rugged but pleasant. This country abounds in *lead mines*, and I passed some very considerable ones about a mile beyond Holywell. The veins of ore, as I was informed, run in directions either north and south, or east and west, but of these the latter are by much the richest. They are found in a matrix either of chert or limestone, and often extend to unknown depths. The common, or lamellated ore, yields above fifteen hundred of lead to twenty of the ore; and, in general, about fourteen ounces of silver to the ton.

Calamine is also found in great quantities in this neighbourhood, and in veins like the lead, sometimes mixed with ore, but frequently alone. Nearly the whole of Flintshire abounds with it, and so entirely ignorant were the inhabitants of its use as, within the last sixty years, even to mend their roads with it. These roads have, however, been since turned up in many places, and their materials converted to more valuable purposes.

I had not passed the lead mines far before I came within sight of an ancient circular building, in form not much unlike a windmill, on the summit of a lofty hill, called Carreg, in the parish of Whitford, and about two miles to the right of the road. This, Mr. Pennant, entreating his friends not to consider him an *antiquarian Quixote* for doing it, conjectures to have been a Roman pharos, constructed to direct the navigators to and from Deva, along the difficult channel of Seteia Portus.*

***

VALE OF CLWYD

About two miles from St. Asaph, I entered the celebrated vale of Clwyd,* and, favoured by a charmingly serene morning, the whole scene, from the side of the hill, appeared to the greatest advantage. Towards the south stood Denbigh, with the shattered remains of its castle crowning the summit of a rocky steep in the middle of the vale; and on the north, clad in its sober hue, I observed the castle of Rhyddlan. The intervening space was enlivened with meadows, woods, cottages, herds, and flocks scattered in every pleasing direction, whilst the whole was bounded by the sea and the dark retiring mountains. This, from the extent of picture, is not a scene fitted for the pencil, though its numerous beauties must attract the attention of every lover of nature. When we enter a rugged mountainous scene, where the shelving sides scarcely afford soil for vegetation, and where the whole character is that of savage grandeur, we are struck with astonishment and awe; but, when nature presents us with a scene like this, which seems to abound in health, fertility, and happiness, every nerve vibrates to the heart the pleasure we receive. Here the pencil fails:

> I admire –
> None more admires – the painter's magic skill,
> Who shews me that which I shall never see,
> Conveys a distant country into mine,
> And throws Italian light on English walls:
> But imitative strokes can do no more
> Than please the eye – sweet Nature ev'ry sense.
> The air salubrious of her lofty hills,
> The cheering fragrance of her dewy vales,
> And music of her woods, – no works of man
> May rival these; they all bespeak a pow'r
> Peculiar, and exclusively her own.*

ST. ASAPH

After enjoying this lovely scene for some time, I descended into the vale, crossed the bridge over the little river Clwyd, and soon after arrived at St. Asaph, or, as it is called by the Welsh, Llan Elwy, *the Church of Elwy*, a name obtained from its situation on the bank of the river Elwy, which runs along the west side of the place. It consists of little more than a single street, the houses pretty uniformly built, up the side of a hill. It has a cathedral and parish church; and, as a city, is, except one or two, the most insignificant in the kingdom. The cathedral, though small, is plain and neat. The episcopal palace is a large and convenient building, under the grounds of which the Elwy runs. The deanery is on the opposite side of the river, and stands due west of the cathedral.

HISTORY OF THE CATHEDRAL

Cyndeyrn Garthwys, or Kentigern, the son of Owain ap Urien Reged, was bishop of Glasgow and primate of Scotland, but was driven thence by the persecutions of one of the Scottish princes. He fled into Wales, where he was taken into the protection of Cadwallon, uncle to Maelgwn Gwynedd, prince of North Wales, who assigned to him Llan Elwy as a place of residence. Here, about the year 560, he founded an episcopal seat and monastery, and became himself the first bishop. On the death of his persecutor he was recalled into Scotland, but first nominated his disciple Asa or Asaph, his successor, from whom both the church and place received their names. In the time of Asa, the number of monks were nine hundred and sixty-five; of these three hundred were labourers in the fields, three hundred servants about the monastery, and the rest were religious. Asa died about the year 596, and was interred in the cathedral.

In the disturbances during the time of the Normans, such devastations appear to have been committed in these parts, that the see remained long unoccupied. Towards the middle of the twelfth century, however, we find that a bishop Gilbert was consecrated to it. Galfrid Arthur, or Geoffry of Monmouth,* was his successor.

About the year 1247, in the wars betwixt Henry III and the Welsh, the bishops both of St. Asaph and Bangor were driven from their sees, and became indebted to voluntary contributions for subsistence. In somewhat more than thirty years after this period, the cathedral was consumed by fire, and two years were occupied in rebuilding it. In the interval, Edward I, at the request of bishop Anian, petitioned the Pope to permit him to remove the see to Rhyddlan, as a place from whose fortifications it would be protected against the fury of the Welsh, whilst in its late situation it had been exposed to all their attacks. He, at the same time, made an offer both of ground for the church, and a thousand marks towards the expences of building it. The design, however, appears to have been frustrated either by the death of the Pope, or the exhortation of the archbishop of Canterbury to rebuild the cathedral on its former site. The roof and upper parts, with the bishop's palace and canons' houses, were again destroyed by Owen Glyndwr in 1404; and they remained in ruins for upwards of seventy years, when they were rebuilt by bishop Redman.

During the protectorship of Oliver Cromwell, the post-master of St. Asaph, who had attached himself to the puritanical party, occupied the palace, in which he kept his office. He used the font belonging to the cathedral as a trough for watering his horses, and, by way of venting his spleen on the established clergy, he tied up his calves in the bishop's throne.

***

MIRACLE

Not many years ago a mark on a black stone in the pavement of the street, about the middle of the hill between the two churches, used to be pointed out to strangers as the print of St. Asaph's horse-shoe, when he leaped with him from Onan-hassa, which is about two miles off. This, however, observes Mr. Grose, who relates the story, seems to have been a miracle performed rather by the horse than by the saint, to whom alone it is ascribed, unless the keeping of his seat at so great a leap may be deemed such. What was the occasion of this extraordinary leap we are not told; whether only to shew the agility of his horse, or to escape the assaults of the foul fiend, who, in those days, took unaccountable liberties even with saints.

VALE OF CLWYD

The tower of the cathedral commands a most extensive prospect of the vale of Clwyd, in every direction; and it is almost the only situation that I could find for seeing it to advantage. The river Clwyd, from which the vale takes its name, is a diminutive stream that meanders along its bottom, scarcely three yards over in the widest part. Its banks are low, and after sudden rains it is subject to the most dreadful overflowings, the torrent at these times, frequently sweeping along with it even the very soil of the land it passes over. From this circumstance it is that much of the land near its banks is let at very low rents. This vale is perhaps the most extensive of any in the kingdom, being near twenty-four miles in length, and about seven in width; containing the three considerable towns of St. Asaph, Denbigh, and Ruthin; and though it is impossible to exhibit a more beautiful scene of fertility, yet, from its great width and its want of water, I believe the painter will prefer to it many of the deep and picturesque glens of Caernarvonshire and Merionethshire.

4

Excursion from St. Asaph to Rhyddlan

From St. Asaph I wandered along the vale three miles, towards the village of Rhyddlan, or the *Red Shore*, so called from the colour of its site. The country all the way was interesting. At the distance of about a mile I looked back upon the little city I had left. Its single street occupied the slope of the hill, at the top of which stood the cathedral; and the intermingled trees and houses, with the turbulent river Elwy flowing at the bottom, under a majestic bridge of five arches, grouped together into an extremely beautiful scene.

RHYDDLAN

Lies in a flat, on the eastern bank of the river Clwyd, about two miles from its influx into the sea. This is here a little extended in width, so as, at high water, to admit of small flat vessels riding up, as far as the bridge. Although Rhyddlan is now a very insignificant village, it was formerly a place of considerable magnitude and importance; but no traces whatever of these are left except in the ruins of its castle. Edward I annexed to it the privileges of a free borough, to facilitate an intercourse betwixt the Welsh and English, for the purpose of allaying the rooted enmity and the unhappy jealousies that had for centuries rent the two countries. In all his proceedings our monarch exhibited strong features of policy. He had been early taught that when stratagem would supply the place of men and treasure, it was at least wise, if not always just, to adopt it. Hence originated likewise the statute of Rhyddlan, and hence was his infant son proclaimed prince of Wales. This statute, which was passed in a parliament assembled here in the year 1283, contains a set of regulations for the government of Wales; it also recites many curious particulars relative to the Welsh customs previous to Edward's conquest, against which it was in a great measure directed. His imposing upon them his son who had, not long before, been born at Caernarvon, for a prince, is an instance of craft which we are surprised to observe in so great a monarch as Edward. He assembled the Welsh barons and chief men, and informed them that in consequence of their long-expressed desire to have a prince, a native of their own country, he had at length determined to indulge them, in nominating one whose whole life had been hitherto irreproachable, and who could not even speak a word of English. Little did they think, when expressing their acclamations of joy and unbounded promises of obedience, that the prince he was about to invest, who was so immaculate, had scarcely been born twelve months, and was at least able to speak as much English as Welsh. The scheme in a great measure succeeded; and, aided by the strength he at that time had obtained in the country, and the additional forces that he brought into it from England, he totally subdued this warlike people. 'I confess, however,' says Mr. Vaughan, of Hengwrt near Dolgelle, 'we have reason to bless God for his mercy to us, in our happy establishment under one monarch. We may well say we were conquered to our gain and undone to our advantage.'

MORFA RHYDDLAN

Betwixt the village and the sea is a large marsh, called Morfa Rhyddlan, *the Marsh of Rhyddlan*, where, in the year 795, a dreadful battle was fought betwixt the Welsh people under their leader Caradoc, and the Saxon forces headed by Offa king of Mercia. The Welsh were routed, and their commander was slain. The Saxon prince, in the heat of his revenge, cruelly ordered all the men and children of the enemy that fell into his hands to be massacred, the women alone escaping their fury. This tragical event is supposed to have been recorded by a poem, written shortly afterwards, copies of which are now extant. The plaintive air called Morfa Rhyddlan,* as we are told by some, had its origin about the same period; but, from its construction, infinitely too artificial for those dark ages, it is easy to discern that it must be attributed to a much more recent date.

RHYDDLAN CASTLE

The castle is of red stone, nearly square, and has six towers, two at each of two opposite corners, and only one at each of the others. One of these was called the *King's Tower*, Twr y Brenin. It had a double ditch on the north, and a strong wall and foss all round. In this wall a tower called Twr y Silod is yet standing. The principal entrance appears to have been at the north-west angle, betwixt two round towers: the two opposite to these are much shattered, but the remainder are tolerably entire.

***

BLACK FRIARY

Not far from the castle was a house of Black Friars, founded some time before 1268; for in that year Anian, who is related to have been prior of the house, was created bishop of St. Asaph. It suffered greatly in the wars betwixt Edward and Llewelyn, but recovered, and subsisted till the dissolution. It does not appear in the valuations either of Dugdale or Speed.* I did not remark when I was here, whether any part of the building was remaining.

From the *port*, (about two miles from the village,) where the river Clwyd discharges itself into the sea, considerable quantities of corn and timber, the produce of the vale and neighbourhood, are annually exported.

DISERTH

The village of Diserth is about two miles and a half east of Rhyddlan. The church stands in a romantic bottom, and is finely overshaded with several large yew trees that grow around it. In the church-yard are many very singular tombstones; two in particular attracted my attention, they were not, as usual, altar-shaped, but had each a semicircular stone on the top. They were of ancient date, and belonged to a family of the name of Hughes. Here was also a curious and much ornamented old pillar, of whose use I could form no conception.

DISERTH CASTLE*

The castle stands on the summit of a high limestone rock, at the distance of about half a mile from the village. Its present remains are very trifling, consisting of nothing more than a few shattered fragments. From hence there is a fine prospect of part of the vale of Clwyd.

Diserth castle, which was formerly a British* post, the last of the chain on the Clwydian hills, had, amongst others, the name of Castell y Craig, *The Castle of the Rock*. The time of its foundation is not known. It was fortified by Henry III about the year 1241; and appears to have been the property of the earls of Chester. In the thirty-first of Henry III on the extinction of this family, it became annexed to the crown; and about twenty years afterwards was destroyed, along with the castle of Diganwy, near Conwy, by Llewelyn ap Griffith.

On the castle-hill I collected some fine specimens of *Veronica*

Spicata, a plant that I had never before met with: its blue spikes appeared very beautiful, mixed with the delicate flowers of *Geranium sanguineum*, or sometimes with the brilliant yellow of the *Cistus helianthemum*, which abounds on this dry calcareous soil. *Cistus Marifolius* was nearly in equal plenty with its relative; and *Thalictrum minus, Conyza squarrosa*, and *Carduus marianus*, with some other plants not so rare, were the principal of my discoveries here.

SIR ROBERT POUNDERLING

In a field somewhat south of this place, I observed a ruinous building, which, on inquiry, I found was called Siamber Wen, *the White Hall*. This was the mansion of Sir Robert Pounderling, a valiant knight, who was many years constable of the castle. This illustrious hero, we are told, was so celebrated for his prowess, that, amongst other challenges, he received one at a tournament in this country from a Welshman, who in the combat struck out one of his eyes. Being afterwards at the English court, he was requested to challenge him in return, but he wisely shewed that he had prudence as well as valour, by declining a second combat, alleging as his excuse, that he had no desire to have the Welshman knock out his other eye.

From this place I retraced my road through Rhyddlan to St. Asaph, from whence the next morning I made my excursion to Denbigh. – I must remark, for the benefit of those who follow me, that in the latter part of this day's ramble from Rhyddlan to Diserth, I received little amusement, except in my botanical pursuits. Neither the village nor the castle of Diserth afford any thing very deserving of attention.

5

Excursion from St. Asaph to Denbigh

> O Denbigh now appeare, thy turne is next,
> I need no gloss, nor shade to set thee out:
> For if my pen doe follow playnest text,
> And passe right way, and goe nothing about,
> Thou shalt be knowne, as worthie well thou art,
> The noblest soyle that is in any part:
> And for thy seate, and castle do compare,
> With any one of Wales, what'ere they are.

So says honest Churchyard in a poetical account of 'the Worthines of Wales,' written about the middle of the sixteenth century, when Denbigh was accounted a place of considerable importance, and when its walls and castle were entire.

I was much disappointed in the walk from St. Asaph to Denbigh. From remarking in the maps that it lay entirely along the vale of Clwyd, I had expected many elegant and varied prospects. The road, however, lies so low, and the vale is so wide, and so much intersected with lofty hedge-rows, that it was only in two or three places that I had any interesting prospect whatever. A woody dell, watered by the river Elwy, and ornamented with a gentleman's seat or two, pleasingly situated amongst the trees on its rising bank, afforded a picturesque scene on the right of the road, about three miles from St. Asaph.

DENBIGH*

The town of Denbigh was hidden by low intervening mountains, till I had arrived within a mile of it. It is situated on a rock, whose summit is crowned by the fine ruins of its castle, nearly in the middle of the vale of Clwyd. All the streets, except one, are very irregular, and the houses are in general ill built. I wandered alone to the castle, but, from the great number of turnings in the narrow streets, experienced some difficulty in reaching it, although I had it in view nearly the whole time. – A late tourist (Mr. Skrine) has remarked, that Denbigh, from its situation, has been thought to resemble Edinburgh.* But though some slight traces of similarity may be found, he is of opinion that the boldness of the position of Edinburgh, and the grandeur of its surrounding objects, far surpass every thing here.

DENBIGH CASTLE

The entrance into the castle is through a large Gothic arch, which was formerly flanked by two octagonal towers, both now in ruins. In an ornamental niche over the arch, is a figure of its founder Henry de Lacy; and over another gate, that formerly stood on the left of this, there was also a statue of his wife, Margaret, the daughter of William Longspee, earl of Salisbury. This castle has once been a most extensive building; and from the strength and thickness of its walls, it appears to have been impregnable, except by artillery or famine. – The breaches in the walls (observes Mr. Grose) plainly shew how they were constructed. Two walls, occupying the extremities, of the intended thickness, were first built in the ordinary manner, with a vacuity betwixt them, into which was poured a mixture of hot mortar and rough stones of all sizes, which, on cooling, consolidated into a mass as hard as stone. This kind of building was called *grouting*.

The parish church of Denbigh is Whitchurch, about a mile distant; but there is a chapel of ease within the walls of the castle, a building which was formerly used as the chapel to the garrison. At a little distance from this there is also part of the body of a church begun by Robert Dudley, earl of Leicester, in 1579. Elizabeth granted to this nobleman the castle and lordship of Denbigh. But having incurred the hatred of the inhabitants by his tyrannical and oppressive conduct, he chose to leave it in its present unfinished state.

From the walls of the castle I had a fine view of all the country for many miles round. From hence the vale, in all its pastoral beauty, is displayed before the eye. The banks of the little river are pleasingly decorated; and the bounding mountains finely contrast their naked barren sides with the delightful scene of fertility between them.

***

With respect to the town of Denbigh, Leland informs us that there had been many streets within the walls, but that in his time (before the middle of the sixteenth century) these were nearly all demolished, the number of householders within the walls scarcely then exceeding eighty. This decay is supposed to have arisen from the joint inconveniences of the want of water, and the steep situation of the old town. It became gradually abandoned till at length it was wholly deserted, and a new town, much more convenient, was formed about the bottom of the rock. – The town walls, like those of the castle, appear to have had great strength. There were only two gates, the Exchequer and the Burgess's Gate. In the former (which was on the west side) the lord's courts were holden; and in the other (which was on the north) the burgesses held their courts. Besides these the walls had only four towers.

This place was endowed with the privileges of a free borough by King Richard II. Queen Elizabeth formed here a body corporate, consisting of two aldermen, two bailiffs, two coroners, and twenty-five capital burgesses, a recorder, and inferior officers. It returns one member to parliament.

WHITE FRIARY

At the east end of the town there was formerly a house of Carmelite, or white friars, dedicated to St. Mary. This is said by some historians to have been founded by John Salisbury, who died in 1289; but, according to others, it was the work of John de Sanismore, towards the close of the fourteenth century.

Whitchurch, the parish church to Denbigh, and about a mile distant, is a white-washed structure of no very elegant appearance. It is chiefly celebrated from containing the remains of sir Richard Middleton, governor of Denbigh castle, under Edward VI, Mary, and Elizabeth, in 1576; and of

HUMPHREY LLWYD,[*]

The antiquary, to whose memory there is a mural monument, containing a figure of himself in the attitude of prayer. This person was a native of Denbigh, and a student of Brason-nose college, Oxford. He adopted the profession of physic, and became family physician in the house of the last Fitzalan, earl of Arundel, the chancellor of the university. He represented his native place in parliament, and died there in the forty-first year of his age. He compiled a map of England for his friend Ortelius, to whom he dedicated his '*Commentariolum Britanniae,*' and his epistle '*De*

Monâ Druidum insulâ, antiquitati suae restituta.' He left in manuscript, among various other tracts, a Welsh Chronicle from king Cadwaladr, and a History of Cambria. He collected many curious books for lord Lumley, (whose sister he married), which form at this time a valuable part in the library of the British Museum. His great grandson, the reverend Robert Lloyd, contended, but without effect, for the barony of Lumley. This latter person was rector of St. Paul's Covent Garden.

The approach to Denbigh from Whitchurch is much more august and grand than from any other side. The castle, from this road, is seen finely situated on the summit of its rock, which being nearly perpendicular, affords one a good idea of the ancient strength of the place. From hence, also, the accompanying scenery appears more open and varied than from any other part of the immediate neighbourhood of the town.

6

St. Asaph to Conwy

My next stage was Conwy. The road now became somewhat more hilly, but it was hard and good, and the surrounding country, for the most part very pleasant. After passing Abergeley, *the conflux of the concealed water*, a small village about seven miles from St. Asaph, I had the sea on the right, and a range of low rocks on the left of the road. From the bottoms of the rocks, for many miles, meadows and corn-fields extended, sloping nearly to the water's edge. – Beyond Llandulas, *The Dark Village*, the road winds round a huge limestone rock, called Penmaen Rhôs.

It is supposed to have been in some of the deep bottoms of this neighbourhood, that king Richard II was surprized by a band of armed ruffians, secreted there by the earl of Northumberland, for the purpose of forcing him into the hands of Bolingbroke, who was waiting the event at Flint.

I had wandered for some time leisurely along this road, my eyes fixed upon the ground in search of plants, when suddenly raising my head, I was astonished with the magnificence of the landscape before me. The fine old town of Conwy, with its gloomy walls and towers, and its majestic, turretted castle, appeared with the wide river in front, and backed by rising, wooded, and meadowy grounds, and beyond these by the vast mountains of Caernarvonshire.

RIVER CONWY AND FERRY

The river Conwy* runs on this, the east side of the town. It is here about half a mile across, and at present passed by means of ferry-boats. Besides the inconveniences naturally attending so wide a stream, in a place subject to all the variations produced by the flowing and ebbing of tides that run sometimes very high, most of the travellers who have crossed here (except the passengers in the mail-coach, who, by order of the post-office, have a boat always waiting for them), know what it is to experience the wilful delays, and the gross and bare-faced impositions of the ferry-men. The charges ought to be *a penny* for every person on foot, except with respect to those who come in the public coaches or in post chaises, who are required, though from what principle I cannot learn, to pay *a shilling* each; *two-pence* for a man and horse, and *half-a-crown* a wheel for gentlemen's carriages. Instead of the latter fare, I have myself known them with the most impudent assurance possible, charge half-a-guinea for ferrying over a gig, and after receiving that, importune in addition for liquor. The ferry is the property of Thomas Williams, Esq. of Llanidan in Anglesea, the member for Great Marlow,* and is regulated by Mr. Hughes of Marl, a place about three quarters of a mile from the ferry-house.

The latter person I met with more than once during the time I was in Caernarvonshire: he informed me the fares were as above, *with what the travellers pleased to give the men besides*; and that they were paid seven shillings a week each from him, but *were entitled to what they could get in addition*. Thus definite are the terms on which these ferrymen are supposed to obtain subsistence. But they are not contented with merely risking the generosity of the traveller, they make him an extra charge, and take the risk for what they can get beyond that, for they very seldom fail to beg something, as they term it, 'for themselves.' These impositions, however, unpleasant as they may be, are trifling inconveniences to those suffered from their wilful and needless delays. In the finest weather, when they have had no excuses to allege from boisterous winds or rough water, persons have frequently waited for them several hours, and indeed instances have occurred of such being under the necessity of remaining at the ferry-house a whole night in consequence merely of their neglect. I have more than once experienced both their impositions and delays myself, and am acquainted with several gentlemen who have suffered infinitely more from them than I ever did. It is however in contemplation to erect a bridge across the stream, which, on account of the narrowness of the channel at low water, is supposed to be perfectly practicable, when all these inconveniences will at once be obviated.*

PEARL-FISHERY

This river was celebrated in former times as a pearl-fishery; and pearls have been found here at different intervals ever since the Roman conquest. It was to obtain these that Suetonius alleges as one of the principal motives for his invasion of our island;* but there is reason to suppose that he was in a great measure disappointed in his hopes, both with respect to their size and quantity. The shell in which they are found is called the

Pearl Muscle, and is the *Mya margaritifera* of Linnaeus. It is peculiar to stony and rapid rivers, burying itself with its open end downwards in the sand; but it is not often found here at present. The pearl is a calculus, or morbid concretion, supposed to be produced by some disease, and is at times found even in the common oyster and muscle. It is sometimes within the body of the animal, and sometimes on the inside of the shell; and one muscle frequently contains more than a single pearl. The shells that bear the best pearls are not smooth and equal like the rest, but are crooked and wrinkled; and the larger the pearls are, the greater is their deformity. Linnaeus informed Mr. Pennant that he had discovered the art of causing the pearls to form: he however refused to communicate it, and it is supposed to have died with him. When there are pearls in the shell, the animals, on being squeezed, will eject them, and they even sometimes spontaneously cast them on the sand of the river. It is reported in the country that sir Richard Wynne of Gwydir presented the queen of Charles II with a pearl from the river Conwy, which was afterwards placed in the regal crown. About twenty-five years ago the late Sir Robert Vaughan went to court with a button and loop in his hat set with pearls from the Conwy. An Irish pearl is mentioned by sir Robert Redding in the Philosophical Transactions, as weighing thirty-six carrats, and valued at forty pounds. The present lady Newborough* has a good collection of the Conwy pearls, and she purchases all the best that are now to be found. – The fish of the pearl muscle is not eaten, being extremely bad and unpalatable.

CONWY

Is, though somewhat gloomy from the antiquity of many of its buildings, a most beautiful and picturesque town. Its walls, which are founded for the most part on the solid rock, and in many places above twelve feet in thickness, are nearly entire. The houses are irregular but by no means bad.

THE CASTLE

Stands upon a rock, two sides of which are washed by the river. Its architecture and situation are truly grand. The heap of rubbish at present remaining in the river nearly opposite to the end of the castle, is the relic of a tower, which terminated a curtain coming from that angle of the town-wall; and at the other end there was a smaller one, which has been long destroyed. The use of these was to prevent the approach of an enemy from the water so near the castle as to become dangerous. Besides these,

Fig. 7. *Conwy Castle*, Caernarfonshire (Gwynedd), engraving after drawing by William Bingley in 1798.

the castle was also defended by eight large circular towers, from each of which formerly issued a slender turret of use as a watch-tower: of the latter only four are remaining. The exterior walls are of the same thickness as those round the town. These, as well as the towers, except one on the south side of the castle, are in appearance tolerably entire. The lower part of that, however, from the stones having been taken away from the foundation, has fallen down the rock. The upper part remains still suspended at a vast height above, and exhibits in the breach, observes Mr. Pennant, 'such vast strength of walling, as might have given to the architect the most reasonable hope that his work would have endured to the end of time.'

The chief entrance into the castle is at the north-west end, formerly over a deep trench and drawbridge.

The hall is the most remarkable part of the building now left, and has once been a magnificent apartment. It is a hundred and thirty feet long, about thirty broad, and upwards of twenty in height. The ceiling was supported by eight flat gothic arches. It was lighted by six narrow windows towards the river, and three much larger and more ornamented towards the court. It appears to have had cellars under the south side and at the east end, the roof of which has long been destroyed. Only four of the arches above the hall are left, and from these and the walls the ivy hangs in the greatest luxuriance. Vegetation seems to be going on in all parts; and the feathered tribe are the only present tenants, whose screams, when disturbed by the abrupt entrance of the traveller, add greatly to the desolation of the scene.

The two towers at the end of the castle opposite to the great gate, are called, one the *King's*, and the other the *Queen's Tower*, from Edward I and his consort Eleanor, who had apartments in them appropriated to themselves. Those of the former are altogether plain; but in the room on the second story of the latter, there is an elegant gothic niche of considerable size in the wall. This is formed by six arches crossing each other, and in the recesses betwixt the pillars which support these have once been seats. In the three middle recesses, which command a prospect of the river, are the remains of three small gothic windows. This is supposed to have been what was anciently called the *Oriel*, and to have contained the queen's toilet. In the front of the towers is a court, from whence probably the royal pair, when at this castle, used to admire together the numerous beauties of the surrounding country.

Edward I, after his conquest of the Welsh, with his queen and great part of the English nobility, spent a Christmas at Conwy castle in all the joyous festivity that a luxurious court could boast. The hall, crowded with warrior knights and damsels, echoed the rude merriment of feudal days. The cup passed quickly round, and tales of feats of arms, of slaughtered foes, and strange adventures, served to beguile the time. Here were they protected in the very heart of an enemy's country, fallen indeed, but still powerful. From hence were issued the edicts of the sovereign against this stubborn people. – But how desolate now the scene of shattered walls and grass-grown towers, of the broken arch and tangling ivy! –

> What now avails that o'er the vassal plain,
>   His rights and rich demesnes extended wide,
> That honour and her knights compos'd his train,
>   And chivalry stood marshall'd by his side.
>
> Though to the clouds his castle seem'd to climb,
>   And frown'd defiance on the desperate foe;
> Though deem'd invincible, the conqueror Time
>   Levell'd the fabric as the founder low.

> Yet the hoar tyrant, though not mov'd to spare,
>   Relented when he struck its finish'd pride,
> And partly the rude ravage to repair,
>   The tottering towers with twisted ivy tied.*

***

THE CHURCH,

Said to have been the conventual church belonging to the monastery, is an inelegant structure, bearing marks of considerable antiquity. There are within it a few modern monuments to the memory of different branches of the Wynne family, formerly of this place. Among other inscriptions, I found one recording an instance of fecundity somewhat uncommon. It was on a plain stone over the body of Nicholas Hookes, of Conwy, gentleman, who was interred here in the year 1637. He is in this asserted to have been the forty-first child of his father, and himself the father of twenty-seven children.* – The tithes of this church are at present vested in three trustees for the benefit of the poor of Conwy, Llandudno, Eglwys Rhôs, and Llan Iestin.

CONWY ABBEY

The remains of the Cistertian abbey founded here by prince Llewelyn ap Iorwerth* in 1185, are at present very few. It was endowed by its founder with many privileges: – the monks were exempt from maintaining for the prince any horses, dogs, or hawks; they had the power of electing abbots among themselves, without the controul or interference of any other persons whatever; they had the benefit of all wrecks on the shores of their property (which would not render them extremely anxious to afford assistance, by their influence with their neighbours, to any vessel in distress); and they were also free from tolls of every description. – In this convent, and that of Stratflur in Cardiganshire,* were kept the Welsh historical records, from 1126 till the year 1270. – The founder was buried in the church of the abbey; but after the dissolution, his coffin was removed to Llanrwst, a town twelve miles distant. In the same church, A.D. 1220, was also interred Cynan ap Owen Gwynedd: his body was inclosed in the habiliments of a monk, holy garments, which in those superstitious days were deemed proof against every power of Satan; and thus, as Moret said of Albertus, 'he turned monk after he was dead.'* –

Edward I, on building the castle, and fortifying the town, removed the religious of this convent to Maenan, a place about ten miles up the river, near Llanrwst, where he had founded for them another abbey, at the same time reserving to the monks all their former lands and privileges. He also allowed them the presentation to their late conventual church at Conwy, now made parochial, on condition that they nominated two able and deserving Englishmen as chaplains, and a third a Welshman, for the benefit of his own countrymen who did not understand English. One of the Englishmen was to be perpetual vicar; and on every vacancy, the person to fill this place was to be named by the convent, and presented by the diocesan.

PLAS MAWR

In the principal street there is a large uncouth pile of building called Plâs Mawr, *The Great Mansion.** This appears to have been erected somewhat more than two centuries ago by Robert Wynne, Esq. of Gwydir. In the front of the house are the letters J. H. S. X. P. S. probably signifying, *Jesus hominum salvator, Christiani populi salus*; and over the gateway a Greek inscription, Ανεχω, άπεχω, *bear, forbear*. The apartments, which are very numerous, are ornamented in a rude style with arms and uncouth figures in stucco work.

Edward made Conwy a free borough; and the mayor for the time being was the constable of the castle. Amongst other privileges, it possessed one, in common with all other English garrisons on the west side of the Clwyd, that when any person committed a crime within that district, he could not be convicted but by a jury empannelled within it.

7

Excursion from Conwy round the Creiddin

Creiddin is a commot, or hundred of Caernarvonshire, situated on the side of the river opposite to Conwy, and forming a considerable promontory into the Irish sea. It is terminated by an extensive rock, on many sides very precipitous, of about two miles in length, called the Great Orme's Head. This is connected to the main land, by a neck of fine fertile ground, altogether so flat, that Leland says 'the way to it is over a made causey, through a marsh often overflown.' This is never the case at present, it is on the contrary supposed to be amongst the finest corn and meadow land in this part of Wales.

After having examined the town of Conwy, I again crossed the river, in company with an intimate friend,* to make the tour of this celebrated cape. We strolled along the shore, botanizing in our progress, for about a mile and a half, till we came to the ruins of ancient

DIGANWY,

Or Dinas Gonwy, *The Fort on the Conwy*, at present called by the common people, though for what reason I cannot learn, *Y Fardre*. The remains are just enough to lead us to some judgment as to the original extent of this castle. The exterior wall inclosed the summits of two high and almost conical rocks, except on one part, where this defence was rendered unnecessary from the depth of the precipice. On the two summits appear to have been the principal buildings; but although it has been well guarded from its elevated situation, and has been successively the habitation of several of the Welsh princes, it is impossible that this castle should have ever been a place of any magnitude. The ruins are now almost covered with earth and shrubs, and in different parts of them the young botanist may meet with much amusement. These rocks are high, and form conspicuous objects from the walls of Conwy. From the summit of the most elevated, we had a good view of the principal parts of the promontory: we saw Gloddaeth in its woods at the foot of a considerable rocky eminence, and in a different direction about two miles east of us the woods of Bodscallon, and again, somewhat south of these, the woods round Marl.

Diganwy is supposed by some to have been a Roman station, the *Dictum*, where the Nervii Dictenses, under the late emperors, had their reserve guard. In the sixth century it was occupied as a place of residence by Maelgwn Gwynedd, and for two centuries afterwards formed one of the royal mansions, till the year 808, when it was destroyed by lightning. It was soon rebuilt, and being thought a post of great strength and consequence, suffered much in the struggles of this country. In the year 1246, Henry III attempted to rebuild this castle, then in a ruinous state; and the English army appears for a considerable length of time to have suffered great distress. A letter, preserved by Matthew Paris,* from a soldier of fashion, describes this in very spirited terms. 'We lie here,' says he, 'watching, praying, fasting, and freezing: we watch in defence against the Welsh, who beat up our quarters every night; we pray for a safe passage home; we fast because we have scarcely any food left, the halfpenny loaf being raised to five-pence; and we freeze from the want of warm clothing, and having only linen tents to keep out the cold.' The army was at length so harassed, that Henry was compelled to retreat, heartily weary of his fruitless attempt. In 1263, the place was completely destroyed by Llewelyn;* and, Conwy castle being erected not long afterwards, it was thought a needless task to commence a new building here.

Near the foot of these rocks, and close upon the shore, is a house belonging to Mrs. Williams, built some years ago, probably in a great measure out of the ruins. To this structure the name of Teganwy, or Deganwy, was given to perpetuate that of the place.*

***

On a rock towards the north of Diganwy we observed a circular watch-tower, of some antiquity.

We now crossed the flat, and under the south-west side of Llandudno rock, passed the shell of a large mansion that, some centuries ago, was a palace belonging to the bishops of Bangor.

ORME'S HEAD, OR LLANDUDNO ROCKS

From thence we were led by steep tracks along the steep and slippery sides of the elevated down of Llandudno, for about two miles, to the

Excursion from

end of the promontory. Here the rocks were for the most part perfectly perpendicular, of amazing height, and extended to a great depth into the sea. It was awful to hear the roaring of the water among the hollows below us, while at the same time we could not see the breakers till we were upon the edge of the steep. The stench of putrid fish, the remains of those with which the sea-fowl on these rocks supply their young, was almost insupportable. Not contented to go away without seeing every thing curious within the bounds of prudence that the place afforded, we each pulled off our boots, and crept with the utmost caution to the very verge of the precipice. A slight trip of the foot might have sent either of us headlong into a corvorant's nest, or amongst the fishermen who were employed with their boats below. The view had enough of sublimity in it;

> The crows and choughs that wing'd the midway air,
> Shewed scarce so gross as beetles.*

The sea dashing in foam against the breakers, the deep hollows, and rude prominences of the rocks several hundred feet below us, were exceedingly tremendous. Our unexpected appearance near their nesting places disturbed the birds, and the flights of so many hundreds, at different depths, with their various harsh and dissonant notes, produced together a grand effect. This was considerably heightened by the contrast of the white plumage of many of them against the gloomy sides of the steep. The fishermen, who were almost immediately under us, appeared in their little skiffs, diminished into children, and it was not without using our glasses that we could well discover their operations. When the sea-fowl had become somewhat familiarized with us, they again quietly settled upon their places on the various ledges below. The corvorants were extremely numerous, and we observed unfledged young in several of the nests. In order to rouse them we pelted the old birds with stones, but as if confident of our inability to injure them with these feeble weapons, they seemed to ridicule our utmost efforts. Though almost close upon them, they always avoided our blows by a short flight, after which they again returned, apparently unconcerned, to their nests. These we could observe to be ranged on most of the ledges at distances of not more than a yard or two from each other. The rock in places was rendered perfectly white with the dung of the birds. The sea reflected a beautiful green colour, and its surface was enlivened by numerous flocks of birds scudding along it in search of prey, and by their whiteness but just visible to us as spots from above. – My companion, I shuddered with horror while he was doing it, descended by means of his hands and knees to a green patch on one of the steep precipices some yards below. To me he seemed scarcely to have footing enough to stand in safety, without clinging to the rock, and to furnish me with a more perfect idea of his situation, he dropped a stone from his hand immediately into the sea. He fixed himself with his left hand firmly to the rock, and with all the force he dared exert, darted a stone at a corvorant that was near him. The effort was rash, and he might have paid dearly for it. With some persuasion, and not without some difficulty, he returned to safety to the top. – On these rocks, which extend entirely along the end of the cape, the samphire, *Crithmum maritimum*, is found in considerable quantity. It is collected by the inhabitants of the adjacent parishes both for home-use and for sale. The process, where it is out of immediate reach, is too well known to need a description here.

LLANDUDNO

Having spent upwards of two hours about the rocks, we directed our course towards the little church of Llandudno, which is on the north-east side of the promontory, and about a mile from the end. It stands alone on an elevated and extensive plain, just above the sea, in the very seat of desolation and barrenness; exposed to every wind that blows, destitute even of a single tree to shelter or protect it. I could not distinguish a hut or cottage of any description in its neighbourhood. – It is dedicated to St. Tudno, who, tradition says, was a Romish recluse of extreme purity of manners and sanctity, that lived and died here. On the very spot where so holy a man had yielded his last breath, it was thought a suitable token of respect to erect a place of worship to his memory. This, therefore, or some former one similar to it, appeared. – Tudno and Cybi the founder of the church at Holyhead, it is said were intimate friends, and that they were accustomed to meet once every week near Priestholme, to join in prayer. The former was called the *White Tudno* from his always going westward, from the sun, and the other the *Tawny Cybi*, because his route led him always to meet it. – Not far from the church are two rows of upright stones called Hwylfar Ceirw, *The High Road of the Deer*. Tradition says of these, that it was a path by which the deer, which once abounded in the mountains of Caernarvonshire, used to descend to a meadow below, long since covered by the sea. This explanation is extremely absurd, and, till some better is found, we must rest in ignorance both as to their origin and use.

Near the road betwixt Llandudno and Eglwys Rhôs, *The Chapel in Rhôs*, is a copper mine, which, though formerly not productive, is now worked to some extent. The miners here descend by shafts, and do not, as in most of the Welsh mines, enter through levels. – By some unaccountable neglect I have mislaid all the particulars that I had obtained respecting it.

GLODDAETH

Not far from the mine is this well-known seat of sir Thomas Mostyn, Bart. built by his ancestor sir Roger Mostyn in the reign of queen Elizabeth. It is situated on an extensive slope, covered with modern plantations, and commanding many delightful prospects. The library, which abounds in valuable manuscripts, principally of Welsh literature, has rendered it very celebrated among the lovers of ancient learning. About the grounds are to be found, in a native state, many plants that are extremely rare in other parts of Great Britain.

My success in the course of this day's short ramble I must give to the botanical reader, in the following extensive list of uncommon plants, and refer him to the catalogue at the end of the work for their particular habitats.

***

From Gloddaeth, without visiting, on account of the lateness of the evening, either Bodscallon, another house belonging to sir Thomas Mostyn, or Marl, we immediately proceeded to the ferry, where, after waiting a considerable time (sufficiently wearied with our excursion), we at length stepped into the ferry-boat, and in about twenty minutes after were landed under the walls of old Conwy. It is needless to say how heartily we eat, and how much we enjoyed ourselves at the harp under the hospitable roof of our kind host Mr. Rous. The remainder of the evening passed swiftly away, and fatigue, which sweetens repose, soon led us to our respective apartments for the night.

8

Excursion from Conwy to Caer Rhun

From Conwy I wandered along the road leading to Llanrwst, for about five miles, to see the village of Caer Rhûn, *The fort of Rhûn*, (ap Maelgwn, prince of North Wales,) and the site of the ancient Conovium; and about three miles farther to a remarkably grand cataract in the mountains on the right of the road.

Having passed the village of Kyffin, I looked back upon the town of Conwy, and saw its black walls and towers, with the river flowing beneath them. They closed the vale, and had the appearance of great strength and grandeur.

THE VALE OF CONWY

Affords many very interesting prospects. It is adorned with all the variety that can arise from a well wooded and highly cultivated country, bounded by lofty mountains. It is more elegant, from its being more varied, and coming more completely under the eye than the vale of Clwyd. The river forms, for a few miles, a broad and expansive water.

CAER RHUN

Is a charming little village on the western bank of the river, and surrounded with wood. – From various discoveries of antiquities in the place and neighbourhood, and from other circumstances, there is good reason for supposing that this was the site of the *Conovium* of the Romans. During the summer of 1801, considerable pains were taken to investigate this station by the owner of the ground, the Rev. H. D. Griffith,* the worthy rector of Llanbeder, who is since dead, and in whom not only his immediate friends, but society and literature, have experienced an irretrievable loss.

In the platform, which was on a low mount, and formed a parallelogram, measuring a hundred and fifty yards in length, and about a hundred in breadth, many apartments were cleared, some of which appeared, as Mr. Griffith informed me, to have been a Roman pottery. He shewed me some of his few discoveries, of which I made no memorandum, as he promised a full account of the place, at the conclusion of his last summer's research, which, however, he unfortunately did not live to complete. I recollect only that there were two small earthen lamps, one of which was very neatly constructed. Some years previous to this, several broken vases, dishes, and other culinary utensils of earthen ware, though none of them entire, were taken up here; some of them stamped with devices of men in armour, others with dogs in chace of the stag; some of them were of a fine sky blue colour, others red, and one in particular, the most perfect of them all, was a sort of hollow dish, with its surface beautifully glazed, and of a lively red colour, bearing the letters PATRICI very visibly stamped in its centre. Its diameter was about six inches. The most curious piece of antiquity found at this time was a brazen shield of a circular form, curiously embossed circle within circle, with small brass studs, from the circumference nearly to the centre, where a sharp piece of wrought iron, about four inches and a half in length, was fixed. This shield, which was somewhat more than a foot in diameter, had on its under side, when discovered, a covering of leather stuffed with hair. – Mr. Griffith thought there were good grounds to contradict the generally received opinion, of a bath and hypocaust having been discovered here.

CATARACT

From the road, near the bridge called *Pont Porthlwyd*, not quite eight miles from Conwy, I observed, high up the mountain on my left, a waterfall of very considerable height, called by the country people Rhaiadr Mawr, *The Great Waterfall*. I ascended along a winding path, which, after about a quarter of an hour's walk, conducted me to the bed of the river, near the station from whence it was to be seen to the greatest advantage. The water in the river, which runs from a pool among the mountains above, called Llyn Eigiau, from late dry weather, was very inconsiderable. The scene, however, was still highly picturesque. From the upper part two streams, one of them much the broadest, descended, at some distance from each other. The range of rock down which the water was thrown was very wide and extremely rude,* being formed, in horizontal ledges, into deep clefts and enormous chasms. Around the whole, and on the various lodgments of the rocks, were numerous pendant shrubs. The dark shades of the clefts, and the irregular brilliancy of the prominent features of the scene, from the reflected rays of the sun, contrasted again with the foaming of the water, were truly grand. The colours of the rock, which were every where also very dark, were rich and highly varied. The streams united a little above the middle of the fall: they rushed from thence in foam over the rocks, and from the deep shelvings, in many places the water was entirely hidden from me below. In addition to this, nearly every different stratum of rock threw it into a fresh direction. In the whole scene there was the utmost irregularity. On the right of the cataract the inclosing rocks were nearly perpendicular, very lofty, and crowned with pendant foliage. Those on the left were very high and towering, adorned on the lodgements with grass and ferns. – I should have made a drawing of this cataract, had it been possible to have expressed it, with any justice, on an octavo plate: this, however, was altogether impossible. The above description is expressed in terms infinitely too feeble to give any correct idea of the scene: – this waterfall is by much the most grand and picturesque of any that I have seen in North Wales.

In descending to the road I had an extensive view along the whole vale of Conwy. It appeared from this eminence to be much varied, and on the whole very beautiful.

9

Conwy to Bangor

In my route from Conwy to Bangor, I began to find myself in a country that was truly mountainous and romantic: the hills of Flintshire and Denbighshire, which I had just passed, bear no comparison in picturesque beauty with the stupendous scenery of Caernarvonshire. The mountains here, instead of being, as those were, gentle in ascent, and frequently covered with grass and verdure to their summits, began to wear the savage and majestic face of nature, – they were precipitous, rugged, and gloomy.

SYCHNANT,

The dry hollow, which commences about two miles from Conwy, is the first scene of mountain horror* that the traveller in this direction is presented with. The road descends along a steep betwixt the rocks. Immediately below it on one side is this deep and narrow vale: from the bottom arises Penmaen Bach, *the lesser Penmaen*, whose head is raised several hundred feet above, and whose broad and sombre front constitutes all the boundary on the right. The ledges of many of the rocks were covered with the flowers of the different heaths, which gave a purple tint to the scene. From the steepness of the road I was almost compelled to descend with a velocity which became very unpleasant. The opening of the rocks towards the bottom, and the gradual unfolding of a distant view of the bay of Beaumaris, the island of Anglesea, and the verdure of the intervening country, however, arrested my progress. The contrast heightened the elegance, and added to it a singularity of character that does not often occur even in mountain-scenery.

PENMAEN MAWR

Near the fifth milestone from Conwy is the celebrated mountain called Penmaen Mawr, *The Great Penmaen*, a huge rock that rises near 1550 feet in perpendicular height above the sea. Along a shelf of this tremendous precipice is formed part of the great Irish road. This is well guarded towards the sea by a strong wall, and supported in many parts by arches turned beneath it, a method, in point of expence, found far preferable to that of hewing it out of the solid rock. Before the wall was built, accidents were continually happening by people falling down the precipices; but, since that time, I believe it has been accounted perfectly safe. Of these accidents the following have been recorded:

An exciseman fell from the highest part, and escaped unhurt.

A clergyman who lived in Anglesea, about forty years ago, fell over with his horse and a midwife behind him. The female and the nag both perished; but the divine, with great philosophy, unsaddled the steed, and marched off with the trappings, exulting in his own preservation.

Somewhat more than a century back, Siôn Humphries of Llanfair vechan, paid his addresses to a female who lived in some part of Creiddin, beyond Conwy. They agreed to meet at a fair at that town. He was thrown down Penmaen Mawr: she was overset in the Conwy ferry-boat, and was the only person that escaped out of more than fourscore. This story seems romantic, but it is well authenticated. They were afterwards united, and lived many years together in the parish of Llanfair. The female died in 1744, at the great age of one hundred and sixteen; and he survived her five years. Their graves are close together in the church-yard, and are yet familiarly shewn by the inhabitants.

At some distance the road appears like a white line along the side of the rock, which towards the sea is in many places so nearly perpendicular, that a stone may be thrown from thence into it without touching below, a height of almost a hundred and forty feet. The pass would, were it not for the wall, be truly terrible; and even yet, to those who can make frights to mock themselves, the amazingly lofty abrupt precipice of rock, towering overhead, with the fragments and ruins that have for ages been falling from it, and seem ready to roll over one, do present a scene of horror. To those unaccustomed to mountain scenes, this steep will not be viewed without considerable tremor. Dryden has a description which may be applied with some propriety to one or two of the most elevated stations:

> As from a steep and dreadful precipice,
> The frighted traveller casts down his eyes,
> And sees the ocean at so great a distance,
> It looks as if the skies were sunk beneath him;
> If then some neighbouring shrub, how weak soever,

> Peeps up, his willing eyes stop gladly there,
> And seem to ease themselves and rest upon it.
> RIVAL LADIES*

On the evening of the 31st of July 1801, during a tremendous storm of thunder, a mass of stone, supposed to weigh several thousand tons, was loosened from its bed, and precipitated with a dreadful crash to the sea; it swept down that part of the wall, and left about a hundred and fifty tons lodged upon the road. A woman and horse narrowly escaped destruction, having but just passed the place before the accident happened. This body of rock appears to have been unfixed by the torrent of water that was pouring down on all sides. I was not many miles from the place at the time, and was informed of the circumstance very soon after it occurred. All the carriages, among which was the mail, were stopped for several hours, till a body of the country people, who immediately set to work upon it, were able to clear away so much of the rubbish as to allow them a passage.

Before this pass was formed, which is now near thirty years ago, the usual mode of going betwixt Conwy and Bangor was either in boats, or, waiting the departure of the tides, to proceed along the sands, at low water. The latter mode was frequently attended with danger, owing to the soft places made by the fresh water streams, and the hollows formed by the tide, of the depth of which, when filled with water, the guides could not always be certain. Few carriages at that time were taken betwixt the two towns, but nearly all the travellers were conveyed on horseback. There were two inns for the convenience of waiting the departure of the tides, the buildings of which are, I believe, both yet standing, but appropriated to other uses. One of these was near the turnpike under Penmaen Mawr, and the other near Penmaen Bach. On the window or sign of each was a distich, said by the people of the neighbourhood to have been the composition of Swift:* that of one was,

> Before you venture hence to pass,
> Take a good refreshing glass.

Of the other,

> Now you're over take another,
> Your drooping spirits to recover.

There was a horse-road along the side of the mountain, but it is said to have been excessively dangerous and bad; in some parts it ran above, and in others below, the present road. Those who went in carriages, or on horseback, along the sands, set out from Conwy marsh, went entirely round the promontory, and passed on the outside of Penmaen Bach.

ASCENT TO THE SUMMIT OF PENMAEN MAWR

From the sixth mile-stone I began an ascent to the summit of Penmaen Mawr. I chose this place that I might have a guide not to the summit merely, but to the spot where I could find a shrub of which I had heard many nonsensical accounts, called by the Welsh Pren Lemwn, *Lemon-tree*. This I had been told grew in a situation almost inaccessible, and bore a fruit resembling a small lemon: that many persons had planted cuttings, and even roots of it, in their gardens, but that these had invariably dwindled and died. I questioned my guide, as we proceeded, as to the figure and colour of its leaves and flowers, and I immediately conjectured it to be, what I soon afterwards found it, nothing more than *Crataegus aria* of Linnaeus, which does not often occur among the Welsh mountains. It grows on the perpendicular rocks just above the road; and of the three small trees that were pointed out to me, one had been cut on all sides, for the purpose of planting into gardens.

From hence I scrambled up a steep ascent, covered entirely with loose stones, which often gave way the moment I thrusted my weight upon them, to the summit; and, as I walked pretty quick, it was not before I had experienced several severe tumbles, and was bruised on all sides, that I reached it. I had frequent occasion, from heat and exertion, to turn round and catch the cool and refreshing breezes that blew from the sea; and in each of these restings, as I gradually rose above the intervening obstacles, I found new objects to admire. From the summit the view was extensive, and, towards the isle of Anglesea, and from thence round to the Cheshire and Lancashire hills, was very beautiful. The whole of the bay of Beaumaris seemed to lie directly underneath, as well as all the coast from the abrupt termination of Ormes Head to the little island of Priestholme. I could just discern the isle of Man. The prospect over the Conwy into Denbighshire was also extremely pleasing; but the mountains towards the south not being sufficiently varied amongst themselves, were destitute of character, and almost entirely of interest.

On the summit, and extending in an oval form from north to south, are some evident remains of antiquity. Many ruins of ancient massy walls, formed apparently without cement, are yet visible; and on the east the fragments of several small circular buildings that seem to have been originally formed for soldiers' huts. On the highest part there are the remains of what appeared to me to have been watch-towers; and near one of these I observed a small square well, in which, although then in the midst of a dry season, I found a considerable quantity of water.

This ruin is called Braich y Ddinas, *The Arm of the City*, and is supposed to have been an ancient British fortification. A correspondent of bishop Gibson* says of it: 'This castle seems to have been impregnable, there being no way to offer any assault to it, from the hill being so high, steep, and rocky, and the walls of such vast strength. The way or entrance into it ascends with many twinings, so that a hundred men might here defend themselves against a whole legion; and yet it should seem there were lodgings within these walls for twenty thousand men. By the tradition of our ancestors, this was the strongest and safest refuge, or place of defence, that the ancient Britons had in all Snowdon, to secure them from the incursions of their enemies.' – Governor Pownall,* contrary to the commonly received opinion, and I think contrary to the fact, conjectures it to have been one of the Druids consecrated places of worship, and that it was never intended for a place of defence.

Penmaen Mawr is not so interesting a mountain, except to the antiquary, as I afterwards found Snowdon, Glyder, and many others in the interior of the country; the prospects from the summit being neither so grand nor so varied as from these.

The easiest places to ascend from are either along a pretty high wall that extends from the road far up the side of the mountain on the extremity nearest to Conwy, or at the other extremity a little beyond the sixth mile-stone. If the traveller is a pedestrian he can ascend one way and descend by the other: this will save him at least a mile or two of journey. The loose stones that lie scattered apparently on every part of the mountain render an expedition to its summit somewhat unpleasant: the distance, however, is so short, that a person who walks pretty quick may overcome it in little more than an hour.

ABER

About nine miles from Conwy stands the pleasing little village of Aber, or, as it is called by way of distinction, Aber gwyngregin, *The Conflux of the White Shells*. Here I found a comfortable little inn. This is a very convenient station for such persons as wish to examine Penmaen Mawr, and the adjacent country, either as naturalists or artists.

On a small artificial mount on the west side of the river, just above the bridge, called the *Mwd*, stood formerly a castle belonging to Llewelyn ap Griffith, prince of Wales; and it was here that he received his summons from our Edward to deliver up the principality to the crown of England. The mount is nearly circular at the top, and not more than twenty yards in diameter.

From this place, persons frequently cross immediately into Anglesea, in a direction towards Beaumaris. The distance is about four miles, and at low water they are able to walk to the bank of the channel, within a mile of Beaumaris, where the ferry-boat plies. In fogs, the passage over these sands has been found very dangerous, and many have been lost in attempting to cross them at such times. As some precaution, however, the bell of the church is now generally rung during foggy weather, which prevents persons from wandering very widely from the line they ought to keep.

A deep glen runs from the village amongst the mountains, at whose extremity I had been informed there was a waterfall. I therefore strolled along the bank of the stream, which passes under the bridge, as the most sure mode of reaching it. The distance I found near two miles. The mountains that inclosed the hollow were some of them clad with wood, which, with the prominences of the rocks, and the verdure of the lower grounds, give a pleasing character to many of the scenes. About half-way is a bridge, over which the road leads to Caer Rhûn and the vale of Conwy. A little beyond this I turned round to take a view down the vale; and when I descended to the bed of the stream, found that I had before me a most charming landscape. The stones of the stream, over which the water broke in a very pleasing manner, with a high bank on the left, formed a rude fore-ground, that in some measure hid from the sight the regular outline of a green mountain on that side. About the middle was the single arch, with a few scattered cottages near it. The road was seen to pass over the mountain-hollow above; and the trees were thinly scattered over one hill, but at the bottom of the rock behind the bridge were collected into a pretty thick and large copse. The background was occupied by this round and lofty, but well varied, rock, in which stony prominences and verdant, but abrupt slopes, were the principal features. This, aided by the purple richness of an evening tint, that I saw in full perfection as I returned, is a scene to which the pencil alone can do justice, description is much too feeble.

RHAIADR MAWR

Following still the course of the stream, I soon came within sight of the fall, Rhaiadr Mawr,* *The Great Cataract*. At a distance this appears to have no one character of picturesque beauty; I fancied it merely a narrow stream falling down the flat and uninteresting face of a lofty rock. It continued in appearance much the same till I had got very nearly to the foot of the cataract. The lower part of the fall is upwards of sixty feet in height: its character is extremely simple, being broken only in places by the seams of the strata. The quantity of water is very considerable, and it is thrown, unless after much rain, in a single sheet from above. At a little distance two or three divisions of the upper rock are seen, but immediately at the foot little more than the lower fall is visible. In the bed of the river, as in those of most mountain torrents, are scattered numerous fragments of rock. On each side of the fall the mountain had the same flat appearance; this, with the nearly regular outline of the whole scene, at the top forming a segment of a large circle, and some other characteristics, gives to it that kind of simple grandeur, though on a much smaller scale, which is conspicuous in Pistyll Rhaiadr, the celebrated waterfall of Montgomeryshire.

> Smooth to the shelving brink a copious flood
> Rolls fair and placid; where collected,
> In one impetuous torrent, down the steep,
> It thundering shoots, and shakes the country round.
> At first an azure sheet it rushed broad;
> Then whitening by degrees as prone it falls,
> And from the loud resounding rocks below
> Dash'd in a cloud of foam, it sends aloft
> A hoary mist, and forms a ceaseless shower.*

LLANDYGAI

At Llandygai, *The Church of Tygai*, a village beautifully situated on the banks of the Ogwen, is a church, one of the neatest in the principality, built in the form of a cross, having the tower in the centre. Its stile is gothic, and it is supposed to have been erected about the reign of Edward III; but its being washed with ochre to render it in some measure correspondent with the neighbouring mansion of Penrhyn castle, gives it unfortunately a modern cast.*

I obtained the key in order to examine the tomb of the celebrated archbishop Williams, lord keeper of the great seal in the reign of James I, who was interred here. This is placed in the wall on the south-side of the chancel, and is protected from the dust by a long green curtain which has a singular appearance. The tomb has lately been ornamented afresh at the expence of Lady Penrhyn, a descendant of the archbishop's family.* He is represented in his episcopal dress at an altar, and (save in the glare of the gilded ornaments) there is a considerable air of elegance about it. On a table monument in the south-east corner, just beyond this, are two antique figures supposed to represent some of the Penrhyn family that were interred here.

***

Near the river Ogwen, and a little above the bridge, are two mills belonging to Messrs. Worthington and Co. of Liverpool. One of these, which has been lately erected, is for the purpose of grinding materials for an earthen-ware manufactory at Liverpool. The other is an oil and paint mill: oil colours are here prepared, from the mineral, entirely in their finished state, and are shipped for Liverpool at Port Penrhyn. The walks that have been formed near these buildings by the company are somewhat pretty; and the planting of the adjacent grounds with trees and shrubs, will, in the course of a few years, render this neighbourhood much more pleasing than it is at present.

PENRHYN CASTLE

On the right of the road, not far from Bangor, is Penrhyn castle, the seat of Lord Penrhyn.* The grounds are entered through one of the most elegant gates I ever beheld. The house is a fine but by no means a superb building, faced with the yellow Devonshire bricks, which give it the appearance of being washed with ochre. It has nothing of state magnificence, or parade about it, but it can boast considerable elegance. The architecture is the military gothic of the reign of Henry VI, with embattled turrets, which rise to some height above the roof. The grounds are well wooded.

Penrhyn is supposed to stand on the site of a palace which in the eighth century belonged to Rodri Moelwynog, the son of Edwal Iwrch, son of Cadwaladr the last king of the Britons. It seems to have been granted, along with Cochwillan, in the adjoining parish of Llanllechid, now in ruins, to Yarddwr, lord of Llechwedd uchaf, about the time of Llewelyn ap Iorwerth; and from him it descended by heirs female to the posterity of Ednyfed Fechan: – the last of the family was *Pierce Griffith*, esq. who lived in the reign of queen Elizabeth. When the Spanish armada threatened destruction to his country, this brave character fitted out a vessel at his own expence, to aid the British fleet, and sailed in it from Beaumaris on the 20th of April 1588. He arrived at Plymouth in about fourteen days, where he was elegantly treated by the admiral, who highly admired his loyalty and public spirit. He remained under sir Henry Cavendish and sir Francis Drake till the defeat of the armada, when he attended the latter in his cruise on the Spanish coast. Griffith accompanied his commander to the gulph of Magellan, where they parted, sir Francis being then employed in his voyage of discovery. A short time after James had obtained the throne, the Spaniards, through their ambassador, complained to the English ministry that Griffith continued to attack their vessels, notwithstanding the proclamation of peace. The prosecutions against him on this account became at length so serious, that he was compelled to sell his estate in order to produce a pardon. This was purchased by archbishop Williams, at that time lord keeper of the great seal; but he dying unmarried, it descended to sir Griffith Williams of Penrhyn, bart. and from him, after several successions, to two sisters of sir Hugh Williams. These were Ann, who married Thomas Warburton, esq. of Winnington in Cheshire, and Gwen, who was married to sir Walter Yonge, bart. of Escott in Devonshire. The present lady Penrhyn* was the only daughter of Hugh Warburton, esq. I believe the estate is now, from the purchase of the other moiety, become the entire property of Lord Penrhyn.

The *stables* at Penrhyn are excellent, and supposed to be among the first in the kingdom for accommodation and utility. They are fronted with the purple slate obtained from his lordship's quarries: which indeed seems to be applied to every possible use on the whole of the property here. The grounds are fenced with it: narrow upright slabs, to imitate palisadoes, are fixed each by two small holdfasts to the railing. The effect is exceedingly neat, but as slate is generally liable to snap, sometimes with a slight blow, and the edges are sharp, I should think them dangerous to sheep in their attempts to escape through the spaces that accident may thus create.

The *chapel* is at a little distance from the house, in the front of one part of the plantation. It is a small gothic building apparently of some antiquity. It formerly stood much nearer the house, but was taken down, and rebuilt of the same materials, put together in the same manner, on its present site. The interior is elegant, and at one end it has a most brilliantly painted gothic window, the performance of Mr. Eggington of Birmingham. The modern porch by no means accords with the other parts.

From the chapel I was led through the grounds to the baths, which are upon the beach, about half a mile distant. In the way I passed the cottage of the under-steward Mr. Lloyd, designed, like all the improvements about this place, by Mr. Benjamin Wyatt.* This station commands a view, though too extensive to be accounted picturesque, yet so enchantingly lovely as scarcely to be exceeded. Nature seems to have crowded here every beauty of mountain, water, wood, and meadow. In front is an expanse of sea, terminated on the right by the Llandudno, or Orme's Head rock, to appearance perfectly insulated, the flat that connects it to the main land not being visible at high water. Penmaen Mawr, along whose side, though near six miles distant, I could plainly distinguish the white line of the road, and the neighbouring mountains, appear rising abruptly from the water's edge: from hence a long range is seen to stretch into the interior of the county, in which Carnedd Llewelyn and Carnedd Ddafydd are peculiarly conspicuous. On the other side is the island of Anglesea from Beaumaris northwards to Penmon, and Priestholme, with the woods of Baron-Hill. The baths are seen at a little distance below, forming part of the elegant landscape. The front of the cottage was trellised, and a few plants and shrubs were training along it. The garden was prettily variegated with flowers: an oval bed on each side of the path leading to the door, was, whimsically enough, inclosed in a green trellised edge, with a handle over the middle, to imitate baskets of flowers. Not a single weed was to be seen that could reproach its owner with neglect. It was in short a terrestrial paradise, and though it affords in itself nothing of picturesque effect, even the artist must confess that it has neatness and uncommon elegance.

I followed the road leading to the *bath*. On the beach, for a considerable way, this is continued by an elevation, walled on each side: at the end is the building. This is plain but elegant. In the middle is a portico, fronted by four columns, which admits carriages underneath. There are three rooms for dressing, &c. The baths are, a circular one open at the top, of size sufficient to allow a person to swim without inconvenience, being apparently about thirty feet in diameter; and a small one that will allow of the water being heated. The latter is within the building, and is lined with white and cream-coloured earthen-ware, from a manufactory near Liverpool: under the window is a large and beautiful oval of the same, with a wreath of oak-leaves within the rim, and a coronet and Lady Penrhyn's initials in the centre. Much expence has been unavoidably incurred in shutting the tide out of the great bath at the times when it was not wanted, and in retaining a proper quantity of water when that of the sea retired. In this building the design of Mr. Wyatt is very evident.

Not far from the bath, and out upon the sands, is an extensive weir occupying several acres of ground, and forming the segment of a large circle, with its ends bending towards the land. It is made by means of stakes driven deep into the beach, secured by stones, and interwoven for many feet above with pliant branches of trees. This is a fishery which produces to those who rent it of his lordship, a comfortable subsistence. It is entirely overflowed by the tide, and at low water is left with only so much as is retained in its mud and sand. The fish are taken at the ebb; and during the herring season the fishermen have their principal harvest. Immense numbers of these are sometimes retained. In one instance so many were taken at a single tide, as, when sold at two shillings, and the worst at eighteen-pence a hundred, produced nearly eighty pounds; besides the quantities that were obliged to be left on the return of the tide, from want of hands sufficient to carry them away, and those that were taken by people who flocked from all parts of the neighbourhood to obtain the refuse fish. – The coast is here very unpleasant to walk upon, being either extremely muddy, or composed of the upright and broken edges of a stratum of slate rock that extends a considerable way into the water.

BANGOR

Passing Port Penrhyn, (a description of which will with more propriety occupy a place in my next than in the present chapter,) I arrived at Bangor, *The chief Choir*. This, although at present only a very small place, had formerly so much importance, as to be denominated from its size Bangor Vawr, *The Great Bangor*, to distinguish it probably from Bangor is-coed in Flintshire.* It is seated in a vale, from the back of which arise the vast mountains of Caernarvonshire. The streets are narrow, and the houses bad and irregular: a spirit of improvement would, however, render it one of the most beautiful places in Great Britain. From the entrance either way it is seen to advantage, the square tower of its cathedral, and some of the best houses which are near it, presenting themselves from among the trees. The cathedral is small, but every thing around it is now kept exceedingly neat. From near the church-yard there is a fine prospect of part of Anglesea, and the town and bay of Beaumaris.

History has recorded, though with what truth it is impossible now to say, that Condagius, a king of Britain, who reigned about eight hundred years prior to the coming of Christ, erected here a *temple*, which he dedicated to Minerva.

On an eminence at a little distance from Bangor was formerly a *castle* built by Hugh, earl of Chester, some time during the reign of William Rufus. It has been so long demolished, that even the period of its destruction cannot be ascertained.

HISTORY OF THE CATHEDRAL

Deiniol ap Dunawd or Dinothus, abbot of Bangor is-coed in Flintshire, founded here some time about the year 525, a college for the instruction of youth and support of clergy, intending it probably as a cell or appurtenant to that celebrated monastery. It had scarcely been founded thirty years, when Maelgwn Gwynedd raised it into a bishopric, dedicated the new church to Deiniol, and created him the first bishop. This prince intended at the time to surrender his dominion to other hands, and to adopt the profession of religion himself: but the world had too many charms to suffer him to leave it, the resolution, therefore, was scarcely formed before it was destroyed. He had been hurried on through his whole life by unrestrained passion, and it was found too severe a forfeiture to surrender himself to the tame unvaried life of a monastery. If, however, we may believe the writers of this period, he became a convert in his latter days; but we have little other proof of this, than his founding several places dedicated to offices of religion, and these alone would have secured their good opinions. In his public character he appears notwithstanding to have always shewn himself a brave man, and a noble and magnanimous prince. – Deiniol died about four years after his creation, and was interred in the isle of Bardsey.

In the tenth century Edgar coming into North Wales, confirmed all the former privileges: he also gave to the college a considerable quantity of land, and founded a new chapel on the south side of the cathedral, which he dedicated to the blessed Virgin. This was afterwards converted into a chantry of singing priests, and is at present supposed to form part of the vicar's house.

The cathedral has been several times destroyed during the troubles in which this country has been involved; in the reigns of William the Conqueror, king John, Henry III, and Henry IV. After the latter demolition, which was by the army of Owen Glyndwr, it remained in ruins near ninety years, when the choir was rebuilt by the bishop, Henry Dean or Denys, formerly prior of Lanthony. He recovered many parcels of land belonging to the see, and was also himself a great benefactor. The tower and the nave, as well as the palace, were built in the year 1532 by bishop Sheffington: the bishop, however, died, and the tower was left at little more than half the intended height.

***

Owen Gwynedd, prince of Wales, who died in 1169, is supposed to have been buried in the south transept, beneath an arch with a flowery cross cut on a flat stone. When Baldwyn, archbishop of Canterbury,* visited Wales, to preach the crusades and invite soldiers to the holy wars, he saw this tomb, and directed the bishop to remove the body out of the church as soon as he conveniently could: this was done on account of his having been excommunicated by Becket for marrying a first cousin, and continuing to cohabit with her till his death. The bishop, in obedience to the charge, made, not long afterwards, a passage from the vault through the south wall of the building, through which he caused the body to be shoved secretly into the church-yard.

At a little distance from the town there was formerly a *house of friars preachers*. This was founded about the year 1299 by Tudor ap Gronw, lord of Penmynydd and Trecastle. Some time during the reign of Edward VI this building was converted into a free school.

St. Mary's de Garthlaman, the ancient parish church, which stood about four hundred yards from the cathedral, appears to have been erected prior to the commencement of the fourteenth century.

BANGOR FERRY,

Called by the Welsh Porthaethwy, *The Ferry of the confined Waters*, is about a mile beyond the town. Here the passengers from England to Ireland cross the strait of the Menai into Anglesea. The ferry-house is situated on the eastern bank of this elegant river, expansive as some of the American torrents, and is certainly one of the most charmingly retired spots in the kingdom. Here is an inn* to which most travellers resort, from the unaccountable want of comfortable accommodation in the town. The views from the house and garden are principally confined to the opposite shore and the intervening stream; but the numerous trading vessels that pass, about the tide of flood, the rocky banks, and altogether varied scene, are too pleasing to be passed unnoticed even by the most tasteless traveller.

It was at this inn that I was, for the first time since my arrival in Wales, entertained with the music of the harp, the indigenous instrument of this country. The evening was approaching, and the sun in retiring had cast a golden tinge over all the objects around. I had seated myself in a window that commanded a full and most delightful prospect of Anglesea, the isle of the Druids, and I listened, in a pleasing melancholy, to the sweetly-flowing tones. A thousand pleasant ideas of times of old, 'of the days of other years,' floated on my imagination: the bardic aera now recurred, and the energetic lines of Gray crossed my thoughts with more than usual force.

> Ruin seize thee, ruthless king!
> Confusion on thy banners wait;
> Though fann'd by Conquest's crimson wing,
> They mock the air with idle state.
> Helm nor hauberk's twisted mail,
> Nor e'en thy virtues, tyrant! shall avail,
> To save thy soul from nightly fears;
> From Cambria's curse, from Cambria's tears!*

In the warmth of fancy I had entirely overlooked the perhaps necessary, though certainly cruel, policy of Edward I, in destroying, (if he did destroy, for it has by no means been satisfactorily ascertained that he did),* a race of men whose songs, deemed almost inspired, could not be heard by the multitude without effects pregnant with the utmost danger to his people.

> Their skill'd fingers knew how best to lead
> Through all the maze of sound the wayward step
> Of harmony, recalling oft and oft,
> Permitting her unbridled course to rush
> Through dissonance to concord, sweetest then,
> E'en when expected harshest.*

In the thirteenth century a *battle* was fought near Bangor Ferry, which none of the historians have mentioned. It is, however, described by a bard who lived about the time, Llywarch Brydydd y Moch,* in a poem on the death of Llewelyn ap Iorwerth. His language is animated and expressive, and may be taken as a specimen of the Welsh bardic style of that period. 'Dark ran the purple gore over the breasts of the warriors: loud was the shout; havoc and carnage stalked around. The blood-stained waves flowed over the broken spear, and mournful silence hung on the brows of the warriors. The briny wave, rolling into the channel, mingled with waves of blood. Furiously raged the spear, and the tide of blood rushed with force. Our attack was sudden and fierce. Death was displayed in all its horrors. Noble troops, in the fatal hour, trampled on the dead, like prancing steeds. Before Rodri was subdued, the church-yards became like sallow ground.'

10

Excursion from Bangor Ferry through Nant Frangon

On the following morning I rose early that I might have sufficient time to examine the romantic vale of Nant Frangon, *The Beaver's Hollow*, and the different commercial undertakings of Lord Penrhyn and others in its neighbourhood. The boundary of my excursion I had fixed at Llyn Ogwen, about twelve miles distant, and the principal objects were to be Port Penrhyn, lord Penrhyn's slate quarries, and the waterfalls of Ben Glog.

I therefore repassed the town of Bangor, and took an early breakfast at the *Penrhyn Arms*, a comfortable and most delightfully situated inn that overlooks

PORT PENRHYN.

This was built by his lordship from a design of B. Wyatt; and had it been large enough for general accommodation, would be a most eligible place for every traveller on pleasure. One end of the house, that commands a view over Beaumaris bay towards the sea, is occupied by a subscription newsroom for the inhabitants of Bangor and its neighbourhood, and few places of this nature possess so much either of internal or external elegance. Mr. Wyatt's taste is here very conspicuous, not only in the neat design of the room, but in the choice of a situation commanding an uncommonly beautiful prospect of land and water. This is the same in general character as that I have described from Mr. Lloyd's cottage in Lord Penrhyn's grounds: but, in addition to all the elegance of that scene, the towers of Penrhyn castle from hence appear in front, rising above the dark surrounding woods. Immediately below the bowling-green, into which the room opens, the observer has the busy scene of the port. Here the appearance of the numerous vessels with which this is at all times crowded, and the bustle and noise that necessarily attend the shipping of goods, form a singular contrast with the other mild and beautiful features.

Excursion from Bangor Ferry

From the inn I descended to the *quay*. On one side of this there is a long yellow building, in which is carried on one of the most extensive manufactures of *writing-slates* in Great Britain. This belongs to Messrs. Worthington and Co. of Liverpool: and Mr. W. (to whose civility and attentions in himself conducting me through all his concerns in this neighbourhood, I acknowledge myself greatly indebted) informed me that as many as between three and four hundred dozen were, on an average, manufactured here every week. A few inkstands, and some other fancy articles, are also made, but these are found not to answer to any extent. The slates used are of the finest quality that the quarries afford. The process of smoothing and framing them is extremely simple, and unnecessary here to be described.

Port Penrhyn is principally used by vessels coming from different parts of the kingdom for the slates obtained from lord Penrhyn's quarries, between five and six miles distant. About six hundred tons are shipped per week. These, for many years, were conveyed to the port at an enormous expence, by means of carts and horses, but his lordship has just completed an iron rail-road that extends all the way from the quarries quite round the quay. Two horses are now able, in fifteen waggons, chained to each other, to draw upwards of twelve ton of slates along the levels. Notwithstanding the general mountainous character of the country, there are no more than four inclined planes (besides those in the quarry) on the whole of the road; and the longest of these extends two hundred and twenty yards. At the top of each there is a windlass, where, by means of a lever pressed against the cylinder, the velocity of the full waggons going down, and drawing up the empty ones, is regulated. Only three waggons, when I saw them, were suffered to go down at once, and in the longest plane the whole fifteen occupied about twenty minutes in passing. By means of this road, as the waggon wheels are concave, and, running on the top of a narrow circular bar, have consequently but little friction, the slates come down in a much shorter time than they did before. Formerly, betwixt three or four hundred horses were used in the work, which is now performed by no more than six or eight. The saving from this is not only very material to lord Penrhyn, but the difference in expenditure of hay and corn, in a country where so little can be grown, and of various other articles of common utility, is of material importance to the people at large. Besides slates, there are shipped at Port Penrhyn, hones, paint, dry colours, chert, &c. to Liverpool and various other parts. – Vessels of about three hundred tons burthen can come up to load at the quay.

Pursuing the rail-road I arrived, after a walk of about two hours, at

LORD PENRHYN'S SLATE QUARRIES,

Which are in a place called Braich y Cafn, in the mountains on the south-west side of Nant Frangon. Here I found several immense openings, with sides and bottoms as rude as imagination can paint, that had been formed in the getting of the slate. On first surveying them, a degree of surprize is excited how such yawning chasms could have been formed by any but the immediate operations of nature; and even on more mature reflection our astonishment at the efforts of man does not altogether subside. But it is also within the last twelve years that this has been chiefly effected, for, previous to that period, the quarries scarcely produced to lord Penrhyn above six or eight guineas a year, some of his tenants here having a lease of the estate for twenty-one years, at the small rent of only a guinea a year each. The unexpired part of this lease his lordship purchased when he first determined to get the slates to a greater extent himself. When he first came into possession of his property in Wales, the quarries were in so low a state, that the annual exports did not exceed a thousand tons: on all his estates in Nant Frangon there were but three carts, and the roads were altogether so bad as to be almost impassable.

As a place to engage the attention of the tourist, few will be found more worthy than this quarry, which, even in singularity of appearance, great depth, and the rude forms of the remaining rocks, will scarcely be found inferior to the copper mines in Anglesea. The bustle of the workmen on the various ledges, the breaking up of the strata, and the noises of splitting and shaping, with at intervals the roar of a blast, and the subsequent crash of the pieces thrown in every direction, will be novel to most of the travellers through this country.

Nearly opposite to the quarry is a small *public house*, where the traveller may obtain such poor, yet acceptable refreshment, as the neighbourhood affords, viz. bacon, eggs, and ale: and he will find the inhabitants, at least equally cleanly, with any among the mountains. – In different parts around are scattered the white-washed cottages of the workmen, built from the designs of Mr. Wyatt, and on the exterior, affording at a little distance, an air of considerable neatness and comfort, but from the broken windows, and the ragged and filthy appearance of the children of two or three into which I ventured to put my head, nothing but the extreme of wretchedness and poverty could be supposed to reign within.

By the road-side, not far distant, lord Penrhyn has erected a large mill for the purpose of sawing the slate into slabs, for grave stones, cottage hearths, mantle pieces, fences, &c.

Descending from the slate quarry, I crossed the road to visit lady Penrhyn's grounds at

OGWEN BANK,

Of which a Welsh writer has said, though perhaps somewhat affectedly, that "'tis an acre of *Tempe* among the rocks of *Norway!*"* In these grounds there is a small ornamental building containing a dining-room and such other accommodations as are necessary for the family or their friends in their visits to the quarry. In front of this the stream of the river Ogwen breaks in a small cascade among the rocks. The grounds are laid out in too *gay* a stile to accord with the bleakness of the surrounding mountain scenery, yet prejudice itself must allow that it is on the whole a most delightful spot.

I do not remember from what exact point it was that the summit of the celebrated mountain

CARNEDD LLEWELYN

Was pointed out to me: it, however, appeared in a direction exactly west, and in a straight line, was scarcely more than three miles distant. Except Snowdon, which exceeds it not more than fifteen or twenty yards, this is the highest of the Welsh mountains. Its rocks are said to afford to the botanist numerous alpine plants, but one in particular, *Ajuga alpina*, that has not hitherto been elsewhere found in Wales. – The neighbouring inhabitants have a tradition, that formerly a giant called Rhitta had his residence on this mountain, and, as in all other stories of giants, that he was the terror of the whole country. They even assert that he wore a garment woven from the beards of several of the princes and most redoubted warriors whom he had slain in combat. – Taking leave of our giant and his residence at the same time, I shall descend into the rude mountain vale of

NANT FRANGON,

The Beaver's Hollow. This tremendous glen is destitute of wood, and almost even of cultivation, except in a narrow slip of meadow, that lies along its bottom. The sides, however, which are truly,

> Huge hills that heap'd in crowded order stand,*

sufficiently repay their want of verdure, by the pleasing and fantastic appearance of the rocks that compose them. These rise abruptly from their base, and stretch their barren points into the clouds, unvaried with trees or shrubs, and uncheered even by the cottager's hut.

In the year 1685, part of a rock of one of the impending cliffs at the upper end of this vale, became so undermined by storms and rain, that, loosing its hold, it fell down in several immense masses, and in its passage along one of the steep and shaggy cliffs, dislodged some hundreds of other pieces. Many of these were intercepted in their progress into the vale, but so much forced its way to the bottom as entirely destroyed a small piece of meadow ground, and several of the fragments were thrown at least two hundred yards asunder. In this accident one great stone, the biggest remaining piece of the upper rock, made in its descent, a trench as large as those in which the mountain streams usually run: this is yet pointed out by the inhabitants of the vale. When it came down to the plain, it continued its passage through a small meadow, and across the river Ogwen, and lodged itself on the opposite bank.

There are many places in Wales that have received their appellation from the beaver, but particularly several pools called Llyn yr Avange, or *Beaver's Pools*. These naturally lead us to suppose that, some centuries ago, the beaver was found wild in the neighbourhood of such places. Indeed Giraldus Cambrensis, in his *Itinerarium Cambriae*, written about the year 1188, has asserted that this was the case; and he mentions that beavers were found in considerable numbers about one of the rivers in Cardiganshire. They were called by the Welsh, with peculiar propriety, Llost-Lydan, or the *Broad-Tailed Animals*; and in the early centuries the skins constituted one of the chief articles of finery that the Britons possessed, and were valued at a price five or six times greater than that of any other animals.

The mountains at the upper end of this vale form a scene singularly grand: on each side the hollow appears guarded by a huge conical rock, Trivaen on the right, and Braich Dû on the left. These, with Glyder Bach and Glyder Vawr, *The Lesser and Greater Glyder*, and some others, fill up the distance, and so close the vale, that no access could possibly be supposed to be had from beyond them.*

WATERFALLS OF BEN GLOG

At the end of the vale the road winds up a steep rock, betwixt Trivaen and Braich Dû, called Ben Glog. And from the bottom, at the distance of about half a mile on the left, may be seen the three falls of the Ogwen. These are called Rhaiadr Benglog, *The Cataracts of Benglog*,* and they are so fine that the traveller in search of romantic scenery will be highly gratified by visiting them. I descended from the road into the bottom of the vale, and went along the bank of the river till I arrived at the foot of the lower cataract. Here the stream roared with vast fury, and in one sheet of foam, down an unbroken and almost perpendicular rock. The sun shone directly upon it, and a prismatic bow was beautifully formed by the spray. The tremendous roar of the water, and the broken and uncouth disposition of the immediately surrounding rocks, added greatly to the interest of the scene. – After a while I climbed a rocky steep to the second or middle fall. Here the river is precipitated, in a fine stream, through a chasm between two perpendicular rocks that each rise several yards above. From the station I took, the immense mountain Trivaen was seen to fill up the wide space at the top, and to form a rude and sublime distance, heightened greatly in effect by a dark aërial tint arising from the extreme heat of the day, and the lowering clouds that were floating around it. The masses of black rocks, surrounded by foam, near the top of the fall, I could have fancied were floating along the torrent, and rushing to the bottom. The stream widens as it descends, and below passes over a slanting rock, which gives it a somewhat different direction. In the foreground was the rugged bed of the stream, and the water was seen to dash in various directions among the broken masses of rock. – The third cataract, to which I now clambered, I found very grand and majestic, yet by no means equal to either of the former. – These waterfalls are scarcely known in the adjacent country, and have been unaccountably omitted even in Mr. Pennant's Tour, although this gentleman accurately describes most of the scenery around them.

Leaving the falls, the trouble of visiting which had been amply repaid by the pleasure I had derived from them, I regained the road. – On crossing the upper end of the vale, I was delighted with a very beautiful and unexpected view for nearly its whole length, where the mountains down each side appeared, to a great distance, falling off in beautiful perspective.

Y TRIVAEN,

The Three Summits, so called from its appearing on one side to have three separate heads, forms, as I have before said, the right boundary of this extremity of the hollow. It is singular from having on its highest point two tall upright stones, which from below have the appearance of two men standing together. These are each about fourteen feet high, and they are not more than a yard and a half asunder. So exact is their resemblance to human figures, (for the eye does not take cognizance of their distance, and consequently their real size is not discovered,) that I am by no means surprized at the circumstance of many travellers having been deceived in fancying them a Welsh tourist and his guide. I was credibly informed that one gentleman who was on horseback, stopped by the edge of Llyn Ogwen, (for this is the place from whence alone they can be seen,) near half an hour to watch their motions; but being somewhat sooner satisfied with gazing at them than he thought they were at the surrounding country, he rode on to Capel Curig, where he related the circumstance, adding an expression of surprize at their remaining so long on one spot. The people at the public house laughed heartily at the joke, and immediately undeceived him. A gentleman of my acquaintance, also, who last summer was in the country, related to me some particulars of his journey, and among other things told me, that having passed through Nant Frangon a little way, he observed on the top of one of the mountains two men that seemed very earnestly engaged in admiring the country. He said, that although he went on very slowly, and was constantly looking back at them, till an intervening rock shut them from his sight, yet they still remained in the same position. This story was told so seriously, that it was not without difficulty I could keep my countenance to hear it to the end; and even when I had, I could scarcely persuade him that his men were nothing but blocks of stone.

LLYN OGWEN,

The source of the little river Ogwen, is a tolerable large pool, for it does not deserve the appellation of lake, well stocked with trout, and some other kinds of fish common to mountain pools. – Near this place the scenery changes its rough aspect, and assumes a more placid, but still rude character, which it retains for some miles.

NEW ROAD

An act of parliament was last year obtained for forming a road from near Llanrwst to Bangor Ferry, on which the mail-coach from London to Holyhead now runs. Till within these few years, the road along these vales was a mere horse-path, and that one of the worst in the country. To the liberality and public spirit of lord Penrhyn it is that the public are

Excursion from Bangor Ferry

indebted for the commencement, and for half the execution of this useful undertaking, for the road from Bangor Ferry to Capel Curig was made a few years ago at his lordship's own expence.* The principal advantages of this new road consist in having upwards of ten miles saved (in thirty-eight) betwixt Capel Voelas and Bangor Ferry; and in its going almost entirely along vallies in the most mountainous and romantic parts of North Wales, and thus avoiding the immense steeps of Penmaen Mawr and Sychnant. There is only one material declivity, that of Ben Glog, (betwixt Llyn Ogwen and Nant Frangon,) the whole way. The principal objection to the road seems to arise from the circumstance of immense drifts of snow in winter rolling down from the mountains into the vallies, and at times entirely blocking up the passage, against which, unhappily, there can be no remedy.

11

Bangor to Caernarvon

Long before I had conceived the thought of making a tour through Wales, I had been told much in praise of the ride from Bangor to Caernarvon. It had invariably been represented to me as affording more exquisite scenery than almost any other part of the country. – For four miles I sauntered along from the inn, expecting every moment to be delighted with a prospect of these boasted scenes, and was indulging some reflections, not altogether favourable to the taste and judgment of my informers, when, on a sudden turn of the road, the straits of Menai, the well wooded island of Anglesea, and beyond these the far distant Rival mountains on one side, opened into a placid scene, whilst the black precipices and shagged sides of the rocks of Caernarvonshire on the other, formed a most delightful contrast. This transition was so momentary, that it seemed almost the effect of enchantment. Proceeding onward, the town and castle of Caernarvon after a while entered the scene, and completed a landscape one of the most charming I ever beheld.

    At Caernarvon I went to the hotel, an inn built a few years ago by the earl of Uxbridge* on a very extensive scale. It is an elegant stone building standing on the left of the entrance into the town, a little above the Menai, of which it commands an extended prospect. This inn affords the best of accommodations; but in so large a house, where an establishment is to be kept through the whole year for the sake of only three of four of the summer months, the tourist must not be surprized in finding the charges somewhat higher than in the *Welsh* inns. – Any person fond of the water may here be accommodated with a little decked vessel containing two beds, and a cabin capable of holding about ten persons. The charge for it is a guinea a day.

CAERNARVON*

Is, on the whole, by much the most beautiful town in North Wales. It is situated on the eastern bank of the Menai, the strait that divides the isle of Anglesea from the other parts of Wales, and is a place extremely well adapted to afford during summer a few months retreat for a thinking mind from the busy scenes of the world. – Its situation between the mountains and the island renders it a convenient place of residence for travellers who wish to visit both.

The walls round the town are even yet nearly entire, and, as well as the castle, seem to bear much the same external appearance which they did in the time of their founder Edward I. They have in them a number of round towers, and two principal gates, entrances to the town. Over one of these is a spacious room, which is used as the town-hall, and in which the dancing assemblies are frequently held. – The houses are, for the most part, tolerably regular, but the streets, as in all other ancient towns, are very narrow and confined. – On the outside of the walls there is a broad and very pleasant terrace walk along the side of the Menai, extending from the quay to the north end of the town walls, which is the fashionable promenade, in fine evenings, for all descriptions of people. – The court-house, in which the great sessions for the county are held, and where all the county business is done, stands nearly opposite to the castle gates. – The custom-house, a small and mean building, is on the outside of the walls, not far from the quay.

From the top of Tuthill, the rock beyond the hotel, I had an excellent bird's-eye view of the town. From hence the castle, and the whole of the town walls, are seen to the greatest advantage; and, on a fine day, the isle of Anglesea, bounded on two sides by the Holyhead, and Paris mountains, appears spread out like a map beneath the eye. Sometimes, even the far distant mountains of Wicklow may be seen towering beyond the channel. On the opposite side to these is the fine and varied range of British Alps, where Snowdon, whose

> Hoary head,
> Conspicuous many a league, the mariner,
> Bound homeward, and in hope already there,
> Greets, with three cheers, exulting,*

is seen to far overtop the rest.

Caernarvon is in the parish of Llanbublic, and the *church* is situated about half a mile from the town. In this, which contains nothing curious except a marble monument, with two recumbent figures of sir William and lady Griffith, of Penrhyn, who died in the year 1587, the service is always performed in the Welsh language. There is an English service every Sunday morning and afternoon, in the chapel of ease to this church, situated in the north-west corner of the town walls, and formerly built for the use of the garrison. The former of these is generally very well attended.

At Caernarvon there is a small, but tolerably good harbour. This is used principally by the vessels that trade there for slates, of which many thousand tons are exported every year to different parts of the kingdom. These slates are brought from Cilgwyn, *The White Recess*, in the parish of Llanllyfni; Cefyn Dû, *The Black Ridge*, in the parish of Llanrûg; and Allt Dû, *The Black Cliff*; in the mountains on the north-east side of the pools of Llanberis.

CAERNARVON CASTLE

The entrance into this stupendous monument of ancient grandeur is through a lofty gateway, over which is yet left a mutilated figure, supposed by most writers to be that of Edward I. In this gate there are the grooves of no fewer than four portcullises, evidences of the former strength of the fortress. The building is large but irregular, and much more shattered within, than, from viewing it on the outside, one would be led to imagine. The towers are chiefly octagonal, but three or four of them have each ten sides: among the latter is the *Eagle Tower*, the largest and by far the most elegant in the whole building. This tower, which received its name from the figure of an eagle yet left (though somewhat mutilated) at the top of it, stands at one end of the oblong court of the castle, and has three handsome turrets issuing from it.

It was in the Eagle Tower that Edward, the first prince of Wales, afterwards Edward II, was born on St. Mark's day, the 25th of April 1284. Pennant says, that the prince was brought forth 'in a little dark room not twelve feet long, nor eight in breadth.' This assertion he alleges to be founded on tradition, but I cannot conceive how that gentleman should retain the opinion after he had once examined the place. This room has indeed had a window and a fire-place in it, but it very evidently was nothing more than a passage-room to some of the other apartments, which, though nearly the most magnificent in the castle, must, during the queen's confinement, have been shut up as useless. There seems to me no doubt, but that, when Edward sent for his queen from England, he provided for her a more magnificent bed-chamber than this, which, besides being extremely inconvenient at such a time, must, from its smallness alone, have been exceedingly unhealthful. If the prince was born in the Eagle Tower, it must have been in one of the rooms, occupying in width the whole inside, in an apartment suitable to the majesty of the heir apparent to the English throne, and not as honest Coleforks, who has the care of the castle, and who pointed out to me the place, said, 'in such a dog-hole as this.' – From the top of the Eagle Tower I was highly gratified by a very extensive view of the isle of Anglesea, the Menai, and the country for many miles round.

At the other end of the court, and opposite to this tower, is a gate called the Queen's Gate. This is said to be that through which the faithful Eleanor, queen of Edward I, first entered the castle. It appears to have been guarded by two portcullises, and it anciently had a communication with the outside of the castle by means of a draw-bridge over a deep moat. At present it is considerably above the level of the ground, owing probably to the moat having been filled up with earth from this part.

The state apartments are larger, and appear to have been much more commodious, than any of the others. The windows were wide, and not inelegant for the times. On the outside, the building containing these apartments is square, but I was surprized, on going into them, to find all the rooms perfectly polygonal, the sides being formed out of the vast thickness of the walls. – The floors and staircases throughout the castle are, except one or two, beaten in and demolished.

A narrow gallery, or covered way, formerly extended round this fortress, by which, during a siege, a communication could be had with the other parts without danger. On one side this gallery remains yet undemolished. It was next to the outer wall, and was lighted by narrow slits that served as stations, from whence arrows, and other missile weapons, could be discharged with advantage upon the enemy.

The castle occupies the whole west end of the town; and was a place of such strength, as, before the introduction of artillery, to withstand the most furious attacks of an enemy. The exterior walls are in general about nine feet thick. It is bounded on two sides by water: the third side appears to have been defended by a ditch, and the fourth was towards the town, where probably the same ditch might formerly have been continued.

From a heap of rubbish near the end of the court opposite to the Eagle Tower, an echo may be heard which repeats several syllables very distinctly. There is only a single reverberation, and it comes from some part of that tower.

Caernarvon castle, it has very justly been observed, from whatever point, or at whatever distance it is viewed, has a romantic singularity, and an air of dignity that commands an awe, at the same time that it pleases the beholder. Its ivy-clad walls appear in some parts to be going fast to decay, while in others they even yet retain their ancient exterior.

It is more than probable that the town of Caernarvon had its origin in the Roman city of Segontium, about half a mile distant, and that it is not, as many have supposed, indebted for its name to Edward I, for *the fort in Arvon*, or in the hundred opposite to Anglesea, as the name indicates, would apply with equal propriety to the ancient city, as to this more modern fortress. The town, however, there is no doubt, was the creation of Edward, and it was most probably formed principally from the ruins of the old station.

***

About half a mile south of Caernarvon there are yet to be seen a few walls, the small remains of

SEGONTIUM,*

The ancient Roman city, mentioned in the Itinerary of Antoninus.* This appears to have been the principal station that the Romans had in North Wales, all the rest being only subordinate stations. It received its name from the river Seiont, which rises in the lower lake of Llanberis, passes under the walls, and discharges itself into the Menai near Caernarvon castle. Its form was an oblong; and it appears originally to have occupied about six acres of ground. The road which leads from Caernarvon to Beddgelert now divides it into two parts.

Not far from hence was the fort which belonged to it: this was also of an oblong figure, and stood upon about an acre of ground. The walls are at present about eleven feet high, and six in thickness, and at each corner there has formerly been a tower.

The Romans constructed their walls in a manner very different from that at present in use. They first placed the stones in order one upon another, generally in two courses, the one regular, and the other zigzag. They then poured boiling mortar upon them, which, from its fluidity, insinuated itself into all the hollows of the work, and thus bound the irregular pieces of stone, they frequently used, into a solid and most durable wall. The mortar of the walls of Segontium has, at this time, almost the hardness of stone.

Along the walls are three parallel rows of circular holes, each nearly three inches in diameter, which pass through the whole thickness: and at the ends are others of a similar kind. Much learned conjecture has been employed as to the original design of these holes. Some antiquaries have supposed them to have been used for discharging arrows through at an enemy, but their great length and narrowness render it impossible that this should ever have been the case. Others have fancied they might have been left in the walls to admit air for the purpose of hardening the liquid cement that was poured in; but this cannot have been so, since there are such at Salisbury that appear to have been closed with stone at the ends, and others have been found even below the natural surface of the ground at Manchester. Mr. Whitaker, in his history of that place, which is a work of consummate judgment and science, says, that he by chance met with a hole that was accidentally laid open from end to end: this, he thought, disclosed the design of all the rest, and he supposes, that as the Romans carried their ramparts upwards, they took off from the pressure on the parts below, and gave a greater strength to the whole, by turning little arches in their work, and fixing the rest of the wall upon them. At Segontium, however, this cannot have been the case, for the holes are not only too small, but are at by far too great a distance from each other to have been of any material use in lightening the work. It appears to me (notwithstanding the circumstance of holes of a similar description being said to be found at Manchester below the surface of the ground), that these were formed for no other purpose than merely to bear the horizontal poles for resting the scaffolding upon, necessary in the building of the fabric: they may have been left unfilled up in order to admit air into the interior of the work, or for some other purpose with which we are not now acquainted. I am the more strongly inclined to this conjecture from their being exactly parallel, and the rows at a proper height above each other to admit the masons to work.

It was the opinion of Mr. Camden that this was the *Setantiorum Portus* of Ptolemy, but that place has been referred with greater propriety to the Neb of the Nefe, a high promontory in the river Ribble, about eight miles west of Preston in Lancashire.

We are informed in the Flores Historiarum,* that the body of Constantius, the father of Constantine the Great, was discovered here in 1283, and afterwards interred in the adjoining church; although in another part of the same work we are told that he died at York.

A chapel is said to have been founded here by Helena, the daughter of Octavius, duke of Cornwall. This was standing so lately as about a century ago.

During part of the fourth century the island of Anglesea was so dreadfully infested with Irish and Pictish rovers that Cadwallo, then prince of Wales, unable to restrain their proceedings, was reduced to the necessity of removing the British court from Aberffraw, where it had been fixed about two hundred years before by Caswallon law hîr, *Caswallon the long-handed*, to Segontium. Here it was continued about a century, till affairs became more settled in the island, when it was again fixed at Aberffraw by Roderic the Great, whence it was never afterwards removed till the country became subject to the English crown.

JUMPERS

Whilst I was at Caernarvon, I was induced from motives of curiosity, more than once to attend the chapel of a singular branch of calvinistical methodists, who, from certain enthusiastical extravagancies which they exhibit in their religious meetings, are denominated *Jumpers*. Their service here is in the Welsh language, and, as among other methodists, commences and concludes with a prayer. It is not till the last hymn is sung that any uncommon symptoms are exhibited. The tune consists only of a single strain, and the hymn having but one verse, this verse is, in consequence, repeated over and over, sometimes for half an hour, and sometimes, if their spirit of enthusiasm is much excited, for upwards of an hour. With this begin their motions. It is sung once or twice over without any apparent effect. The first motion to be observed is that of the upper parts of their body from right to left. They then raise their hands, and often strike one hand violently against the other. Such is the effect produced even on strangers, that I confess whenever I have been among them at these times, my intellects became greatly confused: the noise of their groaning and singing, or oftentimes rather bellowing, the clapping of their hands, the beating of their feet against the ground, the excessive heat of the place, and the various motions on all sides of me, almost stupified my senses. The less enthusiastic move off soon after the hymn is begun: among these, every time I attended them, I observed the preacher to make one; he always threw a silk handkerchief over his head, and, descending from the pulpit, left his congregation to jump by themselves. At intervals the word '*gogoniant*' (praise or glory!) is frequently to be heard. The conclusion of this extravagance, which bears much more the appearance of heathen orgies, than of the rational spirit of Christian devotion, has been described by one of their own countrymen with more justice than I am able to give it. 'The phrensy (he says) so far spreads, that to any observation made to them, they seem altogether insensible. Men and women indiscriminately, cry and laugh, jump and sing, with the wildest extravagance imaginable. That their dress becomes deranged, or the hair dishevelled, is no longer an object of attention. And their raptures continue, till, spent with fatigue of mind and body, the women are frequently carried out in a state of apparent insensibility. In these scenes, indeed, the youthful part of the congregation are principally concerned, the more elderly generally contenting themselves in admiring, with devout gratitude, what they deem the operations of the spirit.' Their exertions on these occasions are so violent, that were they often repeated in the week, the health of the people must be materially affected. When they leave the place, they often seem so much exhausted, as scarcely to be able to support the weight of their bodies; and the hardest labour they could be employed in would not so much waste the animal spirits, or weary their limbs, as an hour spent in this religious frenzy.

Besides these common meetings, they have their general assemblies, which are held twice or thrice in the year at Caernarvon, Pwllheli, and Bala, in rotation. At the latter meetings they sometimes assemble so many as five or six thousand people, who come from all parts of the adjacent country to hear the popular preachers. The general meeting at Caernarvon is holden in the open air, upon the green near the castle. Here, not contented with their enthusiastic extravagancies on the spot, many of the country people have been known to continue them for three or four miles of their road home.*

After so far describing this singular sect of enthusiasts, I may fairly be allowed a few observations on the general increase of methodism, and on what appear to me the modes of conduct to be adopted in order to check the torrent that seems bearing forward to overwhelm us in its vortex, and that appears to strike deeply at the root of government, both in church and state.

***

12

Excursion from Caernarvon to Llanberis

The walk from Caernarvon to Llanberis, *The Church of Peris*, a village about ten miles distant, I found, for the most part, rugged and unpleasant. The road, for nearly half way, lies over a flat barren country; and, beyond that, as far as Cwm y Clo, near the first or lower lake, over mountains, which, affording no varied prospects, are still dull and uninteresting. But when I had passed these, and was arrived in

THE VALE OF LLANBERIS,

A scene presented itself so truly grand, that I do not recollect one equal to it, even in the most romantic parts of Westmoreland or Cumberland. It reminded me most of the scenery about Ullswater; but this view, though much less extensive, is still more picturesque than any thing I saw there. The bold and prominent rocks, which ascend almost immediately from the edges of the lakes, and tower into the sky, cast a pleasing gloom upon the whole landscape. The more distant mountains of the vale, embosoming the moss-grown village, with the meadowy flat around it, are seen retiring in lines crossing behind in the most picturesque manner possible, whilst the intermediate space, betwixt the village and the observer, is filled up with a small lake, whose waters, reflecting the mountains which bound it, contract their sombre hue, and render the scene still more interesting. I could almost have fancied that nature untamed bore here an uninterrupted sway amidst the gloom and grandeur of these dreary* rocks, had not the silence been, at intervals, interrupted by the loud blasts from the neighbouring copper mine, which rolled like distant thunder along the atmosphere.

In my walk to this place, I met on the road several women and boys, who were coming from the mountains with horses, some laden with peat (which is almost the only kind of fuel burnt by the middle and lower classes of people in Caernarvonshire), and others with heath, or, as it is here called, *Grûg*, which the bakers use in heating their ovens. These they carry from a distance of frequently more than six miles, to sell at Caernarvon, where in general they receive about sixpence for each horse-load. – In these journies I have almost always remarked that the women employ themselves in knitting: this makes some small addition to their miserable and hard-earned pittance.

There is no carriage road from Caernarvon nearer to Llanberis than Cwm Clo, which is not quite half way; the road from thence being only a horse-path, and that one of the worst I ever saw. The best mode for those persons who are not able to walk so far, is to go on horseback, or in carriages, as far as the bottom of the lower lake, from whence they may see the waterfall, the old castle of Dolbadarn, or the village. – I have found every part about this romantic spot so extremely interesting, that I cannot too earnestly recommend to all persons who visit Caernarvon to prolong their route by coming here. There are no difficulties to be encountered but what the scenery will amply repay.

In one of my subsequent journies I went up the lakes in a boat. – The vale at the foot of the lower lake is called

CWM Y CLO,

The Vale of the Eminence, from the insulated rock that forms one side of it, on which the Britons had a strong hold called Caer Cwm y Clo. I ascended this rock, and found on its summit the remains of walls, of such a nature as plainly to indicate their pristine use. The fortification seems, however, to have been of no great importance.

From the top of a low rock on the left of this, I had an extensive and a very varied prospect. Towards Llanberis, the vale and the lakes were seen bounded on each side by their lofty and precipitous rocks: on the right was Snowdon, the monarch of the British Alps; he here presented himself the broadest and most tremendous of the group: on the opposite side of the vale were Llider Vawr and Glyder Vawr. Behind all these, in the far distant landscape, I observed the point of Crib Coch, *The Red Ridge*: it was well contrasted by its distance with the sombre mountains that intervened. The narrow isthmus that separates the lakes, and the insulated rock on its right bank, with the remains of Dolbadarn tower, formed distinct features in this interesting scene. The intervening space between the lake and my station was occupied by a dreary extent of moor. On the north-east, over a vast length of wastes, were seen the bay of Beaumaris, the island of Priestholme, and the sea: the isle of Anglesea was visible in its whole range from Abermenai to Penmôn.

Descending from this station, I was requested by the gentleman who attended me,* to examine the cottage of a small Welsh farmer in Cwm y Clo, as he said it was a tolerable specimen of this description of buildings in Caernarvonshire. I entered at a small gate, and first observed a wretched hovel for his cattle: the hay-rick was formed by a large slate, placed near one side, with its edge on the ground: the roof was so broken in and damaged, that only one corner afforded shelter to the miserable beasts from the fury of the mountain storms. I remarked, on the outside of this place, in an angle formed by the junction of two walls, a small slated roof, to protect from the rain the turf intended for fuel. A path between two rude stone walls, adorned with holly hedges, led me to the dwelling. The door was so low, that I was obliged to stoop considerably to enter; and coming out of a bright sun-shine, it was not till some time had elapsed that I was able to distinguish any thing in this hut, except the gleam of light that came down the chimney. This was at least equal to what the six small panes of glass in the window afforded. On the open hearth were a few peat-ashes, the remains of a fire with which the old man had a little while before cooked his dinner. The frame of the roof was formed by branches of trees fixed to larger timbers by straw or hay-bands. This frame was covered with sods, and the whole with slates, which, in the mountains, are obtained in great plenty. The furniture consisted of an old bed, an oak chest, a range of shelves for such poor eating utensils as were necessary in this lowly habitation, some old earthen vessels, some dingy pewter dishes, and a few other things, which, from the darkness of the place, were rendered indistinguishable to me. The whole character of this dwelling was such as clearly to prove the truth of Goldsmith's observation that

Man wants but little here below;

Cheerful at morn he wakes from short repose
Breathes the keen air, and carols as he goes.
At night returning, every labour sped,
He sits him down the *monarch of a shed.**

The day that I visited this cottage I was taken to another about two miles distant, in the same parish of Llanrûg, inhabited by a lame old woman called Mary Morgan. I mention it only for the purpose of relating the singular mode which this old woman *invariably* adopted, till her lameness rendered it too painful, of getting into her house whenever

Excursion from

she mislaid the key of her door. – She mounted the peat-stack at the end of the building, clambered up from thence to the slates, and descended the chimney. – This is an undoubted fact.

We had just seated ourselves in the boat that was to carry us up the lake, when my intelligent friend pointed out to me the cottage that once was inhabited by

MARGARET UCH EVAN.

This is on the left side of the bottom of the lake, near a stable lately built by Assheton Smith, esq.* Few females in this country have attained so great celebrity as Margaret. Being passionately fond of the sports of the chace, she kept a great number of all the various kinds of dogs used in this pursuit. She is said to have destroyed more foxes in one year than all the confederate hunts did in ten. She rowed well; and could play both on the harp and the fiddle. Margaret was also an excellent joiner; and, at the age of seventy, was the best wrestler in the country. She was likewise a good blacksmith, shoe-maker, and boat-builder. She shod her own horses, made her own shoes, and while she was under contract to convey the ore from the Llanberis copper mine, down the lakes, she built her own boats. This wonderful female died a few years ago at a very advanced age. She has lately been celebrated in some pleasant, though not very musical lines, by Mr. Hutton of Birmingham.

> 'Mongst the rocks of Llanberis, where foot comes not nigh,
> Nor eye sees their summit, except a bird's eye;
> Nor ought in the prospect appears to the sight,
> But water and mountain, yet these give delight,
> Quite silent, for miles, through their regions you go,
> Except when the surly wind chuses to blow.
>   Robust are the females, hard labour attends them;
> With the fist they could knock down the man who offends them.
> Here lived *Peggy Evans*, who saw ninety-two,
> Could wrestle, row, fiddle, and hunt a fox too;
> Could ring a sweet peal, as the neighbourhood tells,
> That would charm your two ears – had there been any bells;
> Enjoy'd rosy health in a lodging of straw;
> Commanded the saw-pit, and wielded the saw;
> And though she's deposited where you can't find her,
> I know she has left a few sisters behind her.*

VALE OF LLANBERIS

The entrance into the vale of Llanberis from the bottom of the lower lake is exceedingly grand and romantic. Seated as we were in the boat, nearly on a level with the surface of the water, the lake, on looking along its whole extent, had the appearance of being large and expansive. The mountains arrange in the most beautiful manner imaginable. Among some rocks on the right bank of the lake, about half a mile from the bottom, there is a scene remarkably picturesque. Snowdon, with its deep and perpendicular precipice, and two summits, forms an immense mass of mountain, which constitutes the principal feature. The lake, the round tower of Dolbadarn, the distant vale and mountains, and on the other side the huge rock of Glyder Vawr, lend each its character to heighten the effect of the whole. The beauty of this scene is greatly increased when the atmosphere is sufficiently dense to soften the harsh edges of the rocks. In the broad glare of a noon-day sun, the grand effect of height and distance in the mountains is nearly lost, for every part becoming exposed to the eye, they are in appearance brought much nearer, and their prominences and hollows are not to be distinguished so well as when seen through a medium more dense. In this case too, all the beauty arising from aërial tints is entirely wanting.

The vale of Llanberis is nearly straight, and of no great width throughout. It contains two small lakes, or rather pools; for their size will scarcely admit of the former appellation. The upper pool is about a mile in length, and somewhat less than half a mile across; and the other, though longer, is so very narrow, as to bear more the appearance of a wide river than a lake. These are separated by a small neck of land, but have a communication by a stream which runs from one into the other.

In both the pools the fish called *Char* used formerly to be caught, but, owing to the copper works carried on here, these have all been long since destroyed.

DOLBADARN CASTLE

On a rocky eminence between the two pools stands the old tower of Dolbadarn castle. This is about nine yards in its inner diameter, and, with a few shattered remains of walls and offices, occupies the entire summit of the steep. Its name of Castell Dolbadarn, *The Castle of Padarn's Meadow*, is supposed to have originated in its having been erected on the verge of a piece of ground called Padarn's Meadow, to which a holy recluse of that name retired from the world, to enjoy religious meditation and solitude.

> Just thus in woods and solitary caves
> The ancient hermits liv'd, but they liv'd happy;
> And in their quiet contemplations found
> More real comforts, than societies
> Of men could yield, than cities could afford,
> Or all the lustres of a court could give.*

There are several churches in Wales dedicated to this British saint, of whom we know nothing more at present than that he was buried in the island of Bardsey, and that he must, if the ancient British Triades* are authority, have been descended of a good family; for one of the three curiosities of the island of Britain, is there stated to have been the cloak or upper garment of Padarn, *which would not fit any one but a gentleman!* – This is carrying pride of ancestry to a tolerable length.

Dolbadarn castle very evidently appears, from its construction, to have been of British origin. It was built, no doubt, to defend the narrow pass through the vale into the interior of the mountains; and, from its situation, it seems to have been capable of affording perfect security to two or three hundred persons in cases of emergency. – In this castle it was that Owen Goch, *Owen the Red*, was confined by his brother Llewelyn ap Iorwerth, prince of Wales, upwards of twenty years, for having attempted to excite an insurrection among the people, injurious to his rights and dignity. – It has been long in ruins, for Leland mentions it in his time as only a 'piece of a tower.'

It is highly probable that this was anciently called *Bere Castle*, which some of the historians relate to have been in Caernarvonshire, seated in the midst of a morass, inaccessible but by a single causeway, and not to be approached except through the narrow and rugged defiles of the mountains. About the thirteenth century it was esteemed the strongest castle that the Welsh possessed in this part of the country.

SLATE QUARRY

In the mountain, on the opposite side of the lake, called Allt Dû, *The Black Cliff*, is a large slate quarry belonging to Assheton Smith, esq.* As this is high among the rocks, the men, in conveying the slates down to the lake, are under the necessity, as well as one horse before the cart, to have one yoked behind. This prevents these aukward vehicles from being dashed to the bottom of some of the dangerous steeps in which the mountains abound; for this must inevitably be the case without some such contrivance. It however appears to me, that sledges similar to those adopted in many parts of Westmorland and Cumberland for the same purpose, would not only be less expensive, but would also be found more safe and commodious.

CATARACT

About half a mile south of the castle, at the end of a long and deep glen, there is a tremendous cataract called Caunant Mawr, *The Waterfall of the Great Chasm*. It is upwards of sixty feet in height, and is formed by the mountain torrent from Cwm Brwynog. This rushes through a cleft in the rock above, and after coming for a few yards in a direct line, suddenly takes a turn with a broad stratum of the rock, and thus descends aslaunt, with a thundering noise, into the deep black pool below.

***

LLANBERIS COPPER MINE

Pursuing the path leading from the castle to the village, I came to a copper mine near the edge of the lake, belonging to a company of gentlemen who reside at Macclesfield. The ore here is in general very rich, being worth on an average from twenty to twenty-five pounds per ton, whilst that of the Paris mine is not often worth more than fifteen. The work was commenced in the year 1791; and the number of hands now employed is about a hundred. The ore when got is brought in small waggons to the mouth of the mine: here it is broken into small pieces with hammers. It is then sorted, and the best and smallest pieces are taken out, and conveyed in boats down the lakes, whence it is carted to the Menai, where a vessel is ready to carry it into Glamorganshire, to be melted and wrought into copper. The larger fragments are conveyed to a stamping-mill on the opposite side of the lake, where they are crushed into powder by six stampers, or, as they are called by the Welsh, Dawns Chwech, *Six Dancers*. The more valuable parts are here separated by means of water, and these are afterwards put into small bags, and carried, like the rest of the ore, to be shipped for South Wales. – The proprietors have now a few pits for the corrosion of iron, as in the Paris mines; and they have also lately begun to roast their ore here, which a short time ago were not even thought of.

Whilst I, and three gentlemen, who happened to be with me the day I visited the mine, were watching the women break the ore, a loaded waggon was brought out of the level. This gave us an opportunity of returning in an empty one to examine the interior of the work. We therefore leaped into the waggon that was to convey us, and with one miner before to drag, and two others behind to push us along, we entered the narrow cavern. This was about two hundred yards in length, and in the whole way it was seldom more than six feet wide, and seven or eight high. In some places the rugged arch of the roof was so low, that we were under the necessity of stooping down in order to pass it. The day was one of those excessively hot ones that we frequently have about the middle of August; and the chilling damp which immediately struck us on entering, added not a little to the terrors of the place. The level lying in a direct line, we took no lights along with us. I sat with my back towards the entrance, and the perfect darkness of the place, the confused noise (from the arched and low roof) of the talking of our guides, and the rumbling of the wheels, re-echoed in deep and imperfect sounds along the cavern, added to the frequent jolting of our vehicle, from the badness of the wooden rail-road, inspired me with some ideas not perhaps altogether agreeable. The length of the journey seemed more than double what it really was. When almost at the end of the riding part of the expedition, one of our infernia left us to bring a light from the interior of the mine. He was absent about five minutes, during which time we remained in perfect darkness. When I first saw him at some distance, his candle appeared reflected in the water which was lodged in the middle of the level, and the confused appearance of two lights, the one above and the other below, added to the man's grotesque and dingy countenance, for the other parts of his body were obscured by the gloom, produced an effect that I can scarcely describe, and which I shall not very soon forget. –

When we came to the end of the level we got out of the waggon, and each lighting his candle, followed our guides into a cavern so high, that all our lights did not render the roof visible. The sides were rude as the exterior of the rock, and the black chasms along them, nearly all impenetrable by our lights, rendered it to one of our friends, more timorous than the rest, a scene of horror. A skilful artist might have found us a good subject for his pencil: the glare of light on *our* countenances expressive of inquiry, and not perhaps entirely free from those lines which ideas of terror will create; the blackened visages of our guides; our different dresses; and the rude scenery around, aided by a little picturesque grouping, and that allowable exaggeration which both painters and poets lay claim to in their descriptions, might have produced an admirable picture.*

In the cavern where we were standing, a shaft about sixty feet deep, was driven to a vein of ore below. On looking down this we could just discover in the darkness of the gloom, the reflection of a light from the workmen there. Soon afterwards a light was seen to cross the bottom; and, on calling aloud for it to stop, the man returned, and stood with it immediately below. It was a mere speck, and its rays were just discernible striking on the thick vapour immediately around it. Near the bottom of this shaft, our guides informed us, there was another about fifty feet in depth. We left the cavern, and after visiting another, nearly similar to it, from which all the ore had been got, we ended our adventure by returning along our former road into the light of day.

LLANBERIS

The village of Llanberis is romantic in the extreme. It is situated in a narrow grassy dell, surrounded by immense rocks, whose summits cloud-capped, are seldom visible to the inhabitants from below. 'Nature has here (says Camden, speaking of these parts of Caernarvonshire) reared huge groups of mountains, as if she meant to bind the island fast to the bowels of the earth, and make a safe retreat for the Britons in time of war. For here are so many crags and rocks, so many wooded vallies rendered impassable by so many lakes, that the lightest troops, much less an army, could never find their way among them. These mountains may be truly called the British Alps; for besides that they are the highest in the whole island, they are like the Alps, bespread with broken crags on every side, all surrounding one, which, towering in the centre, far above the rest, lifts its head so loftily, as if it meant not only to threaten, but to thrust it into the sky.'

All the parts immediately surrounding the village were formerly covered with wood; but, except some saplings from the old roots, there are at present very few trees left. In the memory of persons now living there were great woods of oak in several different parts about these mountains. In the tenth century the whole country must have been nearly covered with wood, for one of the laws of Howel Dda,* *Howel the Good*, directs that 'whoever cleared away timber from any land, even without the consent of the owner, he should, for five years, have a right to the land so cleared; and after that time it should revert to the owner.'

Except two tolerable houses in the vale, the one occupied by Mr. Jones the agent to the copper mine, and the other, which is on the side of the lake opposite to Dolbadarn castle, occupied by the agent to the slate quarries, the whole village consists but of a few scattered cottages, and these apparently the most miserable. They are in general constructed of the shaly stone with which the country abounds, and have but just so much cement as to keep out the keenest of the mountain blasts. The windows are invariably small, and many of them that have been broken, are so blocked up with boards, that the light down the chimney is even greater than that from the window.

There are two cottages in this village where the wearied traveller may take such poor refreshments as the place affords. One of these belonged, about two years ago, to John Close, a grey-headed old man, who was born and brought up in the north of Yorkshire. He had occasion to come into Wales with some cattle in his younger days, and preferring this to his Yorkshire home, he resided here the rest of his life. His son now keeps the house. – The other is kept by the parish clerk, who may be employed as a guide over any part of the adjacent country. I found him well acquainted with the mountains, and a much more intelligent man than guides in general are. He does not speak English well, but his civility and attention are a sufficient compensation for this defect. – Neither of these places affords a bed, nor any thing eatable better than bread and butter, or cheese; and, perhaps, eggs and bacon.

The first time that I came to Llanberis, being somewhat fatigued with traversing the adjacent mountains, I went to the former of these houses to rest myself and obtain some refreshment. It was just at the dinner hour, and a scene was exhibited altogether novel to me. At one table were seated the family of the house, consisting of the old host, his wife, and their son and daughter, eating their bread and milk, the common food of the labouring people here: a large overgrown old sow was devouring her dinner, with considerable dissatisfaction on account of the short allowance, from a pail placed for her by the daughter in one corner; whilst I was eating my bread and butter, with an appetite steeled against niceties by the keenness of the mountain air, at a table covered with a dirty napkin, in the other corner. This scene, however, induced me always afterwards to bring with me refreshments from Caernarvon, and enjoy my dinner, in quiet, in the open air.

The widow of old John Close had another suitor within a very few months after his death. Her sons were averse to the connexion, and therefore, though she was more than seventy years old, and her lover upwards of sixty-five, this elegant pair romantically planned a nocturnal elopement. One of the sons, about two o'clock in the morning, was roused by the foot-steps of a horse, and, almost immediately, he heard a man alight, and come to the door. Ignorant of the cause of so strange a circumstance, he sprang out of bed, and on opening the door, found it was the lover, who had brought a horse to convey away his intended bride. The man told his story with great simplicity, but insisted on having his *fair charge* surrendered to him, which with some hesitation was done, and the next morning the clergyman of Llanddiniolen united the happy pair. – It is singular that this man and woman had been lovers in their youthful days, but that prudential motives inducing one of them to marry another person, the other also married not long after. John Close was the woman's second husband, and, after his death, the suitor, being also freed from matrimonial shackles, began his addresses afresh, and at length attained the object of his earliest wishes.

The *church* of Llanberis* was, four years ago, without exception, the most ill-looking place of worship I ever beheld. The first time I came to the village, I absolutely mistook it for a large antique cottage, for even the bell-turret was so overgrown with ivy, as to bear much the appearance of a weather-beaten chimney; and the grass in the church-yard was so long as completely to hide the few grave-stones therein from the view. Since this time it has, however, undergone some repairs, but it is still sufficiently rude to accord excellently well with the surrounding mountains.

THE CURATE

I saw, and was introduced to: he resided in a mean-looking cottage not far from the church, which seemed to consist of but few other rooms than a kitchen and bed-room, the latter of which served also for his study. When I entered the room he was engaged over an old folio volume of sermons. His dress was somewhat singular; he had on a blue coat that long had been worn threadbare, and in various places exhibited marks of the industry of his wife, a pair of antique corderoy breeches, and a black waistcoat, and round his head was tied a blue handkerchief. His library might have been the very same that Hurdis has described in the *Village Curate*.

> Yon half a dozen shelves support, vast weight,
> The curate's library. There marshalled stand,
> Sages and heroes, modern and antique:
> He, their commander, like the vanquished fiend,
> Out-cast of heaven, oft through their armed files,

> Darts an experienced eye, and feels his heart
> Distend with pride, to be their only chief:
> Yet needs he not the tedious muster-roll,
> The title-page of each well known, its name,
> And character.*

From the exterior of the cottage, it seemed but the habitation of misery; but the smiles of the good man were such as would render even misery cheerful. His salary was about forty pounds, on which, with his little farm, he contrived to support himself and his family, and with this slender pittance he seemed perfectly contented and comfortable. His wife was absent, but from a wheel which I observed in the room I conjectured, and was afterwards informed, that her time was principally employed in spinning wool. The account I had from the parishioners of the character of this man was, that he was respected and beloved by all, and that his whole time and attention were occupied in doing such good to his fellow creatures as his very slender circumstances would allow.

> I venerate the man whose heart is warm,
> Whose hands are pure, whose doctrine, and whose life
> Coincident, exhibit lucid proof
> That he is honest in the sacred cause.
> To such I render more than mere respect,
> Whose actions shew that they respect themselves.*

This person, after sustaining a severe illness with the utmost resignation and fortitude, died in the beginning of the year 1801, leaving a widow and one daughter to survive him.

WELSH FUNERAL

During my residence in Caernarvonshire I one day rode with the worthy rector of Llanberis,* to attend the funeral of a girl, a child about seven years old, whose parents resided in the parish of Llanddiniolen, somewhat more than five miles distant. The coffin was tied on the bier, and covered with a sheet, tied also at the corners. It was borne on the shoulders of four men. The number of attendants at the outset was near a hundred, but this increased by the continued addition of men, women, and children, some on foot and some on horseback, till, by the time we arrived at the church, we had more than double that number. At the head of this cavalcade my friend and myself ascended the steep paths of the rocks, passed over mountains, and wound our way along some of the most rugged defiles of this dreary country. To any stranger who could have observed, at a little distance, our solemn procession, in this unfrequented tract of mountains, in one place some hundred feet above the lake of Llanberis, to the edge of which we had to descend, it would have borne much the air of romantic times. When we came to the church, we found that place nearly full of people awaiting our arrival. The service was read in Welsh in a most impressive manner; and the coffin was let down into the grave by four of the female mourners. A more solemn office I had never witnessed, and the circumstance of the body being committed to the bosom of the earth by the hands of relatives or friends was altogether new to me. A few rushes were strewed upon the coffin; and I shall never forget the stifled shriek that was uttered, when, in Welsh, the solemn words, 'we commit her body to the ground,' &c. were read. How enviable were the virtuous feelings of this illiterate peasantry, while thus attending a sister to the verge of peace. – The ceremony being over, the grave was filled up and planted with slips of box and some other evergreens. – The offerings in the church amounted to near two pounds, of which more than thirty shillings were in silver.

At no great distance from the church there is a *well* dedicated to St. Peris, and inclosed within a square wall. In the holes of this a person of the adjoining cottage generally has a small fish, from the appearance or non-appearance of which, when a bit of bread is thrown into the water, the common Welsh people pretend to foretel good or ill fortune. The general reward of a piece of silver from such strangers as visit the place, affords a temptation for them still to keep on foot at least the appearance of this superstition.

I was one day strolling with my friend Williams along the vale, when he pointed out to me a female well known in this village, and who, from the masculine tone of her voice, her manners, and appearance, might have been a descendant of the celebrated Margaret Uch Evan, called

CADDY OF CWM GLAS.

This athletic female does not often visit the town of Caernarvon; but, whenever she does, the boys run after, and call her, 'the woman with a beard.' Caddy resides in Cwm Glâs, a romantic vale, about two miles from Llanberis. She is accustomed to masculine employments of every description, and such is her muscular power, that no man of the village would dare to try a fall with her. Mr. Jones of the copper-mine had often rallied her on the subject of her great strength, and told her that he did not believe half the stories that he had heard related: she, one day, in perfect good humour, came behind him, as he was standing on the bank of the pier, near the stamping mill, and lifting him from the ground, held him in her arm, though by no means a small man, with great apparent ease, over the water. 'Now, Sir, (says she) I suppose you will believe that I am tolerably strong: you must confess it, or I shall throw you in.' He immediately acknowledged her powers, and was relieved from his predicament. – About eighteen months ago, a huge, raw-boned fellow, entered her cottage, during her absence, and had collected together some eatables and clothes, with which he was escaping, just as she returned. Though this cottage is in a very solitary situation, and she was entirely alone, she resolutely went up and insisted on his returning every thing he had taken. He opened his wallet, and gave up the eatables. Supposing these to be all, she returned with them to the cottage. But soon after discovering that a silk handkerchief, which she had left on the table, was gone, she immediately seized one of the bars of a small gate in her hand, and went in pursuit of the thief. She overtook him in the most solitary part of the vale, and, brandishing her cudgel about his ears, with the utmost courage, demanded restitution of the remainder of her property. An answer she did not wait for, but seizing the bag from the cowardly scoundrel, shook the whole contents, with the most contemptuous air, upon the ground. When she had selected her own property, she threw the bag in the fellow's face; and, after bestowing a hearty thwack with her cudgel on each of his shoulders, left her opponent to comfort himself with the idea of having escaped a more sound drubbing, which, as she afterwards declared, she would have inflicted, had she thought it necessary.

CWM GLAS

A bad horse-path* led me from the village of Llanberis into Cwm Glâs, *The Blue Vale*. For four miles I was hemmed in on each side by high rocks that almost approach each other. The sun cast a sloping shade on those of the right, which fully marked all their deepened hollows. Various in themselves, and varied in their tints and colourings, I was at every step interested by their terrific grandeur. They had no characters of softened beauty, there were here none of the delicate features of a cultivated vale, not even a single tree, but rocks towered over rocks, till their summits reached the clouds, whose partial gloominess added still greater sublimity to the scene. Sometimes I beheld above me a gentle hollow, then a few steps further, the deepened precipice and towering basaltic-like columns of an adjoining range of rocks. In some places there appeared three or four ranges, one above another, with the most fantastic outlines imaginable, and receding in distance as in height. The tints on the prominences were of darkened purple, in the hollows sombre, and olive-brown on the nearer ranges. The fore-ground was overspread with masses of rock, and a rapid mountain stream forced its way along the middle of the narrow vale. Such is this tremendous hollow, whose grandeur continues undiminished for almost four miles. The rocks on each side are nearly perpendicular throughout.

About three miles from Llanberis there is an immense stone, that has once been precipitated from above, called

THE CROMLECH.

This stone is of some thousand tons weight, and many times larger than the celebrated mass of rock in Borrowdale, called *Bowdar Stone*. It lies in a place called Ynys Hettws, *Hetty's Island*; and two of its sides meeting at an angle with the ground, it was once used as the habitation of an old woman, who, in summer, resided in the vale to tend and milk her cows. The inclosures are yet nearly entire, and are at present used as a sheep-fold.

Not far from this stone, on the opposite side of the stream, is the cottage of Caddy of Cwm Glâs, the female whom I mentioned a few pages back. There is, at a little distance from the cottage, another very large mass of rock insulated like the former.

GORPHWYSFA,

The resting Place, is an eminence, four miles from Llanberis, that overlooks a considerable part of this vale. It also commands a view into the mountain vale, that joins Nan Hwynan, and the vale of Capel Curig.

From hence I immediately returned to Caernarvon.

The tourist, if he chooses it, may, from this place, proceed onwards nearly in a direct line, through the village of Capel Curig, to Llanrwst; or, adopting another route, may keep the right-hand path, which will lead him through the vale, called Nan Hwynan, to Beddgelert. From Beddgelert, he may either return to Caernarvon, or continue his journey, in a direction towards Dolgelle, or Bala.

13

Excursion from Caernarvon to the Summit of Snowdon

The distance of the summit of Snowdon from Caernarvon is somewhat more than ten miles; and from Dolbadarn castle, in the vale of Llanberis, the ascent is so gradual, that a person, mounted on a little Welsh poney, may ride up very nearly to the top.

From Dolbadarn castle the traveller must go, by the waterfall, Caunant Mawr, to Cwm Brwynog, *The rushy Hollow*. He must proceed up this vale, and then along the ridge immediately over the vale of Llanberis, till he comes within sight of a black, and almost perpendicular rock, with a small lake at its foot, called Clogwyn du'r Arddu, *The Black Precipice*. This he is to leave about a quarter of a mile on his right, and then ascending a steep called Llechwedd y Rè, *The rapid Descent*, he must direct his course south-west to the well, (a place sufficiently known to the guides,) from whence he will find it about a mile to the highest peak of the mountain.*

In my first journey I went from the castle to Cwm Brwynog, but, instead of following the above route, I wandered to *Clogwyn du'r Arddu*, to search that rock for some plants which Lhwyd* and Ray* have described as growing there. The Reverend Mr. Williams accompanied me, and he started the wild idea of attempting to climb up the precipice. I was too eager in my pursuit to object to the adventure, and we began our laborious task without once reflecting on the dangers that might attend it. For a little while we got on without much difficulty, but we were soon obliged to have recourse both to our hands and knees, in clambering from one crag to another. Every step now required the utmost caution, and it was necessary to try that every stone was firm in its place before the weight of the body was trusted upon it. I had once lain hold of a piece of the rock, and was in the act of raising myself upon it, when it loosened from its bed, and I should have been precipitated headlong, had I not in a moment snatched hold of a tuft of rushes, and saved myself. When we had ascended somewhat more than half-way, there seemed no chance of our being able to proceed much farther, on account of the increasing size of the masses of rock above us. We rested a moment from our labour to consider what was to be done. The danger of again descending was much too great, for us to think of attempting it, unless we found it absolutely impossible to proceed. On looking down, the precipice, for at least three hundred feet, seemed almost perpendicular. We were eager in our botanical pursuit, and extremely desirous to be at the top, but I believe it was the prospect downwards that determined us to brave every difficulty. It happened fortunately that the steep immediately above us was the only one that presented any material danger. Mr. Williams having on a pair of strong shoes with nails in them, which would hold their footing better than mine, requested to make the first attempt, and after some difficulty he succeeded. We had along with us a small basket to contain our provisions, and hold the roots of such plants as we wished to transfer to his garden; this he carried behind him by means of a leathern belt fastened round his waist. When, therefore, he had fixed himself securely to a part of the rock, he took off his belt, and holding firmly by one end, gave the other to me: I laid hold, and, with a little aid from the stones, fairly pulled myself up by it. After this we got on pretty well, and in about an hour and a quarter from the commencement of our labour, found ourselves on the brow of this dreadful precipice, and in possession of all the plants we expected to find.

It would be difficult to describe my sensations, when my companion pointed out to me the summit of Snowdon at the distance of only about a mile and a half from us, and, from its great elevation, appearing scarcely more than half a mile. The sight was so unexpectedly pleasant, that I proceeded from hence to the summit with considerably greater alacrity than I should have done had we encountered no dangers, or experienced no interruptions. Thus situated, the well known story of the Pedlar immediately recurred to me, and if he had found relief from the wearisome burthen of his pack by throwing from it the additional weight of a large stone that he had attached to it for the purpose, so I, after the labour of clambering the steep of Clogwyn du'r Arddu, found ascending to the summit of Snowdon perfectly easy. Had I gone along the regular track, I have not a doubt but I should have *fancied* myself much more wearied than I now really felt.

The perpendicular height of this mountain, according to late admeasurements, is 1190 yards (somewhat less than three quarters of a mile) from the level of the sea. It rises to a mere point, its summit not being more than three or four yards in diameter.

The view from the summit I found beyond my expectation extensive. From this point the eye is able to trace, on a clear day, part of the coast, with the hills of Scotland; the high mountains of Ingleborough and Penygent in Yorkshire;* beyond these the mountains of Westmorland and Cumberland; and, on this side, some of the hills of Lancashire. When the atmosphere is very transparent, even part of the county of Wicklow, and the whole of the isle of Man, become visible. The immediately surrounding mountains of Caernarvonshire and Merionethshire all seem directly under the eye, and the highest of the whole appear from this station, much lower than Snowdon. Many of the vales were exposed to the view, which, by their verdure, relieved the eye from the dreary scene of barren rocks. The numerous pools visible from hence, betwixt thirty and forty, lend also a varied character to the prospect. – The mountain itself, from the summit, seems as it were propped by five immense rocks as buttresses. These are *Crib y Ddistil*, and *Crib Coch*, between Llanberis and Capel Curig; *Lliewedd* towards Nan Hwynan; *Clawdd Coch* towards Beddgelert; and *Llechog*, the mountain which forms the south side of the vale of Llanberis, towards Dolbadarn.

The summit of Snowdon is so frequently enveloped in clouds and mist, that, except when the weather is perfectly fine and settled, the traveller through this country will find it somewhat difficult to have a day sufficiently clear to permit him to ascend the mountain. When the wind blows from the west it is almost always completely covered; and at other times, even when the state of the weather seems favourable, it will often become suddenly enveloped, and will remain in that state for hours. Most persons, however, agree that the prospects are the more interesting, as they are more varied, when the clouds just cover the summit. The following description of the scenery from Snowdon when the mountain is in this state, is perfectly accurate.

> Now high and swift flits the thin rack along
> Skirted with rainbow dies, now deep below
> (While the fierce sun strikes the illumin'd top)
> Slow fails the gloomy storm, and all beneath
> By vaporous exhalation hid, lies lost
> In darkness; save at once where drifted mists
> Cut by strong gusts of eddying winds, expose
> The transitory scenes.

> Now swift on either side the gather'd clouds
> As by a sudden touch of magic, wide
> Recede, and the fair face of heaven and earth
> Appears. Amid the vast horizon's stretch,
> In restless gaze the eye of wonder darts
> O'er the expanse; mountains on mountains piled,
> And winding bays, and promontories huge,
> Lakes and meandering rivers, from their source
> Traced to the distant ocean.*

The name of Snowdon was first given to this mountain by the Saxons, its signification is *A Hill covered with Snow*. The Welsh call all this cluster of mountains that lie in the county of Caernarvon, Creigiau yr Eryri, the *Snowy Cliffs*. The highest point of Snowdon is called Yr Wyddfa, *The Conspicuous*. – Most of the old writers who have mentioned this mountain, assert that it is covered with snow through the whole year. This is by no means true, for this, as well as all the other Welsh mountains, has in general no snow whatever upon it between the months of June and November.

Snowdon was formerly a *royal forest* that abounded with deer; but the last of these were destroyed early in the seventeenth century.

The parts of this mountain on which the uncommon alpine plants are chiefly to be found, are the east and north-east sides. These form a range of rocks called *Clogwyn y Garnedd*, which abound in the most dangerous steeps. There is at all times some difficulty in searching them, but when the rocks are rendered slippery from heavy mists or rain, this becomes, from the insecurity of the footing, greatly increased.

***

It is a singular fact that nearly at the top of Snowdon there is a fine *spring of water*, which, I am informed, is seldom increased or diminished in quantity either in winter or summer. From its very elevated situation, this water is the coldest I ever recollect to have tasted.

SNOWDON COPPER MINE

A considerable vein of copper ore was discovered a few years ago in Cwm Glâs Llyn, *The Hollow of the Blue Pool*, near the foot of Clogwyn y Garnedd. Some of the gentlemen of the county associated themselves for the purpose of getting this ore, and the work now goes on with considerable spirit. It is, however, by no means so rich or valuable as that from the Llanberis mine, and this circumstance, together with the expence of conveying it nearly over the summit of the mountain to Caernarvon, may possibly prevent its ever being worked to any extent. The proprietors have made a tolerably good sledge-path from the Beddgelert road, near Llyn Cwellyn, to Bwlch Glâs, a hollow just below the highest point of Snowdon, and from thence a winding footpath down to the mine. To Bwlch Glâs the men carry the ore in bags on their shoulders: here it is loaded on small one-horse sledges, in which it is dragged to the road. – A house has lately been erected near the mine for the accommodation of the workmen during bad weather: some of them live here altogether.

Much difficulty and many hardships are to be overcome by the workmen in the variable climate of these alpine vales. In winter, heavy snows, which frequently drift many yards in thickness; in spring and autumn, the most violent hurricanes; and, in the height of summer, thunder-storms uncommonly tremendous, are to be withstood by the labourers in this copper mine. – In the winter of 1801 the snow drifted so deep before the mouth of the mine, that the men were under the necessity of cutting a level through it, and of thus going to their work under a long arch of snow. Sometimes the mouth of the new level they were forming in the rock was so closed round with snow, that they were not able to tell exactly where it was; and when with difficulty they had found it, it cost some labour to clear an entrance. This snow-drift was in many places near twenty yards deep, and some of it was to be seen in the recesses of the rocks till even the middle of May.

Accidents may also happen in winter from the ice on the rocks: of this an instance has already occurred. A workman was going to the mine from his cottage in Cwm Brwynog early one frosty morning, when, in descending the steep above the mine, he slipped on some frozen snow, and was thrown along the rocks for near a hundred yards. He was there, providentially, stopped by a hovel that had been built to contain the workmen's tools. Almost every part of his body was bruised by the violence of the fall, and one of his eyes was so much injured, that at the time it was doubtful whether he would recover his sight.

I was informed that the wind had often been so furious among the rocks, that the workmen had found the utmost difficulty in preventing themselves from being blown over the edge of the precipices. Sometimes when they heard its approach by the roaring along the vales, they were compelled to fall down on their hands and knees, and, laying fast hold on each other, to wait in this position till the violence of the gust was passed; or, when it was likely to continue, they had to creep along till, under shelter of the side of the mountain, they could proceed in safety. A party of the men were one morning going to the mine, when the wind was heard to roar loudly along one of the hollows. They all, except one man, laid down till the gust had passed by: he ridiculed their cowardice, and holding out his jacket on each side, observed, that 'as a fine breeze was springing up, he should spread his sails, and make the best of his way by scudding before the gale, to work.' The wind in a moment bore him from the ground to the distance of ten or twelve yards, where he was thrown down with the utmost violence. He repented his folly, and though he was not much hurt, the accident had a good effect in teaching the men to act with the utmost prudence in similar perilous situations.

Two Denbighshire gentlemen, who are also partners in this concern, have caused a pretty good mountain horse-path to be made from Gorphwysfa, beyond Llanberis, to the copper mine.* This will now render the ascent to the summit of Snowdon from Capel Curig and the village of Llanberis perfectly easy.

Welsh tourists have been much in the habit of over-rating the difficulties that are to be encountered in the journey to the summit of this mountain. To provide against these, one of them recommends a strong stick with a spike in the end, as a thing absolutely necessary; another advises that the soles of the shoes be set round with large nails; and a third inveighs against attempting so arduous and so difficult an undertaking in boots. I can only say, that to have nails in the shoes, and to take a stick in one's hand, may both be useful in their way, but if a person is in good health and spirits, he will find that he can do very well without either. I should recommend to the traveller to allow himself sufficient time: to be upon the journey by five or six in the morning, when the sun has not yet attained much power, and when the air is cool and refreshing. The chief thing required is a little labour, and this, by going gently along, will be rendered very easy. There is also another advantage in having plenty of time; by stopping frequently to rest himself, he will be enabled to enjoy the different distant prospects as they rise above the mountains, and to observe how the objects around him gradually change their appearance as he rises higher and higher. – It will always be necessary to take a guide, for otherwise a sudden change in the weather might render the attempt extremely perilous to a stranger.

But these changes are of no consequence to the men who are in the habits of ascending the mountain very frequently, for they have marks by which they would know the path in the most cloudy weather. – A sufficient supply of eatables is also absolutely necessary: the traveller will find the utility of these long before he returns.

14

Excursion from Llanberis to the Summit of Snowdon and Ascent of Snowdon from Llyn Cwellyn

In the present excursion I proceeded about a mile beyond the village of Llanberis, and, crossing the brook that runs into the pool, commenced my ascent up the steep mountains on the right. – After some fatigue, for the sun shone bright, and the reflection from the rocks was very powerful, I gained the top of the first range of rocks which overlook the vale I had left. – In a hollow among these mountains I found the little pool called Ffynnon Frech,* *The Spotted Well*. In its bottom were growing in great abundance those rare plants, almost wholly confined to alpine pools, *Subularia aquatica, Isoetes lacustris,* and *Lobelia dortmanna*.

From hence I continued my journey up another steep, and from its top observed two other pools in a vale at a great depth below me, called Llyn Llwydaw, *The Dusky Pool,* and Llyn y Cwm Glâs, *The Blue Pool in the Hollow*. A small island in the former is, in spring, the haunt of the Black-backed Gulls, which here lay their eggs, and bring up their young. I did not descend, as I could observe nothing about them likely to repay me for the trouble, but proceeded onward, for about a mile, along the sloping sides of the mountains, till I came to the hollow called Bwlch Glâs. After leaving this place I was not long in attaining the summit of the monarch of the British Alps.

From the top of the first mountains, after I left Llanberis, till I came within sight of Llyn Llwydaw, the scenery was awfully rude. It was one continued series of rocks, infinitely varied in their figure and disposition. The nimble-footed sheep that brouzed on their dark sides, and skipped along their tremendous precipices, looked down upon us with the utmost composure, fearless of any danger from their seemingly precarious situation. In some places the rocks, overhanging the path, seemed ready to start from their bases, threatening destruction to the travellers who had dared their gloomy shade. I was much pleased with this part of my ramble, for I love

> These lonely regions, where, retired
> From little scenes of art, great Nature dwells
> In awful solitude.*

The latter part of the excursion, along the sloping sides of the mountains, was somewhat unpleasant. The stones I had to traverse for above a mile were so small and loose, as at every step to give way: this not only rendered the walk fatiguing, but sometimes, indeed, dangerous. The scenery was wild, but little interesting. The hollow beneath me, hemmed in by the gloomy mountains around, had, from a few points of view, a considerable degree of grandeur, but, in this respect, it was far inferior to what I had passed. Wandering along this dreary scene, I once or twice heard, sweetly mellowed by the distance,

> The wildly winding brook
> Fall hoarse from steep to steep.*

The light clouds swept briskly over the mountains, sometimes entirely obscuring them, and then again shewing their serrated tops visible through the thinness of the mist.

I descended from Snowdon this time along what may with propriety be denominated a mountain stair-case, down the rocks immediately opposite to the village of Llanberis. This road was for the whole way so very steep and unpleasant, that I would at any time rather go three or four miles round than venture down it again.

ASCENT OF SNOWDON FROM LLYN CWELLYN

On the following day I once again went up to the summit of Snowdon,* and this time I chose, as the place of my outset, the cottage of the mountain guide who lives near Llyn Cwellyn, a pool about six miles from Caernarvon, on the side of the road leading from thence to Beddgelert. – We first went along some meadows which extend up the sides of the mountains for about half a mile. Leaving these, we, after some time, came to Bwlch Cwm Brwynog, *The Hollow of the Vale of Brwynog*, a kind of gap betwixt the mountains, which overlook that vale. This place is reckoned about half way to the top, and persons who visit the mountain on horseback usually ride thus far, leaving their horses here to the care of their servants till they return. – We passed by Llyn Ffynnon y Gwâs, *The Servant's Pool*, so called, it is said, from the shepherd of a farmer in the neighbourhood having some time ago been drowned there as he was washing his sheep. The road then lies along a steep ridge, one of those denominated the buttresses of Snowdon.

The path I found all the way exceedingly tiresome. A little above the pool I had to pass, for near a quarter of a mile, over immense masses of rocks, lying over each other in almost every different direction, and entirely destitute of vegetation. – The sledge-way to the copper-mine (mentioned in the last chapter) will, however now have done away all these inconveniences.

During the whole former part of this excursion the sky was clear, and the sun shone excessively hot: not a single cloud was to be seen on the whole concave of the heavens. Notwithstanding this very favourable appearance, the guide, while we were on the top of Snowdon, suddenly advised that we should hasten our descent, as a storm would otherwise soon be upon us. I ridiculed the idea without once considering that the knowledge of the mountaineers in the symptoms of the weather, must be much more correct than that of an entire stranger, and I had occasion to repent it. The wind had not long before veered round from east to south-west, and a narrow skirt of cloud seemed rising from the ocean. I had already too often experienced the effects of *this* foreboding not now to second the guide's motion, and I was also well aware that we should undergo a thorough drenching before we could possibly arrive at his cottage. We packed up our napkin and eating-vessels in the basket, and footed our way with all possible expedition, springing over the ledges, and among the broken fragments of the rocks, like mountain goats. The cloud increased rapidly, and every time I could take my attention for a moment from my feet, I discovered that it had become more condensed and black than before. Its misty extremity now eclipsed the sun, and from the streaks with which it was marked, it was too plain what we had soon to expect. I advised that we should seek for shelter under two fragments of rock a few hundred yards in front of us, till the fury of the storm passed over. The velocity with which the lower clouds were moved, dashed them among the hollows of the mountains, and whirled them round with great violence. In a few seconds we found ourselves enveloped in a mist so dense that we could scarcely find the stones we had before seen, and under which we intended to seek for shelter. No sooner had we reached them than the torrent descended in mingled hail and rain. The hailstones by rebounding came into my retreat, and the rain so filled the floor, that, in a short time, I found the water flowing over my shoes.

I was, however, under the necessity of quietly submitting to this evil to avoid being wet in other parts. Every moment I expected to be assailed by a tremendous flash of lightning, and deafened by its consequent thunder. Fortunately these did not occur. The clouds blocked up the mouth of my retreat, and left me looking apparently into an expense of air: from the abrupt appearance of the rocks before me, I seemed to be sheltered on the verge of a precipice. In about half an hour the fury of the storm abated, and soon afterwards the heavens again became serene. The brilliancy of the drops of rain on the grass, and the moisture on all sides, rendered the surrounding objects very beautiful. The channels were now filled, and torrents of water were seen pouring down all the mountains into their pools and hollows. Some of the larger streams overflowed their banks into the meadows. Our walking was rendered very uncomfortable from the grass and rocks being so slippery, as several times to throw us on our backs with considerable violence. At length, however, we arrived in safety at the bottom. – After resting myself here about a quarter of an hour, I again returned to Caernarvon.

15

Excursion from Caernarvon to the Summits of the Mountains Glyder and Trivaen

Mr. Jones of Llanberis having obligingly offered me accommodations at his house for a few days, that I might with greater ease and convenience examine every thing remarkable in the neighbourhood of the village, I rose early one morning to undertake, in company with my friend Williams, by far the most laborious walk that I ever ventured upon in the course of one day. This was no less than to ascend the summits of three mountains, Trivaen, Glyder Bach, and Glyder Vawr,* none of them very much inferior to Snowdon.

    About seven o'clock we set out from the village, and directed our route up the mountains on the north-east side of the vale of Llanberis. When we had attained the brow of the first eminence, immediately above the village, we agreed to rest about five minutes, in order to observe the appearance of the vale and mountains. The church, with its half a dozen houses, and a few trees and meadows, were seen almost as on a map. Beyond these, and exactly opposite to us, extended a long range of serrated rocks, marked with innumerable intersecting streaks of red, the effect of the mountain storms. The sun shone with great brilliancy on these rocks, whilst Snowdon, and all the other mountains behind them, were entirely veiled in clouds. The lakes of Llanberis were in part visible. – Having ascended to the eminence next above us, we found that the whole extent of the lakes was now brought into the view. The scene became altogether more extended, for we had now a view over the intervening mountains to the other parts of Caernarvonshire. Part of the island of Anglesea, and the strait of Menai, were to be seen filling up the openings of the mountains. We observed a few light and semi-transparent clouds float down the vale of Llanberis, and over the dark pools, frequently whirled by the wind in eddies. We at length arrived at a very small pool known to all Welsh botanists, called

LLYN Y CWN,

The Pool of the Dogs. This alpine lake was first made generally known from the assertion of Giraldus Cambrensis, that it contained a singular kind of trout, perch, and eels, which all wanted the left eye. Few people seem to have given credit to this account. Mr. Edward Lhwyd,* however, says that a Caernarvonshire fisherman informed him that he had several times caught monocular trout in Llyn y Cwn, and that these had all a distortion in the spine. The honorable Daines Barrington* also declares, that on accurate inquiry he had heard of monocular trout being taken here within the memory of persons then living. There are no fish of any description in the pool at present.

In the bogs near this pool we found the son of the Llanberis guide, and two or three other persons, digging peat; and we observed the mode in which they conveyed it down the mountains to the village. Horses are employed to carry it to the edge of the first steep, where it is loaded on sledges, each managed by one man, to be conveyed to the bottom. These, though tolerably large, and sometimes heavily loaded, seem not difficult to manage by those accustomed to the work. The men even venture to run with them down the less steep parts of the mountains, but when they come to a more sudden descent, they make sudden turns from one side to another, all the way down; this effectually checks the velocity which the sledge acquires; but so much practice is requisite in this work, that a person unaccustomed to it would soon throw himself down. They descend with great velocity, and without any apprehension of danger.

From Llyn y Cwn we proceeded, about three quarters of a mile, along a flat swampy piece of ground, till we came to an immense precipice above a hundred yards in perpendicular height, which forms one side of the hollow that incloses the black waters of

LLYN IDWEL.

This hollow, surrounded on all sides by dark and prominent rocks, is called *Cwm Idwel*. It is said to have been the place where Idwal, the son of Owen Gwynedd, prince of North Wales, was murdered by a person to whose care and protection his father had entrusted him. The shepherds believe the place to be the haunt of demons, and that, fatal as that of Avernus, no bird dare fly over its water.*

We descended along the broken rocks on one side of this precipice to a great depth into the hollow; and turning among the larger masses that lay in rude heaps, somewhat more than half way down, where the descent became more gradual, we soon found ourselves at the foot of a tremendous rent, or chasm in the mountain, called

TULL DU,

The Black Cleft. A more grand, or more sublime scene, the pencil even of Salvator Rosa could not have traced.* The stream that runs from Llyn y Cwn is seen rolling down the deep cleft at a vast height above, and is broken in its descent by a hundred interrupting rocks. There had been much rain the day before we were here, and the accumulated volume of water rushing in a vast cataract, from the astonishing height of *a hundred and fifty yards*,

> In one impetuous torrent down the steep,
> Now thundering shot, and shook the country round.*

Amongst the rocks at the bottom I observed a number of circular holes of different sizes, from a few inches in diameter to two feet and upwards, which had been formed by the eddy of the torrent from above. These hollows are frequently called by the Welsh people *Devil's Pots*, and from this circumstance the place itself is sometimes called the Devil's Kitchen.

We descended from Tull Dû, and crossing the foot of the range of rocks on the east side of Cwm Idwel, came at length so close to Nant Frangon, as to have a view nearly of its whole extent. Still proceeding, after a while we attained the highest part of the rocks immediately surrounding Cwm Idwel. Here we found ourselves on the verge of another mountain hollow, smaller indeed than the last, but equally cheerless and dreary, called *Cwm Bochlwyd*, containing a small black pool, *Llyn Bochlwyd*. From this situation we had the whole conical summit of

TRIVAEN

In view before us. Its sides appeared not greatly inclining from a perpendicular; and the huge masses of rock that covered them seemed destitute of vegetation, except where the clefts gave lodgement to a few mosses, bilberries, and a few species of saxifrage. To ascend its summit appeared, as in truth we found it, a most arduous undertaking: no part of Snowdon, frequented by travellers, can be in any degree compared to it. – We were determined not to be alarmed by appearances, however unfavourable they might be, and though I believe we each felt a secret persuasion that all our attempts would be to no purpose, we crossed Cwm

Bochlwyd, and approached the foot of this upper part of the mountain. Here we mustered all our resolution, and commenced the laborious task; and, after a continued climbing of about three quarters of an hour, for we could scarcely take half a dozen steps together in any place, without at the same time using our hands, we found ourselves on the summit.

Here, from the massy crag, we contemplated all the scene around us, which was rude as mountain horror could render it. We stood on a mere point, and on one side of us was a precipice more deep than any I had before seen. We united our strength, and rolled down it several huge pieces of rock: these continued their thundering noise for several seconds, and by their friction and dashing into hundreds of pieces, emitted a strong sulphureous smell which ascended even to our station. The summit of Trivaen, as I have remarked at the end of my observations on Nant Frangon, in a former chapter, is crowned by two upright stones, twelve or fourteen feet in height, about a yard and a half asunder, and each somewhat more than a yard across at the top. To stand upright on one of these, and look down the side of the mountain, would inspire even a tolerably stout heart with terror: to fall from hence would be inevitable destruction. But my companion stepped from the top of one to the other. I am not easily alarmed by passing among precipices, and my head is, I believe, as steady as that of most persons, but I must confess I felt my blood chill with horror at an act that seemed to me so rash. The force necessary for the leap, without great management in its counteraction, would have sent him a step farther than he had intended to have gone, would have sent him headlong down the precipice. He informed me that a female of an adjacent parish was celebrated for having often performed this daring leap, and when he was standing on one of the stones, dangerous as it was, he was determined to attempt the same.

We descended from the summit, and, crossing a mountain vale, ascended the side of

GLYDER BACH,

The lesser Glyder. This mountain, though considerably higher than Trivaen, is neither so steep, nor, on its exterior, so rocky. On its summit there are several groups of columnar stones, some standing upright, others laid across, and, in short, in all directions. On measuring them, we found many of them to be from sixteen to twenty feet long, and twelve or fourteen broad. In one place there is a particularly large one, laid over some others, and projecting far beyond them. My companion walked to the end of it, and evidently moved it by jumping on it. 'Many of the stones (says Mr. Pennant in his account of this mountain) had shells bedded in them; and in the neighbourhood I found several pieces of lava. I therefore consider this mountain to have been a sort of a wreck of nature, formed and flung up by some mighty internal convulsion, which has given these vast groups of stones fortuitously such a strange disposition, for had they been the settled strata bared of their earth by a long series of rains, they would have retained the same regular appearance that we observe in all other beds of similar manner.'

From hence we passed to the summit of

GLYDER VAWR,

The greater Glyder, and observed in our way several of the same kind of insulated masses of rock scattered in different directions around us. – From this situation we had a grand and unbounded prospect. On one side, the immense mountains of Caernarvonshire and Merionethshire appeared with their towering precipices in such rude order, that they seemed 'the fragments of a shattered world:' these were intersected by green meadowy vales and deep glens. On the other side, towards the town of Caernarvon, we had the whole of the isle of Anglesea in sight, and at a great distance northwards we saw the Isle of Man, resembling a faintly formed cloud. All the intervening space in that direction betwixt us and the sea was filled up by the varied scenery of mountains and vales, interspersed with their lakes and streams. – Glyder Vawr is the most lofty of all the Caernarvonshire mountains, except Snowdon and Carnedd Llewelyn; and in all the scenery of the vale of Llanberis it forms a prominent feature.

Having admired this delightful prospect for some time, we descended, and shortly afterwards came to the bank of Llyn y Cwn. About eight o'clock, after a fourteen hour's ramble, among crags and precipices, we found ourselves once again in the vale of Llanberis, and not a little fatigued with our day's excursion.

As it was not probable that I should remain another night here, after resting myself about a quarter of an hour, I determined to make the best of my time, tired as I was, and watch the close of an

EVENING SCENE IN LLANBERIS.

I left my hospitable friends, and strolled to the end of the lake. Scarcely a breath of air was to be felt. A white fog was extended, in long dense streaks, low down in the vale. The evening clouds appeared across the end of the lakes, tinged with various hues of red and orange, from the refracted rays of the departing sun. These were reflected in full splendour along the water. The rocks reflected various shades of purple, as the prominences were presented to the eye, or as the heath or verdure most prevailed. These colours after a while became one mass of dark greenish blue. The clouds lost their splendour; and the pool began to darken from the shades of the mountains. Scattered clouds now settled on various parts of the rocks, their light colours singularly contrasting with the sombre mountain tints. On looking from the pool towards the village, I was just able to distinguish it in the gloom, its place being marked by the smoke of the peat fires, rising a few yards perpendicularly from the chimneys, and then spreading into a cloud, and hovering directly over it. The rocks and precipices softened by degrees into an uniform mass of shade. The general features now became entirely lost, and only the upper outline was distinguishable in the obscurity. The evening fogs soon after came on, and in a short time so enveloped the whole scene, that not a single former trace was visible.

I shall conclude this chapter with a catalogue of the *plants* that have been found near Tull Du, and about the pool of Llyn y Cwn; and I very much doubt whether any other part of the kingdom, in so small a space of ground, will afford so many uncommon plants as are to be met with here. For the particular habitats, the reader is, of course, as in the two former lists, referred to the catalogue of Welsh plants at the end of the second volume.*

***

16

Excursion from Caernarvon into Anglesea

I crossed from Caernarvon into Anglesea by the ferry-boat, which every day, when the weather will admit, takes passengers over the Menai, *The Narrow Water*, to and from the island. This is a distance of somewhat more than a mile. The boat always goes at high water, and, when ready to set out, one of the men blows a horn in the town, to collect together the passengers.

It was the conjecture of a writer of the sixteenth century, that Anglesea was once joined to the continent of Wales, but that it had been separated by the continual working of the ocean. He says also that, for some time after the disjunction, the inhabitants of Wales and Anglesea probably had a communication, by means of a bridge, till the breach became too wide for such a passage to be any longer maintained. If this ever was the case, and it is by no means improbable, the last point of separation seems to have been near Bangor Ferry, for there the channel is at present much more narrow than in any other part, and at this place there is still to be seen a trace of small rocks jutting out in a line across the channel. Besides these, there are also other great splinters of rocks tumbled down, and really appearing as if the sea had consumed the soil in which they had once been bedded. – In the hollows and cavernous interstices of these fallen and broken rocks, during an hour or two at the beginning of the flood, from the tides flowing in at each end of the straits, and meeting here, the sea violently boils and fluctuates, making it for that time a dangerous whirlpool. This part of the channel is called *Pool Ceris*, and is a place very difficult to be navigated by large vessels, which must not only be conducted by a skilful pilot, but must also embrace the critical moment.

FERRIES

There are six ferries from Caernarvonshire into Anglesea; *Abermenai*, about three miles south-west of Caernarvon; *Tal y Voel*, from Caernarvon;

Moel y Don, about half way betwixt Caernarvon and Bangor Ferry; Porthaethwy, or *Bangor Ferry*; that from the promontory of *Garth*, near the town of Bangor; and from *Aber*, across the Lavan Sands to Beaumaris. – Several accidents have at different times happened at these ferries.

1664. The Abermenai ferry-boat (which is sometimes brought to take passengers from Caernarvon to the Abermenai house, in Anglesea), had arrived at the Anglesea shore from Caernarvon, the oars were laid aside, and the passengers were about to land, when a misunderstanding occurred concerning a penny more than the people were willing to pay. During the dispute the boat was carried into a deep place, where it upset, and although it was at that time within a few yards of the shore, *seventy-nine* of the passengers perished, one only escaping. – The country people believed that this was a visitation of heaven, because the boat was built of timber that had been stolen from Llanddwyn abbey.

1723. The Tal y Voel boat was upset on the thirteenth of April, and *thirty* persons perished. A man and a boy only escaped, the former by floating on the keel of the boat, and the other by laying hold of the tail of one of the horses, was dragged to the shore.

1726. The Bangor ferry-boat was so overloaded with people in their return from Bangor fair, that it sunk, and all the passengers (the number not known) were drowned, except one man and a woman. The latter floated on her clothes till she was taken up by another boat. – She was alive in the year 1798.

1785. In the month of December, the Abermenai boat in going from Caernarvon was swamped in the opposite sand-bank, and all the passengers perished except one, Mr. Hugh Williams, a respectable farmer now living at Tyn Llwydan near Aberffraw in Anglesea.

LOSS OF THE ABERMENAI FERRY-BOAT

The unaffected narrative of the latter melancholy event I received from Mr. Williams himself, and his story is too interesting and too simple to be related in any other than nearly his own words:

'The Abermenai ferry-boat usually leaves Caernarvon on the return of the tide, but the 5th of December being the fair-day, and there being much difficulty, on that account, in collecting the passengers, the boat did not leave Caernarvon that evening till near four o'clock, though it was low water at five, and the wind, which blew strong from south-east, was right upon our larboard bow. It was necessary that the boat should be kept in pretty close to the Caernarvonshire side, not only that we might have the benefit of the channel, which runs near the shore, but also that we might be sheltered from this wind, which blew directly towards two sand-banks, at that time divided by a channel, called Traethau Gwylltion, *The shifting Sands*. These lay somewhat more than half-way betwixt the Caernarvonshire and the Anglesea coast. – It was not long before I perceived that the boat was not kept sufficiently in the channel, and I immediately communicated to a friend my apprehensions that we were approaching too near the bank. He agreed in my opinion, and we accordingly requested the ferry-men to use their best efforts to keep her off. Every possible exertion was made to this purpose, with the oars, for we had no sail, but without effect, for we soon after grounded upon the bank; and the wind blew at this time so fresh as at intervals to throw the spray entirely over us.

'Alarmed at our situation, as it was nearly low water, and as there was every prospect, without the utmost exertion, of being left on the bank, some of the tallest and strongest of the passengers immediately leapt into the water, and, with their joint force, endeavoured to thrust the boat off. This, however, was to no purpose, for every time they moved her from the spot, she was with violence driven back. – In this distressing situation the boat half filled with water, and a heavy sea breaking over us, we thought it best to quit her, and remain on the bank in hopes, before the rising again of the tide, that we should receive some assistance from Caernarvon. We accordingly did so, and almost the moment after we had quitted her, she filled with water, and swamped. – Before I left her I had however the precaution to secure the mast, on which, in case of necessity, I was resolved to attempt my escape: this I carried to a part of the bank nearest to the Anglesea shore, where I observed my friend with one of the oars, which he had also secured for a similar purpose.

'We were at this time, including men, women, and children, *fifty-five* in number, in a situation that can much better be conceived than described. Exposed, on a quick-sand, in a dark cold night, to all the horrors of premature death, which, without assistance from Caernarvon, we knew must be certain on the return of the tide, our only remaining hope was that we could make our distress known there. We accordingly united our voices in repeated cries for assistance, and we were heard. The alarm bell was rung, and, tempestuous as the night was, several boats, amongst which was that belonging to the custom-house, put off to our assistance. We now entertained hopes that we should shortly be rescued from the impending danger; – but how were we sunk in despair when we found that not one of them, on discovering our situation, dared to approach us, lest a similar fate should also involve them. A sloop from Barmouth, lying at Porth Leidiog, had likewise slipt her cable to drop down to our assistance, the only effectual relief we could have received; – but before she floated the scene was closed.

'Finding that our danger was now every moment increasing, and no hopes of help whatever could be entertained, I determined to continue no longer on the bank, but to trust myself to the mercy of the sea. Being a tolerably good swimmer, I had full confidence that, with the mast, I should be able to gain the Anglesea shore. I accordingly went to the spot where I had deposited it, and found my friend there, with the oar in his hand. I proposed to him that we should tie the mast and oar together with two straw ropes, which he also had along with him, and endeavoured to persuade him to trust ourselves upon them. I fastened them together as securely as possible, and finding, after repeated endeavours to prevail on him to accompany me, that he had not fortitude enough to do it, I was determined to make the effort alone. I pulled off my boots and great coat, as likely to impede me in swimming: he committed his watch to my care, and we took a last farewell. I pushed the raft a little off the bank, and placed myself upon it, but at that moment it turned round, and threw me underneath. – In this position, with one of my arms flung through the rope, and exerting all my endeavours to keep my head above water, overwhelmed at intervals with the spray which was blown over me with great violence, I was carried entirely off the bank. When I had been in the water, as near as I could recollect, about an hour, I perceived, at a considerable distance, a light. This I believed to be (as it afterwards proved), in Tal y Voel ferry-house: my drooping spirits were revived, and I made every exertion to gain the shore, by pushing the raft towards it, at the same time calling out loudly for help. But judge of my disappointment when, in spite of every effort, I was carried past the light, and found myself driving on rapidly before the wind and tide, deprived now of every hope of relief. Dreadful as my situation was, I had, however, still strength enough to persevere in my endeavours to gain the shore. These, after being for some time beaten about by the surge, which several times carried me back into the water, were at length effectual. After having been upwards of two hours tossed about by the sea, in a cold and tempestuous night, supported only by clinging hold of the mast and oar of a small boat, I was thus providentially retrieved from otherwise inevitable death.

'I now felt the dreadful effect of the cold I had endured, for, on endeavouring to rise, that I might seek further assistance, my limbs refused their office. Exerting myself to the utmost, I endeavoured to crawl towards the place where I had seen the light, distant at least half a mile from me, but at last was obliged to desist, and lie down under a hedge, till my strength was somewhat recovered. The wind and rain soon roused me, and after repeated struggles, and the most painful efforts, I at length reached the Tal y Voel ferry-house. I was first seen by a female of the family, who immediately ran screaming away, under the idea that she had encountered a ghost. The family, however, by this means were roused, and I was taken into the house. They put me into a warm bed, gave me some brandy, and applied heated bricks to my extremities: this treatment had so good an effect, that on the following morning no other unpleasant sensation was left than that of extreme debility. – Having been married but a very short time, I determined to be the welcome messenger to my wife of my own deliverance. I therefore hastened home as early as possible, and had the good fortune to find that the news of the melancholy event had not before reached my dwelling.

'This morning presented a spectacle along the shore which I cannot attempt to describe. Several of the bodies had been cast up during the night. The friends of the sufferers crowded the banks, and the agitated inquiries of the relatives after those whose fate was doubtful or unknown, and the affliction of the friends of those already discovered, to this day fill me with horror in the recollection: – I, alas, was the only surviving witness of the melancholy event. – Besides those bodies thrown upon the shore by the tide, so many were found in various positions, sunk in the sand-bank, that it was not till after several tides that they could all be dug out. – My boots and great coat were found under the sand, nearly in the place where I had left them. The boat was never seen afterwards, and it is supposed to be even yet lodged in the bank.'

TAL Y MOEL FRE,

Or, Tal y Voel Fre, *The End of the Hill*, where I landed in Anglesea, is so called, from the coast being somewhat more steep there than any where else in its immediate neighbourhood. The river Menai, somewhere off this place, was the scene of a sea-fight about the middle of the twelfth century, that has been celebrated in Welsh verse by a bard of the name of Gwalchmai. His poem was that which Gray has given us in an English dress in,

Excursion from

Owen's praise demands my song, &c.*

A combined fleet of Irish, Danes, and Normans, lay at anchor near this place; and at the ebb of tide Owen Gwynedd came suddenly upon them with his forces, and defeated them before they had time even to arrange themselves in order of battle. Besides this poem of Gwalchmai, there is another Welsh poem describing the event, written by prince Howel, the son of Owen Gwynedd, who was both a bard and a warrior. He seems to have at least had one of the indispensible requisites of a good poet, the inclination to enlarge the magnitude of an event; otherwise I presume he must have viewed the enemy's forces through a multiplying glass, for he describes the defeat of *three hundred ships of war!*

ANGLESEA,

Prior to the invasion of the Romans, had the name of *Môn*, which signified merely an insulation from the continent of Wales; this name they latinized into Mona. It received its first appellation of *Anglesea* on its reduction to the Saxon yoke.

It is denominated 'The Mother of Wales' by Giraldus Cambrensis, for, he says, when all the other parts of the principality failed in their crops of corn, this alone, from its fertile soil and high state of cultivation, was able to supply them. This may have been the case in the twelfth century, when Giraldus visited the country, and when the state of population throughout the whole kingdom was very different from what it is at present. The interior of the island appeared to me to be very ill attended to in this respect: and in addition, much of the land lies in peat-bogs, or is full of low rocks, which cannot be cleared but by blasting, and that at an enormous expence. There are, indeed, some farms in the interior, but it is about the coast that the island is seen in the richest state, and particularly about that part which is opposite to Caernarvonshire. – The general face of the country is low, flat, and unpleasant; and although it has been represented as nearly covered with wood in the time of the Druids, there is now scarcely any other than what is found in the plantations on the south-east coast.

The princes of North Wales had their entire residence in this island, except when driven out for two centuries by the Irish and Picts, till the close of the reign of their last prince. The palace was at Aberffraw; and I have been informed that some few fragments of the walls are yet standing, forming now part of the walls of a barn.*

***

LLANDDWYN ABBEY

In describing the places which I have visited in the island of Anglesea, I shall begin with the Llanddwyn rocks and abbey, at the extreme south point, distant from Caernarvon in a direct line about six miles. It was some days after my excursion through the island that I came here, in the cutter belonging to the hotel, but as it lies out of every other direction, its description will fill this place more appropriately than any other.

The ruins of Llanddwyn abbey are situated about the middle of a sandy flat surrounded by rocks, and also, except on one side, by the sea. Some of the walls are yet standing, but they possess nothing of gothic elegance. If I could judge from the present traces of its site, the erection altogether has never been of any considerable magnitude.

The church was dedicated to the Welsh Venus, *Dwynwen*, the daughter of Brychan Urth. As the tutelary saint of lovers, her shrine was much resorted to in the ages of superstition and ignorance. She was well supplied with offerings, by lovers, to induce her good offices in softening the otherwise impenetrable hearts of the objects of their affection. Dafydd ap Gwilym, in one of his poems, addresses her: 'Dwynwen, fair as the hoary tears of morning, thy golden image in its choir, illumined with waxen torches, well knows how to heal the pains of yonder cross-grained mortals. – A wight that watches within thy choir, blest is his happy labour, thou splendid beauty! With afflictions, or with tortured mind, shall none return from Llanddwyn!'*

This place, I have been informed, is a noted resort of smugglers, and their traces are indeed sufficiently evident in several large and deep holes dug in the sand for concealing the cargoes. I have seen few places more inviting to this species of illicit commerce. Several narrow entrances between the rocks, with a fine sandy bottom, seem particularly calculated to hide their little vessels from the careless eye of the revenue officers of this district. Here they can run in, and (being four or five miles from any inhabited place, and surrounded by eminences,) unload and deliver their cargoes to their emissaries without apprehension.

From the Anglesea coast, near the Tal y Voel ferry-house, the town of Caernarvon, with the straits of Menai in front, and the high grand mountains in the back ground, were strikingly beautiful. Snowdon was, the day I was here, perfectly unclouded, and his red sides, brightened by the sun, were seen gradually sloping till they ended in a point far above the tops of all the adjoining mountains; each of which had its beauty in the disposition of its lights and shades, and of its prominences and hollows.

It was my original intention to have proceeded entirely round the island, by Newborough, Aberffraw, and Holyhead. But on inquiry into the practicability of this scheme, I found that I should meet with considerable difficulty, from the circumstance of a bank having been burst by the sea, near Aberffraw, and several hundred acres of land being constantly flooded at high water. My route was therefore necessarily changed, and instead of making the circuit I had intended, I botanized along the Anglesea coast as far as Moel y Don ferry, from whence I took the direct road to Holyhead.

About three miles from the place where I landed, I passed *Llanedwen*, a village now celebrated principally from its being the place of interment of Henry Rowlands, the learned author of 'Mona Antiqua Restaurata.'* He was instituted to this vicarage in October 1696, and he died in the year 1723. A black slab, near the south end of the church, contains a Latin inscription to his memory: this was his own composition, but it is now nearly obliterated. – The Welsh people have a strange tradition, that the body of a woman *sixteen feet* long, lies buried across the path leading to the south door of the church. The present gardener at Plâs Newydd, to satisfy some inquirers, was induced to dig up the place a few years ago, but no bones, nor any other evidence occurred that could support so ridiculous a story.

The place where the Roman general Suetonius Paulinus first landed, when he invaded this island, is not far from Llanedwen. About two hundred yards from the Menai there is a field yet called Maes Mawr Gâd, *The Field of the Great Army*, and at a little distance eastward, just on the shore, a place still retains the name of Rhiedd, or *The Chief Men's Post*. The foot soldiers are recorded to have passed the straits in flat-bottomed boats; and the horsemen by fording, where the depth of the water would allow it, and by swimming over the middle of the channel. This seems to have been perfectly practicable, for the stream at low water is here very narrow, and so shallow, as in few places to be more than a fathom, or a fathom and a half, in depth.

MOEL Y DON,

The Hill of the Wave, is celebrated as being the place where, in the year

1282, part of the English army experienced from the Welsh a severe defeat, attended with great slaughter. Edward I had led out his men to contend with the Welsh soldiers in the open plains, but, on their retiring to the mountains, he did not dare an attack in their fastnesses. He therefore sent over a party of men into Anglesea, and ordered them to encamp on the bank of the Menai, near Moel y Don; at the same time giving directions for a bridge of boats, of width sufficient for sixty men to march abreast, to be built across the straits. He retired to Conwy castle with the remainder of his army; and the workmen proceeded in their operations. The bridge was so far finished, that part of it only wanted boarding over, when, at the ebb of the tide, several of the English nobility, and about three hundred soldiers, rashly crossed it, and remained on the opposite side till the tide had cut off their access to the bridge. The Welsh soon received information of this circumstance, and, descending in a body from the mountains, rushed with such fury upon the affrighted Englishmen, that every one of them, except for William Latimer, who, from the excellence of his horse, got back in safety, was either put to the sword, or perished in the water. The historians inform us that, besides the common soldiers, the Welsh slew, in this encounter, thirteen knights, and seventeen young gentlemen, probably officers commanding in the English army.

PLAS NEWYDD

I deviated from the Holyhead road about a mile at Moel y Don, to examine the house and grounds of lord Uxbridge at Plâs Newydd, *The New Mansion*. The house is a very elegant building. It stands upon the bank of the Menai, is almost surrounded by woods, and commands from the front windows a beautifully picturesque and extensive prospect of those British Alps, the mountains of Caernarvonshire.

At a little distance are some druidical remains, a large and a small *cromlech*, which stand close together. The former of these is about thirteen feet long, and twelve broad. The upper stone, which, in some parts, is about four feet in thickness, till very lately rested on five upright supporters of stone; but, about two years ago, after some heavy rain, the one at the back suddenly split, since which time it has been necessary to prop it with supporters of wood.

The original design of the cromlech, notwithstanding the contrary opinion of various antiquaries, seems only to have been as a sepulchral monument; for, under several cromlechs in Cornwall and other parts of England, bones have been found deposited. It appears to have been the original of our present altar tombs, which are but a more diminutive and elegantly formed cromlech.

That these erections should have been intended as altars for the druidical sacrifices, seems altogether impossible. The upper stones are, in general, too small, and much too high for a fire to be kindled on them, sufficient to consume the victim, without burning the officiating priest. In addition to this, the horrid rites with which the Druid sacrifice was attended, could not possibly have been performed on so small and so perilous a station. The upper stones of several of them were also so thin, that the intenseness of the sacrificial fire would have cracked and broken them. – Some antiquarians have asserted that they were designed as places of worship; but there seems as little reason for this supposition as the former. In many of them, the space beneath is so small, as scarcely to admit a man even to creep into them; and, besides this, great numbers of them were erected on barrows, or heaps of loose stones; – a very uneasy, and therefore very unlikely, situation for devotional offices.

An attempt has been made to prove that by means of only a lever and an inclined plane, it would be possible to erect some of the largest stone monuments that we have in this island. To do this, we are to imagine that the founders of these erections first formed small mounts of firm and solid earth for inclined planes, which they flatted and levelled at the top. Up the sloping sides of these they might, by means of strong levers, upon fixed fulcra, with heavy weights at the ends, and hands sufficient to guide and manage them, by little and little heave up to the top the stones they intended to erect. These, we are to suppose, they laid down there; then, digging a hole at the end of every stone intended for a column or supporter, as deep as the columns were long, they again applied their levers, raised the stones on end, and let them slip into the holes. These stones being now well closed about with earth, and their tops made exactly level with the top of the mount, the flat cross-stones might then be rolled up to them in the same manner as the columnar ones had been done before. As soon as these were all securely placed across their supporters, the earth was cut away nearly to the bottom, and there would then appear what are called Stonehenge, Rollrick,* and the British cromlech; or, where no incumbent stone was wanted, the upright columns, or pillars, which we now find in many different parts of the kingdom. – This seems the most simple and natural mode that can be conjectured for the erection of those stupendous monuments of antiquity; and it is more than probable that it actually was the mode adopted by the British mechanics, who obtained their knowledge of science from the Egyptians and Phoenicians, with whom they had very early communication.

***

In returning from the house at Plâs Newydd, to the Holyhead road, I observed, at a little distance from the path, a large *tumulus*, which, on subsequent inquiry, I was informed, is generally believed by the country people to have been a druidical place of interment, and to have originally had some connexion with the cromlech. A large upper stone is now exposed, and beneath this, I found a low entrance into a subterraneous recess, apparently ten or twelve feet long, and four wide and high. The sides are formed by flat upright stones, one of which, opposite to the entrance, is said to close the passage into a vault considerably larger than this. This place was first exposed in the time of sir Nicholas Bailey, about seventy years ago; and, when the workmen had opened the entrance into the larger recess, he ordered them to discontinue their operations, as it seemed to contain nothing but bones. A servant of the present earl of Uxbridge, at the request of some gentleman who visited the place about eighteen years ago, dug to the depth of about twelve feet in the bottom of the smaller vault, and discovered a few human bones, and a very old clasp knife, which might probably have been lost by the men who before dug in the same place, for the man could give me no satisfactory description of it.

Having finished my examination of this ancient place of interment, I pursued my journey towards Holyhead; and, evening coming on, I took up my abode for the night at

GWYNDY,*

The Wine House, an inn standing nearly equi-distant from Bangor and Holyhead. – About the reign of Edward IV, and for some years subsequent to that period, the gentlemen of Wales frequently invited their friends in large parties to exercise in wrestling, tournaments, and other feats of activity: but, as these meetings, in consequence of the numbers invited, were usually attended with great expence, they were always held in the house of some neighbouring tenant, who was supplied with wine from his lord's cellar, and this was sold to the visitors, and his master received the profits. These houses were denominated *Gwyndu*, or wine houses; and from this circumstance the present place had its name.

Excursion from

HOLYHEAD

In the morning I proceeded towards this place, distant about thirteen miles. Holyhead is situated on an island, at the extreme west point of Anglesea, but, except at high water, the dividing channel is passable without boats. The island is seven or eight miles long, and, in most parts towards the sea, so rocky, as to be inhabited only by the various species of sea-fowl, which breed among the cliffs. – From being the nearest point of this kingdom that lies towards Dublin, it has always been much resorted to by company passing to and from Ireland. In itself, however, it possesses but few attractions for the tourist on pleasure. – The distance from Holyhead to Dublin is about twenty leagues, which the packets generally make in about twelve hours. They have been known to sail over in six, and in stormy weather, on the contrary, they have been kept at sea for two or three days. The passage, both from Parkgate and Liverpool to Dublin, has been found extremely dangerous, on account of the Welsh coast, along which the packets have to run for more than half way. On this coast, in heavy gales of wind from north-east, they have often been wrecked. The great advantage in sailing from the Head arises from the vessels being able in a short time entirely to clear the land; and also in the length of the passage by water being very considerably lessened.

The name that the Welsh have given to this place is Caer Cybi, *The Fort of Cybi*. They say that it was the residence of Cybi, the son of Solomon, duke of Cornwall, who, being consecrated a bishop for his distinguished zeal against the Arians, settled here about the end of the fourth century, and founded a small monastery. Its name of Holyhead is supposed to have been acquired from its having been, at different times, the place of interment of a great number of holy men.

The church-yard is on a rock directly above the sea: it forms a quadrangle of about ninety yards, by forty. Three sides are inclosed by strong walls, and the fourth is nearly open to the sea, having only a parapet defended by steep rocks. – It is asserted by some writers, that the site of this church-yard was fortified in the sixth century by Caswallon Law Hîr, *Caswallon the Long Handed*, at that time prince of Wales. He had been sent by his father, the king of Cumberland, into Anglesea, to contend with an army of Irish Picts under their chieftain Sirigi, who had, not long before, landed in the island, and put the inhabitants to flight. Sirigi had his fleet at anchor near Holyhead, and not far from hence the two parties met. A severe conflict ensued, which ended in the death of the Irish leader by the prince's own hand, and the entire destruction of his forces.

The church is a handsome embattled edifice, built in the form of a cross. It is supposed to have been once a college of prebendaries, founded by Hwfa ap Cyndelw, lord of Llys Lliven in Anglesea, and one of the fifteen tribes of North Wales, who lived in the twelfth century. The exact number of the prebendaries is not now known; there is evidence, however, that they were at least twelve. The president of this church was one of the three spiritual lords of Anglesea. In the reign of Edward III, the whole of the church, except the chancel, was rebuilt; and this was repaired in the beginning of the last century. This church became the property of Rice Gwynne, esq., who, in 1648, gave the great tythes to Jesus college, Oxford, for the maintenance of two fellows and two scholars. Since that time it has been served by a curate nominated by the college.

A number of cross-roads, sufficiently disagreeable, led me, over a most uninteresting country, to

AMLWCH,

Near the Lake,* a small market town about a mile from the *Paris mountain*, that inexhaustible mine of copper,* a mine of wealth to all its proprietors. Amlwch seems entirely dependent, for its prosperity, on the copper mines, for most of its inhabitants have some concern in them, either as miners or agents. – The church, dedicated to St. Elaeth, a saint of the British calendar, is a neat modern structure. Of the town itself, I observed nothing remarkable except that it was in general a most black and dismal place, from the scoria of the metal, of which all the roads are formed. On the exterior of the town there seems the utmost desolation. The sulphureous fumes from the mine have entirely destroyed the vegetation for a considerable space around, and little else than earth and rock are to be seen even within a short distance of Amlwch. On the Paris mountain, there is not even a single moss or lichen to be found. – When the wind has blown over the mountain, in the direction where I have been walking, I have more than once found the fumes exceedingly oppressive at the distance of at least a mile from the works.

ANGLESEA COPPER MINES

The town of Amlwch is, as I have said, about a mile from the summit of Paris mountain; and on the morning after my arrival, I walked up to this celebrated place. Having ascended to the top, I found myself standing on the verge of a vast and tremendous chasm. I stepped on one of the stages suspended over the edge of the steep, and the prospect was dreadful.

Excursion from

The number of caverns at different heights along the sides; the broken and irregular masses of rock which every where presented themselves; the multitudes of men at work in different parts, and apparently in the most perilous situations; the motions of the whimsies, and the raising and lowering of the buckets, to draw out the ore and the rubbish; the noise of picking the ore from the rock, and of hammering the wadding, when it was about to be blasted; with at intervals, the roar of the blasts in distant parts of the mine, altogether excited the most sublime ideas, intermixed, however, with sensations of terror. I left this situation, and followed the road that leads into the mine; and the moment I entered, my astonishment was again excited. The shagged arches, and overhanging rocks, which seemed to threaten annihilation to any one daring enough to approach them, fixed me almost motionless to the spot. The roofs of the work, having in many places fallen in, have left some of the rudest scenes that imagination can paint: these, with the sulphureous fumes, from the kilns in which the ore is roasted, rendered it to me a perfect counterpart to Virgil's entrance into Tartarus.

> Hac iter Elysium nobis; at laeva malorum
> Exercet poenas, et ad impia Tartarus mittit.

'Tis here in different paths the way divides,
The right to Pluto's golden palace guides;
The left to that unhappy region tends,
Which to the depth of Tartarus descends;
The seat of night profound, and punish'd fiends.*

To look up from hence, and observe the people on the stages, a hundred and fifty feet above one's head; to see the immense number of ropes and buckets, most of them in motion; and to reflect, that a single stone casually thrown from above, or falling from a bucket, might in a moment destroy a fellow creature, a man must have a strong mind, not to feel impressed with many unpleasant sensations. A few days before I was last here, a bucket caught against the point of a rock, emptied its contents on the head of a poor fellow, and killed him on the spot. The sides of this dreadful hollow are mostly perpendicular. Along the edges, and in general slung by ropes over the precipices, are the stages with windlasses, or *whimsies*, as they are here termed, from which the buckets are lowered; and from which those men descend, who work upon the sides. Here, suspended in mid air, the fellows pick, with their iron instrument, a small place for a footing, cut out the ore in vast masses, and tumble it with a thundering crash to the bottom. In these seemingly precarious situations they make caverns, in which they work for a certain time, till the rope is again lowered to take them up.

Much of the ore is blasted by gunpowder, eight tons of which, we are told, was some time ago annually used for this purpose. The manner of preparing for the blasting was entirely new to me, and may be so to some of my readers. A hole is bored in the rock of about the diameter of a very wide gun barrel, and of depth in proportion to the quantity of matter to be thrown up. At the bottom is lodged the gunpowder, and the man then taking a thin iron rod, tapering to a point, and about two feet in length, he places it perpendicularly in the middle of the hole, and fills it up on all sides with stones, clay, &c. ramming these hard down by means of an iron projecting at the bottom, with a nick in it, that it may pass freely round the rod. When this is prepared the rod is taken out, and a straw filled with gunpowder is substituted. A match is then put to it, that will burn so long, before it communicates the fire to the powder, as to allow all the workmen within reach, to escape into different retreats from the danger attendant on the explosion. Several blasts are generally ready at the same time, and notice is given to the workmen to run into shelter, by a cry in Welsh of *fire*. Whilst I was in the mine, the cry was several times given, and I, with the rest, crept into shelter. In one instance six or seven blasts went off in different parts successively, one of which was within thirty yards of my station, and the splinters of the rock dashed furiously past me. I am scarcely a judge of the noise they made, for I took the liberty of stopping my ears, which the men seemed to think a pleasant *joke*, for they laughed very heartily at what they conjectured a mark of my timidity.

When the whole is exploded, information is given to the workmen, and they return to their work. The process of blasting is frequently attended with danger, from the carelessness with which the men retire to their hiding-places: And it sometimes happens that, in ramming down the wadding, the iron strikes against the stone, and fires the gunpowder, which is often fatal to the man employed. During the short time I remained here, I observed upwards of forty men in different places, occupied in preparing for blasting; and I felt somewhat uncomfortable under the idea that in such a number, some one might be careless enough to have his gunpowder take fire before he was aware of it.

There are in the Paris mountain two mines: of these, the one on the east side is the *Mona mine*, the entire property of the earl of Uxbridge. The *Paris mine* is the joint property of the earl of Uxbridge and the rev. Edward Hughes of Kinmael, near St. Asaph. Thomas Williams, esq. of Llanidan, the member for Marlow, has a lease of half the earl's share in these mines; and they work conjointly. Mr. Hughes works his share of the Paris mine alone.

It is generally believed that the Romans got copper ore from this mountain; for vestiges are yet left of what have been taken for their operations; and some very ancient stone utensils have, at different times, been found here.

***

Several of the shafts which have been formed for taking off the water, are driven very deep. One that I saw was upwards of a hundred and sixty feet in depth, below the open bottom of the mine. One of the miners, whilst I was looking at it, brought a lighted candle, and fixed it on the rim of one of the buckets in which they draw up the water. It was curious enough to watch it in its dark and confined descent, till it became a mere speck of light, when, suddenly immersing in the water, it was lost.

The men employed about these mines seemed much more healthful than, from being constantly in the midst of the noxious exhalations from the kilns, it would be natural to expect. – Their complexions are in general somewhat sallow, but much less so than I expected to have found them. Their average wages are about eighteen-pence a day. Some of them get the ore for a certain sum per ton. These are called *bargain-takers*, and if the work is easily wrought, and the ore of good quality, they will frequently earn four or five shillings, whilst the rest earn only their eighteen-pence. The mine companies seem to take great care in providing for all the persons that have any concern whatever in the works. Besides supporting the poor by their own voluntary donations, which now amount to betwixt seven and eight hundred pounds a year, they prevent a great number of the infants, of the aged and infirm from applying for relief, by giving them light and easy employment. This alone is an average expence of more than three hundred pounds a year; and their surgeons and apothecaries bills are generally more than double this sum.

The mines have increased the value of lands in the parish of Amlwch from about fourteen hundred to five thousand pounds *per annum*, and upwards; the number of houses from two hundred to upwards of a thousand; and the population from nine hundred to about five thousand.

VITRIOL AND ALUM WORK

At a little distance from the mine is a building appropriated to the making of vitriol and alum. The proprietor is Dr. Joshua Parr, who resides in Carmarthenshire. The argillaceous earth from which the alum is extracted, is found on the spot, in a stratum about six feet beneath the surface of the ground. About one ton a week was the average quantity manufactured here, and this sold for somewhat more than twenty pounds. A small quantity of white vitriol continues to be made; but the attempts to prepare green and blue vitriol have been attended with no success. Indeed the whole concern has answered so exceedingly ill, that, when I was here, I was informed, it would probably be altogether given up in the course of a very short time.

SMELTING HOUSES AND PORT

These are about a mile from Amlwch. The former contain thirty furnaces: each capable of holding ten hundred weight of roasted ore, which produce not quite one hundred weight of metal. As it is the refuse ore only that is smelted here, it is necessary when it arrives at Swansea, to have it smelted again four or five times before the metal is sufficiently pure.

The port is very small, but excellently adapted to the business of exportation. It is a chasm between two rocks, running far into the land, and has in a great measure been formed by art: Its width is not more than to allow two vessels to ride abreast; it is however sufficiently long and deep to receive thirty vessels of two hundred tons burthen each. This port was first made at the expence of the copper companies, for the convenience of their shipping, and is not therefore frequented by any others than vessels concerned with them.

About two miles east of Amlwch, and not at a great distance from the coast, is the village of

LLANELIAN.

The church is by no means an inelegant structure; and adjoining it is a small chapel of very ancient foundation, that measures in its interior, twelve feet by fifteen, called Myfyr, *the confessional.* – A curious closet of wood of an hexagonal form, called *St. Elian's closet*, is yet left in the east wall, and is supposed to have served both the office of a communion table, and as a chest to contain the vestments and other utensils belonging to the chapel. There is a hole in the wall of the chapel, through which the priests are supposed to have received confessions: the people believe this hole to have been used in returning oracular answers, to persons who made inquiries of the saint respecting future events. – Near the door is placed Cŷff Elian, *Elian's chest*, or poor box. People out of health, even to this day, send their offering to the saint, which they put, through a hole, into the box. A silver groat, though not a very common coin, is said to be a present peculiarly acceptable, and has been known to procure his intercession, when all other kinds of coin have failed! The sum, thus deposited, which in the course of a year frequently amounts to several pounds, the churchwardens annually divide among the poor of the parish.

The wakes of Llanelian were formerly held on the three first Friday evenings in August; but they are now confined to only one of those days. Young persons from all parts of the adjacent country, and even from distant counties, assemble here, most of whom have along with them some offering for the saint, to ensure their future prosperity, palliate their offences, and secure blessings on their families, their cattle and corn.

The misguided devotees assemble about the chapel, and having deposited their offerings, many of them proceed to search into their future destiny, in a very singular manner, by means of the wooden closet. Persons of both sexes, of all ages, and sizes, enter the small door-way, and if they can succeed in turning themselves round within the narrow limits of the place, (which measures only betwixt three and four feet in height, about four feet across the back, and eighteen inches wide,) they believe that they shall be fortunate till at least the ensuing wake. But if they do not succeed, in this difficult undertaking, they esteem it an omen of ill fortune, or of their death within the year. – I have been told, that it is curious enough to see a stout lusty fellow, weighing sixteen or eighteen stone, striving to creep into these narrow confines, with as much confidence as a stripling a yard high; and when he fails in the attempt, to see him, contrary to all reason, fuming and fretting because his body, which contains in solid bulk more than the place could hold, were it crammed into all corners, cannot be got in. But when we consider, that superstition and enthusiasm have generally little to do with reason, we must not wonder at this addition to the heap of incongruities that all ages have afforded us.

Llanelian was formerly a sanctuary, or place of refuge for criminals. This was confirmed by a charter from Caswallon Law Hîr, of which there are copies yet extant. – In digging a grave in the church-yard, about six years ago, a deep trench was discovered, which extended about twenty yards in a transverse direction across. It was found to contain a great quantity of human bones; and is supposed to have been the place of interment of a number of sailors who perished in a storm that drove them upon this coast.

The distance between Amlwch and Beaumaris, by Dulas and Red-wharf bays, is about sixteen miles, and the country, the whole way, was sufficiently pleasant to render the walk very agreeable; but it so greatly resembles the country in many parts of England, that the traveller will not observe its character to be either new or particularly interesting. – I passed, at the distance of about a mile on the right, the village of Llanfair, celebrated as the birthplace of Goronwy Owen.*

***

About a mile from Red-Wharf bay, I passed the village of Pentraeth, *The End of the Sands*. It is pleasantly situated, and its little church is so picturesque, that from this circumstance only, Mr. Grose was induced to insert a print of it in his Antiquities. The ash and sycamore trees around seem to shelter it from the observation of the world. – It is a place of interment of the Panton family,* whose seat, Plâs Gwynn, *The White Mansion*, is about half a mile distant.

In a field near the porter's lodge of Plâs Gwynn there are two stones, at a considerable distance from each other, which were pointed out to me, with what truth I know not, as the place where the tradition says Einion ap Gwalchmai, some centuries ago, obtained his wife by an uncommon exhibition of activity, in leaping *fifty feet*! There were two competitors, and the female decided their claims by taking the man who could leap farthest. Einion, it is said, some time afterwards, went to a distant part of the country, where he had occasion to reside several years, and he found, on his return, that his wife had, on that very morning, been married to another person. He took his harp, and, sitting down at the door, explained in Welsh metre who he was, and where he had been resident. His wife narrowly scrutinized his person, unwilling to give up her new spouse, when he exclaimed:

> Look not, Angharad, on my silver hair,
> > Which once shone bright of golden lively hue:

> Man doth not last like gold, – he that was fair
> > Will soon decay, though gold continue new.
>
> If I have left Angharad, lovely fair!
> > The gift of brave Ednyfed, and my spouse,
> All I've not lost, (all must from hence repair,)
> > Nor bed, nor harp, nor yet my ancient house.
>
> I once have leap'd to shew my active power,
> > A leap which none could equal nor exceed,
> The leap in Aber Nowydd, which thou, fair flower!
> > Did once so much admire, thyself the meed.
>
> Full fifty feet, as still the truth is known,
> > And many witnesses can still attest,
> How there the prize I won, thyself must own,
> > This action stamp'd my worth within thy breast.*

BEAUMARIS

From Plâs Gwynn I had a walk of about five miles to Beaumaris. The entrance into the town was pretty: the bay and castle, with Penmaen Mawr, and the Ormes Head at a distance, are seen in a direct line in front; and the road, which lies down a steep hill, is shaded on each side with trees. The town itself is finely situated on the western bank of the Menai, just where it opens into an extensive bay. The houses are in general neat, and well built, and one of the streets is very good. – On examining the church and church-yard, I found nothing worth notice, except a whimsical inscription on Meredith Davies,

> Who has been our parish clark,
> Full one and thirty years, I say;
> But here, alas! lies in the dark,
> Bemoaned for ever and aye.

BEAUMARIS CASTLE

Is situated close to the town, within the grounds of Baron Hill, the seat of lord Bulkeley.* It covers a considerable space of ground, but its walls are at present so low, that it does not excite much attention. When it was in a perfect state, it consisted of an outer ballium, or envelope, surrounded by a broad ditch flanked by several round towers; and it had on the east side an advanced work, called the gunner's walk. Within these was the body of the castle, which was nearly square, having a round tower at each angle, and another in the centre of each face. The area is a square, with the corners cut off, and measures about sixty yards on each side. In the middle of the north side is the hall, which is twenty yards long, and twelve broad, and has had five elegant windows in front. – There has been a communication round the buildings of the inner court by means of a gallery somewhat more than a yard wide, which is yet in a great measure entire. In recesses in the sides of this gallery are several square openings, which seem to have been furnished with trap doors, entrances to dungeons beneath. The use of these I have not been able to learn: they must have descended by ladders, for there are no remains of steps to be discovered in any of them. The two eastern towers of this building served the purpose of dungeons for the confinement of prisoners. – On the east side of the area are the remains of a very small chapel, arched and ribbed with pointed and intersecting arches. Between each of the gothic pilasters is a narrow window, and, behind some of them, there have been small closets, gained out of the thickness of the wall.

***

When Edward I built the castle, he surrounded the town with walls. He also incorporated it, and endowed it with great privileges, and lands to a considerable value. – It sends one member to parliament.

THE BAY OF BEAUMARIS

Forms a fine opening before the town; and it is so sheltered, that vessels of considerable burthen can lie secure in it, even in stormy weather. The depth of the water near the town is six or seven fathoms, even when the tide is out; but this deep channel scarcely extends more than a quarter of a mile in width. All the rest of the bay, for several miles, is left dry at low water, and has the name of the *Lavan Sands*. These are supposed by the Welsh people to have once formed a habitable hundred of Caernarvonshire, that was first overflowed during the sixth century. It seems by no means improbable that this was the case, for there is decided proof of the sea having incroached very greatly on some parts of this coast. In the church-yard of Abergeley, a village on the coast of

Caernarvonshire, about eighteen miles distant, there is the following inscription:

> Yma mae'n gorwedd
> Ym monwent Mihangel;
> Gwr oedd a'i annedd,
> Dair milltir yn y gogledd.

> Under this stone lieth,
> In this church-yard of St. Michael,
> A man whose dwelling was
> Three miles to the northward.

Another evidence arises from the bodies of oak trees, tolerably entire, having been discovered, at low water, in a long tract of hard loam, far from the present banks of the sea.

BARON HILL

On an eminence behind the town of Beaumaris stands this charming residence of lord Bulkeley, commanding a most delightful prospect of all the northern mountains of Caernarvonshire, of the bay of Beaumaris, and a long expanse of sea. The house stands in front of the woods, and is esteemed by many tourists an ornament to this corner of Anglesea. It was built originally in the reign of James I, for the reception of Henry, the eldest son of that monarch, when on his way to Ireland. But his untimely death so much affected sir Richard Bulkeley, the owner, that he gave up his original and magnificent plan, and used the part only that was then completed, for his family seat. The house has been enlarged, and greatly improved, by its present worthy possessor.*

I was sorry to observe the effect of the elegant view of the Welsh mountains from the house totally destroyed, by the small square building in front, called a *fort*. I cannot conceive how gentlemen should suffer themselves to be so much misled, as to have their agents, without an atom of taste, construct these, singularly called, *ornamental buildings*. The present is a white, church-like castle, an apparent excrescence evidently useless, and glaringly unnatural. Lord Uxbridge has one of these white *ornamental* structures on the side of the Menai, opposite to Plâs Newydd: but superior to all that I have ever seen of this description, is that of Mr. Thomas of Coed Halen, which provokingly obtrudes itself into almost every good view of the fine old walls and castle of Caernarvon. If any of these buildings are to be defended, as I know some of them are, on the score of their being land-marks to the mariner, my objection must cease; utility must ever be considered to supersede elegance. But this is not often the case; lord Uxbridge's building is far distant from the sea, and other eminences near Caernarvon might have been adopted besides the present, being, as it is, almost close to the castle. A friend of mine remarked, to some observations that I had made on this subject, that, in a tour through South Wales, he had almost invariably observed that the only rage for spoiling the scenes by these strange monstrosities, was where the surrounding country was more than usually beautiful. Near old castles, or monastic remains, he had generally been provoked with a deformed castellated pleasure-house, or a lately erected ruin, and invariably in the very place from whence of all others it should have been kept away. The ideas of these gentlemen must be nearly on a par with those of Mr. Pocklington, which stimulated him to improve one of his views by white-washing an oak-tree.* *De gustibus, non est disputandum.** A late tourist to the lakes has whimsically replied, 'As the man said when he kissed his cow.'*

About a mile from Beaumaris, near the seat of sir Robert Williams, bart. and not far from the shore, are yet to be seen, in the walls of a barn, the poor remains of the house of Franciscan friars, founded in the thirteenth century, by Llewelyn ap Iorwerth, prince of Wales, called

LLANVAES,

Or *The Friars*. It is at present principally known as having been the place of interment of Joan,* the wife of Llewelyn, and natural daughter of king John. The stone coffin of this princess, though now removed, served, not long ago, as a watering trough for horses. In this church there were also interred, at different times, a son of one of the kings of Denmark, lord Clifford, and many barons and knights who were slain in the Welsh wars.

The church, and some other parts of the buildings, were destroyed soon after the death of Llewelyn, in an insurrection of the Welsh against the English forces; and Henry IV again nearly destroyed it, on account of the friars having espoused the cause of Owen Glyndwr. His son, Henry V, re-established it, and added a provision for eight friars, of which, however, only two were to be Welshmen. At the dissolution the convent and its possessions were sold: they are at present the property of lord Bulkeley.

PENMON

Two miles north of Friars is the priory of Penmon, at present consisting of little more than the ruinous refectory, and part of the church. This was a priory of Benedictine monks, dedicated to St. Mary, and endowed, if not founded, by Llewelyn ap Iorwerth, before the year 1221. In the twenty-sixth of Henry VIII, the revenues were valued at about forty-eight pounds *per annum*.

The island of Anglesea is celebrated for some of its rare marine productions, and particularly for the variety of its shells and crabs. The places from whence the latter are principally to be obtained are the rocky coasts about Llanddwyn, Roscolin, Holyhead, and Penmon; and the best times for discovering them are at low water, during the spring tides, which sometimes rise and fall near twenty feet. The mode is to turn up the stones, near low-water mark, under which they will be found to lurk, hidden among the sea-weed. The shells are principally taken in the dredges of the oyster-catchers betwixt Beaumaris and the island of Priestholme, and in Red Wharf bay.

***

17

Voyage from Caernarvon to Priestholme

One day, during my residence at Caernarvon, I took the cutter belonging to the hotel, a beautiful little decked vessel, with accommodations for ten or twelve persons, and her pilot, and sailed to the island of Priestholme, off the Anglesea coast, about five miles beyond Beaumaris.

THE MENAI,
As a river, is a remarkably fine piece of water, seldom less than half a mile, and in several places near two miles in width; and, to those persons who are fond of excursions on the water, the sail from Caernarvon to Beaumaris on a fine day, with a brisk wind, will be found extremely pleasant. At different times of the day the scenery will be found very different; and a cloudy and dense, or a transparent and rare atmosphere, render a material change to the appearance of the various scenes that occur in going along this charming water; so that how often soever excursions are made, some new appearance will always occur. The shores, in a few places, are bold and steep; in others, the ascent is gentle and unvaried: sometimes they are barren and rocky, and sometimes adorned with woods and cultivated grounds. The dark wooded banks of the island of Anglesea, sloping gently to the water's edge, afford, in many points of view, an elegant contrast (with the translucent waves between), to the more rude shores of Caernarvonshire. In a brisk side gale, tacking across the stream affords many beautiful views which are lost when sailing before the wind; and when many vessels are on the water at the same time, it is a pleasing sight to observe them going in different directions, and crossing each other in the different tacks.

We had proceeded about five miles, when we passed the front of Plâs Newydd, the seat of the earl of Uxbridge; soon after which the channel straightened very considerably, and the distance was terminated on one side by an almost perpendicular coast, and on the other by a sloping and wooded ascent. Not far from hence are the well known rocks, called, from the numerous currents that set in different directions around them,

THE SWELLY ROCKS.

At low water many of these are to be seen, which, at other times, are hidden by the flood; and the channel betwixt those that are always exposed is very narrow and dangerous. When the lower rocks are covered with water, from the tide running with great rapidity among them, many circling eddies are formed, the vortexes of which the mariners sometimes find it difficult to avoid. When the wind blows directly across the channel, it is often found necessary to row the smaller, and tow the larger vessels through, lest, in tacking, before they are able to get round, they are caught by an eddy, and thrown upon the rock. When this is the case, however, from a strong current setting in a different direction immediately round those rocks that are above water, they are frequently saved; for this, acting like a cushion, breaks the force which would otherwise inevitably destroy them, and gives some little time to the men to get right again.

We had a wind directly across, and in one of our tacks, though I had but just been talking with the pilot on the subject, and every possible precaution was used, the bow of our vessel caught one of the eddies, and, in spite of every effort, bore us directly on the rocks. I seized the helm, and my companion, who was stronger than myself, sprang with a boat-hook to the bow of the vessel, and, before she could touch the rock, so strong was the surrounding current, he pushed her off. A different current bore us furiously against the tide, which now caught our bow, and bringing us again round, with considerable violence, near the deep of the channel, the vessel righted, and we had the good fortune, the second time, entirely to clear these, the Scylla and Charybdis of the Welsh mariners. The circumstances altogether threw us into some little tremor: for the swelling and violent bubbling of the water in some places; the rapid and furious tide-way through the deeps; the roaring of the water in consequence of the submarine rocks, and the dashing of the foam and spray in the various whirlpools, and against the rocks that are exposed, with the noise and turbulence around, are, at some particular times of the tide, of such a nature as scarcely to be described.

LLANDYSILIO CHURCH

At a little distance beyond the Swellies we passed two low rocks, with a flat between them, forming at high water an island called *Bên Glas*. This island, though it affords only a few acres of ground for the grazing of sheep, has on it the small church of Llandysilio. On the Anglesea side there is a causeway to the island, but passable only at low water. What should induce the foundation of a church in so singular and precarious a situation, where the service can only be performed when the tide serves, I am not able even to guess. I fear, when a smart wind blowing in the course of the tide during the service, sets it in sooner than had been expected, as must sometimes happen, the sensations of the congregation are not of the most pleasant nature imaginable. The struggle to escape before they were hemmed in by the tide, would be too ridiculous to be compatible with the sacred duties of public worship; and it is much to be lamented that there should be any necessity for it.

A little beyond Bangor Ferry a fine expansive view opened upon us. Penmaen Mawr here forms, in the distance, a bold end to the wavy ridge of mountains extending into the interior of Caernarvonshire. Beyond this are seen Penmaen Bach, the little Ormes Head, and the great Ormes Head, all presenting their steep sides towards the sea. The town of Beaumaris, appearing just above the level of the sea, on a promontory that forms from hence an extreme point of Anglesea, is observed on the other side of the water. Under the mountains of Caernarvonshire, and sheltered by them nearly on all sides, we observed the town of Bangor; and, a little beyond it, Port Penrhyn, and its numerous vessels. A gale of wind soon drove us past the town of Beaumaris, whose castle appeared, from the water, a large and strong building: these received additional beauty from the high woods of Baron Hill rising behind them.

I happened here to be carelessly leaning over the side of the vessel, when I observed vast quantities of a species of medusae, *sea-blubber*, float past. By means of a small net, I got out two or three specimens, and found them to be *medusa aurita* of Linnaeus, the *sea nettle*. The whole tribe of these animals, in their manners and properties, are extremely singular. They are generally round, smooth, semi-transparent, and gelatinous; appearing, indeed, at first sight, like a lump of jelly. Their mouth is on the under side of the body, and is surrounded by several arms, which serve them as ballast, and by means of which they seize their prey. Their progressive motion, when not aided by any current, is obtained by displacing the water with alternate motions, which render the body at one time flat, and at another convex. This motion is extremely slow, and were not the majority of them preserved by their caustic quality, they would become an easy prey to most species of fish. When handled, they are found to blister and inflame the skin in a most unpleasant manner.

The fishermen, when they find them in their nets, are very careful not to touch them with any exposed part of their body, but generally kick them out with their shoe. I saw one man's hand much inflamed in consequence of laying hold of one of them unawares, and he said it was very painful. An acquaintance of mine irritated his dog to seize one of them in his mouth: the animal soon left his hold, and from the circumstance of his thrusting his nose into the dust, and making a whining noise, it was evident that he suffered much pain. When his mouth was examined, it was found to be considerably inflamed. I recollect Pontoppidan* says, that when some of the species lie on the shore, in a state of putrefaction, if a person comes within their influence, they cause a violent sneezing; and that a boy was nearly blinded by his father's throwing one of them, in a rage, into his face. The Norwegian peasantry prepare from them a poison, by which they kill vermin: some mix them up with clay or mortar, and stop crevices in places where there are bugs, which this composition is said effectually to destroy. A few of the species have no caustic properties.

A tolerably fair wind soon brought us under the rocks of the south side of

PRIESTHOLME.

This island is near three quarters of a mile distant from the Anglesea shore; and is about a mile in length, and half a mile across. On all sides, except that towards Anglesea, it presents steep and inaccessible rocks, inhabited only by various species of sea-fowl. Its interior affords feed for a few sheep. Near the middle of the island there is an old square tower, supposed to have once been an appurtenant to the monastery of Penmôn. There is a considerable quantity of rubbish and stones around it, the remains of other buildings. The island is at present uninhabited by man. I was much surprized, in wandering about it, to find an upright stone, with the following inscription, rudely cut upon it:

> Bar^r. Stout
> belonging to the
> Salley died in
> the small pox
> Novr. ye 3d. 1767.
> N. B. The ship was cast
> away here.

It is called by the Welsh Ynys Seiriol, *Seiriol's island*. This people have a tradition respecting Priestholme, that when what are now the Lavan sands formed a habitable part of Caernarvonshire, their ancestors had a communication from hence across the channel, by means of a bridge; and they yet pretend to shew the remains of an ancient causeway, which they say was made from this place to the foot of Penmaen Bach near Conwy, for the convenience of the devotees who made pilgrimages to the island. – It is at present the property of lord Bulkeley, and is rented of him as a rabbet and puffin warren.

When we had arrived under the rock, and had cast anchor, we fired a swivel gun, to try the effect of the report round the island, when such a scream of puffins, gulls, and other sea birds, was heard, as beyond all conception astonished me. The immense multitudes that in a moment rose into the air, were unparalleled by any thing I had before seen. Here they flew in a thousand different directions, uttering as many harsh and discordant screams: some darted into the water, some scudded about on its surface, others were seen dipping into the deep, others rising out, and others again came flapping almost close to our heads: in short, the air, the sea, and the rocks seemed alive with their numbers. – We landed, and I clambered up the rocks, and walked alone to the other side of the island, when I had a sight that even surpassed the former. Upwards of fifty acres of land were literally covered with *Puffins*. I speak much within compass, when I declare that the number here must have been upwards of 50,000. I walked gently towards them, and found them either so tame or so stupid, as to suffer me to approach near enough to have knocked one or two of them down with a stick.

***

In getting the birds out of their holes, I found it necessary to lay down on the ground, and extend my arm into them; and it was only in a few holes that I found the birds within reach. During incubation, they are not easily driven from their nests; but when the young are hatched, they do not seem to exhibit towards them, as has been said, any extreme attachment, for, whenever they are disturbed, they will either run into a deeper hole, or attempt to fly away. When caught, they will seize on any thing that is near them. The man who was along with me, shot a few of them: One of these had only its wing broken, and when he had set it down in the small boat belonging to the cutter, it hurried to the other end, and bit with great violence several of the dead ones that were laid there. – The young are entirely covered with a long blackish down, and in shape are altogether so different from the parent birds, that no one could, at first sight, suppose them the same species. The bill in these is long, pointed, and black, with scarcely the marks of furrows. Puffins do not breed, till they are three years old; and they are said to change their bills annually. – Their usual food is sprats and sea-weeds, which render the flesh of the old birds excessively rank. The young, however, are pickled for sale by the renters of the island, and form an article of traffic peculiar to this neighbourhood. The oil is extracted from them by a peculiar process, and the bones are taken out, after which the skin is closed round the flesh, and they are immersed in vinegar impregnated with spices. – Dr. Caius* informs us, that in his days, the puffins were allowed by the church to be eaten in Lent, instead of fish, and says that they were usually caught by means of Ferrets, as we now sometimes take rabbits. At present, they are either dug out of the burrows, seized by the hand, or drawn out by a hooked stick.

18

Excursion from Caernarvon to Beddgelert; and thence to Pont Aberglasllyn, into Nant Hwynan, and to the Summit of Snowdon

The distance from Caernarvon to Beddgelert, *the grave of Gêlert*, is about twelve miles, and the road is in general very excellent; being the great road from Caernarvonshire into South Wales.

GLANGWNA

About two miles from Caernarvon, I passed, on the left, Glangwna, one of the most charming retreats in the principality. The house is small, but surrounded with wood, and so completely sequestered, as scarcely to be seen from the road. The grounds are not extensive, but they have an elegant wildness; and the walks through the woods and along the banks of the river Seiont, whose stream dashes in foam among the rocks of its bed, are scarcely exceeded by any on a small scale, that I have yet seen. This beautiful place is the property of Thomas Lloyd, Esq. of Shrewsbury.

From an eminence in the road, about four miles from Caernarvon, I was presented in front with a view extremely fine, along Nant Gwyrfai, *the Vale of Freshwater*. A range of sloping rocks formed the middle distance. The dark and towering rock of Mynydd Mawr, was seen to rise from behind, on the right of the vale; and, on the opposite side, this was well contrasted in the smooth and verdant mountain Moel Aelir. The vale appeared closed at some distance, by part of the side of the lofty Arran. Just at this station, there are several rude, but extremely picturesque cottages, some of which were half obscured by trees. The road is at first hidden, but it is seen at a little distance in front, sloping down into the vale: the latter was intersected by moss-grown walls, and rude hedge-rows.

I left the road for the purpose of ascending the summit of the hemispherical mountain, called

MOEL AELIR,

The frosty hill. This I did without much difficulty, and found the prospect from the top to far surpass my expectations. The Rival mountains appeared quite near, and beyond them the whole remaining extent of the promontory of Llŷn, as far as Aberdaron, was visible. Part of Cwellyn Pool (by the road leading to Beddgelert) was seen just below, from the edge of which the immense Mynydd Mawr reared his black and rugged sides. Beyond this was one of the Nantlle Pools, and near the latter, the small pool of Llyn Cwm Ffynnon. Extending from hence southwards, was a long range of mountain summits, and hollows, some verdant, and others totally destitute of vegetation, but the shades and colours of the whole strikingly grand and beautiful. At some distance was seen part of the yellow sands of Traeth Mawr, peeping in amongst the rocks. The distant mountains of Merionethshire, closed the scene in this direction. On the south-east side of my station, I observed a dreary vale, with nearly perpendicular boundaries, called Cwm Dwythwch, *the hollow of the rapid burrowing river*, containing a small pool, in which the finest and best flavoured of all the Caernarvonshire trout are said to be caught. Beyond this, Snowdon is easily distinguished from his fellow-mountains, by his size and appearance. Part of the vale and lakes of Llanberis, with the castle of Dolbadarn, were visible, in a somewhat different direction. When I was here, Snowdon was covered with a dense black cloud, that seemed to rest on its sides and summit, and gave to it the terrible aspect of a volcano. Dusky intervening clouds passed on with considerable velocity, which rendered the scene as wild as imagination could paint. Heavy showers were pouring into some of the adjacent vales; and light vapours scudded with the wind along the hollows on all sides. Snowdon, and the immediately adjacent mountains, alone remained black and terrific. The intervening rocks received a yellow tinge from the refraction of the light of the sun through the mist; and various other tints and shades were thrown on the vallies and mountains' sides, by different refractions of the light through the more or less dense mediums.

 I descended from this mountain, to the road not far from the romantic little village of *Bettws*, or, as it is sometimes called, for the sake of distinction, Bettws Garmon. Its church is dedicated to St. Germanus, who led on the Britons to the famous '*Alleluia*' victory obtained over the Saxons, at Maes Garmon, near Mold.

NANT MILL

About half a mile beyond Bettws, are a beautiful little cascade and bridge, at a place called Nant Mill. This waterfall would appear to much greater advantage, in almost any other situation than the present; for here the

Fig. 8. *Nant Mill cascade*, near Betws Garmon, Caernarfonshire (Gwynedd), engraving after drawing by William Bingley in 1798.

black and majestic mountain of Mynydd Mawr, on the right, and the more smooth and regular, though still lofty Moel Aelir, on the left of the vale, attract to themselves so much of the traveller's attention, that the little waterfall appears diminutive, amidst such surrounding grandeur.

Beyond the mill, Snowdon is seen on the left, rearing his pointed summit into the sky. His red and precipitous cliffs, and huge bulk, compared with the adjoining mountains, render him easily known from all the rest.

LLYN CWELLYN

On the right of the road, this pool extends itself for about a mile and a half. During the winter season, the *Red char*, a species of fish, which is confined principally to Winander Mere, and Coniston Water, two lakes in the north of England, were formerly caught here in considerable quantities. These fish are called by the Welsh Torgoch, or *Red belly*, from the under parts near the tail being of this colour. They only appear about the time of the winter solstice; and continue to be caught but a very little while, not often more than a fortnight. They seldom wander out of the pool, but traverse it from shore to shore; and they were formerly in such shoals, that sometimes so many as twenty or thirty dozen have been caught during one night, by a single net. The catching of them was, however, so

195

precarious, that perhaps not above ten or a dozen, in the whole, would be taken during the rest of the season. In the frosts and rigours of December, they sport and play near the margin of the pools where they are taken, but in the heats of summer, they confine themselves entirely to the deep and central parts of the water, that abound with large stones and mud. In the Llanberis pools, before the copper mine was established, these fish were so numerous, that the average number annually caught, was a hundred dozen.

On the farther edge of the lake, just under, and forming part of the mountain of Mynydd Mawr, is

CASTELL CIDWM,

Cidwm's fort. This is a high and steep rock, on the summit of which, we are informed, there was once a fortification, one of the guards to the interior of the mountains. This is said to have been founded by the Britons, sometime prior to the sixth century. Whether there are any remains of the fort now existing, I am not able to say: the difficulty of ascending to it, and the small importance of the object, deterred me from attempting to examine it. – The Welsh people have a tradition respecting this rock, that its summit was formerly inhabited by a giant, or a warrior, called *Cidwm.* As Constantine, the son of Helen, was marching in the rear of an army, towards Merionethshire, he was distinguished from his soldiers, by the watchful Cidwm, who was on his station; and though the distance is many times as great, as our modern, degenerated bows, would twang their arrows, yet he aimed one, that with instant celerity, proved fatal. The news of his death was soon carried, along the ranks, to his mother, who was in the van of the army, about ten miles distant. He was interred in the meadow at the lower end of the lake, in a place now called Bedd y mab, *the grave of the son.* On enquiring into the particulars of this unaccountable story, I could neither learn who this Cidwm was, (beyond what I have stated,) nor what the Welsh believe to have been the cause of his enmity to Constantine: in short, it is one of those traditionary legends, that defy all attempts at investigation.

LLYN Y DYWARCHEN

Higher up, amongst the mountains on the right, I visited a small pool, about the size of a good horse-pond, called Llyn y Dywarchen, *The Pool of the Sod,* first celebrated by Giraldus Cambrensis in the account of his journey through Wales, in the twelfth century, as containing a floating island. This is yet in existence, but is not more than eight or nine yards in length; and evidently appears to have been a detached piece of the turbery of which the bank is composed. There is a small willow tree growing upon it; and it is carried to and fro by the action of the wind and water. Sometimes it remains near the side of the pool for a considerable while; and it is so large and firm as to bear cattle upon it. When it has been dislodged by the wind, a sheep or two have often been borne by it to the other parts of the bank.

I passed Llyn Cadair, *The Pool of the Chair, or Eminence*, and, shortly afterwards, crossing a bridge, descended through Nant Colwyn, *The Vale of Colwyn*, to

BEDDGELERT,

A village completely embosomed in mountains, whose rude sides form a fine contrast with the meadows of the vale below. Moel Hebog, *The Hill of Flight*, rises to a point just in front of the village. In a deep hollow high up the side of this mountain, there is a cave in which Owen Glyndwr, on one of his expeditions to harass the English forces, sought, for some time, a shelter from his enemies. – The houses of the village are few and irregular, but the church is one of the neatest of those among the wilds of Caernarvonshire. In the church-yard, among many Welsh inscriptions on the grave-stones, I was surprized by one in English:

> Thousand fates on death attends,
> Which *brings* poor mortals to their ends.

Llewelyn the Great, prince of Wales, is said to have had a hunting seat at this place. Among many others, he possessed one greyhound, a present from his father in law, king John, so noted for excellence in hunting, that his fame was transmitted to posterity in four Welsh lines, which have been thus translated:

> The remains of famed Gêlert, so faithful and good,
>   The bounds of the cantred conceal,
> Whenever the doe or the stag be pursued,
>   His master was sure of a meal.*

During the absence of the family, tradition says, a wolf entered the house;

and Llewelyn, who first returned, was met at the door by his favourite dog, which came out, covered with blood, to salute his master on his arrival. The prince, alarmed, ran into the nursery, and found his child's cradle overturned, and the ground flowing with blood. In this moment of his terror, imagining that the dog had killed the child, he plunged his sword into his body, and laid him dead upon the spot. But, on turning up the cradle, he found his boy alive, and sleeping by the side of the dead wolf. This circumstance had such an effect on the mind of the prince, that he erected a tomb over the faithful dog's grave; on the spot where afterwards the parish church was built, called, from this incident, Bedd Gêlert, or *The Grave of Gêlert*. From this story was derived a very common Welsh proverb; 'I repent as much as the man who slew his greyhound.'

The following beautiful stanzas, which the author, the honorable W. R. Spencer, has obligingly allowed me to insert here, are founded on the above tradition. They were written at Dolmelynllyn, the seat of W. A. Madocks, esq. after a perusal of the story related in my *Tour round North Wales*:*

    The spearmen heard the bugle sound,
        And cheerly smil'd the morn,
    And many a *brach*, and many a hound,
        Obey'd Llewelyn's horn.

    And still he blew a louder blast,
        And gave a lustier cheer,
    'Come Gêlert, come; wer't never last,
        'Llewelyn's horn to hear.

    'Oh! where does faithful Gêlert roam,
        'The flower of all his race,
    'So true, so brave, a lamb at home,
        'A lion in the chace?'

    'Twas only at Llewelyn's board
        The faithful Gêlert fed;
    He watch'd, he serv'd, he cheer'd his lord,
        And sentinell'd his bed.

    In sooth he was a peerless hound,
        The gift of royal John:

But now no Gêlert could be found,
    And all the chace rode on.

And now as o'er the rocks and dells
    The gallant chidings rise,
All Snowdon's craggy chaos yells
    The many mingled cries!

That day Llewelyn little lov'd
    The chace of hart or hare,
And scant and small the booty prov'd,
    For Gêlert was not there.

Unpleas'd Llewelyn homeward hied,
    When, near the portal seat,
His truant Gêlert he espied,
    Bounding his lord to greet.

But when he gain'd his castle door
    Aghast the chieftain stood,
The hound all o'er was smear'd with gore,
    His lips, his fangs ran blood.

Llewelyn gaz'd with fierce surprize,
    Unus'd such looks to meet,
His fav'rite check'd his joyful guise,
    And crouch'd, and lick'd his feet.

Onward in haste Llewelyn past,
    And on went Gêlert too,
And still where e'er his eyes he cast,
    Fresh blood gouts shock'd his view.

O'erturn'd his infant's bed he found,
    With blood stain'd covert rent,
And all around, the walls and ground
    With recent blood besprent.

He call'd his child, no voice replied,

Excursion from

    He search'd with terror wild,
        Blood, blood he found on every side,
            But no where found his child.

'Hell-hound! my child by thee's devour'd,'
    The frantic father cried,
And to the hilt his vengeful sword
    He plung'd in Gêlert's side.

His suppliant looks, as prone he fell,
    No pity could impart,
But still his Gêlert's dying yell
    Pass'd heavy o'er his heart.

Arous'd by Gêlert's dying yell
    Some slumb'rer waken'd nigh: –
What words the parent's joy could tell,
    To hear his infant's cry!

Conceal'd beneath a mangled heap
    His hurried search had miss'd,
All glowing from his rosy sleep
    The cherub boy he kiss'd.

Nor scath had he, nor harm, nor dread,
    But the same couch beneath
Lay a gaunt wolf all torn and dead,
    Tremendous still in death.

Ah! what was then Llewelyn's pain!
    For now the truth was clear,
His gallant hound the wolf had slain
    To save Llewelyn's heir.

Vain, vain was all Llewelyn's woe,
    'Best of thy kind, adieu!
'The frantic blow which laid thee low,
    'This heart shall ever rue.'

And now a gallant tomb they raise,
    With costly sculpture deck't,
And marbles storied with his praise
    Poor Gêlert's bones protect.

There never could the spearman pass,
    Or forester, unmov'd;
There oft the tear-besprinkled grass
    Llewelyn's sorrow prov'd.

And there he hung his horn and spear,
    And there as evening fell,
In fancy's ear he oft would hear
    Poor Gêlert's dying yell.

And till great Snowdon's rocks grow old,
    And cease the storm to brave,
The consecrated spot shall hold
    The name of 'Gêlert's Grave.'

PRIORY

On this spot there was formerly a priory of Augustine monks, of a foundation so ancient, that Anian, bishop of Bangor, who lived in the thirteenth century, asserts it to have been the oldest religious house in Wales, except one. Part of the south walls of the present church were evidently formed from the old building: there are here the remains of two very old arches. In the year 1283, this priory was so much injured by fire, that, in order to encourage benefactors to come forward and contribute towards the rebuilding of it, the bishop gave notice that he would remit to all such persons (who sincerely repented of their sins), forty days of any penance inflicted on them. The revenues at the dissolution amounted to about seventy pounds *per annum*. The name of this priory was Abbey de Valle, S. Mariae Snawdonia.

    The *inn*, or rather public house, that I found at Beddgelert in both my journies, was one of the worst and most uncomfortable houses, in which necessity ever compelled me to take up my abode. In my first journey I found only one bed in the place that was not wretchedly bad. The room in which I slept for three nights (for the other two bed-rooms were occupied), was at the back of the house, and partly over the kitchen.

The floor, the ceiling, and the boarded partition, were all so full of large holes, as to seem only an apology for separation from the rest of the house. I was so intolerably pestered by myriads of fleas, bred and harboured among the filth accumulated in every part, that had I not every night been fairly wearied out with my rambles during the day, it would have been altogether impossible for me to have taken any rest. After I had been here one night, I complained to the servant of the inexcusable negligence that had suffered these animals to become so numerous, as now to defy all attempts at their destruction. 'Lord, sir, (said she,) if we were to kill one of them, ten would come to its burying.' – Nothing, in this state of the house, could possibly have induced a traveller to remain here through the night, but the exquisite scenery around the place. In my second journey I found several very material improvements, in consequence of Mr. Jones of Bryntirion having begun to build a comfortable house for the reception of travellers, on the other side of the river, at a few hundred yards distance. This is now opened, and, I am told, affords excellent accommodations. It is called the *Beddgelert Hotel*. The sign over the door is of a goat clambering among the mountains of Snowdon, and, underneath it, is the motto *'Patria mea petra'*.*

The *guide* from Beddgelert to the mountains is William Lloyd, the village schoolmaster, whose boys, during the summer, are always engaged in rustic employments. He thus explains his summer occupations in a bill wafered on the inn door: 'William Lloyd, conductor to Snowdon, Moel Hebog, Dinas Emrys, Llanberis pass, the lakes, waterfalls, &c. &c. Collector of crystals and fossils, and all natural curiosities in these regions. Dealer in superfine woollen hose, socks, gloves, &c.'

PONT ABERGLASLLYN

Beddgelert is the place to which travellers usually resort who wish to see Pont Aberglâsllyn, *The Bridge at the Conflux of the Blue Pool*, or, as it is usually called, *The Devil's Bridge*. It is about a mile and a half distant, but, as all travellers must cross it in their journey to Tan y Bwlch, many content themselves with merely resting a little while in their progress.

About a mile beyond Beddgelert, the rocks on each side become incomparably grand. The road winds along a narrow stony vale, where the huge cliffs so nearly approach, as only just to leave width sufficient at the bottom for the road, and the bed of the impetuous torrent that rolls along the side of it. Here these lofty rocks, which oppose nothing to the eye but a series of the rudest precipices, 'raised tier on tier, high pil'd from earth to heaven,'* seem to forbid all further access, and to frown defiance on the traveller:

> Fled are the fairy views of hill and dale,
> Sublimely throned on the steep mountain brow
> Stern nature frowns: her desolating rage
> Driving the whirlwind, or swoln flood or blast
> Of fiery air imprison'd, from their base
> Has wildly hurled the uplifted rocks around
> The gloomy pass, where Aberglâsllyn's arch
> Yawns o'er the torrent. The disjointed crags
> O'er the steep precipice in fragments vast
> Impending, to th' astonish'd mind recal
> The fabled horrors by demoniac force
> Of Lapland wizards wrought; who borne upon
> The whirlwind's wing, what time the vext sea
> Dash'd against Norwegia's cliffs, to solid mass
> Turn'd the swoln billows, and the o'erhanging waves
> Fix'd e'er they fell.*

It was, probably, from this very scene, that Giraldus Cambrensis asserted of Merionethshire, that it was 'the roughest and most dreary part of Wales, for its mountains were both high and perpendicular, and in many places so grouped together, that shepherds talking or quarrelling on their tops, could scarcely, in a whole day's journey, come together.'

In the bridge itself my expectations were, I must confess, considerably disappointed. I had somewhere read of an arch thrown across a narrow stream, one end resting on a perpendicular rock in Caernarvonshire, and the other on another in Merionethshire. Perhaps also in some measure confounding it, with what I had heard of the Devil's Bridge, near Hafod, in Cardiganshire, I had formed an idea that I should see an arch thrown across a deep narrow valley, and hanging, as it were, in mid air: but how disappointed to find it a bridge very little out of the usual form! The grandeur of all the surrounding scenery rendered it, indeed, an insignificant object; but even this does not prevent it from forming a beautiful addition to the mountain view. – Many of the ignorant people of the neighbourhood believe that this structure was formed by supernatural agency. They attribute it to the devil, who, they say, proposed to the neighbouring inhabitants, that he would build them a bridge across the pass, on condition that he should take the first who went over it for his trouble. The bargain was made, and very soon afterwards the bridge appeared in its place. But the people were too cunning to adhere to any other than the literal terms of so unequal a bargain; and they cheated the devil by dragging a dog to the spot, and whipping him over the bridge. This, say those who tell the story, was all the recompence this universal agent, in difficult undertakings, was able to obtain for his labour. Hence they account for this structure having the name of the 'Devil's Bridge.'

A few yards above the bridge, the river is thrown over a range of rocks, eight or ten feet from the surface of the lower water. This cataract is chiefly noted as a salmon leap. Salmon come up the fresh water streams to deposit their spawn on the sandy shallows, and, when impeded in their progress by rocks or dams across the water, they have the power of springing to an amazing height above the surface, In order to get over them. This place being only a very few miles from the sea, is frequented by great numbers. In the course of an hour, I have sometimes observed twenty or thirty of them attempt to overcome this barrier; but, on account of a piece of netting which the renters of the fishery place there for the purpose of preventing them, they do not often succeed. Their extraordinary power of leaping out of the water seems to be owing to a sudden jerk which the fish give to their body, from a bent into a straight position. At this place, when the fish are fatigued, from their vain attempts to gain the upper stream, they retire to the still waters below, where they are either taken in nets, or are killed with harpoons. In the latter mode, which seems very cruel, from the lacerations of their flesh, the men are always so sure in their aim, that I have seen five or six fine fish killed by one person in the course of an hour. The general weight of the salmon caught near Pont Aberglâsllyn in August and September, is from one to eighteen pounds. About the month of October they become much larger. – This fishery, I was informed, is the property of Mr. Wynne, who lets it to the fishermen at the rent of twelve pounds a year. The fish, when sold on the spot, are generally thought worth three-pence or four-pence a pound. – In the reign of Henry IV this weir was royal property; and it is by no means improbable that, in old times, it might belong to the princes of Wales; for salmon was the most useful, and consequently the most valuable fish which the Welsh had. It was even reckoned amongst the game, and was perhaps the only species of fish that was preserved by their laws.

I wandered several times from the bridge to the adjacent arm of the sea called Traeth Mawr, *The Great Sands*, and was often amused by the few goats kept in this vale, chasing each other, in playful gambols, among the most dangerous steeps of the rocks. I seldom saw more than from twenty to forty at a time. The goats in this country are all now private property, none of them, as formerly, running entirely wild: they all return regularly to their folds in the evenings. – The varied scene beyond the bridge of wood, rock, and vale, is extremely fine. From several stations

> The mountains huge appear
> Emergent, and their broad bare backs upheave
> Into the clouds; their tops ascend the sky;*

And their rugged files seem here to close, and oppose an invincible barrier into the interior of the country.

Sir John Wynne of Gwydir* conceived the vast design of recovering for cultivation the two arms of the sea, Traeth Mawr, and Traeth Bach, by embanking out the water. For this purpose, in the year 1625, he applied for assistance to sir Hugh Middleton, who, in the Isle of Wight had, not long before, gained upwards of two thousand acres of land from the sea. The affair, however, probably from want of money to execute it properly, was never carried into execution. This object has, however, been in a great measure attained by W. A. Madocks, esq. This gentleman has, within the last four years, recovered above 1500 acres by embanking out the sea.* The land is found exceedingly good, and has already produced excellent wheat, barley, and oats. Some years, however, will elapse before every part of it can be put into high cultivation, and before the trees that are planted will have any effect. The name of the place is *Glandwr*, and the whole length of the land recovered is about two miles.

MOONLIGHT SCENE AT PONT ABERGLASLLYN

During the time I was at Beddgelert, I found myself one evening in want of employment; and as the moon shone beautifully bright, I was tempted to wander alone as far as the bridge. There never was a more charming evening. The scene was not clad in its late grand colours, but was now more delicately shaded, and arrayed in softer charms. The darkening shadows of the rocks cast a gloom around, and the faint rays, in some places faintly reflected, gave to the straining eye a very imperfect glimpse of the surfaces it looked upon; whilst, in others, the moon shot her silver light through the hollows, and brightly illumined the opposite rocks.

The silence of the evening was only interrupted by the murmuring of the brook, and now and then by the shrill scream of the night-owl, flitting by me in search of food.

> The river rushing o'er its pebbled bed
> Imposed silence, with a stilly sound.*

The bridge was deserted, and I hung over its rude battlements, listening to the hoarse fall of the water down the weir, and watching, as the moon got higher, the decreasing shadows of the mountains. The solitude gave rise to reflection, and I indulged almost too long; for, when I arrived at the inn, I found I had been absent near two hours, and from the countenance of the inn-keeper on my appearance, I suspect the family had believed that I should not again return.

EXCURSION INTO NANT HWYNAN

I had not been long at Beddgelert before I strolled through this vale, called also sometimes Nant Gwynant, *The Vale of Waters*; and I found it more beautiful than any other amongst these mountains. It is about six miles long, and affords, in its whole length, such a variety of scenery, of wood, lakes, and meadows, bounded on each side by lofty mountains, that one can scarcely conceive it to be excelled. The vale of Llanberis is the only one that seemed to me to rival it; but the character of the two are so essentially different, and the beauty of each is so exclusively its own, that they cannot be put into comparison.

DINAS EMRYS

On the left of the path, about three quarters of a mile up the vale, the guide pointed out to me a round high rock, with many trees growing from the clefts and shelves of its sides, called Dinas Emrys, *The Fort of Emrys, or Ambrosius*, where

> Prophetic Merlin sate, when to the British king
> The changes long to come auspiciously he told.*

It was to this place that Vortigern retired to hide his shame, and provide for his security, when he found himself under the general odium of his subjects, and unable any longer to contend with the treacherous Saxons whom he had introduced into his kingdom. It is probable, that upon this insular rock he erected a temporary residence of timber (for the country at that time abounded with wood), that lasted him till he went to his final retreat in Nant Gwrtheyrn, or *Vortigern's Valley*, not far from Nefyn, in the promontory of Llŷn.*

Many of the ancient British and monkish writers assert, that, on his coming to Dinas Emrys, he attempted to erect a place of defence, but that, what was built in the day time always disappeared during the night. He therefore consulted his magicians, for such all the men of learning in those dark ages were esteemed, as to the manner in which he ought to act in this dreadful predicament. 'They advise (says the author of the notes on Drayton),* that he must find out a child which had no father, and with his blood sprinkle the stones and mortar, and then the castle would stand as on a firm foundation.' This was a tolerably secure mode of solving the difficulty, for they all had learning and philosophy enough to know that the king might search far and wide for this remedy. They were, however, for once disappointed! Emissaries were sent in all directions through the kingdom, and one of these, as he was going along the streets of the town, since called Caermarthen, overheard some boys quarrelling at play, one of whom reproached his adversary with the epithet of 'unbegotten knave.' This was the very boy that he wanted: he ran up to them, took him from among the rest, and having found out his mother, brought them both to the king. The mother declared that the boy, whose name was Merlin, was the child of an incubus.*

It is generally believed, however, that his father was a Roman consul, and that his mother, being a nun, the daughter of one of the kings of Mathraval, invented this story of his being fatherless to save her reputation and her life, for death was the usual punishment inflicted on those who had violated their monastic vow. The boy was ordered to be sacrificed, but he obtained his liberty by confounding all the magicians with his questions, and himself explaining the cause of the failure of the work. 'He being hither brought to the king (continues the above writer), slighted that pretended skill of his magicians, as palliated ignorance; and with confidence of a more knowing spirit, undertakes to shew the true cause of that amazing ruin of the stone-work. He tells them, that in the earth there was a great water which could endure the continuance of no heavy superstructure. The workmen digged to discover the truth, and found it so. He then beseeched the king to cause further inquisition to be made, and affirmed, that in the bottom of it were two sleeping dragons, the one white, and the other red, which proved so likewise. The white dragon he interpreted for the Saxons whom the king had brought over, and the red one for the oppressed Britons; and upon this event in Dinas Emrys, he began those prophecies to Vortigern, which are to this day common in the British storie.'

The only probable part of this story is, that Myrddin Emrys, for so he is called by the Welsh writers, may have been employed by Vortigern to search out for him a secure retreat from the just vengeance of his injured subjects; and that being a skilful architect and mechanic, he superintended the building of a fortress in this place. – There was another Merlin, frequently mistaken for this, a native of Caledonia, called *Myrddin ap Morvryn* and Myrddin Wyllt, who, in the year 542, when fighting under the banner of king Arthur, accidentally slew his own nephew. In consequence of this accident, he was seized with a madness which affected him every alternate hour during the rest of his life. He retired into Scotland, and in his lucid intervals composed some of the most beautiful pieces of poetry extant. This Merlin afterwards resided in North Wales, where he died: he was buried in the isle of Bardsey.

Vortigern married his own child by his wife Rowena, and had by her one son. Some writers assert that he was afterwards so much affected by this crime, that with his own hands he set fire to his house, and thus, at the same time, destroyed both himself and his partner in guilt. Others say that his palace was destroyed by lightning; and others again, that it was destroyed by Aurelius Ambrosius and Uter Pendragon, two sons of Constantine, who, on discovering the place of his retirement, set fire to it, and consumed along with it Vortigern and his family. – We are not, however, certain that any of these accounts are true; for Vortigern, being considered the author of all the calamities that his country afterwards suffered, he became odious to the people, and the British writers have loaded him with so many crimes, and have represented him as such a monster of iniquity, that it was not fit for him to go out of the world like other mortals. They have therefore invented for him those various kinds of death, that he might appear to depart from the world under the severest marks of divine vengeance.

A little farther in the vale is a pool, in a very charming situation, called

LLYN Y DINAS,

The Pool of the Fort, taking its name from its neighbouring rock of Dinas Emrys. It abounds in large and well-flavoured trout. – Two miles beyond this is *Cwm Llan*, a romantic hollow, extending into the mountains on the left towards Snowdon, the summit of which, above the intervening mountains, is visible from hence. The scene from this station is remarkably fine; there are here many trees about the foreground, and others are distributed among the rising steeps, exhibiting the rocks in various places, and thus elegantly varying the otherwise dull uniformity of the sides of the mountains. – Having passed the entrance into Cwm Llan, I soon afterwards came to another small pool, not even so large as that I had left, called *Llyn Gwynant*. Not far from hence, I believe it was, that a small chapel was founded by John Williams, a goldsmith of London, and a native of this vale, called *Capel Gwynant*. He was an antiquary of some eminence, who after accumulating a considerable fortune in London, retired to the place of his birth, and there ended his days.

IMMENSE STONE

Near the end of the vale I observed two enormous masses of rock, that had once, no doubt, been loosened from some of the high precipices above by rain or frost, and had tumbled from thence into their present insulated situations. One of them was much larger than the celebrated *Bowdar stone* in Barrowdale, near Derwent water. On one side it has the appearance of the gavel end of a house. It projects so far over its base, that an immense number both of men and horses might take shelter under it.

WATERFALL

I ascended the rocks on the left of the vale, to a considerable height, to see the cataract Rhaiadr Cwm Dyli, *The Waterfall of the Vale of Dyli*. There are two distinct falls one above the other. The rivulet that runs from the alpine pool, Llyn Llwydaw, in the mountains above, here breaks in foam and spray down the rugged fronts of the rocks. At the time I was here there had been a succession of dry weather for near a month, and the water was of course very inconsiderable in quantity. The rocks, however, had in themselves sufficient grandeur to compensate for my trouble, and there was still water enough to render the scenes extremely picturesque.

The softened beauties of the vale of Gwynant, or *Nant Hwynan*, are particularly pleasing to a tourist who has lately visited the other more rude vales of Caernarvonshire. The present is varied by all the elegant features that meadows, woods, and cornfields can furnish: it contains two beautiful little pools, and it is bounded by high rocks and mountains. In some places the specimens of picturesque scenery were so perfect, that all the order and beauty of colouring, so well described by Mason, were to be traced in them.

> Vivid green,
> Warm brown, and black opake the foreground bears
> Conspicuous. Sober olive coldly marks
> The second distance. Thence the third declines
> In softer blue, or lessening still, is lost
> In faintest purple.*

During my walk along the vale, I observed, in different places, several men busily employed in cutting down the trees. It is truly lamentable that the practice of taking away the timber should be so general, not only in this country, but, as I some years ago had occasion to observe, even throughout all the north of England, and about the lakes. Avarice, or dissipation, and its inseparable attendant, poverty, a late writer has justly observed, have despoiled the principality of nearly all its leafy beauties. Depriving scenery of wood, is ruinous to picturesque beauty; and if the owners of land do but go on in the manner they have done, for a few years longer, there will be scarcely a tree remaining in all North Wales.

EXCURSION FROM BEDDGELERT TO THE SUMMIT OF SNOWDON

As I had made a determination, soon after I first came into Wales, that I would ascend Snowdon by all the tracks that are usually pointed out to travellers, I, for the last time, undertook the task, along with a party of four others, from Beddgelert.*

The distance from Beddgelert to the summit, being reckoned not less than six miles, and a lady being one of our number, it was thought most eligible for her to ride as far as she could without danger, and for the rest to walk the whole way. In this manner, therefore, we set out, commencing our *mountain* journey by turning to the right, from the Caernarvon road, at the distance of about two miles and a half from the village. – We left the horse at a cottage, about half way up, from whence taking a bottle of milk to mix with some rum that we had brought along with us, we continued our route over a series of pointed and craggy rocks. Stopping at different times to rest, we enjoyed to the utmost, the prospects that by degrees were opening around us. Caernarvon and the isle of Anglesea, aided by the brightness of the morning, were seen to great advantage;

and Llyn Cwellyn below us, shaded by the vast Mynydd Mawr, with Castell Cidwm at its foot, appeared extremely beautiful. In ascending, the mountains, which from below appeared of immense height, began now to seem beneath us; the lakes and vallies were more exposed, and all the little rills and mountain streams, by degrees became visible to us, like silver lines intersecting the hollows around.

Towards the upper part of the mountain, we passed over a tremendous ridge of rock, called Clawdd Coch, *the red ridge*. This narrow pass, not more than ten or twelve feet across, and two or three hundred yards in length, was so steep, that the eye reached on each side, down the whole extent of the mountain. And I am persuaded, that in some parts of it, if a person held a large stone in each hand, and let them both fall at once, each might roll above a quarter of a mile, and thus, when they stopped, they might be more than half a mile asunder. The lady who accompanied us, to my great surprize, passed this ridge without the least apparent signs of fear or trepidation.

There is no danger whatever, in crossing Clawdd Coch in the day-time, but I must confess, that I should by no means like to venture along this tract in the night, as many do who have never seen it. If the moon shone very bright, we might, it is very true, escape unhurt; but a dark cloud coming suddenly over, would certainly expose us to much danger. Many instances have occurred of persons who, having passed over it in the night, were so terrified at seeing it by day-light the next morning, that they have not dared to return the same way, but have gone a very circuitous round by Bettws.* I was informed that one gentleman had been so much alarmed, that he crawled over it back again on his hands and knees.

In the hollow, on the left of the ascent, are four small pools, called *Llyn Coch*, the red pool; *Llyn y Nadroedd*, the adder's pool; *Llyn Glas*, the blue pool; and *Llyn Ffynnon y Gwas*, the servant's pool.

Soon after we had passed Clawdd Coch, we became immersed in light clouds, till we arrived at the summit of the mountain, when a single gleam of sunshine, which lasted but for a moment, presented us with the majestic scenery on the west of our station. It served, however, only to tantalize our hopes, for a smart gust of wind again obscured us in clouds. We now sheltered ourselves from the cold, under some of the projecting rocks near the top, and ate our dinners, watching with anxiety the dark shades in the clouds, in hopes that a separation might take place, and that we should be once more delighted with a sight of the grand objects around us. We did not watch in vain, for the clouds by degrees cleared away, and left us at full liberty to admire the numerous beauties in this vast expansive scene. The steep rock of *Clogwyn y Garnedd*, whose dreadful precipices are, some of them, above two hundred yards in perpendicular height, and the whole rock, a series of precipices, was an object which first struck one of my companions with terror, and he exclaimed, almost involuntarily:

> How fearful
> And dizzy 'tis to cast one's eyes so low!
> The crows and choughs that wing the midway air
> Shew scarce so gross as beetles.*

We now stood on a point which commanded the whole dome of the sky. The prospects below, each of which we had before considered separately as a grand scene, were now only miniature parts in the immense landscape. We had around us such a variety of mountains, vallies, lakes, and streams, each receding behind the other, and bounded only by the far distant horizon, that the eye almost strained itself with looking upon them. These majestic prospects were soon shut from our sight by the gathering clouds, which now began to close in much heavier than they had done before, and it was in vain that we waited near an hour for another opening. We were therefore, at length, obliged to descend, in despair of being any more gratified with these sublime prospects.

We again passed Clawdd Coch, and soon afterwards, turning to the left, descended into the mountain vale, called *Cwm Llân*, which I have mentioned in a preceding part of this chapter. We followed the course of a stream, which runs from thence into Llyn y Dinas, in Nant Hwynan. This little rivulet entertained us much in its descent, being, in many places, thrown over low rocks, and forming small, but sometimes elegant, cascades. – After a walk of two hours, we arrived in Nant Hwynan, the vale that I had traversed with so much pleasure a day or two before; and passing Llyn y Dinas, and Dinas Emrys, soon afterwards reached Beddgelert, not a little fatigued with our mountain ramble.

I observed near a cottage in Cwm Llan, that several children were employed in gathering the berries of the mountain ash (Sorbus aucuparia of Linnaeus). On enquiring of the guide to what purpose this was done, he informed me that the Welsh people brew from them a liquor, which they call *Diod griafol*. This, he said, was done by merely crushing the berries, and putting water to them, which, after remaining a fortnight, is drawn off for use. The flavour, as I understood him, was somewhat like that of perry.

19

Excursion from Caernarvon to the Nantlle Pools

In my visit to the Nantlle Pools, I proceeded along the road from Caernarvon to Beddgelert, till I had passed Llyn Cwellyn, when taking a route westward, between Llyn Cader, and Llyn y Dywarchen, I entered a wild mountainous pass, that led me along a series of sheep tracts, into Nant Lle, *the Vale of Lle*. The mountains rose on each side to an immense height, those towards the north forming a long range of precipices, singularly marked by the innumerable gullies of the mountain storms. The whole scene was that of savage wildness, of nature in her most dreary attire.* It is a narrow pass, encompassed by mountains, uncultivated, destitute altogether of wood, and unsheltered on all sides from the fury of the tempests. – As I proceeded, the scene by degrees, began to extend its limits, and the mountains to attain more varied and elegant forms. At length the two Nantlle Pools, called by the Welsh *Llyniau Nantlle*, and the whole range of the vale, with the gradually declining mountains, became visible nearly to the sea. The prospect was exceedingly beautiful; and the number of trees in different parts, and particularly about the foreground, added greatly to the effect. – On turning round, to look towards the road that I had left, now about two miles distant, I observed that Snowdon closed up the end of the pass, and terminated the view in that direction; its upper parts were, however, so enveloped in clouds, as to render them invisible.

I continued my route along a tolerably good horse-path, between hedge-rows, among meadows and woodland, on the north side of the pools. The trees were chiefly old oaks, that had withstood the fury of near a hundred winters; the limbs shattered, covered with moss, and bared of leaves. Several of the small farmers' cottages among these trees, presented, with the other objects around, scenes peculiarly picturesque. By an ancient over-shot mill, between the pools, I remarked a scene that exceeded all the rest. The mountain grandeur of the vale was broken by the wooded foreground; and the water of one of the lakes, from the rays of the sun, which shot obliquely upon it, glittered through the dark foliage of the trees. The mill, and its rude wooden aqueduct and wheel, with an adjacent cottage or two, overgrown with moss and lichens, and shattered in the walls and roofs, were the other component parts of the landscape.

This was, however, by no means, the last of the elegancies of the vale; in almost every part of my walk, I had something to admire, some new object presented to me, that afforded sources both of reflection and delight. At some distance beyond the farthest lake, the road, which is here wide enough to admit carriages to the neighbouring slate quarries, led me to some little height above the vale. I again turned round to look along the vale in the direction I had come, and was surprised by a view so elegantly picturesque, that even my fancy had scarcely ever led me to imagine one equal to it. The dense clouds that had enveloped all the higher regions of Snowdon, were in a great measure driven away, and those that I now saw, floated below the pointed summit of the mountain, which was visible above. It bounded the end of the vale, and I never before saw this mountain in so much grandeur. A dusky haziness about it, threw it to appearance very different, and added greatly to its effect in height. A gleam of sunshine, passing the valley by Llyn Cwellyn, that crossed by its foot, and softening upwards, formed a fine light in the middle of the scene. The steep black rocks of Mynydd Mawr, on the left, and the craggy summits of the elegant and varied range of the Drws y Coed mountains, on the right of the vale, on whose side I stood, and appearing even still darker than usual, from the light on the mountain beyond them, formed a truly elegant middle distance. The expanse of the water of the two lakes, intersected by a narrow isthmus, appeared in the bosom of the vale. The rude trunks, and weather-beaten limbs of the old oaks around, not only added beauty to the foreground, but varied, by their intervention, the otherwise too uniform appearance of the meadows of the vale, and of some parts of the mountains' sides. This landscape is not exceeded in beauty by any in North Wales.

As the *slate quarries* were not far from this station, I walked up to them, and found a chasm formed in the rocks that, from its peculiar appearance, surprized me almost as much as the excavations in the mountains of Nant Frangon, belonging to lord Penrhyn. This is very narrow, long, and deep, its sides being nearly all perpendicular; and to a stranger, unaccustomed to sights of this nature, it will be found very interesting. The mountain in which these quarries are formed, is called Cilgwyn, *the white retreat*: it is in the parish of Llanllyfni.

In the former part of this ramble (in the hollow near Llyn y Dywarchen), I had observed the cattle, in apparent agony, chasing each other round the foot of the mountains, with their tails erect, and head and neck stretched out, and uttering strange bellowings. The cause of this incident immediately occurred to me, and when they afterwards passed within a few yards the place where I was walking, it was fully explained, by my catching at a fly that was near one of them, which I found to be a species of *gadfly*, the *oestrus bovis* of Linnaeus, that, in summer often torments the oxen, till they almost run mad with terror. If only a single ox is attacked, it runs off bellowing from among the herd, and where water is near, makes immediately to it; for the fly leaves the animal the moment it passes the bank: the rest generally follow, which accounts for all the animals about the same place, usually appearing agitated at the same time. Cattle have been known to plunge from the plough, and in spite of every effort, have run through hedges and thickets, to gain the bank of a stream or pond. Whatever they may happen to be doing, when attacked by these insects, nothing can restrain them from seeking some mode of ridding themselves of them:

> Light fly their slumbers, if perchance a flight
> Of angry gad-flies fasten on the herd;
> That startling scatters from the shallow brook,
> In search of lavish stream. Tossing the foam,
> They scorn the keeper's voice, and scour the plain,
> Through all the bright severity of noon;
> While, from their labouring breasts, a hollow moan
> Proceeding, run low-bellowing round the hills.*

The reason why these flies attack the cattle is, that they may deposit their eggs in the skin. The operation is performed in a few seconds, but probably the pain is extremely severe. The aperture made by the flies, though very minute, does not afterwards close up, but enlarges with swelling. This, when the young grub is produced from the egg, serves both as a breathing place for it, and as a passage, through which the superfluous humour contained in the swelling, discharges itself, which, if confined, would occasion a large abscess, and suffocate the little creature. As soon as the grub has attained its full growth, it works itself out, and dropping to the ground, attains there its chrysalis, and afterwards its perfect, or fly state. – Young and healthy cattle are more liable to the attacks of the gadfly than any others; the first on account of the tenderness of their hides, and the latter, as affording a nidus best suited to nourishing the young insects. Cattle that are found to have a great number of botholes in their skins, are always esteemed by dealers to be the best, and when these occur in the hides, the tanners always find that such make strong and good leather.* The skin heals on the exit of the grub, but it is not with the same matter as that of the original skin; and by the marks that are left, it is easy to know where these holes have been. – The grubs of this gadfly are called by farmers and others, *bots, warbles,* and *wornuls.*

20

Excursion from Caernarvon into the Promontory of Llŷn

The promontory of Llŷn, or that division of Caernarvonshire that juts out into the Irish sea, was the *Langanum* of Ptolemy* and Antoninus. Its Welsh name is derived from an old word, that signifies a long slip of any thing, and more particularly a spear. – In its general character it affords very little interesting matter for the observation of the tourist. In the more northerly parts a considerable quantity of corn is grown; so much indeed as to supply nearly all the rest of the county. Much of the land is there flat and capable of cultivation and improvement. The Rev. Mr. Ellis of Llanslyndwy,* near Criccieth, has introduced in that part of the promontory, the culture of cabbages and turnips, for the fattening of cattle, with some degree of success. This strange attempt has astonished the Welsh farmers, who, wedded to old modes, and altogether ignorant of good management, cannot conceive how it should answer. The same gentleman has also made considerable advances in the irrigation of meadow land. It will probably be long before so good an example will be followed by other farmers; it is hoped, however, that its effect will not be lost. – The most distant extremity of Llŷn is, in general, a bleak, open, and exposed country, in which agriculture can make little progress towards improvement.

DINAS DINLLE,

An ancient fort, about two miles west of Llandwrog, (a village near six miles south of Caernarvon,) was the first place of any consequence that I came to. This is situated on the summit of a green eminence, immediately on the coast. In a stream called Voryd, that runs not far from the place, there are two fords, which, to this day, retain the names of *Rhyd equestre*, and *Rhyd pedestre* (Rhyd being the Welsh word for ford), and are understood by these names, as the horse and foot fords. – The mount on which the fort was constructed, is supposed to have been artificial. It is so near the sea, that at high tides the water comes entirely up to it: on the side towards the water, the bank is very steep. – The fort was of a circular form, and about four hundred feet in diameter. On all sides, except towards the sea, it was defended by a deep foss five or six yards wide. The principal entrance was on the east side. This station not only commanded the whole of Caernarvon bay, its creeks and harbours, but great part of the county of Caernarvon, and of the isle of Anglesea, was also within sight of the garrison. – To this great centre of observation and action (says the late learned vicar of Llanwnda) correspond several other forts, that lie diagonally across the country, some towards the north, and others towards the south; which, like the wings of an army, were of infinite service in time of danger, for its safety and protection. The most considerable on the east are Dinorddwig, in the parish of Llanddiniolen; and Yr Hên Gastell, and Dinas Gorfan, both in the parish of Llanwnda, and about three miles distant. Towards the south, one of the most rocky is Craig y Dinas, on the river Llyfni, about a mile and a half distant. – Dinorddwig, or, as it is now called, Pen Dinas, in the parish of Llanddiniolen, is still entire and strengthened with a double ditch and strong rampart. The excellence of this fort is its strength and compactness, standing, as it were, on tiptoe above all the rest.

Yr hên Gastell, *the old castle*, near the brook Carrog, is a small entrenchment with a single rampart, about fifty paces in length. Dinas Gorfan, near Pont Newydd, *the new bridge*, has merely the name remaining. But Craig y Ddinas, *the rocky fort*, is a circular encampment, about a hundred paces in diameter, very steep towards the river that passes it on the south, as it is also on every other side except the west. The ramparts, with a treble ditch, are of loose stones, exceedingly strong, and not to be taken out even at this day, without great force. The entrance is towards the north side, very narrow, and forty paces in length. This fort is about a mile south-west of the great road that leads from Caernarvon to Pwllheli, and about a quarter of a mile from Lleiar, the ancient family seat of the Twisletons.

Farther on, towards the extremity of the diagonal line, at the foot of Llanhaiarn mountain, and not far from the place where that parish joins upon Llan Gybi, there is a small fort on the top of a high rock called *Caer*. This was a fort of observation, to guard not only the passes of the mountains, but to overlook Llŷn, the ancient division of Caernarvonshire, called Evionedd, and St. George's Channel. – There are other smaller forts interspersed about the country (connected, no doubt, in some shape or other with Dinas Dinlle). These were either the residences of generals, as Gad-lys, in the parish of Llanwnda, or places of observation for some peculiar military uses, as Dinas y Prif, in the parish of Llanwnda, where there is one deep ditch and a western entrance, looking towards the principal fort Dinas Dinlle. – The disposition and economy of these head quarters, savour of the wisdom and sagacity, that seem to run through the whole, being situated, (if the expression may be used,) at proper intervals in the base of a triangle, which the two diagonal lines form, by meeting with the base, in a point at Dinas Dinlle.

On the left of the road, about half a mile beyond the village of Llandwrog, I passed the grounds of *Glynllivon*, the seat of lord Newborough.* The views were over a country in a tolerably good state of cultivation, and were on the whole interesting. At a little distance to the right, was the sea; and on the opposite side, a few miles off, were the mountains around Snowdon.

As I approached the *Rival* or *Eifl* (forked) mountains, they began to assume a very grand aspect. Their conical summits, all nearly of equal height, were obscured by light clouds. They seemed to oppose an impassible barrier, to the still extensive country beyond them. The mountain next the sea, presents a perpendicular precipice to the waves, which seemed to me at a distance, to beat against its foot.

CLYNOG

Is a small village, which, with its elegant gothic church appearing among the trees, and the mountains in the background, forms a picturesque scene, at the distance of about half a mile from the place. The houses are half hidden by the foliage, and the tower of the church rises very beautifully from among them. The sea, on the right, forms an essential part of the view.

The *church*, differing in that respect from every other parish church in Wales, is a large gothic building, with some of the windows of painted glass. In different parts of it, I observed the tombs of several persons of a Yorkshire family of the name of Twisleton, who retired into Wales, and lived chiefly in this parish. A passage called Yr heinous, *the heinous*, (from its having been used as a place of confinement for disorderly persons), leads from the church to a small gothic building, called Eglwys Beuno, *the chapel of Beuno*, supposed to have been originally founded about the year 616. This Welsh saint was the son of one of the kings of Powys, and uncle to Wenefred, the celebrated virgin of Holywell. He is reported to have been interred in the chapel, and an ill worked stone figure, now placed in the belfry, headless and mutilated, was supposed to have covered his grave. In consequence of this opinion, lord Newborough, in the year 1793, ordered the ground to be examined for his remains, but nothing could be discovered. – In the south east corner of the church, near the altar table, there is an old wooden chest, belted with iron, and fastened to the floor, called Cyff Beuno, *Beuno's chest*. This has a slit in the cover, to receive the offerings of money from the devotees of the saint. If a person was affected with any disorder, he made his offering into this chest, usually a four-penny piece, if such could be obtained, and having sat down on Beuno's grave, and addressed his prayers to the saint, he expected immediate relief. This custom is even yet continued by a few ignorant persons. On Trinity Sunday, bread and cheese were usually offered to Beuno; and the church formerly claimed all the calves and lambs that were cast with a slit in their ear.

The other curiosities about this place are, the *well* dedicated to St. Beuno, inclosed in a square wall on the left of the road, about a quarter of a mile beyond the village; a *cromlech*, which is to be seen, a little farther on from the road, in a field near the sea; and a *waterfall* called *Rhaiadr Dibbin Mawr*, in the mountains about two miles distant. The latter I had not heard of when I was here.

From Clynog I directed my route towards the Rivals, and in passing the foot of a smooth and conical mountain called Gyrn Goch, *The Red Point*, observed a number of women and children busily employed in rolling large bundles of heath down the sides, to save themselves the labour of carrying them. – The road led me, up a tolerably steep hill, to *Llanhaiarn*, whose white-washed church on its elevated site, affords a land-mark to the distant mariner. I now wound my way along the hollows of the Rival mountains, and for a considerable distance through a country as desolate and barren as can be well imagined. Emerging from these dreary wilds, I not long afterwards arrived at a small and insignificant borough town, governed by a bailiff and corporation, called *Nevin*, surrounded by mountains, and appearing altogether separated from the world.

I descended from hence to the shore, at Porthynllyn, *The Harbour in Llyn*, about a mile distant. Here are three or four houses situated at the foot of a small semicircular range of low mountains, with, in front, a large and extensive bay. This place is even more secluded from the world than Nevin; it cannot be seen, except from the edges of the hills that immediately surround it. The extent of all the land betwixt the hills and the sea is so small, as scarcely to be more than a mile and a half across, and a quarter of a mile deep. The harbour is chiefly frequented by coasting and Irish vessels.

As I had already seen nearly as much of this uninteresting part of Caernarvonshire as I wished, and as I had previously determined, in the course of a few days, to sail in the cutter belonging to the hotel at Caernarvon, from that place entirely round the promontory, I now cut short my journey by crossing directly over from hence to

PWLLHELI.

This is a small market town supported principally by its coasting trade. Vessels are here built of a tolerably large size; one that I saw on the stocks, I was told, would be registered as of about six hundred tons burthen, but this was the largest that had ever been constructed here. The harbour is a pretty good one, but at the ebb of the tide it is left nearly dry. Pwllheli is the principal town in the promontory, and has in its neighbourhood the seats of several families of great respectability. The surrounding country is more cultivated than in most other parts of Llŷn; and it is in many parts varied with wood. The town itself is very unpleasant, from the extreme irregularity of the houses and streets.

CRICCIETH

Is situated at the north corner of Cardigan bay, about nine miles from Pwllheli. It is an insignificant borough town contributory to Caernarvon; and, except in the few remains of its *castle*, affords nothing which can claim attention from the traveller. This is situated on a rising ground, at the end of a long neck of land that juts into the sea. The entrance to it is betwixt two round towers, which are square within: all the other towers are entirely square. There have been two courts, but neither of them was very large, nor indeed has the whole castle been a building of any other than small extent. At present it is in a very ruinous condition. – From the eminence on which it stands, there is a beautiful view across the bay towards Harlech, where that fine old castle is seen, backed by the high and distant mountains of Merionethshire.

From the architecture of Criccieth castle, it appears undoubtedly to have been of British origin; and its reputed founder Edward I, seems only to have cased the two towers at the entrance, their exterior workmanship being very different from that of the interior. It is conjectured by Rowlands to have been in existence before the sixth century. – The constable appointed by Edward was allowed a salary of a hundred pounds a year, but out of this it was stipulated, that he should maintain a garrison of thirty stout men, a chaplain, surgeon, carpenter and mason.

SIR HOWELL Y FWYALL,

A native of the adjoining parish of Llanstyndwy, and a descendant from Colwyn ap Tangno, one of the fifteen tribes of North Wales, was constable of this castle. This valiant officer attended the Black Prince in the battle of Poictiers,* where, although on foot, and armed only with a battle axe, he performed several acts of the utmost bravery and heroism. The principal of his services was the cutting off the head of the French king's horse, and taking him prisoner. As a recompence for his valour he received the honour of knighthood, and was allowed to bear the arms of France, with a 'battle-axe in bend sinister;' and to add to his name y Fwyall, *the battle-axe*. In further commemoration of his services, it was ordered that a mess of meat should, at the expence of the crown, be every day served up before the axe with which he had performed these wonderful feats. This mess, after it had been brought to the knight, was taken down, and distributed among the poor. Even after sir Howel's death the mess continued to be served as usual, and for the sake of his soul, given to the poor till so lately as the beginning of the reign of queen Elizabeth. Eight yeomen attendants, called yeomen of the crown, were appointed to guard it, who received each eightpence a day constant wages.

The present parish clerk of Criccieth informed a gentleman of my acquaintance, that in digging a grave in the church-yard, about ten years ago, he found a human skull of enormous size, holding in the cavity for the brain more than two quarts of water. He used it for some time, in the place of a more convenient implement, to throw water out of newly opened graves. He supposed it to have been the skull of this renowned hero, but probably, however, without any other reason, than from its enormous size; for the ignorant generally associate the idea of a gigantic figure with the character of a valiant man.

From Criccieth I proceeded about three miles to

PENMORFA,

The Head of the Marsh, a wood-clad village, romantically situated on the western bank of Traeth Mawr. The church contains a small monument to the memory of *sir John Owen*, a valiant commander in the army, and a staunch supporter of Charles I. This hero, after the execution of his royal master, with several of the nobility, was condemned by the parliament to lose his head. During his trial he exhibited a spirit of intrepidity worthy so brave a man; and, after his condemnation, he bowed to the court, and expressed his thanks for the honour they intended him. One of the members asked what he meant, and he replied loud enough to be heard by most of the persons present, 'I think it a great honour for a poor gentleman of Wales to lose his head with such noble lords: –by G––, I was afraid they would have hanged me.' By great good fortune, however, and by the interest of Ireton,* who became his advocate, he was set at liberty, and restored to his friends, after only a few months imprisonment.

There is a ford from Penmorfa, across the two sands, Traeth Mawr and Traeth Bach, to the roads leading to Tanybwlch and Harlech: this saves a very circuitous route to those who wish to go from hence by Beddgelert. Passing this ford is, however, sometimes attended with danger, owing to the tide's not leaving the same level, but sometimes washing deep holes in the sand: and it is never proper for a stranger to attempt to cross it without the attendance of a guide. – The gentlemen of Llŷn have lately entered into a subscription, for the purpose of obtaining an act of parliament, to form a post road from this place, across the promontory, to Porthynllyn, where some Irish packets would then be stationed. The advantage arising from it would be very great to Irish passengers, as from Shrewsbury, (instead of skirting the country by Chester, St. Asaph, and Conwy,) they would pass directly across North Wales, and having saved many miles of land-carriage, they would still have at Porthynllyn a station nearly as good as that of Holyhead.*

***

In my walk from Penmorfa to Beddgelert, on my route to Caernarvon, I passed by the house of *Gesailgyfarch*, formerly the habitation of Jevan ap Robert.* The country on the whole was mountainous and unpleasant.

21

Voyage from Caernarvon to the Isle of Bardsey, and thence to Pwllheli

Having victualled the Flora cutter, belonging to the Hotel at Caernarvon, with provisions for a week's voyage, I went on board one morning in August, on the first of flood, with the intention of sailing to the island of Bardsey, (distant about twelve leagues,) and round the promontory of Llŷn, to Pwllheli.

In the first tide, from want of wind, we only just cleared what is called the bar, a range of sand banks a little beyond the gap of Abermenai. At low water, we were, therefore, under the necessity of coming to anchor off the

LLANDDWYN ROCKS:

And in order to amuse ourselves for a few hours we landed on this point of the island of Anglesea. – As I had examined the place before, I now passed my time in searching for plants and shells. The *purple whelk*, Buccinum lapillus of Linnaeus, was that which first attracted my attention. This was formerly used for dying linen cloth purple. I bruised one of them with a stone, and stained my handkerchief with it. The mark was at first of a yellowish hue, it then became dark green, and after some time assumed its proper colour. The shell is not large, but it is very thick and hard. The colouring matter is contained in a vesicle that lies in a small furrow by the head. The natives of South America, on whose coast this shell is very common, use the juice in dying, and extract it in two ways. They sometimes break the shell, and taking out the animal, lay it on the back of one of their hands, and with a knife press the juice from the head towards the tail, then separating that part of the body into which it is collected, throw the rest away. The usual way, however, is, not to break the shell, but only to squeeze the animal till it throws up the juice; they then return it to the rocks, where it soon recovers from its bruises. After this operation has been repeated about four times, its vigour becomes entirely exhausted. Before the introduction of cochineal from America, this animal was much in request by the dyers not only of our country, but of Europe in general: at present, however, it is merely considered as an object of curiosity. Bede, who flourished about the latter part of the seventh century, says, 'There are snails in very great abundance, from which a scarlet or crimson dye is made, whose elegant redness never fades either by the heat of the sun, or the injuries of rain, but the older it is, it is the more elegant.'*

Amongst the rocks, I picked up two or three specimens of the *common five-fingered sea-star*, or Star-fish, Asterias glacialis of Linnaeus. In their construction and economy, these animals differ very greatly from all others. On an examination, the upper parts of their body are found to be composed of grains of a hard calcareous matter various in figure and size. This covering, when they are fixed close to the rocks or stones, by means of their hundreds of tentacula below, defends them from the attacks of their enemies. The tentacula are short, soft, and fleshy tubes, which may be observed to be pushed out and withdrawn in the same manner as the horns of snails. They are arranged in files from the mouth, which is in the centre of the under part of the body, through the whole length of the branches. Notwithstanding the exterior calcareous covering of these animals, they are able, by the undulation of their rays or branches, both to move on the rocks, and to swim, but their motion is, at all times, exceedingly slow. Their mouth is furnished with five bony teeth, by which they are enabled to break the shells of the animals on which they feed. All the species of star-fish are easily dried, after having been drowned in spirits of any kind, and had their stomach and intestines extracted by a pair of forceps; for they will then come out entire through the mouth.

The rocks were in many places studded over with the shells of the *common limpit*, Patella vulgata of Linnaeus. This is a conical shell known to every one. On a mere inspection, either as fixed on its rock, or when removed from thence by a knife or any other sharp instrument, no one could suppose this animal capable of exerting any locomotive powers. I however observed two or three of them near the edge of the water, left by the tide in the recesses of the rocks, in the act of moving forward, but this was very slowly. When carefully examined, they are found to be furnished for this purpose, with a fleshy mass of fibres, crossing each other in various directions, called a foot or tongue. In this instrument, the superior muscle is composed of two rows of fibres, that meet and form an acute angle upon a middle line, which corresponds to the long diameter of the tongue. The inferior muscle is used in contracting the ellipsis of the tongue, and at the same time in lessening it in breadth; whilst the superior one diminishes the length, but increases the breadth. By means of this singular mechanism it is, that these animals are endowed with progressive powers. They adhere to the rocks by creating a vacuum, from contracting the middle of their bodies into a smaller compass than when they are in motion.

Such are the wonderful operations of the parent of the universe, in these, apparently, the most insignificant parts of the creation. They are, however, by no means less astonishing than what we observe in the greater animals, and can only be overlooked in the want of due reflection on the works of God. It is a pleasing thought, and has often recurred to me, that were we for once actually to observe a fly, of the same bulk and size as an elephant, we should be struck with astonishment at a production so wonderful. But surely all the parts of a fly, or all the parts of the animals of which we are now speaking, are not to be esteemed the less surprizing, because they are so minute as in a great measure to escape the cognizance of our senses. If the larger animals surprize us in their conformation, that of the minute parts of the creation, instead of calling for less attention, ought surely to excite a still greater degree of admiration and wonder.

But to return from these digressions to the main object of my landing, that of collecting plants and shells: I have to remark, that of the former I took away with me several specimens of *Euphorbia Portlandica*, and the bulbs of *Scilla verna*. Of the shells besides those already mentioned, I found only the periwinkle, or *Turbo littoreus*, and *Nerita littoralis*, adhering to the rocks; and *Buccinum reticulatum*, *Cypraea pediculus* (gowries), *Turba terebra*, and *Solen siliqua* (common razor-shell), and *Nerita glaucina*, amongst the rubbish thrown up by the tides.

When I had sufficiently fatigued myself in clambering among the clefts of these rocks, I proposed that we should re-embark. – The moment the tide became again in our favour, we weighed anchor, and to catch the faint breeze over the island, crowded every inch of our canvas. – In a short time we came into a situation that afforded me a most beautiful and extensive view of the whole range of the Caernarvonshire mountains, from Penmaen Mawr towards the north, to an extreme point of the promontory of Llŷn. In this range, which in a direct line occupies upwards of fifty miles, all the primary mountains were visible, namely Snowdon, Glyder, Llyder, Garn, Carnedd Ddafydd, Carnedd Llewelyn, Carnedd Elain, and Penmaen Mawr northwards; and on the south of

Voyage from Caernarvon

Snowdon, Mynydd Mawr, Drws y Coed, Barra dû, the Rivals, Carn Madryn, and Cefn Amwlch. We were proceeding sufficiently slow and steady to allow me to make a tolerably good sketch of their appearance from the sea. – It is perhaps the finest range of mountain scenery that this kingdom affords.

Towards sun-set we found ourselves off Clynog, about six miles from the coast, and as the wind had now entirely failed us, we thought it best to come again to an anchor. This afforded me at least one pleasure, that of watching the departing sun, and the approach of the evening. As the orb became immersed, the horizontal rays of light gleamed along the water, and tinged it with colours uncommonly brilliant. A vessel of some burthen passed, almost along the line of the horizon, before the sun at this moment. Its distance was very considerable, but its situation rendered the whole of its rigging perfectly visible to us: Almost every rope became black and distinct. When it was nearly dark, I ordered a fire to be lighted in the cabin, and retired to rest. This was only interrupted by the sound of 'What cheer?' sung by the man on watch, to a vessel coming in with the tide, and the answer of 'All's well.' All again became still, and I slept till near five o'clock in the morning, when, as we had still a dead calm, I got up and determined to amuse myself with fishing. It was not long after putting out my line, that I caught an immense skait, and after that a dog-fish, squalus catulus of Linnaeus. I was interrupted in this employment, by a breeze springing up, just at the turn of the tide, and was not displeased at laying aside my line, to assist in weighing anchor.

We passed the harbour of Porthynllyn, and in return for the late calm, the weather now became so boisterous, that it was necessary, for our safety, to hold out to sea. We soon approached the island of Bardsey, on which I was desirous to land; but till the wind abated, this was altogether impracticable.

The sudden change in the weather, which at first augured in every respect favourably for us, was now become worse to us than the preceding calm. We suffered ourselves to be driven about during the rest of the day, and all the next night, by the fury of the elements; but in the morning we determined, at all hazards, to enter the strait between the island and the main land, and if possible, get into shelter under the south-east side of the island. In the sound we had, in addition to our heavy gale of wind, to encounter the fury of a violent tide. Here our little bark rose over the tops of the high waves, and was driven into their deep bosoms. The boltsprit several times dipping into the tide, threw the whole spray of the divided wave upon us. A large brig at a little distance was often entirely hidden from our sight by the intervening waves, which seemed about to overwhelm us. But the most unpleasant sensation I experienced, arose from the violent rolling of the vessel from side to side, in which it was with the utmost difficulty I could keep my feet, and then its often pitching suddenly forward, so as sometimes to give me the most violent shocks imaginable. I was completely wet through two great coats, and the cabin floor at one time was two or three inches deep in water. We made several tacks to accomplish the object of our voyage, but, after beating about near twelve hours, we were at length compelled to abandon all further thoughts of it, and to make the best of our way into harbour at Pwllheli. – The reader will, however, experience no disappointment in my not having been able to effect a landing, since the letters of Mr. Jones, the worthy vicar of Aberdaron, to whose parish it belongs, have given me a better account of the

ISLAND OF BARDSEY

Than my own observations could possibly have furnished.

This island, which is the property of lord Newborough, is somewhat more than two miles long, and one in breadth; and contains about three hundred and seventy acres of land, of which near a third is occupied by a high mountain, that affords feed only for a few sheep and rabbits. Its distance from the main land is about a league. Towards the southeast and south-west it lies entirely open, but, on the north and north-east, it is sheltered by its mountain, which to the sea presents a face of perpendicular, and in some parts even of overhanging rocks. Among these precipices the intrepid inhabitants, in the spring of the year, employ themselves in collecting the eggs of the various species of sea-fowl that frequent them. This is usually done barefooted, to prevent them from slipping from heights whence they must be dashed to pieces; and their concern for their own safety, while seizing these eggs, is infinitely less than that of the beholder, sitting securely in the boat below:

> Nor untrembling canst thou see
> How from a scraggy rock, whose prominence
> Half o'ershades the ocean, hardy men,
> Fearless of dashing waves, do gather them.*

These poor fellows do not often meet with accidents, except by the giving way of pieces of the rock, which, however, sometimes, though very rarely, happens. In this case they are irrecoverably lost. The men who venture without ropes are accounted by the natives the most bold climbers: those who are more cautious fix a rope about their middle, which is held by some persons on the top of the rock. By this they slip down to the place where they think the most eggs are to be found. Here, untying it from their body, they fasten it to the basket that is to contain the eggs, which they carry in their hand. When this is filled, they make a signal to their companions to draw them up. In this manner they proceed from rock to rock, ascending or descending as they find it necessary. They adopt the same modes in collecting the samphire, with which the rocks also abound.

On the south-east side of the island, the only side on which it is accessible to the mariner, there is a small, but well sheltered harbour, capable of admitting vessels of thirty or forty tons burthen. In this the inhabitants secure their own fishing-boats.

The soil is principally clayey, and produces excellent barley and wheat: vetches, peas, and beans, are said to succeed sufficiently well, but to oats it is not so favourable. Trees will not grow here, the keen westerly winds immediately destroying the young plants. Indeed, except a small quantity of fine meadow land, all the lower ground of the island is of little value. – No reptile is ever seen in this island, except the common water lizard. None of the inhabitants ever saw in it a frog, toad, or snake of any kind. – Till about four years ago, no sparrows had been known to breed here: three nests were, however, built during the same spring, and the produce have since completely colonized the place.

There are here but eight houses, although the number of inhabitants is upwards of seventy. Two or three of the principal of these rent the island of lord Newborough. They pay for it a hundred guineas a year, and have their land tythe free, and are also freed from taxes and rates of every description. They keep about twenty horses, and near thirty cows. All the former, though greatly overstocking so small a place, are absolutely necessary, on account of the great labour required in carrying up the seaweeds from the coast for manure.

The sheep are small, and, on the approach of a stranger, as Mr. Jones informs me, they squall not much unlike hares. Their activity is very remarkable. In the year 1801, Mr. Jones had one of them on his farm at Aberdaron, that had twice ventured through the sea, though the channel is three miles across, and regained the island. The inhabitants train their dogs to catch them, but if the sheep once gain the rocks, they bid defiance to every attempt for the time, as, rather than suffer themselves to be seized, they will plunge from thence into the sea. At the time of the year when the females usually drop their young, the inhabitants watch them every day, and before these are able to follow their dams, they mark them in the ears: they then suffer them to range at liberty. Without this attention, from the extreme wildness of the animals, the owners would never be able to distinguish their respective property. Some few of the sheep of the island, from having been rendered tame when young, are more easily managed. These alone submit to be folded in the evenings.

Very few of the present inhabitants are natives of the island. Those, however, that are, differ from the new-comers considerably in their tone of voice, which has a distant resemblance to the Irish brogue. Their complexions are in general brown, and their manners, and habits of life, bespeak the little intercourse they have with the world. Their chief employment, beyond managing their land, is fishing. The principal mart for the produce of their labour is Liverpool; to which place they sail in little open boats, and sometimes even in the most boisterous weather.

During the herring season they generally have full employment; but the collecting of *lobsters* and *crabs* it is that occupies the most considerable portion of their time. These they principally take by means of traps made of willows, exactly in the shape of a wire mouse-trap, with the cone inverted. They have weights tied to them, and are let down into the water by means of ropes, a buoy marking their place. The baits of fish, or garbage, are suspended by strings from the sides so near the centre, as to prevent the animals reaching them from without. Tempted by these, they tumble into the traps, or *pots* as they are called, from whence they cannot be released but by the fishermen, who transfer them to other pots, much larger, but constructed exactly in the same manner, where they are kept till a quantity is collected sufficient to be worth the carriage to Liverpool. When the lobsters or crabs are taken, a peg is driven into the moveable joints of each of the large claws, to prevent them from tearing and devouring each other when in confinement. On the English coasts the fishermen usually tie the claws with pieces of hemp. In the preserving pots they are kept without any food, and consequently are better or worse in quality, according to the time they have been immured. – The *sea craw-fish*, cancer homarus of Linnaeus, are frequently found on the coast of Bardsey, and are caught in the same manner as the lobsters. They grow to a larger size then the lobster, and are usually sold at the same rate.

The *oyster-beds* on the Welsh coast lie in eight or more fathoms of water. In the straits of Menai, previous to 1700, it is said no oysters were to be found, but in that year some person threw in about a hundred, which have since so far extended themselves, as perfectly to stock the whole of these coasts. The oysters are, as in England, taken by means of a *dredge*, an instrument about two yards wide, and composed of a net, distended by means of iron rings. The opening in front is of a triangular shape, and the base is a flat piece of iron, which scrapes the oysters from their beds. This dredge, which is of considerable weight, is lowered from the boat by means of a rope attached to the upper angle of the triangle. The boat is then rowed along, and the oysters, as they are scraped off, fall back into the bag of the net. In this operation some care is necessary to bring the boat from deeper into shallower water, as otherwise the net would throw out its contents, and all the labour would be lost.

The modes of taking *cockles* I shall relate nearly in the words of Mr. Jones. The places of these shell-fish are marked in the sands uncovered with water by the depressed spots that they make in opening their shells; but when the fishermen search for them in the shallows, where they lie on the surface of the sand, the eye is directed to the object by a shining line about this size ─────, refracted through the water. The substance that forms this is perfectly clear and very tough, so as not, indeed, to yield to any pressure made by the finger. It is easily removed from the animal by the finger and thumb. The reflection that proceeds from this body is called in Welsh *arlwydd*, the sign or signal: it is not to be seen but during the sunshine; and if a person stands betwixt it and the sun, it is then nearly impossible to discern even the shell of the cockle. The cockles are picked up with the fingers, then put into a basket, and soused in the water till all the sand is completely washed from them. Where they are in tolerable plenty, instead of the men groping for them in the sand, with the fingers, they are dug up, and, along with the sand, put into a basket, and immersed as before.

Curiosity induces many persons to visit this island almost every summer; but the grandest sight the present inhabitants ever witnessed, was at a visit of the proprietor, lord Newborough, about eight years ago, accompanied by lady Newborough,* and several persons of distinction, in the whole to the number of about forty. This company embarked in fishing smacks from Porthor, near Carreg Hall, in the parish of Aberdaron. On their arrival in the island, marquees were immediately pitched. The whole company dined in the open air; and, at the conclusion of their repast, all the inhabitants were assembled. The ensuing scene reminded a gentleman of my acquaintance, who was present, of what he had read respecting the inhabitants of some of the South-Sea islands. They were drawn up into a circle, and lady Newborough adorned the heads of the females with caps and ribbons, whilst lord Newborough distributed hats among the men. The nominal king and queen of the island were distinguished from the rest by an additional ribbon. Part of the day was occupied in strolling over the island, examining the creeks, and picking up shells; and the rest was spent in mirth and pleasantry. On the embarkation it was intended, being in the heat of summer, that the whole party should continue in the island till the next day. The ladies, however, in the evening suddenly changed their resolution, and judiciously ordered the boats to be got ready. The rest of the company followed so good an example, and the night was spent, under the hospitable roof of Mr. Thomas of Carreg, much more agreeably than could have been done in the island.

HISTORY OF BARDSEY

The Welsh name of this place is *Ynys Enlli*. During the violent struggles between the Welsh and English, it was stiled by the poets the Sanctuary, or Asylum of the Saints, and it was sometimes denominated the Isle of Refuge. Some of these poets assert that it was the cemetery of *twenty thousand saints!* The reputed sanctity of this island induced the religious to resort to it from many very distant parts of the country.

It has been asserted by several writers that Roderic Moelwynog, prince of North Wales, first founded here a monastery some time in the eighth century. He might perhaps rebuild or enlarge it, but there are good grounds, from Welsh manuscripts, for supposing that there was a religious house in this island of a much more early date. St. Dubricius, (in Welsh Dyfrûg,) the archbishop of Caerleon on Usk, having resigned his see to St. David, is stated to have retired to Bardsey, with many of his clergy, from the synod of Brevi, which was holden in 522, in order to condemn the Pelagian heresy. Laudatus (Lleuddaf or Lleudad) was then abbot, who did not choose to appear at the above synod, and altogether neglected the summons. This retirement of Dubricius and his followers is mentioned principally by Aneurin, the monarch of the British bards, who himself was living at the same time.

There is an old legend yet extant, written in monkish Latin, which assures us that the Almighty had entered into a particular covenant with Laudatus, in return for the piety of his monks. This granted to all the religious of the monastery of Bardsey, the peculiar privilege of dying according to seniority, the oldest always going off first. By this privilege it is stated, that every one knew very nearly the time of his own departure. The following is a translation of it: – 'At the original foundation of the monastery of this island, the Lord God, who attendeth to the petitions of the just, at the earnest request of holy Laudatus, the first abbot, entered into a covenant with that holy man, and miraculously confirmed his promise, unto him and his successors, the abbots and monks, for ever, while they should continue to lead holy and religious lives, that they should die by succession, that is, that the oldest should go first, like a shock of corn ripe for the sickle. Being thus warned of the approach of death, each of them, therefore, should watch, as not knowing at what exact hour the thief might come; and, being thus always prepared, each of them by turns should lay aside his earthly form. God, who is ever faithful, kept this covenant, as he formerly did with the Israelites, inviolable, until the monks no longer led a religious life, but began to profane and defile God's sanctuary by their fornications and abominable crimes. Wherefore, after this, they were permitted to die like other men, sometimes the older, sometimes the younger, and sometimes the middle-aged first: and being thus uncertain of the approach of death, they were compelled to submit to the general laws of mortality. Thus, when they ceased to lead a holy and religious life, God's miraculous covenant also ceased: and do thou therefore, O God, have mercy upon us.'

The ancient building is now entirely destroyed; but, about the ground where the monastery stood, a great number of graves have even very lately been discovered, lined with white stone or tile, and distant about two feet from each other.

All the religious duties of the inhabitants are now performed in the parish church of Aberdaron. Sometimes, however, in stormy weather, they are under the necessity of interring their own dead in the island.

John Wynne ap Hugh, of the family of Bodvil, standard bearer at the battle of Norwich, in the time of Edward VI, had, for that service, the isle of Bardsey, and a mansion in the parish of Aberdaron, called Court. He was sheriff of Caernarvonshire in the year 1551.

After these observations on the island of Bardsey, I resume the narrative of my voyage to Pwllheli. The wind, as I have already observed, continued still boisterous; it was therefore necessary for us to be very cautious in the management of our little bark. We therefore held off from the Welsh coast for some distance, towards the south, that we might weather the eastern point of the extensive, but dreadful bay, called

HELL'S MOUTH.

I never saw a place which presented so favourable an appearance, and that was at the same time so much dreaded by the mariners, as the present. It is at the very extremity of the promontory, and from point to point is supposed to measure about eight miles: it is also nearly semicircular. None but strange vessels, even in the most boisterous weather, ever seek for shelter here, and when these are so unfortunate, they are soon stranded, and never again return. 'We remember (says Mr. Jones, in one of his letters) more misfortunes to have happened in this bay, and more inhumanity shewn to the sufferers, than we have ever heard of any where else on the Welsh coast.' My pilot, who had been long acquainted with every part of these coasts, informed me, that, from whatever point of the compass the wind blew, out at sea, on account of the surrounding high rocks, it always came into the mouth of this bay; and from whatever quarter the tide flowed, the upper current here always sets inwards! From these circumstances the common tradition is, that the place obtained the appellation of *Hell's Mouth*.

The whole coast, from the Rivals round the end of the land, nearly to Pwllheli, is terminated only by high and steep rocks, inhabited in the summer by a variety of sea-fowl. In one part I could observe some hundreds of martins flitting along the black cliffs and caverns in pursuit of flies and other insects for their young.

Passing the eastern point of Hell's Mouth, we kept as close to the wind as we could, and soon afterwards came in sight of St. Tudwal's, or, as they are usually called, *Studwal's Islands*, of which a considerable sum of money is annually made, as puffin warrens. After a difficult navigation of several hours from hence, on account of the wind blowing almost directly from the west, we at length sailed round the rock of Carreg, at the mouth of the harbour of Pwllheli, and came to anchor in the river just opposite to the town. This was about eight o'clock in the evening of our third day.

From Pwllheli I chose the next morning to make a short passage back, by crossing over the land to Clynog, and walking from thence to Caernarvon. This journey I performed in about five hours. The cutter did not arrive till two days afterwards.

22

Excursion from Caernarvon, by Capel Curig, to Llanrwst; and from thence, by the Vale of Ffestiniog, and Tanybwlch again to Caernarvon

Accompanied by my worthy friend the rector of Llanrûg,* I went from Caernarvon, by way of Nant Frangon and Capel Curig, to Llanrwst.

THE VALE OF CAPEL CURIG

(For I have described all the former part of our route in a previous chapter) is bounded by the British Alps, Snowdon and his adjacent mountains, and affords some of the most picturesque landscape of the whole country.

> Here hills and vales, the woodland and the plain;
> Here earth and water seem to strive again:
> Not chaos-like, together crush'd and bruis'd,
> But, as the world, harmoniously confus'd.*

In this vale, there is that variety both of wood and water, which most of the other Welsh vales so much want to add to their picturesque effect. Here are two tolerably large pools. Near one of these lord Penrhyn has erected, from a design of Mr. Benjamin Wyatt, a small, but very comfortable

INN.

Those tourists who, like myself, have visited this vale a few years ago, when the only place of public accommodation was a mean pot-house, considerably allied to those at Llanberis, and who shall now visit it with the present accommodations, (with which for a mountain country, I was greatly surprized,) will be able with some justice to appreciate the spirited conduct, and truly patriotic exertions of the noble proprietor, who has not only constructed for them an inn, but who was the first to make this part of the country passable in carriages.* – In the inn a book is kept, in which such persons as express themselves satisfied with the treatment insert their names. Among other curious entries, I found the following, with the date of August 3, 1801:

> Heathcote, Impey, and Drake,
> For formality's sake,
> All due commendation bestowing
> On the drinking and eating,
> They had at this neat inn,
> Subscribe to the praises foregoing.

The name of the vale is derived from its chapel, dedicated to a Welsh saint called Curig. He is mentioned in an old Welsh poem, which, however, only intimates his order; and nothing more is at present known of him.

> A certain friar to increase his store,
> Beneath his cloak, *grey Curig's* image bore;
> And to protect good folks from nightly harm,
> Another sells St. Seiriol as a charm.*

When we left Capel Curig, we proceeded about two miles on the road to Llanrwst, and then leaving it, went about three miles southward to see

DOLWYDDELAN CASTLE,

A fortress, some centuries ago, of considerable importance to the Welsh princes. Its mountainous situation rendered it difficult to find, and it was not till after numerous inquiries that we could get into the track that led us immediately up to it.

This castle stands on a rocky steep, nearly perpendicular on one side, and in a vale entirely closed round by mountains. The original import of the name seems to have been the castle in *the meadow of Helen's wood*; for the ancient military road called Sarn Helen, or *Helen's Road*, from Helen,* the daughter of Octavius, duke of Cornwall, passed through the country not far from hence, to the sea-coast of Merionethshire. – It has never been a large building, but it occupied the entire summit of its mount. It formerly consisted of two square towers, each three stories high, having but one room on a floor, and a court-yard, which was betwixt them. The largest of these towers measures within no more than twenty-seven feet in length, and eighteen in width, and the walls are about six feet thick. The walls of the court are entirely destroyed, and very little is now left of the other parts of the building.

HISTORY OF DOLWYDDELAN CASTLE

Who the founder of this fortress was, or what purpose it was originally intended to answer, we have not at this time any documents left to inform us. Most probably, when the feudal system prevailed in Wales, and petty chieftains were engaged in perpetual wars with each other, Dolwyddelan castle, and others similar to it, may have been erected by some of them as places of retreat and refuge, where they could reside in security, attended by their vassals and adherents, in case they should be compelled by superior force to relinquish the plains and more cultivated parts of the country. These castles also answered the double purpose of guarding the passes and defiles of the mountains.

It is a conjecture of Rowlands, that this castle was erected prior to the sixth century. What his grounds for this supposition are, he does not state.

This place was, for many years, the residence of the eldest son of Owen Gwynedd, Iorwerth Drwndwn, or *Edward with the broken nose*. On the death of his father, Iorwerth claimed the crown of Wales as his hereditary right, but was unanimously rejected, and merely from the blemish in his face: so whimsical and indecisive was, at that time, the mode of succession to the Welsh throne. He had, assigned to him, as part of his parental inheritance, the hundreds of Nan Conwy and Ardudwy, and he retired to this sequestered spot to spend the rest of his life. It was in Dolwyddelan castle that his son was born, who afterwards, in the beginning of the thirteenth century, reigned in Wales under the title of Llewelyn the great.

Meredith, the son of Jevan ap Robert,* who has already been mentioned at considerable length, in the account of the promontory of Llŷn, purchased the lease of this castle, and of the inclosures belonging to it, in the reign of Henry VII. It was at that time the property of the executors of sir Ralph Berkenet, late chamberlain of North Wales, having been excepted among those places that had been granted by Richard III and resumed by his successor.

About this period the whole of the surrounding country, was one entire forest overrun with thieves and outlaws. The castle had itself been previously possessed by Howell, ap Evan, ap Rhys Gethin, one of the most noted of these, against whom David ap Jenkin,* whom I have also had occasion to mention before, rose in arms. David, who was likewise an outlaw, contended with him long for the sovereignty of the mountains, and at length, by stratagem, took him in bed, but spared his life, on condition that he should immediately seek refuge in Ireland. In that country he scarcely remained a year, but returned in the ensuing summer with some select adherents. He clothed himself and his followers entirely in green, that they might be the less distinguishable among the forests, and in this disguise, appearing abroad only in the nights, they committed the most dreadful depredations.

The friends of Meredith ap Jevan were greatly surprised that he should think of changing his habitation near Penmorfa, for this castle thus surrounded by multitudes of freebooters. He gave, as a decisive reason, that he chose rather to fight with outlaws and thieves, than with his own immediate relatives. 'If (says he) I live in my own house in Evionedd, I must either kill my own kinsmen, or submit to be murdered by them.' – He had not been here long before he built the house at Penanmen, and removed the church from the thicket in which it formerly stood, to its present more open situation: the church, his house and the castle, thus forming the points of a triangle, each a mile distant from the other. Whenever he went to the church, he took with him, as a guard, twenty stout archers; and he had a centinel placed on a neighbouring rock called Carreg y Big (from whence the church, the house, and the castle, could be seen), who had orders to give immediate notice of the approach of banditti. He never mentioned before-hand when he intended to go out, and always went and returned by different routes through unsuspected parts of the woods. He found it necessary, to his perfect security, to increase the number of his adherents; he therefore established colonies of the most tall and able men he could procure, occupying every tenement, as it became empty, with such tenants only as were able to bear arms. His force, when complete, consisted of a hundred and forty archers, ready to assemble, whenever the sound of the bugle from the castle echoed through the woods, to call for their assistance. These, says sir John Wynne, were each arranged in a 'jacket, or armolet coate, a good steele cap, a short sword and dagger, together with a bow and arrows. Many of them had also horses and chafing staves, which were ready to answer the crie on all occasions, whereby he grew soe strong that he began to put back, and to curb the sanctuary of thieves and robbers, which, at times, were wont to be above a hundred, well horsed and well appointed.'*

Such was the state of Wales in these unhappy times, when every one claimed by a kind of prescriptive right, whatever he had power to seize; and when lives or property were considered of no other value than interest or ambition chose to dictate. Meredith ap Jevan, to enjoy a quiet life, threw himself into the bosom of a country infested with outlaws and murderers, and, comparatively with the state of society about his former residence near Penmorfa, attained his end. He closed his useful life in the year 1525, leaving to survive him twenty-three legitimate, and three natural children.

DOLWYDDELAN

The village of Dolwyddelan is about a mile from the castle, and, from its mountainous situation, it is altogether secluded from the world. Its inhabitants seemed extremely simple, and in their manners, they exhibited signs of great shyness and timidity, probably, however, arising from the unaccustomed appearance of strangers among them. None of them are acquainted with any other language than that of their country: and hemmed in as they are with mountain barriers, it is very probable that three fourths of them never in their lives wandered half a dozen miles from their dwellings. – The village itself is composed of little else than small cottages; for I could only observe one house of any tolerable size in the place.

PONT Y PAIR

We left Dolwyddelan, and came into our former road near Pont y Pair, *the Bridge of the Cauldron*, a singular structure of five arches, not far from the village of Bettws y Coed, *the Station in the Wood*. This bridge, whose arches are irregular and very lofty, is built over the river Llugwy, and has, with the adjoining scenery, a very singular effect. Both above and below it, the bed of the river is covered with such strange masses of rock, as, when the quantity of water is considerable, to exhibit a most pleasing and picturesque scene.

From Pont y Pair, we returned for about a mile, along the road leading towards Capel Curig. Then leaving it three or four hundred yards to the left, and passing over some meadows, we came to the celebrated

WATERFALL OF THE RIVER LLUGWY,

called Rhaiadr y Wenol, *the Cataract of the Swallow*. This fall and the scenery around it, are altogether grand. – The water is thrown in a sheet from above, down a rock nearly perpendicular; but below, its course is changed, by its direction over a smooth and slanting bed. The high and wooded banks were enlivened by the various tints of the oaks, birch and hazels, which hung from the rocks. Had there been more water in the river, we should have seen this cataract to greater advantage than we now did, but the dry weather had diminished all the mountain streams to mere rills. The station on the side of the stream opposite to that on which we stood appeared as if it would take in more of the fall: I made several attempts to get across, but from the rapidity of the current I found it impossible. When the river, after a heavy fall of rain, assumes a more impetuous form than at this time, the cataract must certainly be very grand, as the bed of the stream is at least twenty yards wide; and the innumerable masses of rock, which have at different times been carried along with it, and lodged here, opposing its fury, must throw it foaming into all directions.

At a little distance below the bridge Pont y Pair, the rivers Llugwy and Conwy unite. The latter rises from *Llyn Conwy*, a large pool about three miles beyond the village of Penmachno. Both these streams before their junction, are furious and broken torrents, they are each a truly 'foaming flood,' but from hence they assume a placid form, and glide, in one tranquil current, silently through the vale.

We stopped a while at Bettws y Coed, to see an ancient monument in the church, in memory of Griffith the son of David Goch, who was a natural son of David, brother to Llewelyn, the last prince of Wales. He died in the fourteenth century, and is here represented by a large armed recumbent figure in a recess in the north wall. On one side of the figure, there is yet left this inscription: *'Hic jacet Gruffydd ap Davyd Goch, agnus Dei misere me.'*

VALE OF LLANRWST

The road now led us into the luxuriant vale of Llanrwst, where the gay tints of cultivation once more beautified the landscape, for the fields were coloured with the rich hues of ripened corn and green meadows. Many gentlemen's seats interspersed around, gave an air of civilization to this valley. We had not enjoyed the beauties of this prospect long, before we entered the gloomy woods of *Gwydir*, which afforded a fine contrast to the luxuriance of the vale. The Conwy runs at a little distance from the road, and the silvery reflection of its water through the dark foliage of the trees, gave an additional interest to the scene. On emerging from hence, we had again the same open vale, in which the town of Llanrwst, now before us, formed a conspicuous feature; and the extensive landscape, thus completed, heightened by the dreary rocks, bounding it on each side, has been justly admired by all the lovers of nature, as one of the finest scenes her pencil ever traced.

GWYDIR

About a quarter of a mile from Llanrwst, we passed by Gwydir, the old family residence of the Wynnes. This mansion was erected about the year 1558, by John Wynne ap Meredith, as appears by the date and initials over the gateway. It is an extensive but irregular building. The name is supposed to be derived from the Welsh words Gwy, *water*, and Tir, *land*; part of the grounds being subject to the overflowings of the river.*

At a little distance, among the woods above this mansion, was *Upper Guydir*, a house erected by sir John Wynne, in 1604, apparently for the purpose of enjoying from thence the numerous beauties of the vale, which is here seen in a broad and elegant expanse, nearly as far as Conwy. The house was taken down some time ago, but the family chapel is still left. This is a small building in the gothic stile, sufficiently neat on the outside, but the roof and various other parts within, are decorated with paintings of scriptural figures, most miserably executed.

Both these places are at present the property of lord Gwydir, in right of his lady Priscilla, baroness Willoughby, the eldest sister of Robert late duke of Ancaster. They passed into this family in the year 1678, by the marriage of Mary, daughter and heiress of sir Richard Wynne, with Robert, marquis of Lindsey.

LLANRWST BRIDGE

Betwixt Gwydir and Llanrwst, is the celebrated bridge over the river Conwy, constructed by Inigo Jones.* This bridge was directed to be built by an order from the privy council, in the ninth year of the reign of Charles I. The expences, which were estimated at a thousand pounds, were paid by the two counties of Denbigh and Caernarvon. It consists of three arches, the middle one of which is near sixty feet wide. One of the other two has been rebuilt since Jones's time, and the inferiority of the workmanship is very visible. The inhabitants of Llanrwst *boast*, that their bridge is formed on such nice principles, that if a person thrusts against the large stone, over the centre of the middle arch, the whole fabric may plainly be felt to vibrate: though one cannot from conviction be inclined to concur with them in this assertion, yet allowing it true, would not the bridge have been better built, if it was entirely firm? So many persons have tried the experiment, that the stone is now become quite loose. We attempted it, but except that stone, found the whole bridge as firm as a rock.

THE TOWN OF LLANRWST

Is finely situated on the eastern bank of the Conwy. In itself, it has nothing to recommend it to notice: the streets are narrow, and the houses very irregular.

THE CHURCH

Is a plain, ill-looking structure; but adjoining to it is a *chapel*, built in 1633, by sir Richard Wynne, from a design of Inigo Jones, which has a considerable degree of elegance.

Against the wall of the chapel, there are five brasses, four of them engraved by Sylvanus Crew,* and one by William Vaughan, that are remarkable for the excellence of their execution. Each of these, besides an inscription, contains a portrait of the person to whose memory it was finished. They are the work of the seventeenth century. That on Sarah Wynne, by Vaughan,* is much superior to the rest.

The carved work of the roof of the chapel is said to have been brought from the neighbouring *Abbey of Maenan*.* – Into this chapel has lately been removed, an ancient monument of Hoel Coytmor, which lay before among the rubbish, under the stairs leading into the gallery of the church. It is an armed recumbent figure, with the feet resting on a lion. The inscription upon it is: *'Hic jacet Hoel Coytmor ap Gruff. Vychan ap Gruff. Amn.'* Hoel Coytmor possessed the estates of Gwydir, which were sold by his son David, to Meredith ap Jevan, Welsh nephew, or first cousin once removed to the renowned John ap Meredith, and ancestor to the Wynnes of Gwydir. Hoel was the grandson of David Goch of Penmachno, whose monument we had just seen in the church of Bettws.

Near this monument is placed a large stone coffin, supposed to have been that of Llewelyn ap Iorwerth, denominated from his valiant actions, Llewelyn the great. He was interred in the abbey of Conwy, in the year 1240, but after the dissolution of abbies in the reign of Henry VIII as appears from a brass plate affixed to it, this coffin was removed thence to this place, where it has ever since remained.

Besides these, there are no other monuments in this chapel worth notice, except one, which bears the following singularly long and curious inscription, containing a pedigree of the Wynne family from Owen Gwynedd, prince of Wales, to sir Richard Wynne, who died about the middle of the seventeenth century.

***

The river Conwy runs close past the church-yard of Llanrwst, from whence there is a fine prospect of the bridge, and the high woods of Gwydir behind it. In this river salmon are frequently taken, and in the months of February and March, great numbers of smelts. The tide reaches no farther than to the village of *Trefriw*, about a mile and a half from Llanrwst, to which place only the river is navigable.

In the fifteen years of civil discord during the insurrection of Owen Glyndwr, such were the ravages committed in these parts of Wales, that this place was so entirely forsaken by its inhabitants, that grass grew in the market place, and the deer from the mountains fled for refuge into the church-yard.

INN

The Eagles Inn at Llanrwst, the only one where post horses are kept, is in general found a very comfortable house; but during the summer season it is often so crowded by company, as to render it very unpleasant to the wearied tourist. From this house guides may be had to accompany the traveller to any of the curiosities of the neighbourhood.

About five miles from Llanrwst, leaving the road to Penmachno on the right, we passed over some fields, to see a small *waterfall on the river Conwy*. Its height is not very considerable, being only twelve or fourteen yards. The scene was clad with wood, and the bed of the river excessively rugged.

Somewhat more than half a mile beyond this, we stopped at a fulling mill, near a bridge called Pont y Pandy, *the bridge of the fulling mill*. Here is a

CATARACT

Called *Rhaiadr y Craig Llwyd*, truly romantic and picturesque. It is not very lofty, and the river, from want of water when we were here, flowed in two streams, but the black and rugged rock that separated them, rendered the scene, though not perhaps quite so tremendous, yet much more beautiful than if the whole had been concealed by the water. The high banks on each side are ornamented with pendent shrubs, and a mill, and rude wooden aqueduct (which conveys water to an old overshot wheel), overgrown with mosses and grass, completed this elegant landscape. The descent to the bottom was steep and difficult, but my trouble in scrambling down was well repaid in seeing the fall to much greater advantage than from above. From hence it seemed increased in height, and many of the prominent and pointed rocks, before hidden, came, from this situation, into the view.

The river accompanies the road to some distance beyond this waterfall. Where they parted we left the road, and wandered along the banks of the stream for some time, till we came to a most wild scene of wooded and projecting rocks, overhanging the black and dismal torrent. A grassy ledge on the opposite side, at some height above the water, reminded me very forcibly of the scene where Gray has placed his bard; and all the accompanying features were well suited to such a scene.

> High on a rock, whose haughty brow
> Frowns o'er old Conwy's foaming flood,
> Rob'd in the sable garb of woe,
> With haggard eyes, the poet stood
> (Loose his beard, and hoary hair
> Stream'd like a meteor to the troubled air),
> And with a master's hand, and prophet's fire,
> Struck the deep sorrows of his lyre.*

From hence we returned to the road, and proceeded onwards over a mountainous, though not either very romantic or interesting country, till we reached Penmachno, *The Head of the Machno*, a village singular in its appearance, the houses being built almost in a circle round the church.

At the distance of about four miles from Penmachno, in the road leading from thence to Corwen, is *Yspytty Evan*, now a small village, but so called, it has been conjectured, from its having formerly contained a house belonging to the knights hospitallers, or knights of St. John of Jerusalem.* This had the privilege of a sanctuary, and the place of course became a receptacle for thieves and murderers. It was, says sir John Wynne, 'a wasp's nest, which troubled the whole country, – a sanctuary of robbers, which at times were wont to be above a hundred, well horsed and well appointed.' Being here beyond the reach of invaders, the place was always fully peopled; and extending their plundering excursions on all sides to the distance of twenty or thirty miles, they rendered themselves the terror of the adjacent country. Such were indeed the ravages they committed, that nearly all the inhabitants of the neighbourhood were driven to seek for refuge and security beyond their reach.

From Penmachno, for we did not think it worth our while to visit Yspytty Evan, we continued our journey, over a still mountainous but dreary country, till we came to the village of

FFESTINIOG,

The Place of Hastening. This little place, and the vale near it, have been justly celebrated by the elegant pen of lord Lyttleton, who made a tour through Wales in the year 1756.*

It happened to be during a fair when we were here, and as we chose to suffer any inconvenience rather than be pestered with the vociferous curiosity of a set of drunken fellows, we were taken from the inn into an adjoining building, and shewn up stairs into a bed-room, even worse than that I had slept in at Beddgelert. After we had satiated our thirst as well as we could with what was called brandy and water, but which might indeed have been as easily mistaken for burgundy as brandy, we went by a foot-path which passes through the field, opposite to the end of the house, to see the

FALLS OF THE CYNFAEL.

These are situated, the one about three hundred yards above, and the other three hundred yards below a rustic stone bridge over the river, to which the path led us. – The upper cataract consists of three steeps, over which the water foams into a deep black bason, shadowed by the adjoining rocks. – The other, which I think nearly as beautiful as this, is formed by a broad sheet of water, precipitated down a slightly shelving rock, about forty feet high, and darkened by the foliage around it, which closes in almost to the edge of the stream. After the water has reached the bottom of the deep concavity, it rushes along a narrow rocky chasm; then

> Raging still amid the shaggy rocks,
> Now flashes o'er the scatter'd fragments, now
> Aslant the hollow channel rapid darts,
> And falling fast from gradual slope to slope,
> With wild infracted course and lessen'd roar,
> It gains a safer bed, and steals, at last,
> Along the mazes of the quiet vale.*

Betwixt this cataract and the bridge there is a tall columnar rock, which stands in the bed of the river, called *Pulpit Hugh Lloyd Cynfael*, or Hugh Lloyd's pulpit, the place from whence, the peasantry say, a magician of that name used to deliver his nightly incantations.

***

THE VALE OF FFESTINIOG

From the village of Ffestiniog we descended into Cwm Maentwrog, *The Vale of Maentwrog*, (improperly called by tourists the vale of Ffestiniog,) and wandered leisurely along, enjoying all the way the most sublime pleasure in contemplating the beauties of the scene before us. There are few vales in this country that afford such lovely prospects as this. Many of the high mountains bounding its sides are shaded with lofty oaks; and the silver Dwyryd, *Two Fords*, serpentizes placidly and silently along the bottom, amidst the richest cultivation. The sea, at a distance, closes the view; and Traeth Bach, a wide arm of it, is seen to receive the Dwyryd, a little below Tanybwlch hall, which is situated on a rising ground, and embowered in woods, at the north-west extremity of the vale. The little village of Maentwrog, from whence it takes its name, is seated nearly in the middle. The character of the vale of Ffestiniog is very different from that either of Llanberis or Nant Hwynan: the former is majestic, grand, and sublime; Nant Hwynan bears a middle character, its bottom is varied by insulated rocks, and clad with trees; this is simply elegant, and principally affords charms to the admirer of nature in her most chaste and delicate attire. The bottom is open, and cultivated from end to end, with trees scattered along the walls and hedge-rows. The thick woods on the mountains on the north-side soften very beautifully what would be otherwise a bleak and dreary feature in the scene. 'With the woman one loves, with the friend of one's heart, and a good study of books, (says lord Lyttleton to his friend Mr. Bower,) one might pass an age in this vale, and think it a day. If you have a mind to live long, and renew your youth, come with Mrs. Bower, and settle at Ffestiniog. Not long ago there died in that neighbourhood an honest Welsh farmer, who was 105 years of age. By his first wife he had *thirty* children, *ten* by his second, *four* by his third, and *seven* by two concubines: his youngest son was *eighty-one* years younger than his eldest; and 800 persons, descended from his body, attended his funeral.'

I can add another instance of age and fecundity in this vale, which, though far short of this in point of numbers, is still sufficiently great to prove the healthiness of the place. Jane Price, who died in the year 1694, had at the time of her death *twelve* children, *forty-seven* grand-children, and *thirteen* great grand-children.

We ascended, along with the road, the mountains forming the northern boundary of the vale, on the heights of which stand Tanybwlch inn. Here we dined, and from hence we went the same evening, through Beddgelert, again to Caernarvon.

23

Caernarvon, through Beddgelert, to Harlech

Having remained at Caernarvon a length of time fully sufficient to enable me to visit and examine all the places worth notice within a circle of about thirty miles on every side of it, I now proceeded towards Beddgelert and Harlech, in my journey to the other parts of North Wales. – The road to Beddgelert, together with the scenery around that place, have already been described. I shall therefore, in this chapter, suppose myself proceeding southwards, immediately from

PONT ABERGLASLLYN.

From this celebrated bridge there are two roads to Tanybwlch, the low or *new road*, and the *mountain road*, the former of which occupies about ten, and the latter eight miles. Till within the last two years, carriages were usually taken along the mountain-road, a series of rocky steeps, which were considered so dangerous, that most persons preferred walking for at least five of the eight miles: and several people, to avoid it, have even gone more than forty miles round. For about two miles, this romantic, though rude way, commands several beautiful and extended prospects. From one very elevated situation, I had in my former journey a most delightful view of all the fine and mountainous country around me: Harlech and Criccieth castles were both in sight, and the long extent of ground forming the promontory of Llŷn, was visible even to its extremity.

Beyond the bridge, on the *new road*, which is formed through the more flat and level country towards the sands, the varied scene of wood, rock, and mountain, is uncommonly fine. In some situations the view is confined to the immediately surrounding rocks, whilst in others the eye wanders over a vast expanse of mountains. On one elevation I observed no fewer than six ranges of mountain, one above another, the uppermost at a great distance. I passed on the left two conspicuous and conical summits called *Moelwyn*. This road is on the whole so exceedingly good, as to render it passable in carriages with great pleasure, for the country nearly all the way is very interesting.

TANYBWLCH,

Below the Pass, so called from its being situated on the brow of the hill overlooking the *Vale of Ffestiniog*, or more properly of Maentwrog, consists only of a small but comfortable inn, and an elegant mansion embowered in woods, the property of ——— Oakley, esq. – This vale, watered by the little river Dwyryd, which meanders along its bosom, contrasted with the bleak and dreary mountains on the opposite side, from hence affords a most pleasing prospect. A former traveller was so highly gratified with the scene, as to make the singular remark, 'That if a person could live upon a landscape, he would scarcely desire a more eligible spot than this.'*

The *inn* is a small but good house, occupied by a very civil, attentive, and obliging man of the name of Cartwright. A post-chaise and four horses are kept here.

On the other side of the vale stands the church of Maentwrog, *The Stone of Twrog*, so denominated from a large stone in the church-yard, at the north-west corner of the church. Twrog was a British saint, who lived about the year 610, and was the writer of Tiboeth, a romantic record belonging to St. Beuno, that was formerly kept in the church of Clynog in Caernarvonshire. – Dr. Edmund Prys, archdeacon of Merioneth, who attained considerable celebrity as a Welsh poet, was rector of this place, and is said to have been buried here. I searched both the church and church-yard in vain for some memorial of him, and in my hopes of obtaining intelligence respecting him from the inhabitants I was also disappointed.

I left Maentwrog, and inquiring the road to Harlech, proceeded on my journey. At the distance of about half a mile, I crossed a small bridge. From hence, leaving the road for a while, I wandered along a foot-path up a wooded valley, for about a mile and a half, in search of a

WATERFALL

That had been described to me, called Rhaiadr Dû, *The Black Cataract*. It was not without some difficulty, and after much trouble in ascending and descending the sides of the hills, that I found it. In this cataract, which is surrounded with dark and impending scenery, the water is thrown with vast impetuosity over three black and smooth rocks, each in a different direction. Of its height I could form no idea, for the top of the upper fall, by the winding of the rocks, was not visible from below. The rock that hangs immediately over the fall, was, from its great height and rude form, a fine object in the landscape; and the whole of the hollow, to some distance below the cataract, was extremely grand. I attempted to climb to the upper part, but the rocks were too perpendicular, and too slippery, to suffer the attempt without danger. Therefore contenting myself with seeing as much as I could from below, I crossed the water, and crept along, but not without difficulty, on the shelving rocks, by the side of the stream, for near half a mile. Here the banks closed over my head, leaving but a narrow chasm, from which the light was altogether excluded by the dark foliage from each side, and I found myself entering, to appearance, the mouth of a deep and horrid cavern. The sides were too steep for me to entertain any idea of clambering up, and unless I chose to scramble back again to the cataract, I had no alternative but to penetrate the place. The darkness, fortunately, did not extend far, and I soon found myself in a place where the bank was sufficiently sloping to admit of my ascending to the meadows above; I was not a little pleased in having thus easily escaped from this abode of horror.

Regaining the road I had left, it led me along the side of Llyntecwyn Ucha, *The Upper Pool of Tecwyn*, where I found the scenery pleasant, though less mountainous than what I had passed. This pool is larger than many of those in Wales, and its waters are beautifully clear. On one side there is a range of low rocks, composed of a shivery kind of slate, which had mouldered in many places to the bottom, in small sharp pieces, almost resembling needles.

Afterwards passing the village of Llantecwyn, and Llyntecwyn Isa, *The Lower Tecwyn Pool*, I came to a most lovely little meadowy vale, about three miles distant from Harlech, called (if I understood the guide right) *Dol Orcal*. After the late uncouth scenery, I here enjoyed in the utmost the pleasing effect of the green woods and meads of the vale, and the purple heath which concealed and softened the harsh colouring of the adjacent rocks.

The whole of the walk from Beddgelert to Harlech I found exceedingly pleasant. From the continual varying of the scenery, the attention was fully occupied during every part of the journey. – The road from Tanybwlch is scarcely passable for carriages, but there is another from Beddgelert, at the ebb of the tide, over the sands: a guide, however, must be taken who is acquainted with the track, as it is very unsafe for strangers to venture alone.

HARLECH,

Once the principal town in Merionethshire, is now dwindled into an insignificant village, containing not more than four or five hundred inhabitants. It is in the parish of Llanfair, and on the sea-coast, near Cardigan Bay: the houses and castle are built on a cliff that immediately overhangs the marsh. Not far from the castle, there is an old roofless building, once the town-hall; in which, however, the members of parliament for the county continue still to be elected.

HARLECH CASTLE

This venerable structure is in tolerable preservation. It is a square building, each side measuring about seventy yards; and has at every corner a round tower. From each of these issued formerly a circular turret; nearly all now destroyed. The entrance is betwixt two great rounders. The principal apartments appear to have been over the gate-way, in a building which projected into the court; and at each angle of this building there is yet left a round tower. The castle was defended on the east side by a deep foss; and its situation, on the verge of an almost perpendicular rock, rendered it impregnable in nearly every other part. – From the marsh it is said, except in size, to bear a considerable resemblance to the castle of Belgrade in Turkey.

Fig. 9. *Harlech Castle*, Merionethshire (Gwynedd), engraving after drawing by William Bingley in 1798.

On the evening that I arrived at Harlech, the atmosphere was so perfectly clear, that I could very plainly distinguish the peaked summit of Snowdon, elevated high above all the other mountains. The promontory of Llŷn was visible in almost every part; Criccieth castle seemed scarcely a mile distant; and the fine, though dangerous bay of Cardigan, lay entirely before me.

***

MEPHITIC VAPOUR

In the winter of 1694, this neighbourhood was much alarmed by a kind of fiery exhalation, which came from a sandy and marshy tract of land, called Morfa Bychan, *The Little Marsh*, across the channel eight miles towards Harlech. This injured much of the grass in such a manner as to kill the cattle; and it set hay and corn-ricks on fire for near a mile from the coast. It is represented to have had the appearance of a blue lambent flame, which by any great noise, such as the firing of guns, or the sounding of horns, was easily extinguished. All the damage was invariably done in the night; and, in the course of the winter, no fewer than sixteen hay-ricks, and two barns, one filled with hay, and other with corn, were entirely destroyed by it. It did not seem to affect any thing else, and men could go into it without receiving the least injury. It was observed much more frequently during the first three weeks than afterwards, yet it was seen, at different intervals, for at least eight months. The occasion of this singular phenomenon is not exactly known. It appears most probably to have arisen from some collections of putrid substances, the vapour coming from which might have been directed towards this place by the wind; and yet it is singular that, although the prevailing winds here are from the south-west, which ought to have blown it in a very different direction, it should not have been observed in other parts north of Harlech. Bishop Gibson conjectured that it might have proceeded from the corrupted bodies of a great quantity of locusts which visited this kingdom about that time and were destroyed by the coldness of the climate. He says that a considerable number of them had been seen lying about the shores of Aberdaron, in Caernarvonshire.*

The *public house* at Harlech, for such it can only be denominated, is kept by a very civil man of the name of Anwyl. The provisions, at the time I was here, were homely, but the beds (only two, and those in the same room) were clean and comfortable. – The tourist, in inquiring for a *guide*, will find it worth his while to ask particularly for John Richards, a man who speaks English fluently, is well acquainted with the neighbourhood, and, for his situation, has a very superior understanding.

24

Excursion from Harlech to Cwm Bychan

Conducted by Richards as my guide, I went from Harlech to explore an obscure vale, about four miles distant, called Cwm Bychan, *The Little Hollow*.

About a mile from the town, on a large elevated moor, he pointed out to me a circle of small stones near thirty yards in diameter, with another at some distance, surrounding it. From its form and appearance, I am inclined to suppose that this was one of those

DRUIDICAL CIRCLES

In which were formerly holden the *Gorseddau*, or bardic meetings. These meetings were always in some place set apart in the open air, in a conspicuous situation, and surrounded by a circle of stones, having in the centre a larger one, by which the presiding bard or druid stood. There was here no relic of the middle stone. This kind of circle was called *Cylch Cyngrair*, or the circle of congress. At these meetings, candidates were admitted to the different degrees of bardism, and on these occasions it was that all the oral bardic poems and traditions were recited, and their laws settled. During these ceremonies all the bards stood within the circle, with their heads and feet bare, and clad in their uni-coloured robes.

CWM BYCHAN

Is a grassy dell, about half a mile in length, surrounded by scenery as black and dreary as imagination can draw. On the right of its entrance there is a small pool called *Llyn y Cwm Bychan*, from whose edge, Carreg y Saeth, *The Rock of the Arrow*, (from its being the station where the ancient British sportsmen watched and killed the passing deer,) towers the blackest of all the vale. – I rested myself for a while on a rock above the pool, in a situation whence I could at ease observe the rugged beauties of this romantic hollow. From hence the landscape extended in all its magnificence: the vale was seen embosomed in stupendous rocks, black and barren, and enlivened only by the patches of meagre vegetation lodged on their shelving precipices.

We descended into the hollow, and passing there an ancient mansion, ascended on the other side till we came to a deep mountain hollow called

BWLCH TYDDIAD.

Here the rocks close, and oppose a series of shattered precipices, forming a scene of desolation and barrenness throughout. A few grasses, liverwort, and heath, constitute all the vegetation of this place. We wandered on this rocky cleft, for such it only seemed, till we got beyond the higher mountains, when, on a sudden, a fine open prospect of all the country eastward was extended before us. Here we were treated with a pastoral landscape, bounded by high distant mountains, which formed a majestic barrier around: amongst these, Cader Idris, and the two Arrenigs, were particularly conspicuous.

DRWS ARDUDWY

From hence we made a turn to the right, still continuing our journey over a wretched horse-path, and soon afterwards turning again to the right, we entered another deep glen called Drws Ardudwy, *The Pass of the Maritime Land*, a place well calculated to inspire a timid mind with terror. The sides and bottom were almost covered over with loose fragments of stone, once detached by the force of frost, or the irresistible rushing of torrents, after storms and heavy rain, from the heights above. The fear for personal safety must sometimes, in places similar to this, be accompanied with a tremor; for the mind is not always able to divest itself of prejudices, and disagreeable associations of ideas, and, in spite of every effort of reason and judgment, the unpleasing sensations of terror will sometimes affect us.

After this dreary scene, we entered a more wide and fertile valley, called Cwm Nancoll, *The Hollow of the sunken Brook*. From hence the guide took me, out of the usual track, to see a *cromlech*, in a farm called Gwern Einion. This cromlech is about two miles south of Harlech. It is at present made to form the corner of a wall, and is, on two sides, built up with stones, to prevent the sheep from getting through. There are six supporters, three about six feet, and the other three about four feet in height. The stone that rests upon these is large, flat, and slanting.

CATARACT

A little while before we came to this cromlech, I heard, from the side of the hill on which we were walking, the falling of water in a wood on the opposite mountains, and apparently about half a mile from us. I could also, notwithstanding the distance, plainly perceive a silver line among the trees, formed by the rushing of water down a precipice. The guide, in answer to my questions respecting it, said that it was a cataract of no great height or beauty, and if it had a name he was not acquainted with it. My walk of this day had been very long and laborious, near twenty miles, over the most stony paths that I had yet seen in the country, and I was almost fainting from want of refreshment: I was therefore under the necessity of being satisfied with his account. In almost any other case I should have crossed the vale to examine it, for I am convinced, from its appearance at so great a distance, that it must have been a cataract of very considerable height and beauty.

Betwixt the cromlech and the town of Harlech, I passed another druidical circle, somewhat smaller than the one I have before mentioned, but surrounded with a similar distant circle.

As it happened to be about the ebb of the tide when we returned, the guide pointed out to me part of a long stone-wall, which runs out into the sea from Mochras, a point of land a few miles south of Harlech, in a west-south-west direction for near twenty miles. This is called

SARN BADRWYG,

The Shipwrecking Causeway. It is a very wonderful work, being throughout about twenty-four feet thick. *Sarn y Bwch* runs from a point north-west of Harlech, and is supposed to meet the end of this. The space betwixt these formed, some centuries ago, a habitable hundred belonging to Merionethshire, called

CANTREF GWAELOD,

The Lowland Hundred. The Welsh have yet traditions respecting several of the towns, as Caer Gwyddno, Caer Ceneder, &c. These walls were built to keep out the sea. About the year 500, when Gwyddno Garan Hîr, *Gwyddno with the high Crown*, was lord of this hundred, one of the men who had care of the dams, got drunk and left open a flood-gate. The sea broke through with such force, as also to tear down part of the wall, and overflow the whole hundred, which, since that time, has been always completely flooded. – This is *Cardigan Bay*, (a principal part of which

Cantref Gwaelod formerly occupied,) for many miles so full of shoals, as to render it extremely dangerous for a vessel of any burthen to venture at all near the Merionethshire coast.

25

Harlech to Barmouth

The road from Harlech to Barmouth (ten miles) is even and good; but lying over a flat and disagreeable country, it is beyond measure dull and uninteresting. At a distance towards the sea there are nothing but turfy bogs and salt marshes; and, on the other side, the mountains are low and stony, and in every respect devoid of picturesque beauty.

In a field by the road-side, near Llanbedir, I observed two upright stones standing near each other, the one ten, and the other about six feet in height. These were without inscriptions, and are what the Welsh call *Meini Gwyr*, 'the stones of the heroes;' or the funeral monuments of celebrated warriors slain in battle.

A few hundred yards beyond the fifth mile stone, and at a little distance on the left of the road, two *cromlechs* were pointed out to me. These were very near each other, and placed on barrows, or heaps of loose stones, which are supposed to indicate that some men of ancient note were interred beneath them. These barrows, from the circumstance of the cromlechs being erected on them, are evidently of high antiquity; but I am inclined to suppose, (with a very judicious traveller through this country in the year 1774,) that many of the heaps of stones with which this country abounds, and which are usually taken for barrows, or *carnedds*, as they are here called, 'were originally piled together for no other reason than that the rest of the field might afford the clearer pasture. In the melancholy waste between Pont Aberglasllŷn and Llyn y Wenwn, I observed many modern carnedds, which had been thrown up in large piles by the industrious inhabitants for that profitable purpose.'*

The mode of forming the ancient carnedds in this country was somewhat singular. When the carnedd was considered as the honourable tomb of a warrior, every one that passed by threw on it an additional stone as a mark of respect; but when this heap became disgraced by shielding the body of the guilty, it was still the custom of every one that passed to fling his stone, but, in this case, it was done in token of detestation. –

The original intention of heaping stones over the dead, was doubtless to defend the bodies from being dug up, and devoured by the wolves, with which the wild and mountainous parts of Britain formerly abounded. It was a necessary precaution, to prevent the friends of the deceased from being shocked by the horrid sight of their carcases mangled by these rapacious animals.

I passed *Cors y Gedol*, the ancient family seat of the Vaughans, but now the property of sir Thomas Mostyn, bart., and continuing my journey by Llanaber soon afterwards arrived at

BARMOUTH.

This town is situated in one of the most unpleasant places that could have been chosen for it, near the conflux of the river Maw, or Mawddach.* – Some of the houses are built among the sand at the bottom, and others, at different heights, up the side of a huge rock, which entirely shelters the place on the east. The situations of the latter are so singular, that it is really curious for a stranger to wind up along the narrow paths among the houses, where, on one side, he may, if he please, enter the door of a dwelling, or, on the other, look down the chimney of the neighbour in front. The inhabitants might almost cure their bacon in some parts of this town, by the simple process of hanging it out of their windows. The houses at the foot of the rock are nearly choaked up with sand, which fills every passage, and is blown into every window that is for a moment left open. In rainy weather this sand, on the contrary, renders the place very dirty and unpleasant. The buildings are exceedingly irregular, and in most instances very bad. Notwithstanding all these disadvantages, Barmouth is frequented during the summer season by many genteel families from Wales, and the west of England, as a sea-bathing place. Its origin, as the resort of invalids, has been attributed to persons frequenting the banks of this part of the river for the sake of the scurvy-grass, which grows there in abundance.

The company must necessarily find it a most uncomfortable place, for the inn (the Corsygedol arms) is at times almost buried in sand, and no person can possibly walk many yards without having it over his shoes. Were it not for the civility and friendly attention of Mrs. Lewis, Barmouth would fail in its principal attraction. – I was beyond measure surprized, on being introduced into the dining-room, to find, in this secluded corner of the kingdom, upwards of thirty persons, most of them of fortune and fashion. I found also, on inquiry, that this was by no means all the company at that time in the town; another large and good building, which Mrs. Lewis had in her own hands as a lodging-house, being also quite full. To be thus suddenly introduced, as it were, into the world, after my solitary rambles among the wilds of the country, was a very grateful incident; and I enjoyed the general cheerfulness and affability that prevailed, perhaps the more from its being entirely unexpected.

The lodging-houses in the town, are many of them dirty and miserable places. – There are on the sands three bathing machines, but these are altogether appropriated to the use of the ladies, the gentlemen bathing on the open coast. – The amusements seem to consist principally in going out in parties on the water, and in lounging on the beach or the sands. – The beach is one of the most delightful walks I ever beheld. The wide river Mawddach winds amongst the mountains, forming many, and elegant promontories. These rise to great heights on each side, some clad with wood, and others exhibiting their naked rocks, scantily covered with the purple heath. The summit of the lofty Cader Idris is seen to rise high above the other mountains, in the back ground. Had the town been built here, scarcely half a mile from its present situation, instead of one of the most unpleasant, it might have been rendered one of the most agreeable retirements in the kingdom.

Barmouth is the port of Merionethshire; but it is not so much frequented as it ought to be, on account of the inhabitants (who do not attempt commerce on a large scale), vending their manufactures through the means of factors, who thus seize many of the advantages which the natives might enjoy. Mr. Pennant, however, informs us that prior to the year 1781, flannels to the value of 40,000*l*., and stockings to the value of 10,000*l*., had been exported from hence in the course of a year. – The number of ships at present belonging to the port is about a hundred: and the population of the place is estimated at fifteen hundred.

26

Barmouth to Dolgelle

I had already been highly gratified in my ramble along the beach for about a mile and a half from Barmouth; and, in my walk to Dolgelle, I retraced my steps with additional pleasure. The Mawddach, usually called Avon Vawr, *The Great River*, forms in this place a wide arm of the sea. It was now high water, and from the whole bed of the river being filled, the various scenes that presented themselves for some miles were truly picturesque. The two first miles, at the end of which I was compelled to leave the bank of the river, and proceed along the road, were, however, more interesting than any other part of the journey. In the composition of the views, scarcely any thing appeared wanting: there was every requisite of a fine landscape, mountain and vale, wood, water, meadows, and rocks, arranged in beautiful order. The numerous heaps of peat spread along the green bottom, were the only unpleasing objects in the scene, and these were easily overlooked where every other object was so beautiful. – Beyond the beach the road winds among the low mountains, at a little distance from the river. From the openings or eminences I frequently saw the water, partly hidden by the intervening mountains, in which situations it several times assumed the appearance of a beautiful lake.

From the village of Llanelltyd, about two miles from Dolgelle, there is a road which winds along a dark and gloomy vale towards Tanybwlch; and at a little distance a stile is seen, from whence a foot-path will lead the inquisitive tourist, over the meadows, to the ancient monastic ruin called by the Welsh Y Vanner, and by Tanner *Kemmer Abbey*. This will be described in the ensuing chapter.

Many persons prefer making the excursion from Barmouth to Dolgelle by water. To sit at ease, and enjoy without interruption the pleasures afforded by the picturesque scenes along the Mawddach, must doubtless be highly gratifying to an admirer of nature. The voyage, however, must end at the distance of about a mile from Dolgelle, for here the river becomes so greatly diminished, as not even to admit a small pleasure boat any farther. The company must therefore be contented to walk from thence to the town.

DOLGELLE,

The Holme of the Groves, is a market town, in a commercial view, of some importance, seated in a wide and fertile vale, between the rivers Arran and Wnion, and surrounded on all sides by high, and in many parts wooded, mountains.

A student of Jesus College Oxford, who was a native of Dolgelle, was one afternoon drinking wine with some of his college friends, when, in a bantering stile, they asked what kind of a place it was that had been honoured in giving him birth: – 'There,' says he, flinging on the table a handful of nuts, and setting up a cork in the middle, 'suppose each of these nuts a house, and that cork the church, – you will have some tolerable idea of Dolgelle.'

The analogy holds good, for the streets are as irregular as it is possible to imagine them. The houses in general are low, and ill built. The *church*, which is by much the neatest structure in or about the place, has in itself nothing that can attract particular attention. From various points of view on the outside of the town, the painter will, however, acknowledge, that it is not without its beauty.

We have a singular enigmatical account of Dolgelle, written by Fuller* somewhat more than a century ago.

1. The walls thereof are three miles high.
2. Men go into it over the water; but
3. Go out of it under the water.
4. The steeple thereof doth grow therein.
5. There are more ale-houses than houses.

These five enigmas he solves in this manner: the *first*, he says, is explained by the mountains that surround the place. The *second* implies, that on one side of the town there was a bridge over which all travellers must pass; and the *third*, that on the other side, they had to go under a wooden trough, which conveyed water from a rock, at a little distance, to an overshot mill. For the *fourth*, he says, the bells (if plural) hung in a yew tree; and the *last*, that 'tenements were divided into two or more tipling-houses, and that even chimney-less barns were often used for that purpose.' – I presume in this he alludes to the time in which some fair was held, for the sale and exchange of the manufactures of the place. None of these remarks will apply at present, except the two first.

There are at Dolgelle very considerable manufactories of flannel, which, from the number of hands necessarily employed, have rendered the place very populous, comparatively with other Welsh towns. The principal market for the goods is Shrewsbury, but so great a portion has of late been bought upon the spot, that the inhabitants have had little occasion to send to a market at such a distance.

The best *inn* is the Golden Lion, called likewise Plas Isa, *The Lower House*. The provisions, except the wine, I found good; but the bed into which I was put was intolerable.

During the civil wars of the reign of Charles I, about a hundred of the king's troops attempted to raise a fortification about this town. Mr Edward Vaughan, however, at the head of a small party of the parliament's forces, attacked and routed them, taking prisoners the captain and several of the men.

The neighbourhood of Dolgelle affords many interesting objects to the tourist. The summit of *Cader Idris*, the celebrated Merionethshire mountain, is not much more than six miles distant. A few miles towards the north, and at a little distance from each other, are the three cataracts *Rhaiadr Dû*, *The Fall of the Cain*, and *The Fall of the Mawddach*. These will be described in the next chapter. To all these places guides may easily be obtained at Dolgelle. – The whole of the vale in which the town is situated is remarkable for its picturesque scenery, and beautiful views.

27

Excursion from Dolgelle to Kemmer Abbey and the Waterfalls

The three cataracts mentioned in the conclusion of the last chapter, *Rhaiadr Dû*, in the grounds of W. A. Madocks, esq. of Dolmelynllyn, the *Fall of the Cain*, and the *Fall of the Mawddach*, are all near the road leading from Dolgelle to Tanybwlch. The former is about six, and the other two are about nine miles distant from Dolgelle.

Y VANNER, OR KEMMER ABBEY

In my expedition to these waterfalls, I proceeded near a mile and a half along the road, when, (a few hundred yards before I reached the bridge at Llanelltid,) I left it, and went on a foot-path to the right. This led me over some meadows, for about a quarter of a mile, to an avenue of sycamores, and thence to the remains of an abbey, not visible from the road, called by the Welsh, Y Vanner, and by the old writers, Kemmer abbey.*

> Where pious beadsmen, from the world retir'd,
>   In blissful visions wing'd their souls to heav'n,
> While future joys their nobler transports fir'd,
>   They wept their erring days, and were forgiv'n.*

The present remains of this monastery have little interest for any but the antiquarian: they are altogether devoid of ornament or elegance, and from no point of view are in any degree picturesque. Part of the church only is left, and the space of ground it occupies is very inconsiderable. The ruins of the refectory and the abbot's dwelling, form part of the walls of an adjoining farm-house. The other parts are much shattered, and the farmer, in whose ground the building stands, has patched them in many places with modern masonry, to render them of use in his business. The length of the church is betwixt thirty and forty yards, and the width not more than eight or nine. The east end is more perfect than any other part, and, through its thick covering of ivy, I could discern three small lancet-shaped windows. Against the south-wall there are a few small gothic pillars and arches; and in the wall an aperture where probably the holy water was kept. In this part of the building, opposite to two small arches, there has also been a semi-circular door; and, near this, there is the mutilated head of a human figure. A large plane-tree is now growing from among the ruins of the west-end of the building, whence it should seem to have long been in a ruined state. From the obscurity of its situation, and the want of that kind of elegance usual in monastic ruins, this abbey is scarcely known even at Dolgelle. The tourist will inquire for it in vain as Kemmer abbey, for the Welsh people in general know it by no other name than that of Y Vanner.

It was founded about the year 1200 for some monks of the Cistercian order, from Cwm Hir abbey in Radnorshire, by Meredith and Griffith, the sons of Cynan ap Owen Gwynedd, prince of North Wales. 'This seems (says a Welsh writer) to have been a colony of monks, sent off by that monastery, as bees do when the hive is too full.'*

About thirty years after the supposed period of its foundation, Kemmer abbey appears to have been in a flourishing state. At this time, when Henry III was marching against the Welsh, who had risen, under their prince, Llewelyn ap Iorwerth, and attacked the castle of Montgomery, one of the monks of Kemmer happened to be near, and was questioned as to the situation and strength of the Welsh army. He considered it a duty to befriend his country, rather than assist an enemy, and therefore deceived them so much by his report of the state of the opposing forces, that Henry determined on an immediate attack. The Welsh, at the first onset, feigned a retreat to a neighbouring marsh. The English soldiers, incumbered as they were with their armour, without hesitation, plunged after them, and, as soon as the enemy saw that the greater part were in the marsh, and unable either to act offensively or to retreat, they returned upon them with so much fury, as, after a short conflict, to come off victorious. – This deception naturally enraged the king, and, not long afterwards, as he passed the abbey with his army, he ordered the monastery to be set on fire and destroyed. All the out-offices were consumed, but the abbot saved the rest of the building by his entreaties to the king, and paying down a fine of three hundred marks.

At the dissolution of abbies, the revenues of Kemmer were estimated at betwixt fifty and sixty pounds a year. The site remained in the crown till the reign of queen Elizabeth, who, about the year 1578, granted it to Robert, earl of Leicester. In what manner it has since descended, we have no information.

On a bank nor far distant, there was formerly a British fortress called Castell Cymmer, *The Castle of the Conflux*. This was demolished about the year 1113, not long after its erection, by the sons of Cadwgan ap Bleddyn, on some disagreement with the founder; and it is supposed to have never been rebuilt.

Returning from the abbey to the road, I crossed the bridge at Llanelltid, and proceeded along the vale leading towards Tanybwlch. The first waterfall the guide brought me to was

RHAIADR DU,

The Black Cataract. This, as I have before said, is in the grounds of W. A. Madocks, esq. at Dolmelynllyn, whence it is often called the *Dolmelynllyn Fall.** – The water foams, with a thundering noise, down two rocks about sixty feet high. The scene has a singular appearance from the black adjacent and uncouth rocks being in many places covered with a pure white lichen. The trees on one side of the stream had been lately cut down, but the lively and varied green and brown tints of the other were beautifully contrasted with the almost jet black rocks with which they were intermixed. The torrent rolls into a small deep bason, from whence it dashes itself along the rugged channel to the river Mawddach, which flows at no great distance. – Mr. Madocks has been at the expence of making a good foot-path, both to the bottom, and to the upper part of this cataract, by which the traveller is enabled with comfort to see it to the greatest advantage.

I went about a mile farther on the road, from whence I had a walk, of near two miles, along a foot-path to the right, to the remaining waterfalls, which are within a few hundred yards of each other. From the side of an eminence about half a mile from these, I could observe the river Mawddach rolling down a steep, in a woody vale above, and its hoarse murmuring just reached my ear. Beyond it, at some distance, there was a rude arch, which crossed the glen, and from my station gave a pleasing and romantic cast to the scene.

> Descending now (but cautious lest too fast,)
> A sudden steep upon a rustic bridge,
> We pass a gulph in which the hazels dip
> Their pendant boughs.*

This was a perfectly alpine bridge over the river Cain, formed by the rude trunk of an oak which hung frightfully over the black torrent, that roared amongst the rocks many feet beneath. I had not passed this bridge far, before I found myself at the foot of Rhaiadr y Mawddach.

THE CATARACT OF THE MAWDDACH

The river here forces itself down a rock betwixt fifty and sixty feet in height, whose strata lying in parallel lines several degrees inclined from the horizon, give the scene a singularly crooked appearance. The stream is thrice broken in its descent, and the bason into which it is precipitated is very large. The rocks and trees form an amphitheatre around, and the foreground was finely broken by the large pieces of rock that had been once loosened from above. I had to cross the stream before I could see the upper part of the fall, which was hidden by intervening rocks. In this station the scene appeared complete, and it was certainly picturesque.

PISTYLL Y CAIN,*

The Spout of the Cain, is by far the highest and most magnificent cataract of the three. A narrow stream rushes down a vast rock, at least a hundred and fifty feet high, whose horizontal strata run in irregular steps through its whole breadth, and form a mural front. These, indeed, are so regular, as in a great measure to destroy the picturesque effect of the scene, unless they are nearly hidden by a much greater volume of water than usual. Immense fragments of broken rock at the foot of the fall, scattered in every different direction, communicate a pleasing effect; and the agreeable mixture of tints of the dark oak and birch, with the yellower and fading elm, formed altogether a highly pleasing scene.

My guide to the waterfalls was an Englishman, who keeps a small public house near Dolmelynllyn. His name is Bartlet. He has resided in Wales only a few years, and is yet scarcely able to speak the language of the country.

28

Dolgelle to Machynlleth

From the road leading to Machynlleth, and at the distance of about two miles, the town of Dolgelle is seen to greater advantage than from most other points of view. It appears in the midst of a vale replete with pastoral beauty. The wide river Mawddach in the distance, reflects its silvery whiteness in the bosom of high and dreary mountains. The intervening space exhibits luxuriant woods, meadows, and corn-fields, intersected by the river Wnion, which serpentizes along the vale.

The road now passes over high and swampy moors, and for some miles the scenery is wild, dreary, and comfortless. The lofty Cader Idris, its summit obscured in clouds, formed the entire boundary of these wilds towards the south-west.

THE POOL OF THE THREE PEBBLES*

This is a small pool on the left of the road about five miles from Dolgelle. The Welsh call it *Llyn Trigrainwyn*. It has its name from the three huge fragments of rock that are seen by its side, which the traditions of the peasantry assert to have been what the giant Idris called three pebbles. This huge man, from whom the adjacent mountain had its name, was one day walking round his possessions in these mountains, when, says tradition, he found something had fallen into his shoe that began to hurt his foot. He pulled it off, and threw out these three pebbles, after which he experienced no further inconvenience! One of these *pebbles* is about four and twenty feet long, eighteen broad, and twelve high. – So much for tradition!

The pool is believed to be bottomless; but, though this is not the case, its depth for so small a surface of water is uncommonly great, being, as I was told, upwards of fifty fathoms.

I had not got far beyond this pool, when I found the prospect became somewhat interesting. A pleasing vale now presented itself, which incloses a pool about a mile in length, called Llyn Mwyngil, *The Lake of the Pleasant Retreat*. This is bounded by hills.

THE BLUE LION

As I was anxious to ascend Cader Idris, and, although the weather had become very unfavourable, as I should lose all opportunity of doing it if I proceeded any farther at present, I stopped at the Blue Lion, a small public house, a little beyond the pool of the Three Pebbles. It had begun to rain very hard a little before my arrival, and, as it was then late in the day, I determined to remain here all night, in the hope that before morning the weather might clear up. Not having yet dined, I inquired what I could have to eat, but found, as Dr. Johnson did at Glenelg, in the Highlands of Scotland, that, 'of the provisions, the negative catalogue was very copious.'* I could have no meat (except bad bacon), no eggs, no wine, no spirits. It was needless to inquire further into what I could *not* have, I therefore directed the good woman of the house to bring me any thing that was eatable. Bread and butter, and new ale, taken evidently from the tub in which it was fermenting, constituted therefore my principal fare at this cottage for two days. I have had occasion to remark, through both my journies, that the ale is generally drank within a few days of its being brewed, at most of the small inns in Wales. The labouring people see it taken from the tub with unconcern, and seem to relish it as much, while fermenting, as they would if it was drawn from the cask. If it has but the name of *Cwrw*, they consider its quality a very secondary object. How far this may be injurious to their health, I am not able to say, but the general poverty of the lowest class of the people here is so great, that it is not probable they will ever have their ale of much better quality.

The landlord of the Blue Lion, if I may dignify him with that appellation, is a schoolmaster, a guide, and a cutter of grave-stones, and to his various other qualifications, he adds a very considerable taste for – ale, as the following memoranda of my cheap living at this house will shew:

	s. d.
Two dinners (N.B. bread and butter)	1 6
Tea, supper, and breakfast	1 0
Ale,	2 6
	5 0

This man, whose name is Edward Jones, I found somewhat too talkative, particularly on the subject of his own qualifications. I obtained from him much of the news of the neighbourhood, but little information on which I could rely respecting the country. I smiled several times at his efforts to shew off his learning and talents, these, however, in so obscure a situation, were perhaps excusable.

This house is situated by the road side, immediately under Cader Idris, and is a very convenient place from whence travellers, coming from Machynlleth, may ascend the mountain. If it is not found inconvenient, on account of carriages or horses, they may go over the summit, and down the other way to Dolgelle: this they would do in nearly as short a space of time as it would require to descend again to the Blue Lion. – The bed I slept in was not a very bad one, nor was I here, though in a smaller house, so pestered with fleas, as I had before been at Beddgelert.

ASCENT TO THE SUMMIT OF CADER IDRIS

The morning proved more favourable than I expected; and although it was still cloudy, I was determined to venture on an excursion to the summit of the mountain, under the hopes that the weather might entirely clear up before I arrived at the top. About nine o'clock, therefore, in company with my loquacious host, I commenced my expedition.

I have said that this mountain had its name from a person called Idris, supposed by tradition to have been an enormous giant. The old bardic writings, however, rather represent him great in mind than stature: in these he is said to have been a poet, an astronomer, and philosopher. He is supposed also to have been a prince of these parts; but the period is so remote, that little more than his name and talents are now to be ascertained.* *Cadair Idris*, or the seat of Idris, is thought to imply that he had an observatory, or study, on the summit of the mountain. These suppositions, however, seem founded on a very uncertain basis.

There had been much rain during the night, in consequence of which the guide took me along the side of a rivulet, which flows from one of the hollows above, to see a small cataract. The torrent was thrown down the face of a steep rock in a white sheet of foam, thrice broken in its descent. It might perhaps be more properly denominated a cascade, for, although it was extremely pretty, it was on so small a scale, as to be devoid of much of the grandeur that is usual in waterfalls that boast any degree of picturesque beauty. – Above this, on the same stream, another cascade still more small and contracted was pointed out to me. The height of the latter rock was not more than seven or eight yards, and the whole scene would have appeared very trifling, had it not been ornamented by three majestic oaks, whose branches, whilst they almost concealed the stream, added greatly to its beauty.

Crossing the rivulet, I went for a little way along its bank, and was much pleased with several other cascades that were formed in its descent. After a while I arrived in the mountain hollow, that contains the waters of

LLYN Y CAE,

The inclosed Pool, from the west side of which rises a stupendous, black, and precipitous rock, called *Craig y Cae*, that casts a gloomy shade on every thing below it, and throws upon the water its own dismal hue. Its sullen and majestic front was enlivened only with patches of the moss saxifrage, and a few goats, that were seen skipping carelessly among its dangerous steeps. From its spiry points and deep precipices, it has assumed an appearance that somewhat resembles the age-worn front of a massy ancient cathedral. The whole of the scene, from near the edge of the pool, was truly picturesque and grand.

Whilst I was gazing at the rock, a shower of rain so smart came on, that in a short time my clothes were wet through. Soon after this the clouds rose above the lower parts of the mountain, and the highest peak alone was clouded. – The summit is called Pen y Cader, *The Head of the Seat*. This, like that of Snowdon, is conical, and covered with loose stones. With the utmost patience and composure, I waited on this point, enveloped in mist, for more than half an hour, when, for about ten minutes, the mountain became perfectly cleared. I had from hence a view, if not more extensive, I think more varied, than that from Snowdon. On one side the mountain formed an abrupt and deep precipice, at the bottom of which a small lake or two were lodged. The distant views were of Bala pool, and its adjacent mountains, and beyond these of the long range of Ferwyn mountains, headed by Cader Ferwyn. Towards the south lay the county of Montgomery, which, with its celebrated mountain Plinlimmon, seemed almost immediately under the eye. On the west side I had the whole curve of Cardigan Bay, from St. David's entirely round to Caernarvonshire. I had scarcely looked round, when the gathering clouds swept over me in deeper folds, and all was again hidden from my sight.

The ascent to the summit of Cader Idris is much more easy than that of Snowdon; and I am confident that from Jones's house I could attain the highest point in about two hours. – The perpendicular height of this mountain, measured from the green near Dolgelle, is but 950 yards. – Cader Idris has three high points, the most lofty is called *Pen y Cader*; the next in height *Mynydd Moel*; and the other *Craig y Cae*.

In descending I took a direction eastward of that in which I had gone up, and proceeded along that part of the mountain called *Mynydd Moel*. The path in this direction is sufficiently sloping to allow a person to ride even to the summit. A gentleman, mounted on a little Welsh poney, had done this a few days before I was here.

At the bottom of a hill on the right of the road leading to Machynlleth, and about half a mile from the Blue Lion, I saw another small cataract, which, although scarcely more than seven or eight yards high, was by no means destitute of beauty. The rock is five or six times as wide at the top as it is below, which gives to the scene a very singular effect. In dry weather I should think this would be in want of water: after a heavy shower of rain it may, however, be always seen in perfection.

The road from Jones's cottage to Machynlleth is very level and good; but as I had rain nearly the whole way, and as it lies along a narrow hollow, between a series of wooded mountains, without much variety of character, even this short journey was rendered very unpleasant. The murmuring of the rivulet, which accompanied me for some miles, and here and there a picturesque cottage, seated in the woods, chiefly occupied my attention, till I had arrived within two miles of Machynlleth. Towards evening the rain ceased, the clouds dispersed, and the fine vale in which the town stands appeared exceedingly beautiful. Machynlleth is hidden from the observer in this direction, by intervening mountains, till he is arrived within about a mile of it; and it is first seen on a sudden turn of the road at a little distance from the river.

MACHYNLLETH*

I crossed the Dovey, and shortly afterwards arrived at Machynlleth, a neat, and a much more regularly built town than most in Wales. The town-hall is a plain unadorned structure; and the church (a common fault in this country) is white-washed. From the church-yard there is a pretty view along a green and meadowy vale. – Machynlleth is a place of some trade, and it has an air of greater opulence than most of the Welsh towns.

An ancient building, constructed of the thin shaly stone of this country, and now converted into stables, was pointed out to me as that in which Owen Glyndwr summoned the chieftains of Wales in the year 1402. He was here acknowledged their prince, and as such proclaimed and crowned.

It is highly probable that this town was the site of *Maglona*, the principal Roman station in Montgomeryshire. Near Penallt, about two miles distant, there is a place called Cefyn Caer, *The Ridge of the City*, where Roman coins have frequently been found, and where there has once been a small circular fort.

When on the point of setting out from Machynlleth to Llanydloes, I was informed of a lofty cataract, near a pool called Llyn Pen Rhaiadr, *The Pool at the Head of the Cataract*, about six miles distant; but, as the road lay entirely over the mountains, and I was desirous to reach Llanydloes as soon as possible, I did not take the trouble of visiting it.

If I had not (that I might confine my attention altogether to North Wales, and give to it all the time I had to spare) entered into a resolution not even to set my foot in the southern division of the principality, I should have gone from Machynlleth to

ABERYSTWYTH,

The Conflux of the Istwyth, distant about nineteen miles. This is now a celebrated sea-bathing place, frequented by much company. – It has the remains of a castle, founded at the commencement of the twelfth century by Gilbert Strongbow, but about two centuries afterwards rebuilt by king Edward I.

From hence I should have proceeded to an inn, about twelve miles off, called the Havod Arms, not far from which is the celebrated bridge called Pont ar Monach, *The Bridge over the Monach*, and by the English, *The Devil's Bridge*; and from this place I should have returned into North Wales near Llanydloes. – The excursion altogether would not have been more than fifty miles, and the twenty miles of unpleasant road betwixt Machynlleth and Llanydloes I should by this means have avoided.

***

29

Machynlleth to Llanydloes

The distance from Machynlleth to Llanydloes is about twenty miles, and the road lies over a series of dreary and barren moors. The mountains here have no one character of beauty, and during my whole walk I scarcely saw a single tree. The only pleasing objects were a few patches of corn, sparingly scattered in different parts of the adjacent bottoms. – I had proceeded about five miles, when I arrived at the foot of a lofty hill, along which the road continues on an ascent for near three miles. From the top I had an ample view of all the country around me; but its beauties were very few, it seemed little more than one dismal waste of hill and vale.

Proceeding on my journey, the Montgomeryshire mountain

PLYNLIMMON

Became visible at the distance of four or five miles on the right. Its name appears to have been derived from Pen Lummon, *The Summit of the Beacon*, from its being so much higher than all the surrounding hills. This supposition is aided by the circumstance of its being of the utmost use to the peasantry of the adjacent country, even when the ground is covered with snow, as a known mark by which they are enabled to steer their course. – From the various accounts that had reached me respecting this mountain, there did not appear any probable compensation for my trouble in going so far out of my road to ascend its summit, I therefore continued my route, and only passed it at a distance. – The adjacent mountains being all low, render Plynlimmon much higher in appearance than it really is: from this, and its giving birth to three noted rivers, the Severn, the Wye, and the Rhydol, it seems not improbable that it originally obtained its celebrity. In perpendicular height it is far exceeded by Snowdon, Cader Idris, and many other mountains of the principality.

THE HEAD OF THE SEVERN

The manuscript journal of a very intelligent friend has furnished me with the following short account of the source of this celebrated river. The Severn rises from a small spring on the south-east side of Plynlimmon, and nearly at its summit. The water issues from a rock at the bottom of a kind of large hole, whose sides are formed of peat. The ground around the edges is somewhat elevated. A stream so small issues from this place, that a child four years of age might stride across it. The water, which is of a red colour, is very unpleasant to the taste. –Those persons who wish to trace the Severn to its source, are directed to keep the right-hand stream all the way up the mountain.

In the flat country, betwixt Plynlimmon and the road, I observed a small unadorned pool called Glâs Llyn, *The Blue Pool.*

CATARACT

Having proceeded about half-way to Llanydloes, I was directed to leave the road, and go a mile and a half south, to see a cataract called Frwd y Pennant, *The Torrent at the Head of the Vale.* The rock was nearly perpendicular, and the water, then in plenty, from the late rains, roared down its lofty front with a deafening noise. The shrubs hanging from the adjacent rocks added to its beauty. This waterfall is exceeded in height by few in North Wales.

About four miles from Llanydloes, the appearance of the country began to change, and the woody vales in front, with the little Llyn yr Avangc, *Beaver's Pool,* at a distance among them, formed on the whole a pleasing scene.

LLANYDLOES

The entrance into Llanydloes, *The Church of St. Idlos,* is over a long wooden bridge across the Severn. This was such as not to prepossess me in favour of the town. The streets are wide, but the houses are principally formed by means of timber frames, with their intermediate spaces closed with laths and mud. These in general are very irregular, and I found a greater scarcity of good houses in this place than in any of its size and consequence that I had yet visited. – The town-house is a wretched building, constructed much in the manner of the dwelling-houses.

The width of the streets of Llanydloes is (very singularly) a great inconvenience, for the inhabitants throughout the town, taking advantage of it, accumulate all their ashes and filth in great heaps before their doors. These heaps are, indeed, so large, that in a hot day the exhalation of noxious vapours from them, as I have experienced, must be an abominable nuisance to every person accustomed to cleanliness.

The town is built in the form of a cross, having the market-house nearly in the centre. – The *church* is remarkable only for having six arches, with columns surrounded by round pillars, ending in capitals of palm-leaves. The inhabitants assert that these were brought, some time after the dissolution, from Cwm Hir abbey in Radnorshire.

In Llanydloes there is carried on a very considerable trade for yarn. This is manufactured into flannels, and sent to Welsh Pool for sale.

30

Llanydloes to Newtown

On my leaving Llanydloes, I soon began to find myself in a kind of country that plainly indicated an approach towards England. The road winds along a vale much flatter, and more highly cultivated, than any in the interior of Wales. I saw here several fields both of rye and wheat, two species of corn seldom grown in mountainous countries: the winds and storms are there so violent, that they would shake out the grain from the ears before it could ripen. – I now wandered

> On the gentle Severn's sedgy bank.*

The river was here but a few yards across, and it glided silently and smoothly along, reflecting brightly the green impending foliage of its banks.

> Fields, lawns, hills, vallies, pastures, all appear
> Clad in the varied beauties of the year.
> Meand'ring waters, waving woods are seen
> And cattle scatter'd in each distant green.
> The curling smoke, from cottages ascends,
> There towers the hill, and there the valley bends.*

I passed *Llandinam*, a small village, about seven miles from Llanydloes, which I mention only for the purpose of relating an anecdote of the valour of Edward Herbert, esq., the grandfather of the celebrated lord Herbert of Chirbury.* This gentleman was a strenuous opposer of the outlaws and thieves of his time, who were in great numbers among the mountains of Montgomeryshire. In order to suppress them, he often went with his adherents to the places which they frequented. Some of them having been seen in a public house at Llandinam, Mr. Herbert, and a few of his servants, proceeded thither to apprehend them. The principal outlaw aimed an arrow at him, which struck his saddle, and stuck there. Herbert, with his sword in his hand, and with undaunted courage, galloped up to him, and took him prisoner. He pointed to the arrow, requesting the fellow to observe what he had done. 'Ah! (replied the man,) had not my best bow been left behind, I should have done a greater deed than shoot your saddle.' He was tried for the crime, found guilty, and hanged.

NEWTOWN

In Newtown, or, as it is called by the Welsh, *Tre-Newydd*, I found nothing remarkable. It is a clean, and rather neat place, and the surrounding country is fertile and pleasant. – The manuscript journal of my friend, quoted in the last chapter, contains the following memorandum respecting the church. 'This building has a screen, said to have been brought from some neighbouring abbey. It may be antique, but its gilded ornaments rendered it very unsightly. There is also here a small altar piece, said to have been painted by Dyer the poet.* The subject is the last supper, but it is in part a copy from Poussin, and is bad.'*

A glen about a mile from the town, on the right of the road leading to Builth, was pointed out to me as containing a *cataract*, and some beautiful scenery. I was, however, greatly disappointed in finding these scarcely worth notice. The face of the rock had much the appearance of a shattered wall, thrown aslaunt by one end sinking into the ground. The water scarcely trickled down it, and if I might judge from the muddy pool at the foot, it very seldom descended in quantity sufficient to entitle the scene to the appellation of a cataract.

Returning to Newtown, I crossed the river, and walked along its banks about three miles and a half to

CASTELL DOLFORWYN,

The Castle of the Virgin's Meadow. The remains of this fortress are to be found on a lofty hill, on the north-west bank of the Severn, a situation that commands the whole of the adjacent country. From hence I had a lovely and extensive prospect of the vale of Severn, through which the river was seen to glide in elegant curves, blackened by its high and shady banks. The landscape was enlivened by the luxuriance of woods and meadows; and the towns and villages around lent their aid to decorate the scene.

The castle has been a four-sided building, of no great strength, about fifty yards long, and twenty-five wide; and the exterior walls appear to have been about four feet in thickness. A small part of the north wall, with some trifling remains of the interior of the building, are yet left. The south and the east walls are entirely demolished, and the other parts that are yet standing are greatly shattered.

There have been various conjectures respecting the founder of this castle. Dugdale attributes it to David ap Llewelyn, prince of North Wales, about the middle of the thirteenth century. Stowe says it was the work of Llewelyn; and Mr. Evans,* who is now generally thought to be right, that it was indebted for its origin to Bleddyn ap Cynvyn, some time betwixt the years 1066 and 1073.

In the sixth year of the reign of Edward I, Bogo de Knovill was made governor; and, in the following year, the castle was granted to Roger Mortimer, earl of March, to hold to himself and his heirs on the service of a knight's fee. His son was attainted of high treason, but afterwards, on the reversal of the attainder, it was restored to the family in the person of his grandson. By the marriage of Anne, the sister to the last earl of March, with Richard Plantagenet, earl of Cambridge, this, and some other Welsh castles, became the property of the house of York, and thence descended to the crown.

These are all the memoranda of any importance that I have been able to collect respecting this fortress.

How it first took the name of Dolforwyn, or *The Meadow of the Virgin*, cannot now be ascertained. Circumstances would, however, induce one to suspect, that it had some allusion to the story of Habren, or Abren, the daughter of Locrine, son of Brutus, the first king of Britain, by Essyllt, a daughter of the king of Germany, whom he had taken captive in his wars against the Huns. Previously to the taking of this female he had espoused Gwendolen, a daughter of Corineus, one of the heroes who had entered the island along with Brutus from Troy. The chieftain fearing that Locrine's reported attachment to Essyllt might break off the intended marriage with his daughter, threatened with his army to compel the fulfilment of his promise. Locrine, thus circumstanced, was under the necessity of concealing Essyllt in a cavern, declaring that she had left the kingdom, and, greatly against his inclination, was married to Gwendolen. On the death of Corineus, which appears to have taken place but a short time after the nuptials, he immediately divorced Gwendolen, and acknowledged Essyllt to be his queen. When he died, Gwendolen assumed the government, and she revenged herself for the injuries she had sustained, by causing Essyllt and her daughter Abren to be cast into the river. From this circumstance, the old writers say, the stream assumed the name of Abren; which afterwards, by a slight alteration, became Sabrina, and then Severn.*

> Sabrina is her name, a virgin pure,
> Whilome she was the daughter of Locrine,
> That had the sceptre from his father Brute.
> The guiltless damsel flying the mad pursuit
> Of her enraged stepdame, Gwendolen,
> Commended her fair innocence to the flood,
> That stayed her flight with his cross-flowing course.
> The water nymphs, that in the bottom play'd,
> Held up their pearled wrists, and took her in,
> Bearing her straight to aged Nereus' hall;
> Who, piteous of her woes, rear'd her lank head,
> And gave her to his daughters to embathe
> In nectar'd leaves, strow'd with asphodel;
> And through the porch and inlet of each sense,
> Dropt in ambrosial oils, till she reviv'd
> And underwent a quick immortal change –
> Made goddess of the river: she still retains
> Her maiden gentleness, and oft at eve
> Visits the herds along the twilight meadows,
> Helping all urchin blasts, and ill-luck signs
> That the shrewd meddling elf delights to make,
> Which she with precious viol'd liquors heals;
> For which the shepherds at their festivals
> Carol her goodness loud in rustic lay,
> And throw sweet garland wreaths into her stream,
> Of pansies, pinks, and gaudy dafodils.
> And as the old swain said, she can unlock
> The clasping charm, and thaw the numbing spell,
> If she be right invoked in warbled song;
> For maidenhood she loves, and will be swift
> To aid a virgin, such as was herself,
> In hard besetting need.*

31

Newtown to Montgomery

From Newtown I had a fine cultivated country all the way to Montgomery. The infant Severn accompanies the road nearly half the way, in some places approaching, and in others bending from it, and hidden by intervening trees and hedges.

The few houses at Abermule, *The Conflux of the River Mule*, about five miles from Newtown, were delightfully situated on the bank of the Severn, surrounded by hills, and decorated by woods, in all the luxuriance of foliage. From hence the road gently ascends, and from the eminence a view so extensive and beautiful bursts on the sight, as to defy the utmost expression of the pencil to represent it. A vale in high cultivation is seen to extend for several miles, the Severn appearing in different parts from among the trees and meadows: The whole scene was bounded by distant hills. The descent continues still beautiful; and, near the town of Montgomery, the fine ruins of its castle formed a very interesting addition to the prospect. – The road is so much elevated immediately above the town, as to afford the traveller a bird's eye view into almost every street.

MONTGOMERY,

From the neatness of its houses, seemed to me to be inhabited principally by persons of small fortune, who had settled here to lead a life of retirement. It is clean, and well built; and seems capable of affording the comforts and conveniences, without any of the bustle and noise of a large town. All the adjacent country is decorated with the most lively and luxuriant scenery.

The church is an elegant cruciform structure, dedicated to St. Nicholas, and contains an ancient monument, to the memory of Richard Herbert, esq. the father of the very celebrated lord Herbert of Chirbury, and his lady. The two figures are recumbent, under what has once been a magnificent and much ornamented canopy. In an adjacent corner of the church, I observed a large collection of legs, arms, heads, and trunks of other monumental figures, but all of them so much shattered, that I could make nothing out of them. On the grave-stones in the churchyard I remarked more epitaphs than I had usually seen together before. Among such a number, many were of course ridiculous.

In the year 1092, a few of the Norman barons that were settled in the Marches, were allowed to wrest all the territory they were able from the Welsh, on condition that they should hold it as tenants, *in capite*, under the crown. Roger de Montgomery, earl of Shrewsbury, entered Powisland, and took possession of this place, then called Tre-faldwyn, or *Baldwyn's Town*, from its having been built, and fortified with a castle by Baldwyn, lieutenant of the Marches to William the Conqueror. The earl did homage to the king for these possessions, fortified the place afresh, and called it, after himself, Montgomery.

MONTGOMERY CASTLE

The castle is situated on an eminence on the north side of the town, and appears to have once been a grand and majestic building. It is, however, at present so much demolished, that it is impossible to trace its extent with any degree of accuracy. It stood on a rock precipitous on one side, and so elevated as to overlook all the immediately adjacent country. The present remains consist of a small part of a tower at the south-west angle, and a few low and shattered walls. In this tower I observed several small holes, similar to those I have mentioned as found in the walls of the Roman fort at Segontium near Caernarvon; and these served more clearly to convince me that they were all originally formed for no other purpose than to rest in them horizontal poles, for the support of the scaffolding used in the erection. Some of these are near six feet deep. This fortress seems to have been defended by four fosses, cut in the rock, each of which had formerly its drawbridge.

HISTORY OF MONTGOMERY CASTLE

I have already remarked that Tre-faldwyn, or, as it was afterwards called, Montgomery, was built and fortified with a castle during the reign of William the Conqueror, by Baldwyn, lieutenant of the Marches; and that in 1092, the place was fortified afresh as the property of Roger de Montgomery, earl of Shrewsbury. In the following year, the Welsh mustering all their force, rose in arms, seized and ransacked the castle. William Rufus marched with an army to the relief of the English, retook and repaired the castle; but, in his encounter with the Welsh, having lost a great number both of men and horses, he was compelled to return into

England to recruit his forces. Montgomery castle was at this time believed to be the strongest fortress in Wales, and the Welsh, after William's retreat, again commenced an attack upon it. The Norman soldiers gallantly defended it for many days, but the Welsh, having found means to undermine the walls, took it by storm, and after putting the whole garrison to the sword, levelled the fortress to the ground. The English struggled ineffectually against this hardy people for near four years. At length they obtained a decisive victory. The castle was immediately rebuilt by the earl of Shrewsbury; but in little more than a century afterwards was again destroyed.

It appears that in 1221, Henry III, in order to restrain the predatory excursions of the Welsh, erected a castle at Montgomery, which he granted to his justiciary, Hubert de Burgh. – About seven years subsequent to this period, as some of the garrison's soldiers were attempting, with the assistance of the country people, to open a road through an adjoining forest, which had long afforded to the Welsh a secure asylum; from whence issuing, they frequently murdered and plundered travellers through the country; they were on a sudden attacked by a body of the natives, who with great slaughter compelled them to seek refuge in the castle. The party then invested, and laid regular siege to it, on which Hubert de Burgh, alarmed at his situation, sent to Henry for succour, who brought an army to his aid, on the arrival of which the Welsh immediately fled.

In the year 1231, a party of Welshmen having made an excursion into the lands adjoining the castle, they were intercepted by the English, and many were taken prisoners, and beheaded. Prince Llewelyn ap Iorwerth, in retaliation for this injury, assembling an enormous force, laid waste all the English borders. During the general consternation, Hubert de Burgh evacuated the castle; it was immediately seized by the Welsh, who set fire to and destroyed it, and shortly afterwards attacked and demolished some of the castles in South Wales.

In a conference held at Montgomery, in the year 1268, a peace was established betwixt Llewelyn ap Griffith, then prince of North Wales, and king Henry III. That prince paid down a fine of 32,000 marks, and in return received four cantreds, or hundreds, in Wales, which during the wars he had lost.

From an inquisition taken on the reversal of the attainder of Roger Mortimer, earl of March, in the year 1345, it appears that he had been possessed of Montgomery castle at the time of his death. It was in consequence restored to the family, and passed, with his other castles and property, by the marriage of Anne, the sister of the last earl, into the house of York, and thence to the crown.

This fortress was held by the immediate ancestors of lord Herbert of Chirbury, as stewards for the crown, and it was their principal place of residence.

In the civil wars of the reign of Charles I, lord Herbert was made governor. On the arrival of the army of the parliament in 1644, under the command of sir Thomas Middleton, he declared himself of that party, and on treaty permitted the men to enter the castle. Not long after this transaction, lord Byron advanced with the king's forces, consisting of about four thousand men, on which Middleton was compelled to flee to Oswestry, leaving his foot-soldiers with lord Herbert to defend the castle. The royalists commenced their attack; but sir Thomas having been joined by sir John Meldrum, sir William Brereton, and sir William Fairfax, returned with about three thousand men to the relief of the place. Lord Byron brought forward his men to engage them, but, after a dreadful conflict, which lasted more than eight hours, the parliament's army obtained a complete victory. The routed troops fled towards Shrewsbury, and the pursuit was continued near twenty miles. In this battle betwixt three or four hundred of the king's party were slain, and above a thousand taken prisoners. Sir William Fairfax, major Fitzsimons, and about sixty men belonging to the parliament, were killed, and about a hundred others dreadfully wounded. – The castle met the fate of all others, in being dismantled by order of the Commons. Lord Herbert, however, received from the parliament a satisfaction for the loss of his property.

RURAL SCENE

It was on a fine, serene morning in the beginning of September, that I happened to be at Montgomery; and I was so much delighted with the extensive and varied prospect from the castle, that I rested under the cool shade of one of its walls for near an hour, feasting my eyes with the lovely picture before me. The scene, which was calculated for almost Arcadian felicity, was enlivened by the busy work of harvest, and the merry carol of the reapers floated cheeringly through the air. The rustic swains and damsels were all assiduously employed in gathering the yellow riches of the summer. Some were cutting, others binding; and the gleaner,

> With bended shoulders traversing the field,*

Followed the loaded waggons, storing up with care every ear that fell. – I love to contemplate these rustic sights.

> Hail, therefore, patroness of health and ease,
> And contemplation, heart-consoling joys,
> And harmless pleasures in the throng'd
> Abode of multitudes unknown! Hail, rural life!
> Address himself who will to the pursuit
> Of honours, or emoluments, or fame;
> I shall not add myself to such a share,
> Thwart his attempts, or envy his success.*

THE TOWN OF MONTGOMERY

Was formerly defended by a circumambient wall, strengthened with towers. Leland, in the sixteenth century, thus describes it: 'The soyle of the ground of the towne is on mayne slaty rocke, and especially the parte of the towne hillinge toward the castell, now a late re-edified, whereby hathe been a parke. Great ruines of the waulle yet apere, and the remains of foure gates, thus called, Kedewen Gate, Chirbury Gate, Arthur's Gate, and Kerry Gate. In the waulle yet remayne broken tourets, of the which the white tower is the most notable.'

King Henry III granted to Montgomery the privileges of a free borough. – The town is now governed by two bailiffs, and twelve burgesses, or common-council men; and it sends one member to parliament, who is elected by the burgesses, and returned by the bailiffs.

CUCKING-STOOL

In Blount's Ancient Tenures and Jocular Customs,* I find that this singular instrument of justice was once in use at Montgomery. Whenever any woman was found guilty, in the judgment of the free burgesses of the town, of causing strifes, fightings, defamations, or other disturbances of the public peace, she was adjudged to the goging-stool, or cucking-stool, there to stand, with her feet naked, and her hair dishevelled, for such a length of time as the burgesses should think proper, as a public warning to all who beheld her. This is the same kind of instrument which was used among the Saxons. It was called by them scealfing, or scolding stool, that is, a chair in which they placed scolding women as public examples; but, in addition to this, if the enormity of the case required it, this people also plunged them over the head in water. The engine in general consisted of a long beam, or rafter, that moved on a fulcrum, and extended towards the centre of a pond: at its end was fixed the stool, or chair, on which the offender was made to sit. It was called by the Welsh Y Gadair Goch, *The Red Chair.*

> Ye vixen dames, your neighbour's pest,
> Unless your tongues in future rest,
> Know that with all your faults, your fate
> Is the *red-chair*'s degrading seat.*

***

32

Montgomery to Welsh Pool

Leaving Montgomery, I went over rich champaign country, about ten miles, to Welsh Pool. I passed on the left Powis castle, situated on the narrow ridge of a rock, about a mile from Pool. For three or four miles of the road this building is a striking object in the scene.

WELSH POOL

Is a large and populous place, and from its vicinity to England, it has assumed much the appearance of an English town. The houses are in general well built, and principally of brick. There is one long and handsome street, in which stands the county hall, an elegant structure, erected by subscription a few years ago. The manners of the inhabitants of this town are so completely English, that even the language of the country seems scarcely known here. An air of opulence unusual in Wales may be observed throughout the place, owing to the trade in Welsh manufactures, which is carried on to a great extent. It is principally resorted to as a market for Welsh flannels, which are manufactured here, and in various adjacent parts of the country: from hence these are sent into England, and principally to Shrewsbury and Liverpool. – The Severn is navigable to a place called Pool Stake, within a mile of Welsh Pool, although upwards of two hundred miles from its mouth in the Bristol channel.

The *church*, apparently a modern structure, is singularly situated at the bottom of a hill, and so low, that the upper part of the church-yard is nearly on a level with its roof. This church has a chalice which was presented to it by Thomas Davies, some time governor-general of the English colonies on the western coast of Africa. It is formed of pure gold brought from Guinea, and is valued at about a hundred and seventy pounds. Notwithstanding the evidence of its inscription to the contrary, the sexton informed me, with much assurance, that this chalice had been given to the church by a transported felon, who, from industry and application during his banishment, had returned to his country the possessor of considerable wealth. – I was somewhat surprized in observing in the choir a few branches of ivy that had penetrated the roof, and were permitted to hang entwined round each other in a cylindrical form, to a length of more than eighteen feet. The neatness of the place was not in the least injured by them, and I presume their singularity was the cause of their preservation.

POWIS CASTLE

Has been originally built of a reddish stone, but in order to keep the structure in repair, this has of late years been so plaistered over with a coat of red lime, that at present very little of the stone is visible. This red coating gives to the building so much the appearance of brick, that it was not till I almost touched it, that I was undeceived in supposing it such. The antique grandeur of this castle is much injured by the great number of chimnies, and by the striking and harsh contrast betwixt the walls and the modern sash windows.

The ascent to the castle is up a long and laborious flight of steps, much out of repair when I was there; and the principal entrance is a gateway betwixt two large round towers. The edifice is kept in repair as an habitable mansion, but its owner very rarely visits it. The apartments have a heavy and unpleasant appearance, from the great thickness of the walls; and the furniture is chiefly in the ancient stile of elegance. In some of the chambers the old and faded tapestry is yet left. There are, in different rooms, several portraits, chiefly of the family, the best of which are the work of Cornelius Janson.* Among them there is one of king Charles II painted by sir Peter Lely,* two of the earl of Strafford, one of lord Herbert of Chirbury, and others of various other celebrated characters. In the gallery, which is near a hundred and twenty feet in length, there is a small collection of antiques, some of which are supposed to be valuable.

The gardens were laid out in the wretched French taste, but in 1798, when I saw them, they were greatly out of repair.

The prospects from the terrace are very extensive, this situation commanding all the beautiful and spacious country eastward, intersected by the Severn, and the Breiddin hills; with much of the cultivated and well wooded county of Salop.

***

33

Welsh Pool to Oswestry

About six miles from Welsh Pool I passed a group of three lofty mountains called the

BREIDDIN HILLS.

The highest and most conical of these has the name of *Moel y Golfa*; the second *Craig Breiddin*; and the third *Cefyn y Castell*. On one of them an obelisk was erected a few years ago, from a subscription of several of the neighbouring families, in commemoration of lord Rodney's defeat of the French fleet,* under the command of the Count de Grasse.

Just before I arrived at Llanymynech, I had to cross the furious little river *Virnwy* by a ferry.

LLANYMYNECH,

The Village of the Miners, is a small white-washed village, standing on the northern bank of the Virnwy. Its name was evidently derived from the mines in which the neighbourhood formerly abounded, and which were worked in the adjoining hill, called *Llanymynech Hill*, even so early as the time of the Romans. Of this there are undeniable proofs. One vestige of their work is a large artificial cave, of immense length, called Ogo, from whence they obtained considerable quantities of copper. – The windings of this cavern are very numerous and intricate. Some years ago, two men of the parish, endeavouring to explore it, were so bewildered in its mazes, that, when they were discovered by some miners who were sent in search of them, they had thrown themselves on the ground, in despair of ever again seeing the light. – Previously to this period, some miners who were searching for copper, found in the recesses of the cavern several skeletons; and near them some culinary utensils, a fire-place, and a small hatchet. These too plainly indicated that the unfortunate wretches had for some time dragged on a life of misery in this gloomy mansion. One of the skeletons had a battle-axe by his side, and round his left wrist there was a bracelet of glass beads, like those druidical rings called Gleiniau Nadroedd, *Snake's Beads*. About fifteen years after this first discovery, other miners found human bones, and in one instance a bone of the arm clasped by a golden bracelet. Several Roman coins of Antoninus, Faustina, and others, have also been discovered in this cavern.

The hill, besides copper, affords zinc, lead, calamine, and so much lime, as to supply the whole county of Montgomery, and great part of Shropshire. In the summer of 1795, upwards of eight thousand tons were exported from hence to different parts of the adjacent country. About a hundred and fifty men are usually employed here during the summer in burning the lime, and about fifty in winter in breaking and raising the stone. – The lead and zinc obtained here, have of late years been conveyed by the Stourport canal to Birmingham, Macclesfield, and other places.

From the summit of Llanymynech hill I had an extensive view over the plains towards Shrewsbury on the east; and, on the other side, of the rough and uncultivated parts of Montgomeryshire, in which I either could, or fancied I could, discern the lofty cataract called Pistyll Rhaiadr, lighted by the beams of the morning sun, and glittering like a stream of light down the black front of its rock. Below me was the Virnwy, sweeping in elegant curves along the meadows; and towards the south of the Breiddin hills, I had a view in Montgomeryshire of a series of wooded and pleasant vales.

OFFA'S DYKE

Under the west side of this hill runs the rampart constructed by Offa, king of Mercia, for the purpose of dividing his country from Wales, called Clawdd Offa, *Offa's Dyke*. This commences from the river Wye, near Bristol, and extends along Herefordshire, Radnorshire, part of Shropshire and Denbighshire, and ends near Treyddin chapel in Flintshire. From the time of its formation, till nearly the conquest, Offa's dyke was considered as the dividing line betwixt England and Wales: in 1064 a law was made by Harold, directing that if any Welshman, coming into England without licence, was taken on the English side of Offa's dyke, he should be punished with the loss of his right hand. It has been conjectured by some of our historians that this rampart was intended to protect the kingdom of Mercia from the inroads of the Welsh. 'But,' says Mr. Lewis Morris, 'how came the king of Mercia to build this wall across the island? There must have been other kings to join him; and it seems the Welsh were *plaguy* troublesome when there must have been a wall to separate them. But I cannot be of the common opinion, that this was a defence against the Welsh, for how soon would they have demolished a mud wall if they were such terrible creatures? If they were a parcel of poltroons, as some modern wits will infer from this silly fortification, what occasion was there for any wall against such worthless animals? Doth it not seem more likely, that upon a peace betwixt the English and British princes, this was an everlasting boundary line between the two nations, and that they all concurred in forming it?'*

OSWESTRY

Is a considerable market town in Shropshire, and a place that during the Saxon times was much celebrated. – A little distance from the town I passed a large and elegant brick building, a *house of industry*, erected a few years ago by the joint subscription of several of the adjacent parishes, for the use of their poor. From every present prospect, this place promises to afford greater comforts to the poor, and in time to be much less expensive to their maintainers, than if they were supported in their respective parishes.

This town was anciently called *Oswaldstre*, a name that it is said to have obtained from the following event: In the year 642, the contending armies of Oswald king of Northumberland, and Penda, the ferocious king of Mercia, met here: the former was routed, and Oswald fell on the field of battle. Penda, with unexampled barbarity, caused the breathless body of Oswald to be cut in pieces, and stuck on poles, as so many trophies of his victory. Thus the place was called *Oswald's Tree*, and some time afterwards Oswestry.* – In a manuscript account of the town written in 1635, I find the following note: 'There was an old oake lately standing in Mesburie, within the parish of Oswestry, whereon one of king Oswald's armes hung, say the neighbours by tradition.'

Oswald had been a great benefactor to various monasteries, and his character was so much revered by the monks, that a short time after his death he was canonized; and the field in which he was slain became celebrated for the numerous miracles that were believed to have been wrought in it.

On the place of martyrdom, as the monks have termed it, a *monastery* was founded, dedicated to St. Oswald; but there are no evidences at present extant of the time either of its foundation or dissolution. In the reign of Henry VIII no part of the building was left, for Leland, who then visited this place, says that the cloister only was standing within the memory of persons then living.

This accurate writer likewise informs us, that when he was here, the houses of the town were principally formed of timber, and slated. – On the south-west side of the church there was, he says, a free school founded by a lawyer of the name of Holbech, steward of the town and lordship. – Not far from the church there was a fine spring of water, surrounded by a stone wall, (having a chapel over it,) called *Oswald's Well*. Of the origin of this well, the inhabitants had a tradition, that when Oswald was slain, an eagle tore one of the arms from the body, and making off with it, fell and perished on this spot, whence a spring of water immediately gushed up, which has remained ever since a memorial of the event. – The town was defended by walls, and was moated round, but in the walls there were no towers except those of the four gates. – This place, he says, was also principally supported by its trade in woollen cloth.

Of the town of Oswestry, and of the Welsh people, we have a curious encomium by Churchyard:

        Oswestry's a pretie towne full fine,
Which may be lov'd, be likte, and praysed both.
It stands so trim, and is maintaynd so cleane,
And peopled is, with folke that well doe meane:
That it deserves to be enrould and shrynd
In each good breast, and every manly mynd.

The market there, so farre exceedes withall,
As no one towne comes neare it in some sort:
For looke what may be wisht or had at call,
It is there found, as market men report.
For poultrie, fowle, of every kind somewhat,
No place can shew so much more cheape than that:
All kind of cates that countrie can afford,
For money there is bought with one bare word.

They hacke not long about the thing they sell,
For price is knowne of each thing that is bought:
Poor folke, God wot, in towne no longer dwell,
Than money had, perhaps a thing of nought.
So trudge they home, both barelegge and unshod,

With song in Welsh, or els in praysing God.
O sweete content, O merrie mind and mood,
With sweate of brow, thou lov'st to get thy food.

O plaine good folke, that have no craftie braines,
O conscience cleere, thou knowst no cunning knacks:
O harmless hearts, where feare of God remaines,
O simple soules, as sweete as virgin waxe.
O happie heads, and labouring bodies blest,
O sillie doves of holy Abraham's brest:
You sleepe in peace, and rise in joye and blisse,
For heaven hence, for you prepared is.*

OSWESTRY CASTLE

On an artificial mount, at the outside of the town, are the remains of this fortress; but they are at present little more than a confused heap of shattered walls and rubbish.

According to the Welsh historians, it was founded in 1148 by Madoc ap Meredith ap Bleddyn, prince of Powis, an ally of Henry II. The English records, however, assign to it a more ancient date. They inform us that it was in being before the Norman conquest, and that William the Conqueror, shortly after that event, bestowed it on Alan, one of his Norman friends. The artificial mount on which it was placed, indicates it to have been earlier than the Norman era. The Britons and Saxons gave their fortresses this species of elevation. The Normans built on the firm and natural soil, or rock; but often made use of these mounts, which they found to have been the site of a Saxon castle. This appears to have been the case with that in question.

In the year 1214, a complaint was laid to the archbishop of Canterbury by Llewelyn ap Griffith ap Madoc, against the constable of Oswestry castle, for compelling him to put to death two young noblemen, in derogation of their birth and extraction; 'which disgrace (he states) their parents would not have undergone *for three hundred pounds sterling!*' He alleges also, that the constable had twice imprisoned sixty of his men, when each man was compelled to pay ten shillings for his liberty; and that when the Welsh people came to Oswestry fair, the constable would seize their cattle, by driving them into the castle, and refuse to make any satisfaction.

Two years after this the town was destroyed by order of king John, on account of Llewelyn, prince of Wales, having refused to aid him in the contentions with his barons. It experienced a similar disaster in the reign of Henry III, in being burned during an insurrection of the Welsh.

In the subsequent reign, that of Edward I, Oswestry was surrounded with walls, that it might be less liable to suffer from the plundering excursions of this people.

These, however, do not appear to have altogether restrained them, for during the rebellion of Owen Glyndwr, in the beginning of the fifteenth century, it was again plundered and burnt. – Oswestry has likewise thrice suffered dreadfully by accidental fires in the space of thirty years. In 1542, two long streets were thus consumed; two years afterwards there was a fire more destructive than this; and in 1567 two hundred houses were burnt to the ground, namely, a hundred and forty within the walls, and sixty in the suburbs, in only two hours, betwixt two and four o'clock in the morning.

The contests, robberies, and disturbances in the *marches* of Wales, appear to have been continued with little interruption till a very late period. Both Welsh and English seem to have considered every thing as lawful plunder which they could seize in each others territory. In consequence of this, the stewards, the constable, and the lieutenant of Oswestry, and Powys, entered into covenants in the year 1534, to restrain these plundering excursions. It was agreed that if, after a certain day then fixed, any person of one lordship committed a felony in the other, he should be taken, and sent into the lordship where the offence was committed, to receive his punishment; and that if any goods or cattle were stolen from one lordship and conveyed into the other, the tenants, or inhabitants of that lordship, should either pay for the same within fifteen days, or otherwise four principal men should remain in bail or mainprise till they were either paid for or recovered. – Among the records of the draper's company at Shrewsbury, there is the following order: '25 Elizabeth, 1583. Ordered that no draper set out for Oswestry on Mondays before 6 o'clock, on forfeiture of 6*s*. 8*d*.; and that they wear their weapons all the way, and go in company. Not to go over the Welsh bridge before the bell toll six.' William Jones, esquire, left to the company one pound six shillings and eight-pence, to be paid annually to the vicar of St. Alkmunds's church for reading prayers on Monday mornings before the drapers set out for Oswestry market.

The town of Oswestry was rendered by its walls a place of considerable strength; and during the civil wars of the reign of Charles I, it was in possession of the royalists till June 1644. It was then besieged by general Mytton and the earl of Denbigh with a force consisting of two troops of horse, and two hundred foot soldiers. These were so furious in their attack, that in the short space of an hour, and with the loss of only one or two men, a breach in the wall was effected, by which they entered the town. The inhabitants, in consternation, fled for shelter to the castle; but an attack was immediately commenced on it by cannon. A daring youth, of the name of Cranage, was persuaded by some of the parliament's officers to fasten a *petard* to the castle gate. Being well animated with sack, he undertook the desperate enterprize. With the engine hidden, he crept unperceived from one house to another, till he got to that next the castle, whence he sprang to the gate; he fixed his engine, set fire to it, and escaped unhurt. This, by the force of its explosion, burst open the castle gate, and the place was immediately taken. The deputy governor, four captains, and about three hundred soldiers, were made prisoners. From hence the parliament's soldiers hastened into Lancashire to other service there.

Previously to the attack, the governor pulled down the tower and part of the body of the church, which stood within the walls, lest the enemy should use them to the annoyance of the garrison.

About a fortnight after its surrender, the king's forces, consisting of about three thousand foot, and fifteen hundred horse, under the command of colonel Marrow, attempted to retake this place. Intimation of their approach was immediately sent to sir Thomas Middleton, who hastening to the assistance of the garrison, attacked the king's troops, and completely routed them. After the death of the king the castle was demolished.

Oswestry has at different times been favoured with many privileges from its lords. Its most extensive charter was however granted in the year 1406, by Thomas, earl of Arundel, at that time owner of the place. From this the inhabitants derived several advantages which they had not before enjoyed. The chief of these were, that neither the lord nor his heirs should seize on or confiscate the effects of any person in the corporation that died without making a will; and that none of the inhabitants of the lordships of Oswestry, Melverley, Kinardsley, Egerley, Ruyton, and eleven adjacent villages, at that time called the *eleven towns*, should convey cattle or goods to any other fair or market without having previously exposed them for sale in the town of Oswestry, under the penalty of six shillings and eight-pence for each offence.

Till about the end of the sixteenth century there was a very considerable market at Oswestry for Welsh flannels: Shrewsbury, however, soon after this period, deprived it of the principal part of this trade.

Oswestry and its hundred, at the making of Domesday, formed a part of Wales. They were taken thence, and annexed to England in the eighth year of the reign of Edward I.

***

34

Oswestry to Ruabon

The village of *Chirk* is situated on the brow of a hill; and from the numerous coal-works and other undertakings in the neighbourhood, it appears to be a place of some business.

The Ellesmere canal passes within half a mile of the village, and is carried over the river and vale of Ceiriog by a long aqueduct.*

In the *church* at Chirk there are several marble monuments in memory of the Middletons of Chirk castle: the best of these was erected for sir Thomas Middleton, one of the commanders in the army of the parliament during the civil wars.

***

CHIRK CASTLE

Is about a mile and a half from the village. This building, like that of Powys, still retains a mixture of the castle and mansion. It stands in an open situation, on the summit of a considerable eminence, which commands an extensive view, into *seventeen* different counties. On the exterior it retains much of its primitive aspect. It is a quadrangular structure, having five towers, one at each corner, and the fifth for the gateway, in front. The entrance is into a spacious court yard, a hundred and sixty feet long, and a hundred broad; and on the east side of this there is a handsome colonnade. The principal apartments are a saloon, a drawing-room, and gallery; in the latter of which there is a large collection of paintings, consisting, however, almost entirely of family portraits.

In a room adjoining to the gallery I observed a singular landscape, in which *Pistyll Rhaiadr*, the waterfall in Montgomeryshire, is represented as falling into the sea. I asked the cause of this strange impropriety, and was informed that the painter was a foreign artist; he had been employed by one of the Middletons to take a view of that cataract, and when the piece was nearly finished, it was hinted that a few *sheep*, scattered in different parts, would probably add to its beauty. The painter mistook the suggestion, and nettled that a person whom he judged ignorant of the art should presume to instruct him, replied with considerable tartness, 'You want some *sheeps* in it? Well, well, I will put you some *sheeps* in it!' He soon dashed out the bottom of the picture, and introduced the sea, and several *sheeps*, (ships) some of which are represented as lying at anchor close to the rocks.*

There is a dungeon to this castle, as deep as the walls are high: it is descended by a flight of forty-two steps. – The building is on the whole low and heavy, and wants magnitude to give consequence to its appearance.

***

About two miles from Chirk, in the road to Ruabon, I was much pleased with a view down a woody dell, in the bottom of which ran the river Dee. It was the first time that I had seen this stream surrounded by those romantic features for which it is so justly celebrated.

This scene was interesting, but at

NEW BRIDGE,

About half a mile farther on, it was greatly exceeded. Out of the road, about a hundred yards above the bridge, such a scene presented itself, that with the pencil of a Claude,* I could have sketched one of the most exquisite landscapes the eye ever beheld. The river here dashed along its rugged bed, and its rocky banks clad with wood, where every varied tint that autumn could afford added to their effect, cast a darkening shade upon the stream. With the green oak, all the different hues of the ash, the elm, and the hazel, were intermingled. Above the bridge arose a few cottages surrounded with foliage. The evening was calm, and the smoke, tinged by the setting sun, descended upon the vale, whilst the distant mountains were brightened by his beams into a fine purple. I sat down on the bank of the river, and contemplated these beauties till the declining sun had sunk beneath the horizon, and twilight had begun to steal over the landscape, and blend into one every different shade of reflection, and to cover the whole face of nature with its sober grey. – I forced myself away, and pursued my journey to Ruabon, my intended residence for the night.

RUABON

Is a village pleasingly situated on a rising ground, and has around it the residences of several persons of fortune. I spent two or three days very agreeably in this place, and in little excursions around the neighbourhood.

The *church* is a good building: it contains an organ, an instrument very unusual in Welsh churches, which was given by the late sir Watkin Williams Wynne.* – At its east end I observed a table monument of marble, with the date of 1526, in memory of John ap Elis Euton, and Elizabeth Clefeley, his wife:

> A tombe, it is right rich and stately made,
> Where two do lye, in stone and aunciect trade.
> The man and wife with sumptuous solemne guise,
> In this rich suit, before the aulter lies

> His head on crest, and warlike helmet stayes,
> A lion blue, on top thereof comes out;
> On lion's necke along his legges he layes,
> Two gauntlets white are lying there about.
> An aunciect squire he was, and of good race,
> As by his armes appeeres in many a place:
> His house and lands, not farre from thence, do show
> His birth and blood were great, right long ago.*

Besides this, there are four other marble monuments, two of which deserve particular attention. One of these is in memory of the late sir Watkin Williams Wynne, and the other of his wife, lady Henrietta Williams Wynne. The latter is represented by a beautiful figure of Hope, reclining on an urn: the inscription is on a pedestal, within a serpent with its head and tail united, expressive of eternity. If I am not deceived in the recollection, they are both the workmanship of Roubiliac.*

DR. DAVID POWEL,

The Welsh historian, was instituted to this vicarage in the year 1571, and lies buried here. – He was born about the beginning of the reign of queen Elizabeth; and after he left Oxford, obtained the living of Ruabon, and was made a prebendary of St. Asaph. Thus rendered easy and independent in his circumstances, he studied with great assiduity the ancient history of Britain. For this he was well qualified by his extensive acquaintance with the Welsh and other languages. – He translated into English the History of Wales written in Welsh of Caradoc of Llancarvan; and edited the writings of Giraldus Cambrensis, which he illustrated, and corrected by many learned and valuable notes. He died in 1590, leaving behind him a large collection of ancient manuscripts.

35

Excursion from Ruabon to Bangor Iscoed

From Ruabon, I wandered into the grounds of sir Watkin Williams Wynne, baronet, at

WYNNSTAY.*

These grounds are brought close up to the village; they are well wooded, and about eight miles in circumference. I observed here some immensely large oak, ash, and birch trees: the trunk of one of the oaks was near fifty feet in girth in the smallest part.

I ascended, by its well-staircase, to the top of a handsome, lately erected stone column, of very considerable height. I had entertained hopes that from thence I should have had a fine view of the surrounding country, but was disappointed: the prospect was sufficiently extensive, but in no degree interesting.

At a little distance from the column there is a tolerably large pool. The rivulet that supplies it is thrown over some artificial rock-work, and forms not an inelegant cascade.

The house is deficient both in elegance and uniformity, having been erected at different periods, and in different stiles of architecture. – From the ancient rampart called Watt's Dyke, which passes through the grounds, this place was formerly called Wattstay: but, on the marriage of sir John Wynne with Jane, the daughter of Eyton Evans, and heiress of this property, he changed its name to Wynnstay. He inclosed the park, in the year 1678, with a stone wall for deer, and planted the avenues. Sir John died about forty years afterwards, and was buried at Ruabon. He bequeathed all his estates to his relative Watkin Williams, afterwards sir Watkin Williams Wynne, bart., the grandfather of the present owner.

This place was anciently the property and residence of Madoc ap Griffith Maelor, the potent lord of Bromfield, and founder of Valle Crucis abbey, near Llangollen.

NANT Y BELE,

The Dingle of the Martin, within the grounds of Wynnstay, is a deep and wooded hollow, The sides are precipitous and rocky; and the waters of the Dee, which roll along the bottom, are blackened by the shady banks, and for the most part concealed from the eye of the observer, by the thickness of the foliage. In the distant background, I observed Chirk castle, and the country around it, clad in lively colours; whilst, to the westward, I had a view of Castell Dinas Brân, crowning the summit of its steep. The whole vale of Llangollen, as far as the town, lay nearly in a straight line, and was richly varied with wood, rock, and pasture. The scene was closed in the horizon by the far distant British Alps, which bounded the sight. – From this station I proceeded along the bank of the Dee, clambering over hedges and ditches, till I found myself at Pen y Llan, the seat of Mr. Lloyd, whence I had another charming view of the country.

I returned to Ruabon, and rambled from thence to Bangor Iscoed, *Bangor under the Wood*, a village about ten miles distant. In this excursion I passed through

OVERTON,

A picturesque little village, seated on an eminence at a small distance from the Dee. Near the bridge I had another fine prospect along this romantic stream.

In the church-yard I saw several fine old *yew trees*. These, from their size and beauty, have been accounted among the wonders of Wales. – If the poems of Ossian can be considered as authority, the custom of planting yews in burying-places was adopted in a very remote period. He thus speaks of two lovers: – 'Here rests their dust, Cuthullin; these lonely yews sprang from their tomb, and shade them from the storm.'* – A short inquiry into the origin of this custom may deserve attention.

***

Sir Thomas Brown, in his Urn Burial,* says, 'it may admit conjecture, whether the planting of yew trees in church-yards, had not its original from ancient *funeral rites*, or as an emblem of resurrection, from its perpetual verdure.'

An intelligent writer has remarked, that in this country there was formerly a procession (as in Catholic countries there still is) on Palm Sunday, in memory of the entrance of Christ into Jerusalem, where branches of palm-trees were strewed in his way. We have authority that *palms* were borne in the procession with us till the reign of Edward VI. An old manuscript states, that in this country, from want of olive, that 'berith greene leves,' *palm* was used to be carried in its stead. From these intimations it is evident that something green, called *palm*, was carried in procession on Palm Sunday, which is sometimes so early in the year as the 15th of March, and never later than the 18th of April, when very few plants are in leaf: and in some church-yards in east Kent the yew-trees are to this day called *palms*. It is therefore more than probable that the palms were no other than the branches of yew-trees, which are not only always green, but usually in bloom about this time; and one or two trees, the number usually found in each church-yard, would be amply sufficient for the purpose.

Yew-trees may also have been considered emblematical of the state of mankind. The leaves having a most poisonous quality, may have been thought representative of mortality; whilst the durable foliage, and the long period through which they flourish, of two or three centuries, are not unaptly significant of immortality and eternity.

BANGOR ISCOED

Is somewhat more than two miles beyond Overton. It is situated on the banks of the Dee, which here flows under an elegant stone bridge of five arches.

This place has its chief celebrity from having been the site of the most ancient monastery in Britain, founded, as the old writers assert, by Lucius, the son of Coel, and first Christian king of Britain, somewhat prior to the year 180.* Lucius formed it an university, for the increase of learning, and the preservation of the Christian faith in this realm; and it produced for an age so unenlightened many learned men. It is said by some writers to have been converted into a monastery about the year 530 by Cynwyl or Congelus, who was created the first abbot. Others say that Pelagius the monk, a native of Wales, who had studied here in his youth, after having travelled through France, Italy, Egypt, Syria, and various other countries, was made a bishop, and on his return to England converted this house.

The monastery of Bangor was rich in manuscripts, and universally celebrated for its valuable library: and Speed states, that from its great age, and the number of its learned men, it was acknowledged to be the parent of all the other monasteries in the world.

At the arrival of Augustine, who was missioned about 596, from pope Gregory I, to convert the English Saxons to Christianity, this monastery appears to have been in a very flourishing state. There were at this time as many as 2400 monks: a hundred of these, in turns, passed one hour in devotion, so that the whole twenty-four hours of every day were employed in sacred duties. Bede says there were just so many, that being divided into seven parts, each of these contained three hundred men, which, with their proper rulers, passed their time alternately in prayer and labour.

The monks of Bangor were dissenters from the Romish church; and, on a conference betwixt Augustine and its governors, the imperious monk demanded of them that they should keep the feast of Easter at the same time the papists did; that they should administer baptism according to the ceremonies of the church of Rome; and 'preach the word of life with him and his fellows.' In other things, he said, they would be allowed to retain their ancient customs, insolently concluding, that 'if they would not accept of peace with their brethren, they should receive war from their enemies, and by them, without reserve, should suffer death.' They refused obedience to his injunctions, and resolutely maintained the original rites of their church. Shortly after this period followed the dreadful massacre of above twelve hundred of the monks by Ethelfrid, king of Northumbria, at the memorable battle of Chester. This unmanly slaughter the British annals and songs ascribe to the instigations of Augustine.

Not long after this event the monastery became neglected, and went entirely to decay. William of Malmesbury, who lived shortly after the Norman conquest, asserts, that even in his time, there remained only some relics of its ancient magnificence: there were, he says, so many ruined churches, and such immense heaps of rubbish, as were not elsewhere to be found. – Leland says of it, in the reign of Henry VIII, that its site was in a fertile valley on the south side of the Dee; but that the river having since changed its course, then ran nearly through the middle of the ground on which it stood. The extent of its walls, he says, was equal to that of the walls round a town; and the two gates, the names of which had been handed down by tradition, had been half a mile asunder. Within the memory of persons then living, the bones of the monks, and pieces of their clothes, had been ploughed up, in the cultivation of the ground, as well as pieces of squared stones, and some Roman money.

***

TYSILIO

While I am speaking of the monastery of Bangor, and its eminent men, I ought by no means to leave this writer unnoticed. Tysilio was a British bishop, the son of Brochwel Ysythroc, prince of Powis, and was nearly contemporary with Nennius.* He was the author of a British history intitled *Brut y Brenhinoedd*, or the traditions of the British bards. It commences with the descent of the Trojan colony, and ends with the reign of Cadwaladr, the last king of the Britons. This history, about the year 1150, fell into the hands of Galfrid Arthur, or Geoffry, archdeacon of Monmouth, and afterwards bishop of St. Asaph, who translated it into Latin, inserting in his translation all the monkish fables that he could collect. In this state the work took the name of the translator, and has suffered the most violent abuse by all the English, since the time of Camden, that have written on the British history, and by various French and Dutch writers. This, however, has been done without any acquaintance with the original work in the British language, which is essentially different from the translation both in general matter, and in the statement of facts.

36

Ruabon to Wrexham

I left Ruabon, and proceeded on my journey towards Wrexham. In order to pass through the grounds of *Erddig*, belonging to Philip Yorke, esq.* I left the carriage-road, and went along a foot-path, over the meadows on the right. I observed considerable taste displayed at Erddig, but all the efforts of art are so infinitely inferior to the majestic operations of nature, which I had lately seen in so much variety, that I cannot say I derived much pleasure from these grounds. – Watt's Dyke runs through them; and not far distant is the fragment of a wall, conjectured to have been part of a Roman fort.

WREXHAM

Is a populous market town, and of such size and consequence as to have obtained the appellation of the metropolis of North Wales. The streets and buildings are in general good; and the adjacent country is so beautiful, as to have induced many families to fix their residence in its vicinity. The centre street, in which the market is held, is of considerable length, and of unusual width for an ancient town. The common hall is a large and convenient building. This place was known to our Saxon ancestors by the name of Wrightesham, or Wrightlesham. A few centuries ago it was noted as the resort of buckler, or shield makers.

The *church* was formerly collegiate, and is yet a most elegant structure. On the exterior it is richly ornamented with gothic sculpture. The tower, which is about a hundred and forty feet in height, is particularly beautiful. On three of its sides there have been statues as large as life, of no fewer than thirty saints: two have been destroyed by falling from their niches. Miss Seward, in her verses on Wrexham, has finely expressed the elegance of this building:

> Her hallow'd temple there religion shews,

>That erst with beauteous majesty arose,
>In ancient days, when gothic art display'd
>Her fanes in airy elegance array'd.
>Whose nameless charms the Dorian claims efface,
>Corinthian splendor and Ionic grace.*

The interior of the church is plain, but exceedingly neat, being devoid of the load of ornaments common in gothic churches. It contains, among other monuments, two of the elegant workmanship of Roubiliac.* One of these, having the date of 1747, was erected to the memory of Mary, the daughter of sir Richard Middleton. A female figure is represented in the act of bursting from the tomb: the countenance is truly angelic, and the mixture of surprize and admiration is so delicately, and at the same time so firmly expressed, that after gazing for some moments stedfastly on the face, I could almost have fancied it more than stone. The sainted maid,

>Amid the bursting tomb
>Hears the last trumpet shrill its murky gloom,
>With smile triumphant over death and time,
>Lifts the rapt eye, and rears the form sublime.*

Against the wall, an ancient pyramid, a building, from its solidity, calculated to resist the efforts of time, is represented as falling into ruin. The ridiculous little figure blowing the trumpet might have been omitted without any derogation from the merit of the sculpture. On the whole, however, it is so uncommonly beautiful, as to demand the admiration of every lover of the art. – The other piece of Roubiliac's performance, is a medallion containing two profile faces of the reverend Thomas Middleton, and Arabella his wife. – Nearly opposite to the former of these monuments there is a recumbent figure of *Hugh Bellot*, of the ancient family of Morton in Cheshire. He was bishop of Bangor, was afterwards translated to the see of Chester, and died in the year 1596. Bellot was one of those divines who adhered to the monastic austerities long after both law and custom had rendered them unnecessary: during the whole of his life he would never admit a female into his family. – There is under the belfry an antique monument, which was some years ago discovered in the ground by the workmen who dug for a foundation for the iron gates of the church-yard. The figure is of a knight in complete armour; his feet rest on some kind of animal, and round his shield there is an inscription, but this is at present illegible.

The altar-piece is a fine painting of the institution of the sacrament. It was brought from Rome, and given to the church by Elihu Yale,* esq. a native of America, who went on speculation to the East Indies. Of this person, it is recorded by one of the travellers in India, that he ordered his groom to be hanged for having ridden his horse on a journey of two or three days for the sake of his health: he was tried for this crime in the English courts, and escaped with a high pecuniary punishment. He died in London in the year 1721, but was interred in this church-yard with the following inscription on his tomb:

> Born in America, in Europe bred,
> In Afric travelled, and in Asia wed;
> Where long he liv'd and thriv'd – in London dead.
> Much good, some ill he did, so hope all's even,
> And that his soul through mercy's gone to Heaven!
> You that survive and read this tale, take care
> For this most certain exit to prepare,
> Where blest in peace, the actions of the just
> Smell sweet, and blossom in the silent dust.

The present church at Wrexham was finished, except the tower, before the year 1472: the latter, from a date that there is upon it, does not seem to have been completed till about thirty-four years afterwards. In 1647, during the civil wars, this venerable building was used for some time as a prison, and several of the committee-men were confined in it by the parliament's soldiers, who had mutinied for want of pay.

At this town there is a noted annual fair, held in the month of March, which lasts nine days. This is frequented by traders from various, and even very distant parts of the kingdom. The commodities brought by the Welsh people are chiefly flannels, linen, linsey-woolsey, and horses and cattle in abundance. Traders from other parts bring Irish linen, Yorkshire and woollen cloths, and Manchester and Birmingham goods of all kinds. For the accommodation of those who have goods to sell, there are two squares, or areas, furnished with little shops or booths.

The two principal inns are the Eagles and the Red Lion, both good houses. At the former I had excellent accommodations, and experienced the most obliging treatment.

In the neighbourhood of Wrexham there are several manufactories of military instruments; and in particular a large cannon foundery not far from the town.

37

Excursion from Wrexham to Holt

From Wrexham I made an excursion to *Holt*, an obscure village on the west bank of the Dee, about six miles distant. This was once a market town, and a place of some consequence; and it still continues to be governed by a mayor and aldermen. The former is usually some gentleman of respectability who resides in the neighbourhood. – The town was incorporated in the year 1410, by a charter of Thomas earl of Arundel, which, however, restricts the burgesses from being Welshmen: – the charter runs in this singular form: 'To the burgesses of our town, and to their heirs and successors, being *Englishmen*.' This arose, no doubt, from the hatred which the lords marchers entertained towards the Welsh people, on account of the insurrection of their hero Glyndwr, at that time scarcely suppressed.

This place has also the name of *Lyons*. The castle was anciently called Castrum Leonis, which appellation Camden conjectures to have been derived from the Roman twentieth legion having been stationed at a little distance higher up, and on the other side of the river.

The two villages of Holt and Farndon are divided only by the Dee, and have a communication by a very ancient bridge of ten arches. – All the scenery of this neighbourhood is flat and unpleasant. The Dee flows through meadows, without any of the beauty or grandeur of rocks, or foliage, that adorn its banks in the more mountainous parts of the country.

HOLT CASTLE

Was situated close to the river, and defended on three sides by a moat forty or fifty yards wide, cut out of the solid rock: the present remains consist of little else than rock, for this originally seems to have formed the first eight or ten yards of the castle. The stone used in the building appears to have been that obtained in making the moat. – The fortress consisted of five bastions, of which four were round, and the remaining one, facing the river, square. The entrance was by a drawbridge on the west side. So little of the masonry is left, that in the present state it is impossible to form any idea of its ancient strength. The site is by no means extensive; and as it stood on a piece of ground level with the town, it must have had its principal strength in the deep and perpendicular sides of its moat.

The lands of Holt and Chirk, in the reign of Henry III, and the commencement of the reign of Edward I were the property of Madoc ap Griffith, a native of Wales who had espoused the English cause. On the death of Madoc, two sons were left, both of them under age; and Edward gave one of them to the guardianship of John, earl of Warren, and the other to the care of Roger Mortimer, the son of lord Mortimer of Wigmore. To the former boy belonged the lordship of Bromfield and Yale, in which Holt stands, and the castle of Dinas Brân; and to the other the property of Chirk and Nanheudwy. – The villainous guardians, to disburthen themselves of their charge, and get possession of the estates of the children, caused them both to be murdered. Their inhumanity, so far from meeting its just reward, was freely pardoned by Edward, who came in for a share of the spoil. He confirmed to Warren the castle of Dinas Brân, and the lordship of Bromfield and Yale; to Mortimer he gave the property of Chirk; and the castle and demesnes of Caergwrle, or Hope, he reserved to himself. Warren and Mortimer immediately began to secure their possessions by erecting on them places of defence. The latter built Chirk castle, and Warren commenced this fortress, but dying soon afterwards, it was finished by his son.

In the ninth year of Edward II, John earl Warren, the grandson of the founder, having no issue, gave this castle, with that of Dinas Brân, and the lordship of Bromfield, to the king. He was soon after divorced from his wife, and he obtained a regrant of them to himself, and Matilda de Nereford, his mistress, for life, with remainders to his illegitimate children, and their heirs. Matilda was the last survivor, and therefore at her death, in the following reign, the property reverted to the crown. It was, not long afterwards, given to Edward Fitz Alan, earl of Arundel, who had married the sister of the late owner. In this family it remained for three generations; but on the execution of Richard it appears to have been forfeited to the crown. When, in 1399, after this event, Holt castle was delivered to the duke of Hertford, there were found in it jewels to the value of two hundred thousand marks, and a hundred thousand marks in money. These had been deposited there, as a place of safe custody, by the unfortunate Richard II previously to his expedition into Ireland.

The estates and title were restored in the succeeding reign, and they once again escheated to the crown. Henry VII granted them to sir William Stanley; but on his execution resumed them, and took in this castle plate and money to the value of above forty thousand marks, which Stanley had obtained from the plunder of Bosworth Field.

The lordship of Bromfield and Yale afterwards became the property of Henry Fitzroy, duke of Richmond, the natural son of Henry VIII; and in the reign of Edward VI, of Thomas Seymour, brother to the protector Somerset, who formed here a magazine of military stores. On his execution it once more fell to the crown.

During the civil wars Holt castle was garrisoned for the king, but in 1643 was seized by the parliament. It was afterwards retaken, and in February 1645–6 was again besieged by the parliament's forces. The governor, sir Richard Lloyd, defended it for more than a month with the utmost bravery, but was at length compelled to surrender. Towards the end of this year this castle, with four others, was dismantled by order of the parliament.

The lordship of Bromfield and Yale is at present the property of the crown; and sir Watkin Williams Wynne, bart. is the steward.

The inhabitants of Holt contribute with those of Ruthin and Denbigh, towards sending a member to parliament.

38

Wrexham to Mold

About five miles from Wrexham I passed through a romantic glen, which would have had considerable picturesque effect, if this had not been destroyed by several white-washed cottages obtruding themselves on the sight from among the trees. A little beyond this scene I passed a neat bridge of a single arch, which appeared very beautiful, accompanied by the rustic cottages overshadowed with trees on the bank of the stream. – The country I now journied through was somewhat mountainous; but beyond this vale it became again flat and uninteresting.

CAERGWRLE

> Comes right now to passe my pen,
> With ragged waulles, yea all to rent and torne:
> As though it had been never knowne to men,
> Or carelesse left, as wretched thing forlorn;
> Like beggar bare, as naked as my nail,
> It lies along, whose wrecke doth none bewayle.*

Caergwrle, like Holt, was once a flourishing town, but it is dwindled into an insignificant village. – Its parish church is about a mile distant.

There is good reason for supposing that Caergwrle was a Roman station, probably an outpost to Deva. Camden discovered here an hypocaust, hewn out of the solid rock, six yards and a quarter long, five yards broad, and somewhat more than half a yard in height. On some of the tiles were inscribed the letters LEGIO XX., which seem to point out the founders. This is further corroborated by the name of the place. Caer gawr lle, *the camp of the great legion*; Gawr lle being the name by which the Britons distinguished the twentieth legion.

The *castle* stood on the summit of a high rock. Its present remains are very inconsiderable; they are, however, sufficient to indicate that it could never have been a fortress of any great importance.

The founder has not been ascertained; but from its construction it has been evidently of British origin. – In the reign of Edward I we find it possessed by the English crown, for that monarch bestowed it, along with the lordship of Denbigh, on David, the brother to prince Llewelyn. Whilst in his hands, Roger de Clifford, justiciary of Chester, cut down the adjacent woods, and endeavoured to wrest the castle from its owner: this, however, he was prevented from doing by the timely interference of the king. – When David, in 1282, insidiously took up arms with his brother against his former benefactor, he left a garrison of some strength in the castle; but it was besieged by a division of the English army, and was shortly afterwards surrendered to them.

In the preceding account of Holt I have remarked that Caergwrle castle was excepted from the grant which was made to John earl of Warren of the property of one of the children of Madoc ap Griffith. Edward annexed it, with the tract of land in which it is situated, to Flintshire: it continued to form a part of this county till Henry VIII separated, and added it to the county of Denbigh. It was, however, not long afterwards restored to its proper county.

Edward I after the surrender of the garrison that David left in it, gave the castle to his consort, Eleanor, from whom it acquired the name of *Queen Hope*. She lodged here in her journey to Caernarvon; and either during her abode in the castle, or very shortly afterwards, it was by some accident set on fire, and burnt.

In the first year of the succeeding reign, this castle and manor were granted to John de Cromwell, on condition that at his own expence he should repair the castle. – Some years afterward they were given to sir John Stanley.

The town of Hope received its first charter from Edward the Black Prince, in the year 1351. By this charter it is directed that the constable of the castle for the time being should also be the mayor, and he was to choose annually from the burgesses two persons as bailiffs. – All the privileges which the inhabitants enjoyed from this charter were afterwards confirmed by Richard II. – Caergwrle and Hope, in conjunction with Flint, Caerwys, Rhyddlan, and Overton, send a member to parliament.

MOLD

Is a small market town, consisting principally of one long and wide street.

The *church* is a neat building, ornamented all round the top of the outside walls with gothic carvings of animals. The body was erected in the reign of Henry VII, but the tower is of more modern date. The pillars in the interior are light and elegant, and its whole appearance was exceedingly neat. There is a good monument of Richard Davies, esq. of Llanerch, who died in the year 1728. He is represented in an upright attitude, but, unfortunately, the figure has lost its nose from an accidental stone thrown through the window. – The epitaph on Dr. William Wynne of Tower, some time fellow of All Souls college Oxford, who died in the year 1776, deserves a place here, not from its eccentricity, so much as its recording an example of an express direction against interment within the walls of the church, which ought to be generally followed:

> In conformity to ancient usage;
> from a proper regard to decency,
> and a concern for the health of his
> fellow-creatures, he was moved to give
> particular directions for being buried
> in the adjoining church-yard,
> and not in the church.
> And as he scorned flattering of others
> while living, he has taken care to prevent
> being flattered himself when dead,
> by causing this small memorial to be
> set up in his life time.
> *God be merciful to me a sinner.*

There is also in this church an ancient cenotaph to the memory of Robert Warton, or Parfew, who was abbot of Bermondsey, but in 1536 was translated to the see of St. Asaph. He was interred at Hereford, but having been a considerable benefactor to the church of Mold, this cenotaph was erected as a grateful memorial of his beneficence.

MOLD CASTLE

From the church-yard a lofty mount called the Bailey Hill, was pointed out to me as the site of the castle. Of the building there are not now, I believe, the smallest remains. The hill was planted on its summit, and round the bottom, with larches, firs, and other evergreens.

The castle appears to have been founded during the reign of William Rufus, by Robert Montalt, the son of the high steward of Chester. From him the place received its name of Mont Alt, or De Monte Alto.

In the year 1144 it was seized and demolished by Owen Gwynedd, prince of Wales, and in little more than a century it appears to have several times changed owners. At length, in 1267, Griffith ap Gwenwynwyn wrested it from the hands of the English, and again destroyed it. It was soon rebuilt, and restored to the barons of Montalt. – In 1327, the last baron having no issue, conveyed it to Isabel, the queen of Edward II, for life, with remainder to John of Eltham, a younger brother of Edward III. But on his death, without issue, it reverted with his possessions to the crown.

The lordship became some time afterwards the property of the Stanley family. The earls of Derby possessed it till the execution of James, after which it was purchased, along with the manor of Hope, by some persons whose names I have not been able to learn, who enjoyed them till the restoration. At the conclusion of the civil wars, the earl of Derby agreed to pay eleven thousand pounds for these manors; but afterwards retracting, the king ordered the former purchasers to be confirmed in their possession. The Derby family, however, by some means regained the manor of Hope, but that of Mold was lost to them for ever.

MAES GARMON

About a mile west of Mold, and not far from Rhual, the seat of the Griffiths, is a place which to this day retains the name of Maes Garmon, The Field of Garmon or Germanus. On this spot, in Easter week 448, was fought the celebrated battle between the joint forces of the Picts and Scots against the Britons, headed by the bishops Germanus and Lupus, who had about two years before been sent into this kingdom. Previously to the engagement, Germanus instructed the soldiers to attend to the word given them by the priests on the field of battle, and to repeat it with energy through the whole army. When the forces were prepared for the critical onset, that was to decide the important fate of the day, Germanus pronounced aloud ALLELUIA! The priests repeated it thrice, and it was afterwards taken up by the voices of the whole army, till even the hills reverberated the sound. The enemy, confounded, affrighted, and trembling, fled on every side. The Britons pursued, and left few alive to relate the dismal story. Most of them fell by the sword, but many threw themselves into the adjoining river, and perished in the flood.* This victory has been called by all the historians Victoria Alleluiatica. – A pyramidal stone column, erected on the spot in 1736 by Nathaniel Griffith, esq. of Rhual, commemorates the event in the following inscription.*

***

The date of this battle seems to have been mistaken both by Mr. Griffith and Mr. Pennant, who each fix it to the year 420. Matthew of Westminster,* from whose work the preceding account is extracted, says expressly that it took place in 448, and that Germanus and Lupus did not arrive in this kingdom till about two years before this time. He mentions nothing of the Saxons having any share in the business; nor indeed does it appear very probable that they should, since their army was not introduced by Vortigern till the following year. What has been said, that the Saxons here engaged might have been such as came over on some predatory excursion, prior to the invitation of Vortigern, can have little validity when such evidence both direct and circumstantial is to be adduced to the contrary. The arrival of the Saxons prior to that period, seems however of much less importance in the proof than the arrival of the bishops, for they evidently were not in the kingdom till twenty-six years after the generally supposed time of the event.

39

Mold to Ruthin

From Mold I went again to Denbigh, in order to pursue a regular track through the remainder of North Wales to Shrewsbury, which was the place I had fixed as the termination of my pedestrian ramble, and from whence I intended to take coach immediately to London.

I was highly delighted with my walk along the vale of Clwyd, from Denbigh to Ruthin. The views all the way were of the elegant, rich, and here picturesque vale, bounded by the distant Clwyddian hills. The day was peculiarly favourable to this kind of scenery; it was dark and hot, and the rolling clouds that hung heavily in the atmosphere, tinged the mountains with their sombre shade, which gave an indescribable richness to the scenes.

LLANRHAIADR

I arrived at Llanrhaiadr, *The Village of the Cataract*,* which is situated on a small eminence in the midst of this fertile vale.

The *church* is a handsome structure, with a large and somewhat elegant east window, containing a representation of the genealogy of Christ from Jesse. The patriarch is painted as sprawling upon his back, with the genealogical tree growing from his stomach. – I was wandering carelessly about this building, when I cast my eyes on a tombstone containing the following inscription, which affords a memorable instance of the pride of ancestry which is inherent in the Welsh character:

> Heare lyeth the body of
> John, ap Robert of Porth, ap
> David, ap Griffith, ap David
> Vaughan, ap Blethyn, ap
> Griffith, ap Meredith,
> ap Iorwerth, ap Llewelyn,
> ap Ieroth, ap Heilin, ap

Cowryd, ap Cadvan, ap
Alawgwa, ap Cadell,
the
KING OF POWIS,
who departed this life the
xx day of March, in the
year of our Lord God
1643, and of
his age xcv.

About a quarter of a mile distant there is a celebrated spring called Ffynnon Dyfnog, *The Well of Dyfnog*. There was on this spot a bath, and formerly a chapel dedicated to this Welsh saint.

RUTHIN

I proceeded on my journey, and found the scenery all the way to Ruthin, *The Red Fort*, extremely beautiful. – This place, like St. Asaph and Denbigh, is pleasantly situated on a considerable eminence nearly in the middle of the Vale of Clwyd. At a little distance behind the town, the mountains seem to close up the end of the vale. From different situations in the outskirts of the town I had several fine prospects of the adjacent country. The little river Clwyd runs through this place, and is here scarcely three yards across. – Ruthin is a large and tolerably populous town, having two markets in the week, one on Saturday for meat, and the other on Monday principally for corn. The county-gaol for Denbighshire is here: it is a neat and well-constructed building.

The *church* was originally conventual, belonging to a house of Bonhommes, a species of Augustine monks. It was made collegiate in 1310 by John, the son of Reginald de Grey, lord of Dyffryn Clwyd, who endowed it with upwards of two hundred acres of land, granted to it many privileges, and established seven regular priests, one of whom was to serve the chapel of the garrison. In this state it probably continued till the dissolution, but neither Dugdale nor Speed have mentioned its valuation. – The apartments of the priests were joined to the church by a cloister, part of which is built up, and now serves as the mansion of the warden. – The tower is of a much later date than the rest of the building.

It is believed that there was formerly a *house of white friars* in this place: of this there is nothing left except the name.

RUTHIN CASTLE

Was situated on the north side of the town, and on no great elevation. Its present remains are a few foundations of the walls, and the fragments of a tower or two. Some parts of the building appear to have been of vast strength and thickness. The stone of which it was formed was of a brick red colour, whence the place had the name of Rhudd Ddin (or Dinas), *The Red Fort*. On the area of the castle there is at present a meadow, and in another part a five's court, and bowling-green. The walls afford a fine prospect of the vale. – The following is a description of this fortress during the sixteenth century, previously to its demolition:

> This castle stands on rocke much like red bricke,
> The dykes are cut with tool through stony cragge,
> The towers are high, the walls are large and thicke,
> The worke itself would shake a subject's bagge,
> If he were bent to build the like againe.
> It rests on mount, and lookes o'er wood and playne,
> It hath great store of chambers finely wrought
> That tyme alone to great decay hath brought.
>
> It shews within by double walls and wayes,
> A deep device did first erect the same;
> It makes oure worlde to think on elder dayes
> Because one worke was form'd in such a frame.
> One tower or waull the other answers right,
> As though at call each thing should please the sight:
> The rocke wrought round where every tower doth stand
> Set forthe full fine by head, by heart, and hand.*

The town and castle of Ruthin appear to have been founded by Reginald Grey, second son to lord Grey de Wilton, to whom Edward I had given nearly the whole of the vale of Clwyd, as a reward for his active services against the Welsh. His posterity, who received the title of earls of Kent, resided here, till earl Richard, having dissipated his fortune by gambling, sold the whole property to king Henry VII. – From this time the castle, being unroofed, fell into decay, till, along with large revenues in the vale, it was bestowed by the bounty of queen Elizabeth, on Ambrose earl of Warwick. By him it was repaired, and again rendered tenable.

During a fair that was holden at Ruthin in the year 1400, the soldiers of Glyndwr suddenly entered the town. They set it on fire in various places, plundered the merchants, and again retired in safety to the mountains.

In the civil wars the castle was retained by the royalist party till February 1645–6: it was then attacked, and, after a siege of near two months, was surrendered to general Mytton. Colonel Mason was made governor; but in the same year it was ordered by the parliament to be dismantled.

40

Ruthin to Llangollen

I left Ruthin early in the morning. The clouds began to collect, and a drizzly rain came on, which lasted without intermission till I arrived within four miles of Llangollen. I thus lost several probably fine views from the high mountains that form the eastern barrier of the vale of Clwyd, over which the road winds. During the greatest part of this journey I was so enveloped in clouds and mist, that I could not, literally, discern objects that were twenty yards distant from me.

VALE OF CRUCIS

About ten miles from Ruthin I descended into this, one of the most charmingly secluded vales that our kingdom can boast, surrounded by high mountains, and abrupt rocks towering rudely into the sky. The bottoms of these were, in many places, clad with wood and verdure. In this vale are seated the venerable ruins of Llan Egwest, or Valle Crucis abbey; and from the road, at a little distance, the fine gothic west end, embowered in trees, and backed by the mountain, on whose summit stand the shattered remains of Castell Dinas Brân, form a scene finely picturesque. The adjacent precipices were enlivened by the browsing flocks, which were scattered along their sides, and by

> Kites that swim sublime
> In still-repeated circles, screaming loud,*

whilst from below I was entertained with

> The cheerful sound
> Of woodland harmony, that always fills
> The merry vale between.*

The rugged and woody banks of the Dee, upon my proceeding onward, soon added a fresh interest to the scenery of this beautiful retreat. – The vale extends nearly to Llangollen; and at the distance of about a mile, the town, with its church and antique bridge, romantically embosomed in mountains, whose rugged summits pierced the clouds, became additional features in the landscape.

PILLAR OF ELISEG

The vale of Crucis is indebted for its name to this cross, or pillar, which is to be found in a meadow near the abbey; and just opposite to the second mile-stone from Llangollen.* This pillar is very ancient. It appears to have been erected upwards of a thousand years ago, in memory of Eliseg (the father of Brochwel Yfeithroc, prince of Powis, who was slain at the battle of Chester in 607), by Concenn, or Congen, his great grandson. The inscription is not at present legible. The shaft was once above twelve feet long, but having been thrown down and broken some time during the civil wars, its upper part, only about seven feet in length, was left. After these commotions it was suffered to lie neglected for more than a century. At length, in 1779, Mr. Lloyd of Trevor Hall, the owner of the property on which it now stands, caused this part of it to be raised from the rubbish with which it was covered, and placed once again on its pedestal.

VALLE CRUCIS ABBEY,

Or, as it is called by the Welsh, Llan Egwest abbey, is about a quarter of a mile from the pillar of Eliseg. It is a grand and majestic ruin, affording some elegant specimens of the ancient gothic architecture. Miss Seward has addressed this abbey in language finely poetical and descriptive:

> Say ivy'd Valle Crucis, time decay'd,
>   Dim on the brink of Deva's wandering flood,
> Your riv'd arch glimmering thro' the tangled glade,
>   Your gay hills towering o'er your night of wood,
> Deep in the vales's recesses as you stand,
> And desolately great the rising sigh command.*

There are still remaining of the church the east and west ends, and the south transept. In the west end there is an arched door-way, that has been highly and very beautifully ornamented: over this, in a round arch, there have been three lancet windows; and above these a circular, or marigold one, with eight divisions. The east end, from its stile of

Fig. 10. *Valle Crucis Abbey*, Denbighshire, engraving after drawing by William Bingley in 1798.

architecture, appears of higher antiquity than the other; and its three long, narrow, and pointed windows, give it a heavy appearance. The cloister on the south side, which a century ago was only a shell, is now converted into a dwelling-house, the residence of the person who farms the adjacent land. Three rows of groined arches, on single round pillars, support the dormitory which is now a loft for containing corn, approached by steps from without. The floors are here so thick, from their being arched beneath, that when the doors are shut, and the threshers are at work, even in that part directly over the present kitchen, they cannot be heard below. – Part of a chimney in one of the bed-chambers is a relic of a sepulchral monument. – The ornaments to the pillars and arches are of free-stone, and many of them are perfectly fresh and beautiful. The area of the church is overgrown with tall ash-trees, which hide from the sight some parts of the ruin, but contribute greatly to its picturesque beauty.

> I doe love these auncient ruynes,
> We never tread upon them but we set
> Oure foote upon some reverend historie;
> And questionless here, in this open courte

> (Which now lies naked to the injuries
> Of stormy weather) some men lye interred
> Who lov'd the church so well and gave so largely to't,
> They thought it should have canopied their bones
> Till dombesday: but all things have their end;
> Churches and cities (which have diseases like to men)
> Must have like death that we have.*

> This sober shade
> Lets fall a serious gloom upon the mind
> That checks but not appals. Such are the haunts
> Religion loves, a meek and humble maid,
> Whose tender eye bears not the blaze of day.*

Valle Crucis was a house of Cistertian monks, dedicated to the virgin mother. It was indebted for its foundation, about the year 1200, to Madoc ap Griffith, a prince of Powis, who, after various successes, and acquiring much booty by the reduction and ruin of English castles, dedicated a portion of his plunder to the service of religion! He was interred here. At the dissolution the revenues appear to have amounted to about two hundred pounds *per annum*.

***

LLANGOLLEN

From these elegant and beautiful scenes I wandered into the dirty, ill built, and disagreeable town of Llangollen. The streets are narrow, and all the houses are built of the dark shaly stone so common in North Wales. The situation of this place is, however, truly delightful to the admirer of nature; it stands on rocks that overlook the Dee, and is surrounded by high and bold mountains.

The *bridge*, which consists of five narrow and pointed arches, was originally erected about the middle of the fourteenth century, by John Trevor, bishop of St. Asaph. It is built on the rock, and in a place where it would almost seem impossible to fix a foundation sufficiently firm to withstand the furious rapidity of the current, which has worn the shelving masses to a black and glossy polish. During late years it has undergone considerable repairs.

In the *church* I found nothing deserving of attention. The name of the patron saint, who has left behind him a legend worthy even of the Koran, is pretty enough, and of no great length! *Collen, ap Gwynawc; ap Clydawc, ap Cowrda, ap Caradawc Freichpas, ap Llyr Meirim, ap Einion Urth, ap Cunedda Wledig*! – From the church-yard, the lofty mountains, on one of which stands Castell Dinas Brân, and the woody banks of the Dee, whose rapid stream winds along the valley, form a scene by no means inelegant.

PLAS NEWYDD

About a quarter of a mile south of Llangollen is Plâs Newydd, the charming retreat of lady Eleanor Butler and Miss Ponsonby,* which, however, has of late years been probably too much intruded upon by the curiosity of the multitudes of tourists who every summer visit Llangollen. Lady Eleanor Butler was, I am informed, the youngest sister of the late, and is consequently aunt to the present earl of Ormond. – Miss Ponsonby is the grand-daughter of general Ponsonby, who was slain in the battle of Fontenoy. Her father, Mr. Chambre Ponsonby, married Miss Louisa Lyons, a most elegant and accomplished woman, the second daughter of captain John Lyons, clerk of the council of Dublin. This lady lived but a few years after her marriage, and left the present Miss Ponsonby, her only child. – These two females, delighted with the scenery around Llangollen, when it was little known to the rest of the world, sought here a philosophical retirement from the frivolities of fashionable life, erected a dwelling that commands a fine mountain prospect, and have resided here ever since.

CASTELL DINAS BRAN

Is situated on a high, and somewhat conical hill, about a mile from Llangollen. This hill is so very steep on all sides, towards the summit, as to render the walk to the castle not a little fatiguing. – The building has been about a hundred yards long, and fifty in breadth; and it formerly occupied the whole crown of the mountain. From its extremely elevated situation it must have been a place of vast strength. On the side which is least steep it was defended by trenches cut through the solid rock. The present remains consist of nothing more than a few shattered walls. The views from hence on every side are very grand. Towards the east I could look along the whole vale of Llangollen, through which the Dee was seen to foam over its bed of rocks; and, beyond the vale, I could see all the flat and highly cultivated country that extended for many miles. Just beneath me lay the town of Llangollen. Towards the west I overlooked the vale of Crucis, and the mountains beyond it were all exposed, their dark sides agreeably varied with wood and meadow. On the north-west I was much struck with the singular appearance of a vast rock called Craig Eglwyseg, *The Eagle's Rock*, from a tradition that formerly a pair of eagles had their nest, or aëry, here. Leland has mistaken this rock for that on which the castle stands, where he says, 'there bredith every yere an egle. And the egle doth sorely assault hym that destroyeth the nest; going downe in one basket, and having another over his hedde, to defend the sore stripes of the egle.' For upwards of a mile this rock lies stratum upon stratum, in such a direction as to form a kind of horizontal steps, denominated by naturalists *saxa sedilia*. – The inhabitants of Llangollen assert, that in one part of the rock there is an opening, whence a long arched passage leads to the foundation of the castle. The latter part of this assertion is evidently false from the situation of the building; and I could scarcely even credit the report of a cavern in the rock, for, though such is generally believed to exist, I was not able on frequent inquiry either to find any person who had himself seen it, nor could any one point out its situation to enable me to examine it.

HISTORY OF CASTELL DINAS BRAN

This fortress, from the stile of its architecture, was evidently the work of the Britons. It is supposed by some writers to have been founded by Brennus, the Gaulic general, who is reputed to have come into this country to contend with his brother Belinus. The similarity of names seems, however, the only foundation for the conjecture, and the most accurate historians believe it to have originated at a much later period. – The mountain river Brân runs at the foot of the hill, but whether the fortress derived its name from the stream, or the stream from the fortress, would be no easy matter to decide at the present day: Mr. Edward Lhwyd,* a justly celebrated antiquary, who lived upwards of a century ago, considers the former to have been the case.

Castell Dinas Brân was the principal residence of the lords of Yale, and probably was founded by one of them. – In the reign of Henry III, Griffith ap Madoc resided here. He had married the daughter of James lord Audley, by which his affections were alienated from his own country; and he took part with the English against the Welsh prince. This induced a persecution, which compelled him to seek for security in this aërial retreat, and confine himself to the walls of his castle. The Welsh writers say that grief and shame, not long afterwards, put an end to his life. – His son possessed the property; and, after his death, the guardianship of his two children was given by Edward I to John earl of Warren, and Roger Mortimer. In the account of Holt castle, I have stated that the iniquitous guardians caused the boys to be murdered, and then seized the estates to their own use. Castell Dinas Brân was part of Warren's share in the plunder.

In the ninth year of Edward II, the grandson of the earl of Warren having no issue, surrendered this and other fortresses to the king. Being, however, afterwards separated from his wife, he obtained a regrant of the estates to himself, and his mistress, Matilda de Nereford, for life, with remainder to their children. Matilda was the last survivor, and therefore on her death, in the thirty-third year of Edward III, they reverted to the crown. – Not long afterwards they were given to Edward Fitz Alan, earl of Arundel; and from him they seem to have followed the succession of the lords of Bromfield.

In 1390, Castell Dinas Brân was the habitation of Myfanwy Vechan, a very beautiful and accomplished female, a descendant of the house of Tudor Trevor. She was beloved by Howel ap Einion Lygliw, a Welsh bard, who addressed to her an ode full of sweetness and beauty:

>'Mid the gay towers on steep Din's Branna's cone,
>>Her Hoel's breast the fair Myfanwy fires,
>Oh! harp of Cambria, never hast thou known
>>Notes more mellifluent floating o'er the wires,
>Than when thy bard this brighter Laura sung,
>And with his ill-starr'd love Llangollen's echoes rung.
>
>Thus consecrate to love in ages flown,
>>Long ages fled, Din's Branna's ruins shew,
>Bleak as they stand upon their steepy cone,
>>The crown and contrast of the vale below,
>That screen'd by mural rocks with pride displays
>Beauty's romantic pomp in every sylvan maze.*

At what period this castle was demolished, we have no information. Churchyard, who visited it in the sixteenth century, calls it 'an old and ruynous thing.'*

VALE OF LLANGOLLEN

In order that I might see the beauties of the vale of Llangollen to as great an advantage as possible, I determined to walk round it. This led me through a circuit of about eleven miles. – I crossed Llangollen bridge, and went along the road leading to Ruabon and Wrexham, on the north side of the river. The scenery in this direction was pretty, but from the lowness of the road it had nothing particularly interesting. The most beautiful prospects were those that I had by looking back towards the town. In these the castle, from its great elevation, formed a very conspicuous feature; and in many places the Dee added considerable beauty to the scene. – I passed Trevor Hall, the family seat of the Lloyds, seated on an eminence above the road.

I had proceeded somewhat more than four miles when I turned to the right, along a road which led over the Dee at Pont y Cyssyllte. Near this bridge I saw the columns of the famous *aqueduct* formed for conveying the water over the river Dee and the vale of Llangollen. At the time I was here* there were eleven erected: they were of stone, and square, and the two that stood in the bed of the river were each about a hundred and twenty feet high. From a tablet on one of them I copied the following inscription, which will sufficiently explain the nature of the undertaking:

The Nobility and Gentry of
the adjacent counties
having united, their efforts with
the great commercial interest of this country,
in creating an intercourse and union, between
England and North Wales,
by a navigable communication of the three rivers,
Severn, Dee, and Mersey,
for the mutual benefit of agriculture and trade,
caused the first stone of this aqueduct of
Pont Cysyllty,
to be laid, on the 25th day of July, MDCCXCV.
when Richard Middleton of Chirk, Esquire, M.P.
one of the original patrons of the
Ellesmere Canal,
was Lord of this manor,
and in the reign of our sovereign
GEORGE THE THIRD,

> when the equity of the laws and
> the security of property,
> promoted the general welfare of the nation,
> while the arts and sciences flourished
> by his patronage, and
> the conduct of civil life, was improved
> by his example.

I returned to Llangollen by the Oswestry road on the south side of the river. This is considerably elevated above the bottom of the vale, and from hence all the surrounding objects are seen to great advantage. From these steep banks the Dee's transparent stream is seen to wind in elegant curves, along the wooded meadows beneath. The mountains on the opposite side of the vale, are finely varied in shape and tints; and Trevor Hall, seated on its eminence, embosomed in woods, lent its aid to decorate the scene. From hence Castell Dinas Brân, and its conical hill, seem to close up the end of the vale, and imperiously to hold in subjection all the surrounding country. This sylvan vale, justly celebrated for its numerous beauties, affords many picturesque and highly romantic scenes.

The Hand* is the only tolerably good *inn* in Llangollen, but in summer I have more than once found it very unpleasant, from the crowd of travellers that are constantly passing on the great roads to and from Ireland, and from the number of Welsh tourists that visit Llangollen. I never yet heard any one say that he received either civility, or good accommodation, at this house: I have often heard, and I have experienced the contrary.

41

Llangollen to Corwen

All the country betwixt Llangollen and Corwen is exceedingly beautiful. The road, for about a mile, extends along the picturesque vale of Crucis, which, through its whole length, is adorned with woods, and in many places enlivened by neat little cottages peeping from among the trees. – I had not passed this vale far before I entered *the valley of the Dee*, Glyn Dyfrdwy, celebrated as, some centuries ago, the property of the Welsh hero, Owen Glyndwr.* The mountains are high, and their features bold and prominent. From the winding of the river, and the turnings of the vale, almost every step presented a new landscape.

I passed Llandysilio hall, the family seat of the Jones's, seated on a woody flat, near the opposite edge of the Dee. From its situation in the bosom of the mountains, it is secluded from the world, but there is so much elegance around it, that it appeared to me a charming retreat. – This Tysilio,* to whom the parish church is dedicated, and from whom the hall takes its name, was a Welsh saint, and held in such veneration, that no fewer than six churches have been dedicated to him. He was the son of a prince of Powis, and the writer of the most ancient history of Britain now extant.

Looking back upon the country I had left, I saw Castell Dinas Brân, and its accompanying rock, Craig Eglwyseg, at the head of the vale. The latter forms from hence a very conspicuous object.

About half a mile beyond Llandysilio, I clambered to the top of a lofty hill on the left of the road. I was considerably deceived in its height. I fancied that it extended no higher than the ridge visible from the road; but I had no sooner attained this, than I had another eminence before me: I persevered, and found two others equally high beyond this.

From the summit of this eminence I had a view of the whole vale and its various windings, with its still more serpentizing river, immediately beneath me. Castell Dinas Brân was very evidently lower than my present station. I could carry my eye along the entire vale of Llangollen, and over the flat country for many miles beyond, to the far distant mountains on the verge of the horizon.

I descended to the road, and continued my journey. – Beyond the fourth mile-stone, the vale began to change its appearance. The road, instead of winding amongst mountains, now lay in a direct line.

About three miles farther on, an oak wood on the left, and a small clump of firs on an eminence on the right of the road, mark the place near which the palace of 'the wild and irregular'* Owen Glyndwr once stood. There are at present no other remains of it than a few scattered heaps of stones. Iolo Goch, Owen's bard, about the year 1390, wrote a poem containing a description of this palace. He says it was surrounded by a moat filled with water, and that the entrance was by a costly gate over a bridge. The stile seems to have been of gothic architecture, for he compares one of the towers to a part of Westminster abbey. It was a Neapolitan building, containing eighteen apartments, 'a fair *timber* structure, on the summit of a green hill.'*

***

For two miles before I arrived at Corwen the vale had completely changed its aspect. It was here destitute of wood, and the low and verdant mountains were cultivated nearly to their summits. The river Dee had assumed a placid form, and glided silently and smoothly within its flat and meadowy banks.

CORWEN,

The White Choir, is a disagreeable little town, with a white-washed church. Its situation is under a rock at the foot of the Berwyn mountains. – It is a place much resorted to by anglers, who come here for the advantage of fishing in the Dee, which abounds in salmon, trout, and various other species of escuculent fish.*

The church contains an ancient monument to the memory of Iorwerth Sulien, one of the vicars. In the church-yard there is an apparently very old square stone pillar, that has once had much carved work upon it, but from the effects of time and weather, this is now nearly obliterated. – There is also, joining upon the church-yard, an alms-house, founded in 1709 by William Eyton, esq. of Plâs Warren, in Shropshire, for the use of six clergymen's widows of Merionethshire.

A mill on a stream at the back of the inn I found a picturesque object;

and some of the cottages near it are rude, and singularly built. The young artist would find here a good study or two.

Corwen is celebrated as having been a place of rendezvous to the Welsh forces under their prince Owen Gwynedd; who from hence, in 1165, put an end to the invasion of Henry II.

CEFYN CREINI

Near the summit of a hill on the opposite side of the river, called Cefyn Creini, *The Mountain of Worship*, there is a vast circle of loose stones, which bears the appearance of having once been a British fortification. This is called Caer Drewyn and Y Caer Wen, *The White Fort*. It is near half a mile in circumference, but the walls are at present in such a state, that at a distance they appear like huge heaps of stones piled round the circumference of a circle. Owen Gwynedd is believed to have occupied this post, whilst Henry II had his men encamped among the Berwyn mountains, on the opposite side of the vale. It is also related that Owen Glyndwr made use of this place in his occasional retreats. – The whole circle is perfectly visible from the road leading to Llanrwst, at the distance of about two miles from the town.

GLYNN BRIDGE

From Corwen I made an excursion of six miles to Pont y Glynn, *The Bridge of the Glen*, on the road leading to Llanrwst. The scenery along the whole walk had numerous beauties; but from one situation I had an uncommonly fine view along the beautiful vale of Edeirnion, bounded by the lofty Berwyn mountains, and adorned with the most pleasing cultivation. – The woody glen, at the head of which stands Pont y Glynn, with its prominent rocks, nearly obscured by the surrounding foliage, after a while presented itself; and then, almost in a moment, on a sudden turn of the road, appeared the bridge, thrown over the chasm. Beneath it was the rugged and precipitous bed of the river, where, amongst immense masses and huge fragments of rock, the stream foamed with the most violent impetuosity. The transition to this romantic scene was so momentary, as to seem almost the effect of magic. The cataract is not very lofty, but from its being directly under the bridge, where the foam and spray was seen dashing among the dark opposing rocks, and having the addition of pendant foliage from each side, a scene was formed altogether finely picturesque and elegant. The bridge rests on two nearly perpendicular rocks, and appears to be at least fifty feet above the bed of the stream. – The view from thence down the hollow was grand and tremendous.

42

Corwen to Bala

The distance from Corwen to Bala, along the usual road, is about eleven miles; but as there was another that for some miles accompanied the Dee, I was induced to prefer it. This road, as I had imagined from my map, extended along the *vale of Edeirnion*, which I had so much admired in my late ramble to Glynn Bridge. I found it so bad, as in some places to be nearly impassable. From its very low situation I had few opportunities of seeing the elegancies of the vale; but whenever the road passed over an eminence, I found much to admire.

WATERFALL OF CYNWYD

At the village of Cynwyd, *The Source of Mischief*, (probably so called in consequence of the courts which formerly were held there by the great men of the neighbourhood, to settle the boundaries of the adjacent commons, and to take cognizance of encroachments,) I left the road about half a mile, and proceeded along a deep glen that led me to Rhaiadr Cynwyd, *The Waterfall of Cynwyd*. The water dashed from precipice to precipice, among the wood and rocks, in the wildest and most romantic manner imaginable. The scene was so varied from the confusion of the water foaming in every direction, and partly hidden by the shrubs and trees growing on the ledges of the rocks, that the pen cannot describe it with justice, and even the efforts of the pencil could only give a faint conception of its elegance. Many detached parts of it afford excellent studies to the admirers of picturesque beauty.

I resumed my journey, passed Llandrillo, *The Church of St. Trillo*; and afterwards crossing the river, arrived at *Llanderfel*, another small village, whose church is dedicated to a British saint, called

DERFEL GADARN.

The church once contained a vast wooden image of this, its patron saint, which was formerly held in such superstitious veneration, that people from very distant parts made pilgrimages to it, and on these occasions offered not only money, but sometimes even horses or cattle. The Welsh people believed that Derfel Gadarn had the power of once rescuing each of his votaries from the torments of hell. On the 5th of April 1537, the festival day of this saint, no fewer than betwixt five and six hundred persons, some of them from a great distance, came to Llanderfel to make the accustomed offerings.

***

The Welsh people had extant a prophesy concerning this image, that it should 'make a *forest* blaze,' and in the ensuing year an opportunity occurred not only of depriving them of the cause of their superstition, but even of completing the prophesy, in a manner, however, that they little expected. A friar observant, whose name was *Forest*, was condemned to the stake for having denied the supremacy of the king. The name was thought by the heads of the church a fortunate occurrence, and it was advised that the image should be immediately brought to London to consume this wretched friar. To the stake on which he suffered was affixed the following elegy:

> David Darfel Gatheren,
> As sayth the Welshmen,
>> Fetched outlawes out of hell.
> Now is he come, with spere and shield,
> In harnes, to burne in Smithfield,
>> For in Wales he may not dwell.
>
> And Forest the friar,
> That obstinate lyar,
>> That wilfully shall be dead,
> In his contumacie,
> The gospel dothe deny
>> And the king to be supreme head.

At Llanfawr, *The Great Village*, two miles from Bala, is the supposed place of interment of

THE WELSH BARD, LLYWARCH HEN,*

Who flourished in the seventh century. He was nearly allied to the Welsh princes, and to his bardic character united that of a warrior. His whole life was spent in a series of vicissitudes and misfortunes, and he died about the year 670, at the great age of a hundred and fifty years. Somewhat more than a century ago an inscription was found upon the wall, near which his remains were supposed to have been deposited: this wall is now covered with plaster. – Not far from hence there is a circle of stones called Pabell Llywarch Hên, *The Tent of old Llywarch*, where it is probable he had a house, and spent the latter part of his days. He had been one of king Arthur's generals, and a member of his council. In his activity in opposing the encroachments of the Saxons and Irish, he was deprived of his whole patrimonial possessions, and lost every one of his four-and-twenty sons. Having now no friends, he retired to a hut at Aber Cuog (now Dôlguog, near Machynlleth,) to soothe with his harp the remembrance of misfortune, and to vent in elegiac numbers the sorrows of old age in distress. One of his poems, particularly, describes his misfortunes, and his deplorable situation, in the most simple and affecting language. It opens with the representation of an aged prince, who once ruled in magnificence, now robbed of his possessions, and wandering in a strange country, oppressed with wretchedness and poverty. Overcome with fatigue and hunger, he is supposed to rest his wearied limbs on the top of an eminence, and to contemplate there the varied and unhappy events of his life. This elegy has appeared in an English dress: what follows is a selection from it, as the whole would be too long for insertion here:

> Hark! the cuckoo's plaintive note
> Doth thro' the wild vale sadly float;
> As, from the rav'nous hawk's pursuit,
> In Ciog rests her weary foot;
> And there, with mournful sounds and low,
> Echoes my harp's responsive woe.
>
> Returning spring, like opening day,
> That makes all nature glad and gay,
> Prepares Andate's fiery car,
> To rouse the brethren of the war;
> When as the youthful hero's breast
> Gloweth for the glorious test,
> Rushing down the rocky steep,

Corwen to Bala

See the Cambrian legions sweep,
Like meteors on the boundless deep.

    Old *Mona* smiles
Monarch of an hundred isles.
And *Snowdon* from his awful height,
His hoar head waves propitious to the fight.

But I – no more in youthful pride,
Can dare the steep rock's haughty side;
For fell disease my sinews rends,
My arm unnerves, my stout heart bends;
And raven locks, now silver-grey,
Keep me from the field away.

But see! – He comes, all drench'd in blood,
Gwên, the Great, and Gwên, the Good;
Bravest, noblest, worthiest son,
Rich with many a conquest won;
Gwên, in thine anger great,
Strong thine arm, thy frown like fate;
Where the mighty rivers end,
And their course to ocean bend,
There, with the eagle's rapid flight,
How wouldst thou brave the thickest fight!
Oh, fatal day! Oh, ruthless deed!
When the sisters cut thy thread.
Cease, ye waves, your troubled roar;
Nor flow, ye mighty rivers more;
For *Gwên*, the Great, and *Gwên*, the Good,
Breathless lies, and drench'd in blood!

Four and twice ten sons were mine,
Us'd in battle's front to shine;
But – low in dust my sons are laid,
Nor one remains his sire to aid.

Hold, oh hold, my brain, thy seat;
How doth my bosom's monarch beat!

Cease thy throbs, perturbed heart;
Whither would thy stretch'd strings start!
From frenzy dire, and wild affright,
Keep my senses thro' this night.*

BALA,

The Outlet of the Lake, is a market town containing about two thousand inhabitants. It consists principally of one long and wide street, and is situated at the bottom of a pool, the largest in the country, called Llyn Tegid, *The Fair Pool.* It is principally noted for its manufacture of woollen stockings, and as the autumnal resort of grous shooters. Lord Lyttleton asserts its celebrity for the beauty of its women, and that he saw some of the prettiest girls here that he ever beheld.*

Near the town I passed a lofty artificial mount called Tommen y Bala, *The Tumulus of Bala.* This is supposed to have been of Roman origin, and to have been formed here, with a small castle on its summit, to secure the pass towards the sea, and to keep the mountaineers in subjection. The Welsh taking advantage of it, made it one of their chain of fortresses which extended through the country to the coast of Flintshire. – The history both of this place and of the town is little known. I only find that the mount was fortified in the year 1202 by Llewelyn ap Iorwerth, prince of North Wales. – On the eastern bank of the Dee, not far distant, there is another mount called Castell Gronw Befr o Benllyn, *The Castle of Gronw the Fair, of Penllyn,* a Welsh chieftain who lived in the sixth century.

BALA LAKE,

Llyn Tegid, or Pimblemere, for this pool has these various names, is about a quarter of a mile south of the town of Bala. It is by much the largest of the Welsh lakes, being about four miles long, and in many parts near a mile in breadth. The scenery around it is mountainous, but not sufficiently rude to render it very picturesque. It reminded me of the low mountain-scenery surrounding Winandermere, in the north of England. From the bottom, however, the diversified shores present to the eye a pleasing scene. On the west are seen the summits of the lofty Arrenigs. Arran Benllyn, beyond the upper end of the pool, stretches his black and rocky front into the clouds; and in the extreme distance, in fainter colours, are seen the three summits of Cader Idris.

This pool is well stocked with fish of various kinds, but in particular with trout, eels, and a species found only in alpine lakes, called, from the whiteness of its scales, *Gwyniadd*. It is a gregarious fish, the Salmo lavaretus of Linnaeus. Its greatest weight seldom exceeds three or four pounds. With respect to the taste, this fish is generally said to be insipid: the noble traveller quoted in a preceding page, asserts, however, that it is so delicate, that his friend would prefer the flavour of it to even the lips of the fair maids of Bala. The time of spawning is in the month of December. These fish usually keep at the bottom of the water, where they feed on small shells and aquatic plants. – It is generally believed by the inhabitants of the neighbourhood, that although the Dee runs directly through this pool, the gwyniadds are never to be caught in the river; nor, on the contrary, are the salmon with which the river abounds, ever taken in the pool. Hence Churchyard;

> A poole there is thro' which the Dee doth passe,
> Where is a fish that some a whiting call:
> Where never yet no salmon taken was,
> Yet hath good store of other fishes all.
> Above that poole, and so beneath that flood
> Are salmons caught, and many a fish full good,
> But in the same there will no salmon bee,
> And neere that poole you shall no whiting see.*

This is a singular circumstance, but there appears some truth in it. The honourable Daines Barrington,* who made many inquiries respecting it, observes to the assertion, that they *never* encroach upon each other; that he had seen a salmon caught in the lake more than two hundred yards from the bridge, and that he had been authentically informed of several of the gwyniadds having been caught in the Dee near Llandrillo, eight miles from Bala. – The fishery of Bala lake is the property of sir Watkin Williams Wynne.

The overflowings of this pool are at times very dreadful. These, however, seldom take place, except when the winds, rushing from the hollows of the mountains at the upper end, drive the waters suddenly along. In stormy weather great part of the vale of Edeirnion will sometimes be overflowed. By the united force of the winds and mountain torrents, the water towards the bottom of the pool has been known to rise six or eight feet in perpendicular height. On the contrary, in calm and settled weather, it is always very smooth. There have been some instances, in severe winters, of its being entirely frozen over; and when covered with snow, it has been mistaken by travellers for an extensive plain.

EXCURSION ROUND BALA LAKE

In this excursion, of about ten miles, I crossed the bridge over the Dee, and proceeded along the eastern bank of the pool. From near the church of Llangower, a pleasing vale was seen to open on the opposite side, bounded by mountains, and closed at the end by one of the Arrenigs.

I had passed the head of the pool somewhat more than half a mile, when I found the narrow lane which leads to Llanwchllyn, *The Church above the Lake*. I left the road, and soon afterwards entered the *Vale of Twrch*. Nature is seen in all her majesty here; but as lord Lyttleton observed of the Berwyn mountains, 'it is the majesty of a tyrant frowning over the ruins and desolation of a country.' There were no marks of habitations or culture; and heath, moss, lichens, and a few grasses, seemed the only vegetation. The surrounding mountains were as rude as description can paint: the most prominent of these was Arran Benllyn, which here presented only a series of naked crags and precipices. – From hence I crossed the river Twrch, *The Burrower*.*

PHENOMENON CALLED DAEAR-DOR

My guide now pointed out a piece of land, of considerable extent, nearly covered with innumerable masses of broken rocks. These, he said, had all been conveyed thither in the summer of 1781, by what the inhabitants call Daear-Dor, *a breaking of the earth*. The daear-dor is a dislodgement, by means of water, of a vast quantity of the surface of the ground, or, as in the present instance, of a considerable part of some of the rocks among the higher mountains. An unusual volume of water descending suddenly from the clouds becomes lodged in some confined situation: by degrees it penetrates the earth, and this loosening, the whole mass is swept along before the torrent, till it meets with resistance in some of the vales below, where it is therefore deposited. The accident near Llanwchllyn happened after a violent storm of thunder. The banks of the Twrch were overflowed, and the torrent carried every thing before it that was not actually embedded in the rock. Seventeen cottages, ten cows, and a vast number of sheep, besides the soil of all the meadows and corn-fields along its course, were overwhelmed and destroyed. This meadow, in which the river deposited its chief contents, was rendered totally unfit to be any more cultivated. The dimensions of some of the pieces of rock borne here by the fury of the torrent, are almost inconceivable. Two of the stones came in contact, which were each near twenty feet long, eight broad, and six deep, and by the collision one of them was split. Eight other stones, about half this size, were carried near nine hundred yards beyond. Five bridges were swept away; and had not the inhabitants of Llanwchllyn, providentially, received timely alarm, every one of them would have been destroyed. The only person missing was a poor old woman, who was confined to her bed by sickness.

Whilst speaking of the neighbourhood of Llanwchllyn, I must digress a little from my subject to relate a whimsical adventure which happened to a gentleman of my acquaintance, Mr. D., an artist, and his friend, whilst at this village a few summers ago. – These gentlemen, in a pedestrian excursion round Bala lake, found themselves, on their arrival at Llanwchllyn, fatigued and hungry. As neither of them could speak a word of Welsh, they were compelled to have recourse to signs in order to make themselves understood. These so far answered their purpose, that a man whom they met in the village exclaimed in answer, 'eze' (intended doubtless for 'yes'), and pointed with his finger to a kind of hut, from the rafters of which two or three dirty candles, and a few bits of bacon were suspended. On entering they again made the signs of eating and drinking, and the woman, though beyond measure astonished at their manners and appearance, had sense enough to conduct them to what they conjectured to be the public-house. Here their attention was fixed upon some fragments of bacon, which had hung so long, that all the strings had nearly cut their way through. They explained by signs, as well as they were able, what it was they wanted, and the female of the house brought out *three* eggs. This was a slender supply for two hungry men. They both called out 'more,' the woman answered 'eze,' but brought out the frying-pan. They shook their heads, she fetched a sauce-pan. Here they found a difficulty that they knew not how to encounter. A bright thought suddenly came into the other gentleman's head: – 'D., you can draw, *ask the woman for a piece of chalk*, and *draw* an egg.' The absurdity of the idea was such, that Mr. D. could not refrain from a loud and hearty laugh. It was, however, at last agreed, that the woman should be suffered to boil the three eggs, but that when she brought them to the table, D. was to snatch them from her, and pretend to eat them all himself. The plan succeeded; the woman laughed immoderately at the contest, and running out with a cry of 'eze, eze, eze,' soon afterwards brought in four eggs more. There was no difficulty in making the payment for this rude cheer: Mr. D. held out some silver in his hand, from which the honest Welshwoman took eighteen pence for the seven eggs, and a quart of ale!

On the summit of a high and craggy rock, at some distance from the road, and about a mile from Llanwchllyn, are the remains of *Castell Corndochon*, an ancient British fort. It was of a somewhat oval form, and has consisted of a square tower, and another oblong, but rounded at the extremity. I have met with no historical data whatever respecting this fortress.

In my return I observed an eminence on the west side of the head of the pool, which the guide informed me was called Caer Gai. There was on this spot a fort that belonged to Cai Hir ap Cynyr, or, as Spencer has called him, Timon:* he was the foster-father of king Arthur, who during his youth resided here. The Romans are supposed to have had a fortress on this spot; and many of their coins have been dug up in the neighbourhood. This place of defence was doubtless constructed to guard the pass through the mountains. Of its history I am altogether ignorant.

THE RIVER DEE

The source of the Dee is under one side of Arran Benllyn, the high mountain at the head of Bala pool. – Its name is thought to have been derived from the Welsh word Dwy, which signifies something *divine*. Some centuries ago it was held in superstitious veneration by the inhabitants of the country, from what were then believed the miraculous overflowing of its banks at times when there had been no preceding heavy rain: and from its being believed to have foretold some remarkable events by changing its channel. History informs us, that when the Britons, drawn up in battle array on its banks, have been prepared to engage with their Saxon foes, it was their custom first to kiss the earth, and then for every soldier to drink a small quantity of the water. – The name is certainly not derived, as many have supposed, from Dû, *black*; for, except when tinged by the torrents from the mountain morasses, its waters are perfectly bright and transparent. In Spencer's description of Caer Gai, the dwelling of old Timon, the foster-father of Arthur, the colour of the Dee is considered very different from black:

> Lowe in a valley green,
> Under the foot of Rawran, mossie o'er,
> From whence the river Dee, as *silver clene*,
> His tumbling billows rolls with gentle roar.*

That lover of the marvellous, Giraldus Cambrensis, informs us very gravely, that the river Dee runs through Bala lake, and is discharged at the bridge near the town, without their waters becoming mixed. He doubtless means to say that the river might be traced by its appearance from one end of the lake to the other. Giraldus believed every thing that the inhabitants chose to impose upon him.

43

Bala to Shrewsbury

Leaving Bala, I turned my steps towards England, and occupied two days in the journey from hence to Shrewsbury. These, from severe rain that set in when I had got about ten miles from Bala, and lasted with little intermission till I arrived at Shrewsbury, were rendered two of the most unpleasant days I had spent in the country. – At my outset the morning was, however, very serene. The sun, in exhaling the dews, gave a delightful air of freshness to all the surrounding objects. The whole scene was enlivened by the music of the birds, whose various tones and elegant strains would have interested less ardent admirers of the works of nature than myself. Every thing seemed to partake of a general sprightliness. The thrilling tones of the sky-lark were heard on every side: the notes of the blackbird echoed from among the distant foliage,

> Whilst now and then sweet Philomel would wail,
> Or stock-doves plain, amid the forest deep,
> That drowsy rustled to the sighing gale;
> And still a coil the grass-hopper did keep.*

These rural objects continued, however, for very few miles; for I then entered on a succession of dreary and open moors, which might have charms for the sportsman, but they had none for me.

About a mile and a half from Bala, I passed a bridge called *Pont Cynwyd*. The bed of the turbulent little stream is here crowded with huge masses of rock, deeply excavated into circular hollows by the furious eddying of the water. In one situation these rocks, with the stream rushing down amongst them, form a small but pleasing cascade.

A little beyond the bridge stands Rhiwedog, *The abrupt Ascent*. This was an ancient family seat; and a vale in its neighbourhood was the scene of that severe battle betwixt the British and Saxon forces, in which the aged Llywarch took an active part, and lost his only surviving son.

From the side of a steep, on the edge of the moors, I was presented with a distant view of the vale of Edeirnion, whose verdure and fertility formed a striking contrast with my bleak and dreary situation. – The road now led me over Trûm y Sarn, *The Causeway of the Ridge*, a place that has its name from being near a lofty heath-clad mountain, which I passed at a little distance towards the south. It is one of that immense range of mountains which extend fifteen or sixteen miles, and are called *Berwyn Mountains*. The two most elevated summits are Cader Ferwyn, and Cader Fronwen. – I arrived at a noted bwlch, or pass, which divides the counties of Merioneth and Montgomery, called Milltir Gerig, *The Stony Mile*.

LLANGYNOG

I had now a view into the curious and romantic *vale of Llangynog*, a hollow so completely inclosed on all sides by mountain barriers, as apparently to afford no outlet to the residents in its bosom. The mountains seemed in many place nearly perpendicular, and their cliffs too steep to be scaled by any other than those most active of all British animals, the sheep and goats. These I observed browsing along the sides with the utmost unconcern. The bottom was entirely in a state of cultivation, but principally as meadow land: it was interspersed with the houses of the farmers and their labourers.

A tolerably good road took me from the edge of this vale, by a descent, somewhat steep, first into the hollow, and then to the small and comfortless village of Llangynog, *The Church of St. Cunog.*

SLATE QUARRIES

From a stupendous rock, which rises on the north side of the village, are obtained those slates for which this neighbourhood is celebrated through all the adjacent counties. The quarries are situated high up in the mountain. I observed that the mode of conveying them to the vale was different from that practised near Llanberis, which I have already described, but it appeared much more dangerous. The slates are loaded on small sledges, which are to be conveyed down the side of the mountain, along winding paths formed for the purpose. Each of these sledges has a rope by which it is fastened to the shoulders of a man who has the care of conveying it. He lays firm hold with his hands, and thus, with his face towards it, begins to descend. The velocity which the sledge acquires in its descent is counteracted by the man's striking forcibly against the

Fig. 11. *Pistyll Rhaiadr,* Denbighshire/Montgomeryshire, engraving after drawing by Edward Dayes (1804).

prominences with his feet. This manoeuvre, since he goes backward, and has at the same time some attention to pay to the sledge to keep it in the track, must be difficult to attain, and long practice alone can render it easy. The danger to an observer seems very great: on inquiry at the village, I was, however, informed that a serious accident had scarcely ever been known to occur from it.

LEAD MINES

At Craig y Mwyn, about two miles and a half from Llangynog, somewhat more than a century ago, a vein of lead ore was discovered, so valuable as to yield to the Powis family, for forty years, a clear revenue of at least twenty thousand pounds a year. It had been worked to the depth of about a hundred yards, when on a sudden the water broke in, and became so powerful, that the proprietor was compelled to abandon the undertaking. Ever since that time the mines have continued nearly filled with water, but some gentlemen a few years ago determined to attempt their recovery, and for this purpose levels were to be driven in various parts of the mountain, if possible, to drain off the water. Whether they have proceeded in the attempt, or given it up, I have not the means of being informed. – Besides these there are some mines, but of less importance, near the village, which were worked when I was at Llangynog. The produce of these I was informed was very trifling.

On my leaving Llangynog, the clouds gathered round the summits and sides of the mountains, and the rain soon afterwards began to descend in torrents. This village appeared, however, so wretched a place for a wearied traveller, that I had no inducement to return for shelter. In the greatest misfortunes we are generally able to find some object on which we can rest with satisfaction: it soon occurred to me that the drenching of my clothes would be amply compensated by the increased volume of water at the cataract of *Pistyll Rhaiadr*, which I intended to visit in the morning. The idea of this gave me so much pleasure, that when I became fairly wet to the skin, I was altogether careless as to personal comfort; and now the faster and more heavily the rain descended, the better a great deal I was pleased with it.

LLANRHAIADR

In this state it was that, after about two hours slippery walking, and my clothes dripping with wet, I arrived at Llanrhaiadr, *The Village of the Cataract*, situated, like Llangynog, in a deep hollow, surrounded on all sides by mountains, whose summits were now entirely obscured by clouds. This hollow is called Mochnant, *The Vale of the rapid Brook*. The houses, or rather cottages, of the village are irregular; but, as most of them were old and overgrown with vegetation, it had from many points of view an appearance highly picturesque.

I found very tolerable accommodations, even for the night, at the *Coach and Horses*, an inn, or rather public-house, whose exterior does not bespeak the good opinion of the traveller.

Dr. William Morgan, who first translated the Bible into the Welsh language, was vicar of this place. He was afterwards rewarded with the bishopric of Llandaff, and in 1601 with that of St. Asaph.

PISTYLL RHAIADR,

The Spout of the Cataract, the most celebrated waterfall of this country, rushes down the front of an almost perpendicular rock, that terminates a vale at the distance of about four miles from the village. The vale is narrow and well wooded; it was watered by the little river Rhaiadr, which here constitutes the boundary line betwixt the counties of Denbigh and Montgomery, and it affords many pleasing and beautiful scenes. The upper part of the cataract, when the sun shines upon it, is visible to a great distance; and along this hollow its silvery and linear appearance give an air of singularity to many of the views. – Pistyll Rhaiadr is upwards of two hundred and ten feet high; and for near two thirds of this height, the water is thrown down the flat face of a bleak, naked, and barren rock; from thence it rages through a natural arch, and betwixt two prominent sides into the small bason at its foot. The whole scene is destitute of wood, but it has so much simple grandeur, that trees would injure, rather than heighten the general effect. When visited after very heavy rain, a singular occurrence is to be remarked. The water in its descent is obstructed by the mass of rock, through which it seems by time to have forced a passage, and it is said to burst through it with a vast quantity of spray, appearing like smoke from the explosion of a cannon.

I was told that the late worthy vicar of Llanrhaiadr, Dr. Worthington, with a view of gratifying the curious, had a pair of flood-gates fixed on the stream, above the cataract, occasionally to obstruct the passage of the water: when a sufficient quantity had been collected behind them, they were suddenly thrown open, and the rushing down of the flood is said to have afforded one of the grandest spectacles imaginable. – This gentleman also erected a small building at the foot of the rock for the accommodation of visitors, which is found very convenient to those who bring refreshments along with them.

On my return from the cataract, I left Llanrhaiadr, and proceeded along the road which leads through the *vale of Llangedwen*. I passed Llangedwen hall, a handsome stone edifice, the property of sir Watkin Williams Wynne. This place was a favourite residence of the late baronet, but it is seldom visited by the present owner.

I now arrived once again at *Llanymynech*. Betwixt this village and Shrewsbury I had so much rain, as to render the journey in every respect dreary and uncomfortable. Through the thickness of the mist I could but just discern the *Breiddin Hills*, at the distance of a few miles on the right: their summits were perfectly obscured in clouds.

KNOCHIN,

A village about five miles from Llanymynech, has once been a place of some celebrity. The hall was the residence of the family of L'Estrange, who built the town. They had on its site a castellated mansion so early as in the reign of Henry II. The last of the family was Joan, who married George Stanley, the eldest son of the first earl of Derby. The following occurrence is said to have taken place, some years ago, in the neighbourhood of Knochin:

A man of the name of Elkes was left guardian to his brother's son. This boy was very young, and the only obstacle to Elkes becoming possessed of considerable property. He had long revolved in his mind the manner in which he could rid himself of this incumbrance, and at length hit upon the following inhuman expedient: a poor child of the village was directed to take the boy to a distant corn-field to play and gather flowers. Elkes met them near the spot, and directed the other child to return immediately home. He then took his ward up in his arms, walked with him to the end of the field, where he knew there was a tub nearly full of water, and forcing his head into it, held him in that position till the child was suffocated. The neighbours soon observed that the boy was missing; the *poor* boy who had accompanied him to the field told his simple story, and a party of them, on searching the place, discovered the body. Information soon reached them that Elkes had fled towards London. Two horsemen were therefore immediately dispatched in pursuit of him. These men were riding along the road near South Mims in Hertfordshire, when they were surprized by the singular actions of two ravens, that were perched on a cock of hay in an adjoining field. The birds made an unusual noise, and furiously pulled about the hay with their beaks. Curiosity alone, the men said, induced them to alight, and see what could be the cause of such singular actions. They threw down the heap of hay, and were astonished to discover beneath it the man of whom they were in search. He asserted that these two birds had followed him incessantly, from the time that the murder had been committed. This unhappy victim of avarice was conveyed to Shrewsbury, tried, condemned, and afterwards hung in chains on Knochin heath.

KYNASTON'S CAVE

A few miles from Knochin I passed under a high rock of red free-stone, called Ness Cliff. In the south-east side of this rock there is a cave, which has the name of Kynaston's Cave. This was a place of occasional retreat to Humphrey, the son of sir Roger Kynaston, constable of Harlech castle, and a party of his mad companions. He was outlawed in the sixth year of the reign of Henry VII, was pardoned in the year following, and died in 1534. He is remembered by many strange pranks, and still continues the talk of the neighbouring peasantry.

Leaving this rock, I soon afterwards saw, by the road-side, a small building, from which several boys were coming. An inscription over the door arrested my steps for a moment:

> God prosper long this public good,
> A school erected, where a chapel stood.

In what this originated I did not learn.

I crossed the Severn at Montford bridge; and in about an hour afterwards ended my pedestrian excursion at Shrewsbury.

Explanatory notes

Abbreviations

FLS: Fellow of the Linnean Society of London
NLW: The National Library of Wales / Llyfrgell Genedlaethol Cymru, Aberystwyth
ODNB: *Oxford Dictionary of National Biography* (online)

(Bingley's footnotes are shown in inverted commas.)

43   *Welsh pronunciation*: I have copied this from Bingley's 1804 edition, vol. II, in his chapter on the Welsh language. He probably had it approved/corrected by Rev. Peter Bailey Williams: see note to p. 55.

43   *Owen's Welsh Dictionary*: William Owen Pughe (1759–1835), born near Barmouth (he added the surname 'Pughe' after receiving an inheritance), was one of the scholarly pillars of the London Welsh Gwyneddigion society, and was acquainted with William Blake, Walter Scott and Robert Southey. But he also swallowed crazy ideas, including about etymology and spelling, which marred his Welsh Dictionary (1793–1803). He edited the works of Dafydd ap Gwilym and Llywarch Hên, and was editor of the *Cambrian Register*, which Bingley used as a source. Gwyn A. Williams remarked: 'He often wrote moonshine, but it always sparkled' (*Madoc*, 1979).

50   *James Edward Smith*: Dr Smith (1759–1828; knighted in 1814) was founder and first president of the Linnean Society of London. He had a long correspondence with Bingley and encouraged the younger man. See Introduction.

52   *Evans's map*: In his 1800 Preface, Bingley recommended the map by John Evans, dedicated to Sir Watkin Williams Wynn, 5th Baronet (1772–1840). The large map was published in 1795 (available online at NLW), and the smaller one after Evans's death in 1797. However, in his 1804 edition, Bingley remarked how expensive it was, and instead his new publishers provided a fold-out map showing Bingley's route in red (see map on pp. 44–7).

52   *chapter on the language*: I have omitted his chapter on the Welsh language, which he recognized as Celtic but derived erroneously from Hebrew; his 'force of the letters' (pronunciation of some Welsh letters) is on p. 43.

52   *Mr. Pratt*: Samuel Jackson Pratt (1749–1814), English author of *Gleanings through Wales, Holland and Westphalia* (1795), was a failed clergyman, actor, prolific writer and fabricator. See Introduction.

52   *Mr. Warner*: Richard Warner (1763–1857), English clergyman, wrote *A Walk through Wales, in August 1797* (1798) and *A Second Walk through Wales* (1799). Bingley is equally scathing about him and Pratt. Warner also compiled two volumes of *Literary Recollections* (1830). See Introduction.

Notes to pages 53–5

53   *Mr. West's Guide*: Scottish-born Jesuit priest Thomas West (c.1720–79) wrote a popular *Guide to the Lakes* (1778) which went through many editions. See Introduction.

53   *Mr. Pennant*: The naturalist, travel writer and antiquarian Welshman Thomas Pennant (1726–98) wrote pioneering works on his tours of Scotland and Wales, as well as zoology. His *A Tour in Wales* (2nd edn, 1784) was Bingley's main source and inspiration for his first edition of 1800. See Introduction.

54   *Dr. Aikin*: John Aikin, MD, *A Description of the Country from Thirty to Forty Miles round Manchester* (1795). I have omitted Bingley's description of Chester in this edition.

54   *Mr. Jones ... Bards*: Edward Jones, 'Bardd y Brenin' (1752–1824), was a harpist and music historian. He was appointed harpist to the Prince of Wales (later George IV) after he moved to London in the 1770s. His most significant books are the three editions of *The Musical and Poetical Relicks of the Welsh Bards* from 1784. The 1802 edition was entitled *The Bardic Museum*. Bingley used his books as sources.

54   *Owen ... history of bardism*: Bingley was wise to be sceptical since the section on bardism was written by Iolo Morganwg (Edward Williams; 1747–1826), who invented the Gorsedd of the Bards, and who was revealed in the twentieth century as a brilliant literary forger.

55   *Lord Lyttleton ... Letters*: Bingley did not include Lyttelton's two letters about Wales in his 1804 edition, but he does quote from them. George Lyttelton (1709–73; Bingley misspells his name) was a poet, politician and patron of poets, including James Thomson. The tall, lanky Lyttelton toured North Wales in July 1756. His first letter to Archibald Bower (6 July), enthusing about the girls of Bala and the Vale of Ffestiniog, was published in 1775 in the *Annual Register for 1774*, which also contains a memoir. Both letters were published in his collected works, edited by George Edward Ayscough. He climbed Cadair Berwyn and Moel Hebog, but it was too wet to climb Snowdon. He was elevated to the peerage later that year. In 1767–71 he published the *History of the Life of Henry the Second*, which Bingley used as a source. Lyttelton was a steadfast friend to Scottish-born (apparently) writer Bower, who constantly converted between Jesuitism and Protestantism, and was involved in a pamphlet war at this time. The well-known quote about living with the woman one loves in the Vale of Ffestiniog (p. 247) is poignant, since his first wife, whom he loved, died in childbirth in 1747 and he was having a miserable time with his second wife, who flaunted her affairs.

55   *Peter Williams*: a prominent figure in Caernarfonshire (1763–1836), graduate of Jesus College, Oxford, rector of Llanrug and Llanberis, and younger brother of Eliezer Williams, vicar of Lampeter and schoolmaster. Both were Anglicans, unlike their Calvinistic Methodist father, and both were thanked as 'zealous supporters' in the first volume of the *Cambrian Register* (1796). A seemingly indefatigable walker and mountain climber, Peter Williams befriended Bingley on his first tour in 1798. Williams later wrote *The Tourist's Guide through the County of Caernarvon* (1821), which mentions Bingley only in passing. See Introduction.

55   *John Wynne Griffith, Esq. F.L.S*: country gentleman of Denbigh (1763–1834), graduate of Trinity Hall, Cambridge, and a botanist who specialized in lichens,

later a member of parliament. In his 1800 edition, Bingley gives references for all the plants in his 'Catalogue of the More Uncommon Welsh Plants', and even though Griffith had not published anything, Bingley mentions him there seven times. In a letter to Dr Smith (February? 1799), several months after his return from Wales, Bingley notes that he had called three times at Griffith's home near Denbigh, but he was out. There is a letter from Bingley to Griffith, dated 22 July 1798 from Caernarfon, mentioning that he had called and requesting habitats of certain plants and specimens of plants that had gone out of flower: 'the Despair of obtaining them by any other means almost obliges me to do what I certainly could not otherwise have thought of doing' (that is, Bingley is unsure about the propriety of writing to him). In August 1799, a year after his first tour, he is still hoping for a list of plants from Griffith and others. Bingley possibly saw Griffith's name acknowledged in William Withering's book of British plants (3rd edn, 1796), which was his main botanical source in 1800.

55   *Hugh Davies, F.L.S.*: Anglesey-born botanist and clergyman (1739–1821), who published *Welsh Botanology* in 1813. He accompanied Thomas Pennant to the Isle of Man in 1774 and became known as the Welsh Linnaeus. See Bingley's letter to Dr Smith of 10 May 1801 on p. 11.

55   *Evan Lloyd, of Maes y Porth*: Anglesey-born antiquarian, clergyman, botanist and poet (1728–1801).

56   *great Irish road*: 'Except only in going from the village of Northop to Flint, and thence to Holywell, in the whole not more than eight miles.' Regular coaches operated in the 1770s from London to Holyhead through North Wales, crossing the Afon Conwy and Menai Strait by ferry, and then by sea to Dublin. Thomas Telford's bridges at Conwy and over the Menai Strait opened in 1826.

57   *Mr. Aikin*: Bingley quotes in his book from the Lancashire-born natural scientist Arthur Aikin (1773–1854), whose *Journal of a Tour through North Wales and Part of Shropshire; with observations in mineralogy and other branches of natural history* was published in 1797. Bingley remarked in 1800 that as regards the Devil's Bridge near Aberystwyth, Aikin's was 'the only account I dared to rely upon for accuracy'. See Introduction.

57   *Mr. Skrine*: Well-off Oxford graduate Henry Skrine, 'Esq. of Warley in Somersetshire' (as on his title-page; 1755–1803), published *Two Successive Tours throughout the Whole of Wales* in 1798 after writing travel books on the north of England and Scotland. It is a description of summer tours he took over several years in Wales and through some English towns and counties, with curious spellings. It is a sympathetic, short account, with a whiff of condescension. He didn't climb Snowdon or Cadair Idris, blaming it on the weather, but, he shrugged, 'the elevation is too great for any display of picturesque beauty'.

57   *The Itinerary*: I have not included this. It is a seventeen-page summary of Bingley's route, the attractions and inns, including mileages.

58   *quoted many books*: Bingley hits back at a reviewer. I have omitted his list of reference works, which range from Gerald of Wales to recent Welsh publications.

60   *Leland*: John Leland (c.1503–52), London-born poet and antiquary, studied in Cambridge, Oxford and Paris and became a royal chaplain. In 1533, Henry VIII gave him a commission to examine the manuscripts in religious houses, before their dissolution, many of which he later rescued. By c.1539 his interest moved to

Notes to pages 60–5

local history and topography and he spent six years travelling through England and Wales. His notes circulated widely, influencing Stow, Camden and Dugdale, and were finally published as *The Itinerary of John Leland the Antiquary* in 1710–12. Leland went insane some years before his death.

60 *Owen Gwynedd*: Owain Gwynedd (Owain ap Gruffudd, b. c.1100), ruler of Gwynedd from 1137 until his death in 1170; he was called *rex* (king) and later 'prince of the Welsh'. The Battle of Ewloe (or Coleshill) in Flintshire took place in July 1157 as the new king Henry (in his mid-twenties) tried to halt Owain's expansion into Powys and was confronted by two of Owain's sons, Dafydd and Cynan. But Owain ultimately had to pay homage to Henry. However, in another campaign in August 1165, Henry was defeated in the Berwyn Mountains by the Welsh and torrential rain.

61 *Flint*: 'It is not worth the while of any tourist to follow my route to Flint, as he will find there scarcely any thing worth his notice.'

62 *Camden*: London-born William Camden (1551–1623) was Bingley's main source after Pennant's *Tour*. Alongside a troubled relationship with Oxford University, Camden became a master at the prestigious Westminster School (one of his pupils was Ben Jonson) while he wrote his famous *Britannia*, which investigates Britain's past. From the 1570s he travelled extensively through Britain, researching for his book, which was first published in 1586 (in Latin) and had numerous later editions. In 1590 he travelled in Wales. Camden focused on accurate scholarship and primary sources, transforming the study of history, and discredited the Brutus myth of the origins of Britain. Just as Bingley was to do, Camden interweaved poetry into his work as another kind of truth. Bingley quotes from his Latin edition but largely relied on Edmund Gibson's English translation of 1695, which included notes on Wales by Edward Lhuyd (or Lhwyd; see note to p. 146), and Richard Gough's of 1786.

62 *Fabian*: Referring to *The New Chronicles of England and France* (1516) by prosperous London draper Robert Fabyan (d. c.1512). The posthumous third edition (1542) ends: 'the first day of Julye was a Welshemanne hung, drawne and quartered for prophesiyng of the kyng his majesties death'.

62 *Stowe*: The meticulous historian John Stowe or Stow (c.1525–1605) was born in the City of London – Thomas Cromwell stole half of his father's garden when erecting a mansion – and worked first as a tailor. He was a self-taught scholar, committed to historical accuracy, and an avid collector of manuscripts, travelling on foot to investigate old buildings and to search for historical records. He was acquainted with Ben Jonson and Camden, but says nothing about Shakespeare. He died in poverty. His most famous work is his innovative *Survey of London* (1598), invaluable to modern archaeologists and historians. Bingley used his *Annales of England* (1592), augmented in 1631.

62 *Llewelyn and his brother David*: Llywelyn ap Gruffudd, prince of Wales, 'Llywelyn the Last' (d. 1282) and Dafydd (d. 1283).

65 *Mr. Grose*: Bingley used as a source *Antiquities of England and Wales*, 10 vols (1784) by Francis Grose (c.1731–91). Half-Swiss and half-English, Grose was born in London and enlisted as a soldier, hence he was usually called Captain Grose. He began sketching buildings, which led to the publication of his *Antiquities* from 1772, which included descriptions, as well as engravings by other artists. Witty and amiable, he declared in his early sixties that he was too fat to ride a

horse, though he toured Scotland from 1788 and became friends with Robert Burns, who wrote verses about him.

65 *Wenefred*: 'The Welsh name of this female was Gwenvrewi; Tudur Aled, a Welsh bard who flourished about A.D. 1450, has celebrated her sanctity and the reputed miracles of her well, in a poem still extant.'

66 *she bare*: Michael Drayton, *Poly-olbion* (1612). The poet Drayton (1563–1631) was the son of a butcher or tanner in Warwickshire. He collaborated in writing plays for the Lord Admiral's Men in London, though the story that he had a drinking session with Ben Jonson and Shakespeare just before the latter's death is probably apocryphal. *Poly-olbion* was his *magnum opus*, describing the rivers, forests and mountains of Britain, with notes by John Selden commenting wryly on some of the legends (see note to p. 207).

66 *Drayton*: See note above.

67 *Linnaeus*: Carl Linnaeus, influential Swedish botanist (1707–78), the father of modern taxonomy. Thomas Pennant corresponded with him. James Edward Smith (see note to p. 50) apparently began the study of botany as a science on the day of Linnaeus's death, at the age of eighteen. Smith borrowed money from his father to buy Linnaeus's collection in 1783 – books, plants, minerals, insects and letters. There is a legend that the King of Sweden sent a ship to intercept the vessel carrying the precious cargo, but failed (see Fig. 2).

67 *Dr. Powel*: Bingley wrote a biographical sketch of Welsh historian and clergyman David Powel (c.1552–98; see pp. 300–1), who was descended from an ancient family in Denbighshire. Powel may have been the first to graduate from Jesus College, Oxford, and he helped William Morgan translate the Bible into Welsh. His *Historie of Cambria, now called Wales* (1584), based on Welsh chronicles, was the first printed history of Wales and the authority until the nineteenth century for the period down to 1282.

67 *Giraldus Cambrensis*: Gerald of Wales (c.1146–c.1223), prolific writer and archdeacon of Brecon (1175–1203). Born in the castle of Manorbier, Pembrokeshire, he was three-quarters Norman and one-quarter Welsh through his grandmother Nest, daughter of Rhys ap Tewdwr, king of Deheubarth. He studied and lectured in Paris, and in 1188 (Bingley made an error with 1187) accompanied Archbishop Baldwin on a preaching tour of Wales to recruit soldiers for the third crusade, described in Gerald's *Journey through Wales* (written in Latin as *Itinerarium Cambriae*, 1191).

67 *Dr. Fuller ... improbable untruths*: Thomas Fuller, 'The Worthies of Wales', in *The History of the Worthies of England*, edited by his son (1662), the first English biographical dictionary. Clergyman and historian Dr Fuller (c.1608–61) served as a chaplain in the royalist army but continued preaching and writing during the Interregnum.

67 *prince ... lost her head*: Thomas Pennant, *History of the Parishes of Whiteford and Holywell* (1796). He is referring to James II, the last Catholic monarch of Britain (from 1685), deposed in the Glorious Revolution in 1688.

68 *Brass Company*: 'Since this work was sent to the press, Mr. Williams is dead, and the property has been advertised for sale.' Thomas Williams (1737–1802) started out as a lawyer in his native Anglesey and became the enormously wealthy 'copper king' of the Parys mine. He needed water-power for smelting and manufacturing

Notes to pages 68–73

the copper and turned in part to the Holywell stream in Flintshire in the 1780s.

68 *manillas … legs of the negroes*: The future Prime Minister of Trinidad and Tobago, Eric Williams, in *Capitalism and Slavery* (1944), remarks that 'manelloes' were 'metal rings worn by the African tribes' and mentions briefly the Holywell works; one of his sources was indirectly Bingley.

68 *Parys Mine Company*: also spelled 'Paris'. Thomas Williams was the managing partner from the 1770s. See note to p. 68 above.

70 *last embrace*: George Keate, 'Netley Abbey: An Elegy' (1764). The poet and painter George Keate (1729–97) had a gift for friendship, which included Voltaire (whom he met on his Grand Tour in the 1750s), the actor David Garrick and the artist Angelica Kauffman. The ruins of Netley Abbey, built by Cistercian monks, are close to Southampton Water. Thomas Gray was fond of the ruins: he commented in a letter in 1764 that the ivy 'hangs flaunting down among the fretted ornaments & escutcheons of the Benefactors'.

70 *Tanner*: Wiltshire-born Thomas Tanner (1674–1735), Bishop of St Asaph (1732–5) and antiquary, compiled *Notitia monastica, or, A Short History of the Religious Houses in England and Wales* in 1695, which updated Dugdale's work (see note below). He met Edmund Gibson at Oxford, who became a lifelong friend (see note to p. 62). Bingley used the 1787 edition with additions.

70 *Dugdale*: Sir William Dugdale (1605–86), antiquary and herald, born in Warwickshire. At first in collaboration with Roger Dodsworth (until the latter's death in 1654), he compiled *Monasticon Anglicanum* (1655–73), a history of all the monasteries, which also printed their surviving charters and land benefactions. Some protested that it was a covert plea for the restoration of Catholicism. Dugdale was a great scholar, writing also, among many other works, *The Baronage of England* (1676–7; which Bingley used) and a history of Warwickshire. He was knighted in 1677.

70 *Llewelyn prince of North Wales*: Llywelyn ab Iorwerth, 'the Great' (d. 1240).

72 *pris'ner streight*: Thomas Churchyard (c.1523–1604), soldier and poet, born in Shrewsbury. His long potpourri of a poem (it contains prose extracts, some in Latin) *The Worthines of Wales* (1587) is quoted by Bingley several times (from the 1776 edition), and was carried by Joseph Hucks on his walking tour of Wales with Coleridge in 1794 (see Introduction). Churchyard's experience of being both besieger and besieged gave him an appreciative soldier's eye for castles and regret at their ruin. He dedicated it to Queen Elizabeth, describing it as 'a worke in the honour of Wales, where your highnes auncestors tooke name' and commending Wales's 'noble soyle and nation', but lamenting that the castles 'doe dayly decay, a sorrowful sight'. The work also includes lengthy praise of towns and castles in Shropshire and several stanzas in praise of mountains. The widespread interest in mountains did not occur until the mid-eighteenth century, but Churchyard, two hundred years before, declared that 'who so sits, or stands on mountayne hye, / Have halfe a world, in compasse of his eye' and 'highest hilles are best'.

73 *Seteia Portus*: I have omitted here a long 'Memoranda' (biographical sketch) on the naturalist, writer and traveller Thomas Pennant, who had lived at his mansion, Downing, in Flintshire. See notes to pp. 53, 67, and Introduction.

73 *vale of Clwyd*: 'Called by the Welsh Dyffryn Clwyd, *The Vale of the Flat.*'

74 *exclusively her own*: William Cowper, *The Task* (1785), Book 1. The poet Cowper (1731–1800) was born at a rectory in Hertfordshire. His life is a troubled tale of depression and suicide attempts. His mother died when he was five; he was later sent to Westminster School, where he was fairly happy, then made to follow the law as a career and forbidden to marry the cousin he loved. In his fifties, a year after his first volume of poems was published, the widowed Anna, Lady Austen inspired him to write *The Task*, famously giving him the subject of a sofa ('I sing the Sofa,' the poem starts), which leads to six books of reflections on himself, God and Nature – against the tasteless 'Improvement' of landscape designers like 'Capability' Brown; on the rural life in contrast to the 'noisome sewer' of 'gain-devoted cities'; on affected or vicious clergymen, and against geologists and astronomers who were trying to displace God the Creator; on the 'ignorance in stilts' at universities; on domestic happiness and gardening; against war leaders, racism, slavery, blood sports and cruelty to animals. Poet Laureate Robert Southey compiled the *Works* of Cowper in the mid-1830s, with a biography, noting that *The Task* had made Cowper 'the most popular poet of his age'. Cowper was also an influence on Jane Austen, especially in *Mansfield Park*.

75 *Galfrid Arthur, or Geoffry of Monmouth*: Galfridus Arturus or Geoffrey of Monmouth was born probably in Monmouthshire. His life is sketchy but it is documented that he gained election to the see of St Asaph in 1151 and died c.1155. He is best known as the author of the hugely popular *Historia regum Britanniae* (c.1139; *The History of the Kings of Britain*). He claims it was a translation from an ancient 'British' book, but he doesn't seem to have known Welsh and no older manuscript has been found. It made internationally famous the figures of Arthur, Merlin and King Leir, and claimed that Brutus of Troy founded Britain. The account finishes around the seventh century. See note to p. 306.

78 *Morfa Rhyddlan*: 'The Marsh of Rhyddlan' is one of the 'Sixteen Admired Welsh Airs' in Bingley's book, though not included here. He supplied English words in his 1800 edition, from a fragment in Anon., *Letters from Snowdon* (1770); see Introduction.

79 *Speed*: English historian and cartographer John Speed (c.1551–1629). He published *History of Great Britain* (1611) and an accompanying atlas volume, *The Theatre of the Empire of Great Britain*. He was helped in his researches by William Camden and other antiquaries.

79 *DISERTH CASTLE*: 'The word Diserth seems to be derived from the Welsh *dy*, very, and *serth*, steep, from the elevated situation of its castle.'

79 *British*: For Bingley's use of 'British' see Introduction.

81 *DENBIGH*: 'Dinbech, the present Welsh appellation, signifies a small hill, which this is, when compared with the adjacent mountains.'

82 *Skrine ... Edinburgh*: See note to p. 57. As far as is known, Bingley never travelled in Scotland.

83 *HUMPHREY LLWYD*: antiquary and map maker (1527–68), born in Denbigh, graduated from Brasenose College in 1551. He was probably not a physician to the Earl of Arundel, but was a member of his household. He wrote an English adaptation of the medieval *Brut y tywysogyon* (*The Chronicle of the Princes*), which was used by David Powel (see note to p. 67). Llwyd's *Commentarioli Britannicae* is a short geographical and historical description of Britain (1568). He defended

Geoffrey of Monmouth's book and wrote two works in Welsh.

85 *Conwy*: 'The *Conovius* of Antoninus.' See note to p. 127.

86 *Thomas Williams ... Marlow*: 'Mr. Williams is dead since this work was sent to the press.' See note to p. 68.

86 *erect a bridge ... obviated*: 'From information that I have received since this part of the work was written, it is to be feared that the public will for some years longer be disappointed in this advantage.' Scottish-born engineer and amateur poet Thomas Telford's suspension bridge across the Conwy was opened in July 1826.

86 *Suetonius ... invasion*: Bingley seems to muddle the historian Gaius Suetonius Tranquillus (c.AD 70–c.140) with the general and governor of Britain (from AD 58), Gaius Suetonius Paulinus, who defeated Boudica, fought the Ordovices tribe in Wales and attacked the Druids in Anglesey. The historian Suetonius mentions pearls as the lure for Julius Caesar's earlier invasion (in 55–54 BC) in *De Vita Caesarum* (*The Twelve Caesars*).

87 *lady Newborough*: See note to p. 220.

90 *twisted ivy tied*: John Cunningham, 'An Elegy on a Pile of Ruins' (1761; Bingley rearranged the order of these stanzas). Dublin-born Cunningham (c.1729–73) was a poet and untalented actor, who also wrote a farce, *Love in a Mist* (1747), performed in Dublin. He published his *Poems, Chiefly Pastoral* in Newcastle in 1766, where he died aged forty-four.

90 *Nicholas Hookes ... children*: In 1794, Samuel Taylor Coleridge walked through Wales with his Cambridge college friend Joseph Hucks. When they got to Conwy, Hucks wrote: 'I there paid a visit to the tombs of my ancestors, some of whom lie buried in the church belonging to the town. Observe that this visit must not be attributed to superstition, or ought of peculiar veneration for their memory, but the effect of mere curiosity; for there is a singular monument of one of them, who was the father of forty-one children, by two wives. I took down the inscription with a pencil, and then left my prolific ancestor to his uninterrupted repose' (Hucks, *A Pedestrian Tour*, p. 29). Bingley may have been acquainted with Hucks and read his book. See Introduction.

90 *Llewelyn ap Iorwerth*: Llywelyn the Great (d. 1240).

90 *Stratflur in Cardiganshire*: Strata Florida / Ystrad Fflur, Ceredigion.

90 *Moret ... Albertus ... monk after he was dead*: Bingley may not have known who Moret or Albertus were, apart from the latter being a prince. He copied it from William Seward's popular *Biographiana* (1799). Seward (1747–99) travelled the Continent picking up anecdotes and was a friend of Samuel Johnson, Welsh-born Hester Thrale Piozzi and Fanny Burney.

91 *Plâs Mawr*: is in the care of Cadw, and called 'the finest surviving Elizabethan town house anywhere in Britain', built between 1576 and 1585. Bingley's adjective 'uncouth' (however it is translated into modern English) is an example of our change in taste, as is his criticism of towns as 'irregular'.

92 *intimate friend*: Bingley doesn't give his name; maybe it was Rev. Peter Williams.

93 *Matthew Paris*: historian, cartographer and Benedictine monk of St Albans (c.1200–59), probably English-born, used as a source frequently by Bingley,

along with 'Matthew of Westminster'. It was not known then that this was the same man. Paris says he argued with Henry III; in 1248 he was sent to Norway to sort out problems at a monastery. His major work was *Chronica majora*, a universal chronicle; his *Flores historiarum* was an abridgement, both first printed (in Latin) in the sixteenth century. According to the current *ODNB* author, he was irritated by the devious Welsh but admired their bravery in contrast to the imbecility of the English.

93   *1263 ... Llewelyn*: Llywelyn ap Gruffudd.

93   *of the place*: I have here omitted legends of the sixth-century bard Taliesin.

94   *gross as beetles*: Shakespeare, *King Lear*, Act IV (written c.1605–6): Edgar, disguised as poor mad Tom, speaking to his blinded father Gloucester, pretending that they are on the edge of a cliff at Dover. This quote is repeated by Bingley on the summit of Snowdon.

97   *Rev. H. D. Griffith*: Hugh Davies Griffith (d. 1802), BA Christ Church, Oxford 1787, Vicar of Llanbedr with Caerhun from 1798. He matriculated at Christ Church in 1784 at the age of eighteen, so he was in his mid-thirties when Bingley met him in 1801.

98   *rude*: rough, irregular, rugged.

100   *horror (mountain)*: roughness, ruggedness; a thrill of awe.

102   *Dryden ... RIVAL LADIES*: poet, playwright and translator John Dryden (1631–1700). *The Rival Ladies* was his second play, a tragicomedy first performed c.1664, set in Spain and involving two girls (the rival ladies), dressed as boys, in love with the same man, more than happy to scratch each other's eyes out. The speech comes in Act V by 'Hippolito' (Honoria) as they decide to escape a pirate ship by seizing its rowing boat. Dryden was born in Northamptonshire in a puritan family and went to Westminster School and Cambridge. He attended Oliver Cromwell's funeral in 1658 alongside John Milton, but welcomed Charles II at the Restoration, and later became a Roman Catholic. After the reopening of the theatres he became the leading dramatist, and was made Poet Laureate in 1668. Among his many translations were *The Works of Virgil* (1697), which was regarded as a national event. It took him three years, during which he may have been suffering from cancer. Bingley could have found the passage in *A Poetical Dictionary; or, the Beauties of the English Poets* (1761), under the heading 'Cliff', or from *The Modern Universal British Traveller; or a new, complete, and accurate tour through England, Wales, Scotland, and the neighbouring islands* (1779), the sections on Wales by David Llewellyn Rees.

102   *Swift*: Jonathan Swift (1667–1745), author of *Gulliver's Travels* (1726) and Dean of St Patrick's Cathedral, Dublin. He would have travelled many times through North Wales.

104   *bishop Gibson*: referring to Gibson's edition of Camden's *Britannia*. See note to p. 62.

104   *Governor Pownall*: Thomas Pownall (1722–1805), born in Lincoln, England, Governor of Massachusetts (1757–9), later member of parliament. He wrote on a variety of subjects, including Roman antiquities and the article Bingley refers to in *Archaeologia*.

106   *Rhaiadr Mawr*: also known today as Aber Falls.

106 *ceaseless shower*: James Thomson (1700–48), 'Summer', *The Seasons*. After the relaxation of copyright in 1774, there was an explosion in bookselling and the Scottish playwright and poet Thomson's *The Seasons* (all four poems were published in 1730; revised finally in 1746) was said to be read by shepherds. He was J. M. W. Turner's favourite poet, and in 1797–8 Turner added lines from *The Seasons* below his painting of *Buttermere with a Rainbow* in the Academy catalogue, preoccupied with the theory of colour. Thomson moved to London as a young man and became very successful. He was a close friend of Alexander Pope and George Lyttelton (who became his patron; see note to p. 55) and travelled on the Continent. He wrote the words to 'Rule Britannia' in one of his plays. Indolence, overeating and hard drinking helped bring about his death at his home in Richmond, Surrey. An ode after his death by William Collins begins: 'In yonder grave a Druid lies'.

106 *Penrhyn castle ... modern cast*: This is not the castle that exists now. See Introduction.

107 *archbishop Williams ... Lady Penrhyn*: I have omitted Bingley's biographical sketch of John Williams (1582–1650), born in Aberconwy, made Archbishop of York in 1642 after spells of imprisonment. During the Civil Wars he defended Conwy Castle. For Lady Penrhyn, see Introduction and note below.

107 *Lord Penrhyn*: Richard Pennant, Baron Penrhyn of Louth (c.1737–1808). The medieval manor house known as Penrhyn Castle was reconstructed by Samuel Wyatt (1737–1807) from 1782, 'an architectural radical employed by the most progressive groups in late eighteenth-century England', who also designed the stables, entrance-lodge and estate cottages (John Martin Robinson, *The Wyatts: An Architectural Dynasty* (1979), pp. 28, 258). Only parts of the house remain within the neo-Norman castle built by Penrhyn's successor from 1820. See Introduction.

108 *lady Penrhyn*: Ann Susanna née Warburton (1745–1816) was a descendant of Ednyfed Fychan (d. 1246), steward to prince Llywelyn ab Iorwerth; she was joint heiress to the Penrhyn estate. See Introduction.

109 *Benjamin Wyatt*: The Wyatts were a prolifically talented family. Their descendant, the politician and journalist Woodrow Wyatt (1918–97), commented that from the 1750s 'in England they dominated architecture, the highest form of art. Twenty-eight Wyatts were architects, all of skill and mostly of distinction ... Few important constructions were contemplated without asking for a design or advice from a Wyatt.' As for Benjamin Wyatt, Samuel's youngest brother and Lord Penrhyn's agent, 'though not a professional architect, whenever he needed a harbour, or an inn, or a farm building just designed and built it himself' (Woodrow Wyatt, 'Foreword', in Robinson, *The Wyatts*, pp. vi–vii; see also pp. 136–40).

110 *Bangor Vawr ... Bangor is-coed*: Bingley has deleted here his 1800 criticism of the tour writer Rev. Richard Warner: 'Mr. Warner, a late tourist, whose average rate of walking of about twenty-five miles a day seems to have rendered him liable to a thousand errors, has, amongst others, mistaken this place for Bangor in Flintshire. He speaks of its being watered by the "Deva's wizard stream," which flows under an elegant bridge, of five arches. He says that this was the site of the antient Roman station, *Bouvium*, that here was the monastery, 1200 of whose monks were slain by Ethelfred, and that this formed a part of the kingdom of

Notes to pages 110–14

Powis!!' (Bangor in Caernarfonshire/Gwynedd on the North Wales coast is 65 miles north-west of Bangor-on-Dee/Bangor-is-coed near Wrexham.)

112 *Baldwyn, archbishop of Canterbury*: Gerald of Wales accompanied Baldwin on his preaching tour of Wales in 1188. See note to p. 67.

112 *inn (Bangor Ferry)*: 'The charges at this inn are somewhat high, but the accommodations are fully equivalent.'

113 *Cambria's tears!*: This is the start of Thomas Gray's 'The Bard' (1757). London-born Gray, poet and Cambridge scholar (1716–71), who went on the Grand Tour with his schoolfriend Horace Walpole (with whom he was probably in love), was the most famous poet in England after the publication of 'Elegy Written in a Country Church-yard' in 1751. 'The Bard' deals with a Welsh legend – a massacre by Edward I of the bards in the 1280s – in the framework of a Pindaric Ode (nine stanzas). The bard places a curse on Edward's line, which will culminate in the death of his final descendant Richard III, the restoration of the Welsh to the throne under the Tudors and the revival of poetry under Queen Elizabeth.

113 *Edward I ... if he did destroy*: Bingley has added this bracketed caveat about whether Edward I did indeed massacre the bards; the scepticism is not in his first edition. In correspondence between the bishop Thomas Percy and the bard Rev. Evan Evans (both acquainted with Gray) in 1761, it is mentioned that Gray found a hint about the massacre in Thomas Carte's *History of England* (1747–55), and was grateful for Evans's later confirmation of the story, which Evans found in the 'History of the Gwydir Family' by Sir John Wynn, written after 1580, some 300 years later (see notes to pp. 168 and 205). Bingley used Carte as a source on several occasions.

113 *expected harshest*: William Mason, *Caractacus, a Dramatic Poem* (1759), adapted for the London stage in 1776. Mason (1725–97), born in Hull, Yorkshire, became a friend of Thomas Gray at Cambridge, whose work and (censored) letters he published (he also destroyed many). He was ordained and held a living in the West Riding but later inherited a large estate and became financially independent. His great work was the blank verse *The English Garden* (1772–81), also quoted from by Bingley. Mason was also a successful garden designer in the picturesque, informal manner (he was a friend of William Gilpin: see Introduction). In the poem, set in AD 50, King Caractacus has sought refuge on Mona (Anglesey) among the Druids after fighting the Romans for nine years. Two sons of Cartismandua (usually spelled Cartimandua), queen of the Brigantes, a tribe in the area of Yorkshire, have been taken hostage to betray the king to the Romans. This passage is spoken by the Chorus (the chief Druid), summoning the bards with their harps to help reveal the truth of Cartismandua's apparent appeal for military help from Caractacus to save Britain from tyranny. The poem ends with the capture of the king by the Romans. It bears little resemblance to Tacitus' account of his defeat in *The Annals of Imperial Rome*, but Mason does give readers a taste of the famous speech by Caractacus to the Emperor Claudius in Rome, quoted (or invented) by Tacitus some sixty years later, which saved his life.

114 *Llywarch Brydydd y Moch*: Llywarch ap Llywelyn (Prydydd y Moch; fl. 1173–1220), the chief court poet of Gwynedd. Bingley perhaps saw the whole poem (in Welsh) in *The Myvyrian Archaiology of Wales*, vol. I (1801), edited by William Owen Pughe and Edward Williams (Iolo Morganwg). Bingley doesn't name the translator.

118 *Norway!*: Richard Llwyd, note to his poem 'Beaumaris Bay' (1800). Llwyd (1752–1835), poet and antiquarian, was born in Beaumaris in Anglesey; while still a child, sometime after the death of his father, he began work as a domestic servant. However, he educated himself enough to become a clerk, before retiring with his savings to Beaumaris. He was visited by several tourists and writers interested in the antiquities of Anglesey, including the Duke of Somerset and Sir Richard Colt Hoare, who was preparing an edition of Gerald of Wales. Llwyd's topographical poem made his name; in it, his Muse travels anticlockwise around the bay, starting and ending at Priestholm / Ynys Seiriol / Puffin Island, and he became known as the Bard of Snowdon. Around 1807 he moved to Chester, later meeting the Welsh scholarly elite in London, and always remaining a passionate Welshman. See also note to p. 287.

118 *crowded order stand*: Author untraced, with confusing evidence from 1780 onwards. The poem describes a climb of Ben Lomond in the Trossachs. It is headed 'Descriptive Lines, written on a pane of glass at an inn in the neighbourhood of Ben Lomond, near Glasgow' in the *Lady's Monthly Magazine* (September 1799).

119 *beyond them (Nant Frangon)*: 'Near this place, by a little gothic cottage, there is a small *hone quarry*. The stones obtained here are said to equal the Turkey hones in quality. These are taken to a mill at Llandygai to be sawn and ground into shape. When I was here, the quarry was worked by only a single man.'

120 *Cataracts of Benglog*: '*Benglog* signifies a skull; and the name is here taken from the appearance of the rocks.'

122 *road from Bangor Ferry … own expence*: See Introduction about Lord Penrhyn.

123 *earl of Uxbridge*: Henry Bayly-Paget (1744–1812), of Plas Newydd in Anglesey. He was Lord Lieutenant of Anglesey and created Earl of Uxbridge in 1784. His eldest son became the 1st Marquess of Anglesey, after losing his leg at the Battle of Waterloo. The first earl was much involved in the mining of copper on Parys Mountain with Thomas Williams and others since he inherited some of the land, for example as partner in the Mona Mine and Parys Mine Companies. The inn he built in Caernarfon still exists, though swallowed by a later hotel.

123 *CAERNARVON*: 'This name is properly *Caer yn Arfon*, which signifies a walled town in the district opposite to Anglesea: *Ar fôn* or *Ar môn* implies opposite to Mona.'

124 *three cheers, exulting*: Cowper, *The Task*, Book I. See note to p. 74.

127 *SEGONTIUM*: 'This place is called by the Welsh *Caer Custeint*, the Fort of Constantine, and *Caer Segont*, the Fort of the river Seiont.'

127 *Itinerary of Antoninus*: *Itinerarium Antonini Augusti*, perhaps early third century. The Antonine Itinerary describes the roads of the Roman Empire; it mentions one road in North Wales: from Segontium (Caernarfon) to Deva (Chester).

128 *Flores Historiarum*: by Matthew Paris. See note to p. 93.

130 *road home*: 'The following is an extract from a letter, well deserving of notice, inserted in the Gentleman's Magazine, for September 1799. It is dated from Denbigh, and has the signature W. M. B. – "What renders this sect particularly dangerous is, that the preachers are, in general, instruments of Jacobinism, sent into this country to disseminate their doctrines; and, I assure you, that *Paine's works*, and other books of the like tendency, *have been translated into Welsh, and*

secretly distributed about by the leaders of this sect. These are facts which may be depended on, and which are well known to many in this country as well as to myself.'" See Introduction.

131 *dreary (rocks)*: dismal, gloomy.

133 *gentleman who attended me*: 'The Reverend Peter Williams, the rector of Llanrûg and Llanberis, who was my companion in most of my rambles among the mountains.'

133 *monarch of a shed*: Oliver Goldsmith, 'The Traveller' (1764). Goldsmith (c.1728–74) was born in Ireland, about 70 miles west of Dublin. His father was a Protestant clergyman in an area that was mainly Roman Catholic. Goldsmith had a receding chin and was disfigured by smallpox, but one woman who heard 'The Traveller' read by Dr Johnson declared: 'I never more shall think Dr Goldsmith ugly.' He studied medicine in Edinburgh and the Netherlands (though not too seriously), which he criticizes in 'The Traveller' for its love of gain. He walked through France, Switzerland (the location of the 'shed' in the poem), Germany and Italy, largely financing his journey with gambling and busking with his flute. He then worked as a hack writer in London, and became close friends with Samuel Johnson and Joshua Reynolds. His only novel, *The Vicar of Wakefield*, was published in 1766; to his surprise, his comedy *She Stoops to Conquer* had a successful run in 1773, though a letter in a newspaper, shortly after the first performance, describing Goldsmith as an orang-utan and maligning a female friend led to a fight with the London Welsh publisher Thomas Evans in his shop. In the poem, the traveller looks for a country where real happiness can be found, but discovers that 'Our own felicity we make or find', and living in a Swiss 'shed' is stunting.

134 *Assheton Smith, esq.*: See note to p. 136.

134 *sisters behind her*: William Hutton, 'The Welsh Wedding' (1799). Hutton (1723–1815) was born in Derby and worked in a silk mill from the age of seven. He taught himself book-binding and set up as a bookseller in Birmingham. His wife and his daughter Catherine, the future novelist, visited Wales often and he became a friend of Richard Llwyd (see note to p. 118). His *History of Birmingham* was published in 1782. Hutton was a dissenter among a group of radical thinkers. In the Church and King Riots in Birmingham of 1791, aimed at nonconformists, his town and country houses were destroyed. Bingley possibly saw the poem in the *Gentleman's Magazine* (June 1799). In 1803 Hutton published it again in his travel account, *Remarks upon North Wales*, which he dedicated to Lord Penrhyn (see note to p. 107).

136 *court could give*: Thomas May, *The Old Couple, a Comedy* (first performed at court 1636; published 1658). May (c.1596–1650) was an English playwright, poet, translator (from Latin) and historian; he sided with Parliament against the royalists and was given a state funeral but dug up at the Restoration. It is part of a soliloquy in Act II by young Eugeny, beloved of Artemia, who is hiding in the woods, afraid that he has killed a man (but who in fact recovered and is in disguise). The villainous old couple (in their eighties) are his uncle – an old covetous rich knight – and Lady Covet.

136 *British Triades*: a compendium of traditional lore, *Trioedd Ynys Prydein*, compiled in the twelfth century.

136 *Assheton Smith, esq.*: Thomas Assheton Smith (1752–1828), landowner and member of parliament; the quarries were inherited by his son, also Thomas.

138 *admirable picture*: Perhaps Bingley had seen the dramatic lighting effects in the paintings by Joseph Wright of Derby (1734–97), such as *The Orrery* (1766), now at the Derby Museums.

139 *Howel Dda*: Hywel (Dda = the Good) ap Cadell (d. c.949), ruler of Deheubarth (south-west Wales), who extended his power north into Gwynedd and Powys. Some legal manuscripts suggest he codified the law, which might not be reliable, but he was remembered for doing so.

141 *church of Llanberis*: 'This is dedicated to Peris, a cardinal missioned from Rome as a legate to this island. He is said to have settled and died here.'

142 *And character*: James Hurdis, *The Village Curate* (1788). Hurdis (c.1763–1801) was born in Sussex and, after his father's death when he was six, attended school in Chichester before going to Oxford in 1780. After ordination, he was a curate at Burwash in the High Weald of Sussex, where he lived with three of his sisters, a landscape described in his poem. The wealthy rector did not allow him to use his library; just as George Rose MP did not allow another curate, Bingley, to use his. Hurdis became friends with William Cowper and met, and disliked, the radical Tom Paine. In 1793 he was elected professor of poetry at Oxford, but his argumentative nature curtailed any further preferment until just before his death. While sometimes Bingley may have spotted suitable verse extracts amongst the many poetry anthologies, it is possible that the title had drawn him to read the poem, which dwells on morality and the ideal life of a country curate who is anti-slavery and abhors cruelty to animals. In the poem, commenting on the belief that the Welsh were the true descendants of the ancient Britons, Hurdis wrote that his English curate 'has not clomb the high and hoary tops / Of Snowdon or Plinlimmon, yet in heart / A truer Briton lives not'.

142 *respect themselves*: Cowper, *The Task*, Book II. See note to p. 74.

142 *rector of Llanberis*: Rev. Peter Williams.

144 *bad horse-path*: now the A4086.

146 *highest peak of the mountain*: 'This is called Yr Wyddfa, *The Conspicuous*.'

146 *Lhwyd*: Edward Lhuyd or Lhwyd (1660–1709) not only contributed sections on Wales to Gibson's edition of Camden's *Britannia* but was an eminent naturalist and Celtic philologist. One twentieth-century historian considered him to be the greatest scholar that Wales had produced. He spent his early life in the Welsh part of Shropshire before going to Jesus College, Oxford in 1682. There he became keeper at the Ashmolean Museum, which had just opened to the public, where he spent the rest of his life. (It was not then in its present building.) He corresponded with John Ray, especially about fossils, and proposed writing 'The Natural History and Antiquities of Wales' and an *Archaeologia Britannica*. He spent five years on fieldwork in Wales, Scotland, England and Brittany, but only one volume of his *Archaeologia*, with an emphasis on Celtic languages, was published before his premature death. Above Cwm Idwal he discovered the small white lily now known after him as *Lloydia serotina* (Snowdon lily). Prys Morgan states that he gave the Welsh language 'the status of an impeccable ancient pedigree' (*Eighteenth Century Renaissance*).

146 *Ray*: John Ray (also Wray) (1627–1705), celebrated naturalist and theologian, born in Essex, became a lecturer at Cambridge and studied botany and natural history. In 1658 and 1662 he travelled in North Wales, remarking on the puffins of Priestholm and climbing Snowdon with a guide, where he found 'diverse rare plants'. For Ray, geology, botany and zoology displayed the action of a benevolent deity. His many botanical works influenced Linnaeus.

148 *Ingleborough and Penygent in Yorkshire*: Bingley mentions in a letter to Dr James Edward Smith on 18 August 1799 that he had climbed these and other mountains in Yorkshire in his search for plants.

149 *distant ocean*: William Sotheby, 'A Tour through Parts of South and North Wales' (1790). London-born Sotheby (1757–1833), who inherited an estate near Epping Forest and joined the army, went on a walking tour of Wales with his naval officer brother in 1788, publishing afterwards his first collection of poems. He entertained many young authors, such as Scott, Coleridge and Byron (who later was scathing about him), and was also a successful translator but unsuccessful playwright, which included the (not surprisingly) unperformed *The Cambrian Hero, or Llewelyn the Great: An Historical Tragedy* (printed 1800), which is instead about Llywelyn 'the Last' ap Gruffudd, which hurtles from Edward I's coronation in 1274, after his return from Crusade, to Llywelyn's death in 1282 (here stabbed by an evil childhood friend). Before Bingley's extract, Sotheby cries: 'Thee, *Snowdon!* king of *Cambrian* mountain hail' as he is guided to the summit by a guide with 'hoary brow'. Probably the best element of the poem (and the play) is his enthusiasm and sympathy for Wales.

151 *horse-path ... copper mine*: the Miners' Track.

153 *Ffynnon Frech*: known today as Llyn Bach.

154 *awful solitude*: Thomson, 'Summer', *The Seasons*. See note to p. 106.

154 *steep to steep*: Thomson, 'Autumn', *The Seasons*. See note to p. 106.

154 *summit of Snowdon*: the Ranger Path.

157 *Trivaen, Glyder Bach, and Glyder Vawr*: Bingley climbed Glyder Fawr with a guide in 1798 and uses here some of his description from his 1800 edition, but there is no reason to doubt that Peter Williams accompanied him up that mountain again, as well as Glyder Fach and Tryfan on the same day.

158 *Edward Lhwyd*: See note to p. 146.

158 *Daines Barrington*: referring to an article on Cambrian fish in *Philosophical Transactions* (1767). Barrington (c.1727–1800) was an antiquarian and naturalist, born in Berkshire, son of the 1st Viscount Barrington. He was appointed judge of great sessions for Meirionnydd, Caernarfonshire and Anglesey in 1757. He wrote many articles, including one on Welsh castles in 1770 and another on Mozart, whom he met. He was a friend of Thomas Pennant and Gilbert White of Selborne, whom he encouraged, as he did Evan Evans, sending specimens of his work to Thomas Gray (see note to p. 113).

158 *Avernus ... water*: See Virgil's *The Aeneid*, Book 6.

159 *Salvator Rosa*: Italian artist (1615–73), whose dramatic landscapes, often depicting banditti, were collected by the Grand Tourists, and influenced the Sublime and Picturesque movements. See Introduction.

Notes to pages 159–75

159 *country round*: Thomson, 'Summer', *The Seasons*. See note to p. 106.

162 *second volume*: Bingley's list of plants here, and his catalogue of Welsh plants, are not included in this edition.

168 *Gwalchmai ... Gray ... my song, &c.*: Gwalchmai ap Meilyr (fl. 1130–80), court poet on Anglesey, who sang to Owain Gwynedd (d. 1170). Thomas Gray had been made aware of the translations by the scholar, clergyman and poet Evan Evans (Ieuan Fardd; 1731–88), later published in his *Some Specimens of the Poetry of the Antient Welsh Bards* (1764). Gray turned, for example, 'I will extol the generous hero descended from the race of Roderic ...' into 'Owen's praise demands my song, / Owen swift, and Owen strong; / Fairest flower of Roderic's stem, / Gwyneth's shield, and Britain's gem ...' in his 'The Triumphs of Owen' (written c.1761; published 1768), which acknowledged Evans's pioneering work in rescuing old Welsh poetry from manuscripts.

168 *walls of a barn*: I have omitted here 'Memoranda of Dafydd ap Gwilym' (c.1315–c.1350): 'this celebrated Welsh bard'; 'His works possess harmony, invention, elegance, and perspicuity', says Bingley.

169 *from Llanddwyn!*: Bingley saw this translated extract from Dafydd ap Gwilym's 'Galw ar Ddwynwen' in Edward Jones's *Bardic Museum* (1802; see note to p. 54), but there are several differences. The poem in Welsh (and in English translation) can be found at Dafydd ap Gwilym.net: https://dafyddapgwilym.net/eng/3win.php.

170 *Rowlands ... Restaurata*: Henry Rowlands (1655–1723), vicar of Llanidan, antiquary and author of *Mona Antiqua Restaurata: An Archaeological Discourse on the Antiquities, Natural and Historical, of the Isle of Anglesey, the Antient Seat of the British Druids* (1723). He corresponded with Edward Lhuyd (see note to p. 146), but after Lhuyd's death, although Rowlands was a good field archaeologist, he became obsessed with Druidism, while believing in the Creation and Deluge (as most did) and that Welsh was derived, erroneously, from Hebrew, and he developed strange derivations of Welsh words. His book tells the story of Brutus as founder of Britain, and that Druidism was brought to Anglesey by one of Noah's sons. It was an extremely influential work, which Bingley used in his first edition, but less frequently in his second. John Aubrey (1626–97) was the first to assign megalithic monuments to the Druids rather than the Danes or Romans. But the study of geology and fossils, and Charles Darwin's work, in the nineteenth century, together with the study of stone tools, led to the realization that human history was far longer than the accepted notion of 6,000 years. The burial chambers (Bingley calls them cromlechs) on Anglesey are now dated to the Neolithic period, which lasted there until c.1700 BC.

172 *Rollrick*: the Neolithic Rollright Stones on the Oxfordshire/Warwickshire border.

173 *GWYNDY*: Thomas Telford's new Irish road across Anglesey to Holyhead, built in the 1820s, ran south of this inn and it fell into disuse.

175 *AMLWCH, Near the Lake*: 'This loch, or lake, from which the town has its name, was situated betwixt the church and the port. It has been long drained, and is now in a state of cultivation.'

175 *inexhaustible mine of copper*: The mine was actually almost exhausted. There was a rapid decline from about 1799, after the peak of output in the mid-1780s.

Notes to pages 176–92

176 *punish'd fiends*: John Dryden's translation from Virgil's *Aeneid*, Book 6, in which Aeneas descends to the Underworld to see his dead father. For Dryden see note to p. 102.

181 *Goronwy Owen*: I have omitted here a biographical sketch of the poet Goronwy Owen (1723–69): 'A man inferior in talent and genius to none which Wales has produced', Bingley states, and 'As a Welsh poet he ranks superior to all since the days of Dafydd ap Gwilym.'

181 *Panton family*: Paul Panton (1727–97) was a barrister from an old Welsh family; Plas Gwyn came into the Panton family through his marriage, though he spent most of his time in Flintshire. He was a friend of Thomas Pennant, was interested in antiquities and early Welsh literature, and a collector of manuscripts, despite his limited knowledge of Welsh. He was a patron of Evan Evans (see note to p. 168), and given thanks in the first volume of the *Cambrian Register* (1796). His son, also Paul (1758–1822), made Plas Gwyn his main home. He was also a barrister, and took a keen interest in Welsh antiquities. The first volume of *The Myvyrian Archaiology of Wales* (1801) was dedicated to him.

182 *Einion ap Gwalchmai ... within thy breast*: Einion ap Gwalchmai (fl. 1203–23), poet, probably son of Gwalchmai ap Meilyr (see note to p. 168).

182 *Baron Hill ... lord Bulkeley*: The Bulkeleys were one of the most powerful families in North Wales, arriving on Anglesey before 1450 from Cheshire and becoming Irish Viscounts in 1644. Thomas James Warren Bulkeley was raised to the peerage of the United Kingdom in 1784, dying in 1822 without issue, when the long line of Bulkeleys of Baron Hill ended. His half-brother's son inherited, adding Bulkeley to his surname Williams. Princess Victoria and her mother, the Duchess of Kent, stayed in Anglesey during the summer and autumn of 1832, and on 29 August the 13-year-old Victoria handed out medals on the terrace of Baron Hill to winners at the Beaumaris Eisteddfod, which, according to her journal, she didn't attend.

184 *worthy possessor*: See note above. Bingley here gives a footnote to Richard Llwyd's poem 'Beaumaris Bay' and its notes (not included in this edition; see note to p. 118).

185 *Mr. Pocklington ... white-washing an oak-tree*: Joseph Pocklington, of a banking family, bought an island on Derwentwater in Cumberland in 1778 and was keen on whitewash. See Malcolm Andrews, *The Search for the Picturesque* (1989), pp. 190–1.

185 *De gustibus, non est disputandum*: In matters of taste, there can be no dispute; or Everyone as they like.

185 *tourist ... cow*: an old proverb, dating back to at least 1546. I have not been able to trace the tourist.

185 *Joan*: wife of Llywelyn ab Iorwerth. The marriage (in 1205) was hugely prestigious for Llywelyn, who by then was in control of Gwynedd. Joan called herself *domina Wallie* (lady of Wales) and she was involved in Anglo-Welsh politics into the reign of her half-brother Henry III. She died in 1237.

190 *Pontoppidan*: Erik Ludvigsen Pontoppidan (1698–1764), Bishop of Bergen, author of *The Natural History of Norway* (1752–3).

192 *Dr. Caius*: John Caius (born Kays), English physician to Edward VI, Mary

Notes to pages 192–205

and Elizabeth, and naturalist (1510–73), second founder of Gonville and Caius College, Cambridge. Shakespeare possibly used his name for the comic French doctor in *The Merry Wives of Windsor* (c.1600), who challenges the Welsh parson-schoolmaster to a duel.

197 *sure of a meal*: a Welsh *englyn*, in Jones's *Musical and Poetical Relicks* (see note to p. 54). In Jones's 1784 edition the greyhound owner is 'Prince Llewelyn ap Gruffudd ap Llewelyn', which is changed in 1794 to Llewelyn ab Iorwerth ('the Great') and he adds a note on the legend.

198 *Spencer ... Dolmelynllyn ... Madocks*: The Hon. William Robert Spencer (1770–1834) was an Oxford friend of William Madocks, who had built a cottage at Dolmelynllyn, near the waterfalls north of Dolgellau, in the 1790s (see also note to p. 205). Spencer was the grandson of the Duke of Marlborough and one-time pupil of William Gilpin (see Introduction). The attachment of this legend to the village of Beddgelert was investigated by D. E. Jenkins in 1899, in *Bedd Gelert: Its Facts, Fairies, and Folklore*, who combined the poet Spencer, Bingley, Edward Jones (in the 1794 edition of his *Musical and Poetical Relicks*, where Bingley found the story), the first landlord of the new hotel, David Pritchard (significantly, apparently, a South Walian), and the hotel's builder Thomas Jones. A similar legend may have been known elsewhere in Wales, but Spencer's ballad made it famous and the crowds flocked to see the hound's 'grave' in Beddgelert that was probably erected after Bingley's Welsh tour of 1801. See also Elizabeth Beazley, *Madocks and the Wonder of Wales* (1967).

202 *Patria mea petra*: (My homeland is rock.) The hotel, now known as the Royal Goat Hotel, opened c.1802, after Bingley's visit. In July 1854, Charlotte Brontë, on her honeymoon with Arthur Nicholls, may have stayed or taken refreshment here. She wrote in a letter: 'On the day of our marriage we went to Wales. The weather was not very favourable there – yet by making the most of opportunity we contrived to see some splendid Scenery – One drive indeed from Llanberis to Beddgelert surpassed anything I remember of the English Lakes.'

203 *earth to heaven*: Henry Carey, *The Tragedy of Chrononhotonthologos* (1734), a satirical play about George II, Queen Caroline, Robert Walpole and bizarre operatic plots. The lines in the play describe the marching of Antipodean armies (obviously upside down), but probably Bingley found it in a book of quotations with no mention of armies.

203 *Fix'd e'er they fell*: Sotheby, 'A Tour through Parts of South and North Wales'. See note to p. 149.

205 *tops ascend the sky*: John Milton (1608–74), *Paradise Lost* (1667), Book VII, in which the archangel Raphael explains to Adam how the world was created by God.

205 *Sir John Wynne of Gwydir*: Sir John Wynn (1553–1627) attended Oxford and then studied law in London. On his father's death in 1580 he inherited Gwydir in the Conwy valley and was involved in the public life of North Wales as high sheriff and member of parliament. He was created a baronet in 1611. His 'History of the Gwydir Family' (written after 1580) was first published in 1770, edited by Daines Barrington (see note to p. 158), and reprinted in his *Miscellanies* (1781), including a letter from Sir John about embanking Traeth Mawr. Sir John's uncle Robert Wynn built Plas Mawr in Conwy (see note to p. 91).

205 *Madocks ... embanking out the sea*: Bingley is referring to Madocks's first embankment of 1800. William Madocks (1773–1828), of Welsh heritage, bought land near Penmorfa in 1798 in his mid-twenties and had an embankment built which enclosed areas of the marsh of Traeth Mawr up the estuary of the Afon Glaslyn. His later 'Great Embankment', known as the Cob, was begun in 1808 after Bingley's tour, as were his town of Tremadog and port of Porthmadog.

206 *stilly sound*: John Home, *Douglas*, Act V. Home (1722–1808) was a Scottish playwright and minister. The tragedy was first performed to great acclaim in Edinburgh in 1756 and then in Covent Garden, London, a year later and often revived. It foreshadows the Gothic revival in its atmosphere of a Scottish castle surrounded by woods during a Danish invasion, perhaps in the thirteenth century, and its mystery of what had happened eighteen years earlier. The lines are from Norval/Douglas's soliloquy in a moonlit oak grove, having discovered his true, noble parentage. On 23 December 1801, cultural icon Sarah Siddons played the tragic heroine, Lady Randolph, at the Theatre Royal, Drury Lane, a role she had played for many years. Bingley may have seen the play on one of his trips to London.

206 *auspiciously he told*: Drayton, *Poly-olbion*. See note to p. 66.

207 *Llŷn*: 'Vortigern was king of Britain from the year 449 to 465.'

207 *author of the notes on Drayton*: John Selden (1584–1654), lawyer, linguist, poet and scholar, friend of Drayton and Ben Jonson.

207 *incubus*: 'He was called Ambrosius from the circumstance of his being patronized after Vortigern's death by Ambrosius, his successor to the British crown.'

210 *faintest purple*: William Mason, *The English Garden: A Poem*, Book 1 (1772). See note to p. 113.

210 *from Beddgelert*: the Rhyd Ddu Path.

211 *Bettws*: Betws Garmon, north-west of Llyn Cwellyn (not Betws-y-Coed).

212 *gross as beetles*: Shakespeare, *King Lear*, Act IV. See note to p. 94.

214 *dreary attire*: gloomy attire.

216 *round the hills*: Thomson, 'Summer', *The Seasons*. See note to p. 106.

217 *good leather*: Bingley's father was a saddler, and although he died when Bingley was twelve, Bingley may well have learnt about hides during his childhood in Doncaster.

218 *Ptolemy*: Greco-Egyptian geographer and astronomer (c.AD 100–70).

218 *Llanslyndwy*: Llanystumdwy.

220 *lord Newborough*: Thomas Wynn, 1st Baron Newborough (1736–1807), member of parliament successively for Caernarvonshire, St Ives and Beaumaris; he was raised to the peerage of Ireland in 1776; his seat was at Plas Glynllifon. Lady Newborough was his second wife: Italian-born Maria Stella (1773–1843), allegedly the daughter of Louis Philippe, Duke of Orléans (Philippe Égalité). She was a child actress in Florence and married Wynn at the age of thirteen. She later married an Estonian baron. She died in poverty in Paris and her parentage remains a mystery.

223 *Black Prince ... Poictiers*: The Battle of Poitiers, in western France, was a major

victory against the French in the Hundred Years' War, on 19 September 1356, under the eldest son of the English king Edward III.

224 *Ireton*: Henry Ireton (1611–51) was an English general in the Parliamentary army during the Civil Wars, and son-in-law of Oliver Cromwell; he was one of the commissioners who signed King Charles I's death warrant. Ireton's corpse was exhumed and mutilated by the orders of Charles II in 1661.

224 *Porthynllyn ... Holyhead*: William Madocks (see note to p. 205) was heavily involved in promoting Porth Dinllaen near Nefyn, in the Llŷn peninsula, as the main port for Dublin. His biographer, Beazley, wrote in 1967: 'It is difficult now, with Holyhead so long established and Porthdinllaen once more just a rocky bay, to realize how close was the contest between these two claimants to Dublin's traffic.'

224 *Jevan ap Robert*: Ieuan ap Robert, whose brother- and sister-in-law kept trying to kill him. I have omitted Bingley's section on bloody and revengeful 'Caernarvonshire Feuds' in the fifteenth century, which he found in Sir John Wynn's 'History of the Gwydir Family': see note to p. 205.

226 *Bede ... elegant*: the Venerable Bede (c.673–735) of Northumbria. The quotation is from his *Historia ecclesiastica gentis Anglorum* (*Ecclesiastical History of the English People*), completed c.731.

229 *gather them*: A seemingly careless copying from John Philips, *Cyder* (1708). English poet Philips (1676–1709) was from a royalist Herefordshire family; he studied natural history while at Oxford and was influenced by Milton in his poetry. *Cyder* is about farming, gardening and cider-making, with a subtext of political commentary; he also praises 'Indian Weed' – perhaps tobacco rather than cannabis. Later in the poem he hails Henry VII, 'Of Tudor's race, whom in the womb of time / Cadwallador foresaw'. Suffering from consumption and asthma, Philips died at the age of thirty-two. *Cyder* influenced Pope's 'Windsor-Forest' (see note to p. 236). A 1791 edition renders Philips's lines: 'Ev'n on the cliffy height / Of Penmaen Mawr, and that cloud-piercing hill, / Plinlimmon, from afar the traveller kens, / Astonish'd, how the goats their shrubby browse / Gnaw pendent; nor untrembling canst thou see, / How from a scraggy rock, whose prominence / Half overshades the ocean, hardy men, / Fearless of rending winds, and dashing waves, / Cut samphire, to excite the squeamish gust / Of pamper'd luxury.'

232 *lady Newborough*: See note to p. 220. If this picnic visit occurred around 1796, then Newborough's Italian wife was in her early twenties, while her husband was in his early sixties.

236 *rector of Llanrûg*: Rev. Peter Williams.

236 *harmoniously confus'd*: Alexander Pope, 'Windsor-Forest' (the first part written 1704 when he was a teenager). London-born poet Pope (1688–1744) moved with his Catholic family to Windsor Forest as a child, where he was largely self-taught. He contracted tuberculosis of the bone, perhaps from infected milk, which inhibited his growth, making him a hunchback and often ill. The poem is in praise of the end of the European wars under Queen Anne, daughter of the exiled Stuart Catholic monarch James II; the completed poem was published in 1713, just before her death. Samuel Johnson said of Pope, in his *Lives of the Poets* (1779–81), that he had 'all the qualities that constitute genius'.

236 *inn ... carriages*: See Introduction on Lord Penrhyn.

237 *Seiriol as a charm*: Bingley gave the source for this verse in his 1800 edition: a letter from Lewis Morris (1701–65) printed in the *Cambrian Register* (1799). It was written to his brother William in Anglesey while Lewis was en route to London, possibly in 1757. The three Morris brothers (Richard moved to London) were hugely influential in the revival of Welsh culture, which has been called the Welsh renaissance.

237 *Helen*: 'This Helen is supposed by Camden to have been the mother of the emperor Constantine the Great. She was sometimes called by the Britons Elen Luyddawc, or *Elen with the great Army*; which she led out of Britain on an expedition to Jerusalem, where she is said to have found the holy cross on which Christ suffered. She lived in the latter end of the third, and the beginning of the fourth centuries.'

238 *Meredith ... Jevan ap Robert*: See note to p. 224.

238 *David ap Jenkin*: I deleted Bingley's account of 'Caernarvonshire Feuds' (see note to p. 224), where he describes him as 'an outlaw, and a man of great valour'.

239 *well appointed*: 'The sanctuary here alluded to, was the hospital which will be hereafter mentioned, at y Spytty Evan, of the knights of St. John of Jerusalem.'

242 *Gwydir ... river*: The modern editor of 'The History of the Gwydir Family' (1990) says that it is now believed that the name derives from 'gwedir' (low-lying land).

242 *Inigo Jones*: architect and theatre designer (1573–1652), born in a Welsh-speaking family in London. He collaborated for many years with the poet and playwright Ben Jonson (1572–1637) on court masques.

243 *Sylvanus Crew*: Sylvanus Crue (d. 1681), Wrexham goldsmith.

243 *Wynne ... Vaughan*: Lady Sarah Wynn (d. 1671); William Vaughan (fl. 1653–78). The three unsigned brasses are now attributed to Robert Vaughan, London engraver of Welsh origin (c.1600–c.1663). Thomas Pennant remarks in his *Tour* that the portrait of Sarah Wynn, daughter of Sir Thomas Middleton, is 'far the most beautiful piece of engraving I ever saw'.

243 *Abbey of Maenan*: 'This abbey stood about three miles north of Llanrwst. On its site was erected a house, at present the property of lord Newborough. It was founded by Edward I after he had fortified the town of Conwy, for the purpose of removing into it the religious of the Cistertian abbey there.'

245 *sorrows of his lyre*: Gray, 'The Bard'. See note to p. 113.

245 *Jerusalem*: 'The word *spytty* being probably derived from *hospitium*.'

246 *Lyttleton ... 1756*: See note to p. 55.

246 *quiet vale*: Thomson, 'Summer', *The Seasons*. See note to p. 106.

250 *spot than this*: 'Wyndham's Tour through Monmouthshire and Wales in the summers of 1774 and 1777.' The antiquarian Henry Penruddocke Wyndham (1736–1819), of a county family in Wiltshire, went on the Grand Tour for two years in 1765–7, reaching as far as Sicily. He published his first 'tour' of Wales in 1775 anonymously: *A Gentleman's Tour through Monmouthshire and Wales, in the Months of June and July, 1774*; his intention was 'a desire of inducing his

countrymen to consider Wales as an object worthy attention'. For his next edition he toured Wales again in 1777 with Swiss artist Samuel Hieronymus Grimm, and published engravings of his work in a folio-sized edition in 1781. There were further portable editions of his first text of 1775. He also published a guide to the Isle of Wight (1794) and became a member of parliament in 1795. See also Introduction.

253 *Gibson ... Caernarvonshire*: in Gibson's edition of Camden's *Britannia*. See note to p. 62.

259 *profitable purpose*: Wyndham's *Tour*. See note to p. 250.

260 *Maw, or Mawddach*: 'From this river the town is sometimes called Aber Maw, *The Conflux of the Maw*. This was shortened into 'Bermaw, and corrupted to Barmouth.'

263 *Fuller*: Fuller, 'The Worthies of Wales'. See note to p. 67.

265 *Kemmer abbey*: 'Or, variously, Cymmer, Cymner, Cwmner, Kinner, Kinmer, and Kymmer Abbey. *Kymer*, in the ancient British language, signified the meeting of two or more rivers.' It is now known as Cymer Abbey / Abaty Cymer.

265 *were forgiv'n*: Keate, 'Netley Abbey'. See note to p. 70.

266 *hive is too full*: letter by Lewis Morris (the same letter as in the note to p. 237), found by Bingley in the *Cambrian Register* (1799).

267 *Dolmelynllyn Fall*: See note to p. 198.

267 *pendant boughs*: Cowper, *The Task*, Book I. See note to p. 74.

268 *PISTYLL Y CAIN*: 'The word *Pistyll*, in the Welsh language, signifies a narrow stream of water, somewhat resembling that which issues through a spout.'

269 *POOL OF THE THREE PEBBLES*: William Condry wrote in the 1960s: 'Craig y Llam, the shattered precipice that hangs over the once famous Lake of the Three Pebbles, now better known as Llyn Bach, and today mostly filled in by road construction' (*The Snowdonia National Park*).

270 *Dr. Johnson ... copious*: Samuel Johnson, *A Journey to the Western Islands of Scotland* (1775).

271 *ascertained*: 'He is sometimes called *Cawr Idris*, or king Idris, *Cawr* being an old Welsh word for king.'

273 *MACHYNLLETH*: 'This word implies *the place near the river Cynllaeth*, which was the ancient name for the Dovey.'

278 *sedgy bank*: Shakespeare, *King Henry IV, part I* (first performed c.1597; set around 1403), Hotspur's speech in Act I. One writer in 1784 considered it Shakespeare's best play, and it was performed at Drury Lane in 1802, so Bingley probably assumed that his readers would know where the line came from, and they would have heard of one of the characters in the play, the 'great magician, damned Glendower': see note to p. 333. In this speech, the rebel Henry Percy (Hotspur), son of the Earl of Northumberland, reports to the king a hand-to-hand fight between Lord Mortimer and Glendower, who becomes Glendower's son-in-law. Glendower's daughter speaks (and sings) in Welsh in Act III, to whom Glendower replies in Welsh. It is not scripted, but Shakespeare's company, the Lord Chamberlain's Men, probably had at least one actor who spoke Welsh.

278 *valley bends*: Author not traced. Bingley may have found these lines in George Augustus Walpoole, *The New British Traveller* (1784).

278 *lord Herbert of Chirbury*: I have omitted his 'Memoranda' at the end of Chapter 31. Edward Herbert (1583–1648), soldier, linguist, ambassador, historian and poet, born at Montgomery Castle, 'a singular and celebrated character', states Bingley, and 'vanity was his prevailing foible'.

279 *Dyer the poet*: John Dyer (c.1699–1757) was born in Carmarthenshire and went to Westminster School. He studied painting in London, wrote poetry, spent over a year in Italy and became a clergyman. His most famous poem is 'Grongar Hill'. Some of his paintings survive.

279 *Poussin*: either the French artist Nicolas Poussin (1594–1665) or his Italian brother-in-law, who used the name Poussin, Gaspard Dughet (1615–75); they were often muddled.

280 *Mr. Evans*: 'Evans's Dissertatio de Bardis.' In *Some Specimens* (see note to p. 168), Evan Evans included an essay on bards in Latin.

281 *Severn*: 'This event is said to have taken place above 1000 years before the birth of Christ. The most ancient account of it extant is found in Tysilio's History of Britain from the settlement of the Trojan colony in the reign of Cadwaladr, the last king of the Britons. This work is intitled *Brut y Brenhinoedd*; it was written about the year 620, and is the same that Geoffry of Monmouth afterwards published, but with innumerable alterations, in Latin.'

281 *besetting need*: John Milton, *Comus*, first presented at Ludlow Castle in September 1634. Milton was then a graduate of Cambridge in his mid-twenties. The masque was in honour of the inauguration of the Earl of Bridgewater as Lord President of Wales and celebrates chastity, virtue and temperance. The water nymph, the 'virgin pure' Sabrina, who 'sways the smooth Severn stream', frees the virtuous Lady, who has been captured by the evil seductor Comus, son of Circe and Bacchus. See also note to p. 205.

285 *traversing the field*: Author not traced.

286 *envy his success*: Cowper, *The Task*, Book IV. See note to p. 74.

286 *Blount ... Jocular Customs*: The last work of Catholic writer Thomas Blount (1618–79) was *Fragmenta antiquitatis: or, Ancient tenures of land, and jocular customs of some manors* (1679), enlarged by Josiah Beckwith in 1784. It contains sometimes humorous snippets from legal manuscripts. Blount was legally trained but not allowed to practise. Bingley may have come across his law dictionary (1670) while he was training as a lawyer, before he went to Cambridge.

287 *degrading seat*: 'Welsh epigram of William Phylip, translated by Mr. Lloyd, the author of Beaumaris Bay.' See note to p. 118 for Richard Llwyd. The *pennill* in Welsh in Llwyd's notes to his poem is: 'Chwi'r gwragedd rhyfedd eu rhoch, ysgeler / Ysgowliwch pan fynnoch, / E'ch bernir, a'ch bai arnoch, / Gyda'r gair i'r gadair goch.' Phylip (c.1579–c.1669) was a royalist, born and buried in Meirionnydd.

289 *Cornelius Janson*: London-born portrait painter of Dutch heritage, Cornelius Janssens van Ceulen (usual surname Johnson) (c.1593–1661), prolifically active in England c.1618–43. The only painting by him at Powis Castle listed by the National Trust is that of Richard Herbert, 2nd Baron Herbert of Chirbury.

289 *Peter Lely*: celebrated portrait painter (1618–80), born in Westphalia, who used 'Lely' as a pseudonym. He came to London around 1643. He did paint Charles II, but the National Trust assign the portrait at Powis Castle to Sir Godfrey Kneller (1646–1723) and studio.

290 *Rodney's defeat of the French fleet*: Admiral Sir George, 1st Baron Rodney (1718–92): Battle of the Saintes in April 1782 off Dominica, during the American War of Independence, which saved Jamaica from a French invasion. Numerous places are named after him.

292 *Lewis Morris ... forming it*: 'Letter of Mr. Lewis Morris to Dr. Robert Vaughan of Nannau, near Dolgelle.' Bingley found the letter, dated February 1742, in the *Cambrian Register* (1799); there are some copying errors. See note to p. 237.

292 *Oswestry*: '*Oswaldstre*, as a Welsh word, signifies only *Oswald's town*. Previous to the death of Oswald, this place was called Maeserfelth, or Maeserfield, in the kingdom of Mercia.'

294 *for you prepared is*: Churchyard, *The Worthines of Wales*. See note to p. 72.

298 *Ellesmere canal ... aqueduct*. The 1790s was an era of canal mania for transporting goods. In 1791 a meeting was held in Flintshire to discuss a canal to link the Mersey and Dee at Chester and the Severn at Shrewsbury. The problem of carrying the canal over the valleys of the rivers Dee and Ceiriog was solved by Thomas Telford; he called it 'the greatest Work, I believe, that is now in hand in this kingdom'. See note to p. 330.

299 *close to the rocks*: The oil painting is still at Chirk Castle, with a modern title, *Capriccio of a Rocky Coast with Llanrhaeadr Falls and Ships*, as if to suggest that the artist knew it was a fantasy; but maybe the person who showed Bingley around had been passed on an authentic story. After several previous attributions the National Trust now assign it to the Dutch artist Adriaen van Diest, c.1700, who moved to England in the 1670s. It is indeed a strange painting, with a weird mismatch between the waterfall on the left and the seascape on the right.

299 *pencil of a Claude*: It was a cliché in this period to invoke Claude or Salvator Rosa (see note to p. 159) when looking at a landscape, but it was shorthand that the reader would understand and the writer feel aesthetically and emotionally (as well as showing off their taste). French painter Claude Lorrain (c.1600–82) spent most of his life in Italy, and his works (or copies of them) were snapped up by Grand Tourists. See Introduction.

300 *sir Watkin Williams Wynne*: (usually Wynn), 4th Baronet (1749–89), whose seat was at Wynnstay, owned a huge estate in North Wales that extended into Shropshire. He went on the Grand Tour for nine months (1768–9), and on his return married Lady Henrietta Somerset, who died a few months later aged twenty-two. There is a group portrait of him and his two gentlemen companions on the Tour by the fashionable Italian artist Pompeo Batoni (1768) in the National Museum of Wales, Cardiff. Sir Watkin, aged nineteen, has ginger hair, expensive clothes and a prominent tummy (though he is much plumper in other contemporary portrayals). He was a cello-player and a great patron of the arts (which led to enormous debts), including the harpist Edward Jones, Welsh artist Richard Wilson, and his drawing master, the English artist Paul Sandby, with whom he made a two-week tour on horseback of the land he owned in North Wales in summer 1771. Sandby first published aquatint views in the 1770s and

was partly responsible for the start of tourism to Wales. The family harpist was blind John Parry (d. 1782), who inspired Gray to finish 'The Bard'. Watkin's eldest son, by his second wife, also Watkin, the 5th Baronet (1772–1840), was known as the 'Prince in Wales'. He was at Westminster School with William Madocks (see note to p. 205) who visited Wynnstay frequently and took part in the amateur theatricals. Madocks carried on the theatrical tradition at his new town of Tremadog in the first decade of the nineteenth century. The 5th Baronet's brother Charles was at Westminster with Robert Southey and inspired him to write a long poem about a twelfth-century Welsh prince who sailed to America, *Madoc* (1805). Wynnstay was destroyed by fire and rebuilt in the mid-nineteenth century; the Williams Wynns finally left Wynnstay after the Second World War.

300 *right long ago*: Churchyard, *The Worthines of Wales*. See note to p. 72.

300 *workmanship of Roubiliac*: The monument to Lady Henrietta is instead by Joseph Nollekens (1737–1823). The monument to the 3rd Baronet is by Michael Rysbrack (1694–1770), Roubiliac's main rival. See note to p. 308.

302 *WYNNSTAY*: See note to p. 300.

303 *Ossian ... storm*: Ossian is the narrator and supposed author of a cycle of poems, possibly set in the third century, published together by Scottish poet James Macpherson (1736–96) in *The Works of Ossian* (1765). They were allegedly based on ancient manuscripts and oral tradition in Scottish Gaelic, which he said he had translated. There were doubts at the time and the poems are usually now considered to have been largely written by Macpherson. The poems were an international phenomenon and influential on the Romantic movement.

303 *Thomas Brown ... Urn Burial*: Sir Thomas Browne's *Hydriotaphia: Urn Burial, or, a Discourse of the Sepulchral Urns lately found in Norfolk* (1658) is a meditation on burial practices, largely classical. London-born writer and physician Browne (1605–82) coined numerous words and believed in witchcraft and alchemy. Coleridge, Virginia Woolf and Jorge Luis Borges were among his admirers. The Saxon urns are in the British Museum. Bingley's quotation is a slight paraphrase.

304 *year 180*: 'According to the account left us by Rowlands, Lucius was converted to the Christian faith from the preaching of Timothy, the son of Claudia Ruffina, a British female of distinction, who had been a disciple of St. Paul.'

306 *Tysilio ... Nennius*: Tysilio was a seventh-century Celtic saint. The Welsh chronicle *Brut y Brenhinedd* (Chronicle of the Kings) is instead a collection of versions of Geoffrey of Monmouth's *Historia regum Britanniae* (see note to p. 75), dating at the earliest from the thirteenth century. The *Brut Tysilio*, also based on Geoffrey's work, became better known at the beginning of the nineteenth century after its publication in *The Myvyrian Archaiology of Wales*, bedevilled by Iolo Morganwg's forgeries. See notes to pp. 54, 281. Nennius was a ninth-century Welsh monk traditionally considered as the author of *Historia Brittonum*.

307 *Philip Yorke, esq.*: 'The author of a valuable history of the Five Royal Tribes of North Wales.' Yorke (1743–1804), of English ancestry, was born at Erddig and schooled in England. He was elected to the Society of Antiquaries in 1768, a year after he inherited Erddig, and was an enlightened landlord. His interest in Wales derived from his Welsh wife. He published *Royal Tribes of Wales* in 1799, was a dreadful horseman and enjoyed performing in amateur theatricals at Wynnstay

(see note to p. 300).

308 *Seward ... Ionic grace*: 'Verses on Wrexham, and the inhabitants of its environs', *Llangollen Vale, with other poems* (1796). Anna Seward (1742–1809), 'the Swan of Lichfield', was a comfortably off, unmarried, poet and correspondent, with a long, acrimonious relationship with Samuel Johnson (her grandfather's pupil). She visited the Dee valley in 1795 where she met the 'Ladies of Llangollen', Lady Eleanor Butler and Miss Sarah Ponsonby (see note to p. 327). She subsequently wrote two Welsh-themed poems: 'Llangollen Vale' (see note to p. 324) and this one.

308 *Roubiliac*: Louis François Roubiliac (1702–62), born in Lyons, was arguably the most important sculptor working in Britain in the eighteenth century. The marble monument to Mary Myddelton (who died in 1747 aged fifty-nine, according to the inscription) was commissioned in 1751 for £300 and was later moved to another part of the church. The medallions of Rev. Thomas and Arabella Myddelton (d. 1754 and 1756) were placed near their graves and those of three of their children who died young.

308 *form sublime*: Seward, 'Verses on Wrexham.'

309 *Elihu Yale*: (1649–1721), born in Boston, Massachusetts, of Welsh ancestry, he moved to England as a child. Yale was a merchant and administrator in India for the East India Company. His increasingly autocratic behaviour made him unpopular and he returned to London in 1699 a wealthy man. He maintained his father's country house near Wrexham and was appointed high sheriff of Denbighshire. As a philanthropist, he helped found Yale University at New Haven, Connecticut. He died in London and his body was taken to St Giles church, Wrexham, where his parents are buried.

314 *none bewayle*: Churchyard, *The Worthines of Wales*. See note to p. 72.

317 *perished in the flood*: 'The river is at present so very shallow, that it would scarcely drown a dog: this battle might have taken place during an overflowing of the water in consequence of heavy rains.'

317 *inscription*: I have omitted the Latin inscription.

318 *Matthew of Westminster*: Matthew Paris: see note to p. 93.

319 *Village of the Cataract*: 'This is the literal translation of the Welsh word: whence the name can have been derived I know not, as there is no cataract near the place.'

321 *by heart, and hand*: Churchyard, *The Worthines of Wales*. See note to p. 72.

323 *screaming loud*: Cowper, *The Task*, Book I. See note to p. 74.

323 *merry vale between*: Hurdis, *The Village Curate*. See note to p. 142.

324 *Llangollen*: 'Buck says the vale took its name from the circumstance of the abbey having possessed a piece of the true cross. This, we are informed, was given to Edward I, who, in return for so valuable a present, granted to the abbey several immunities. Buck's Antiquities.' Yorkshire brothers Samuel (1696–1779) and Nathaniel Buck (fl. 1724–59) made topographical drawings and copper engravings of many of the towns and ruins in England and Wales, touring the latter c.1739–41 (published 1742) and 1748. In 1774 the printmaker Robert Sayer published three volumes of their prints, entitled *Buck's Antiquities*. The introduction comments that 'there is something in ancient Ruins that fills the

mind with contemplative melancholy'.

324 *sigh command*: Anna Seward, 'Llangollen Vale'. The poem was 'inscribed to the right honourable Lady Eleanor Butler, and Miss Ponsonby' (see notes to pp. 308, 327). The poem moves from Owain Glyndŵr and bloody battle in the early fifteenth century to the virtue and friendship in the home of the Irish 'Ladies of Llangollen'.

326 *death that we have*: John Webster, *The Duchess of Malfi* (1613/14). This revenge tragedy by Webster (c.1580–1632) was seldom performed in the eighteenth century. Instead there was a bowdlerized version by Lewis Theobald, called *The Fatal Secret*, in the 1730s in which the Duchess is not strangled on stage but lives happily ever after with her former steward Antonio. But in the 1770s the antiquarian Francis Grose used Antonio's original speech in Act V – who is at the ruins of an echoing, ancient abbey in Italy – as an epigraph to his multivolume *Antiquities of England and Wales*, curved below an engraving of two men gazing at a tomb in a ruined abbey (see note to p. 65). Bingley possibly came across the quotation there. See Introduction.

326 *blaze of day*: This extract from Hurdis's *The Village Curate* (see note to p. 142) has been squashed below the Webster extract, and the first line replaced with Bingley's phrase after he (presumably) removed an emotional passage from his 1800 edition about his feelings at the abbey ruins. He seldom names the authors of poetic extracts but this is oddly careless. The first line should read: 'The sober twilight of this winding way'. See Introduction.

327 *lady Eleanor Butler and Miss Ponsonby*: Lady Eleanor Butler (1739–1829) and Sarah Ponsonby (1755–1831), known as the 'Ladies of Llangollen', eloped from Ireland in 1778. Less than two years later they found a place of retirement on the river Dee in Denbighshire. They Gothicized their house, Plas Newydd (especially with rescued wood carvings), and created a picturesque, romantic garden. They were visited by all the good and the great, including the Duke of Wellington, Wordsworth and, bizarrely, the runaway schoolboy Thomas De Quincey in 1802.

328 *Edward Lhwyd*: See note to p. 146.

329 *sylvan maze*: Bingley here gives a footnote reference to Pennant's *Tour*, which indeed has an English version of the poem by Hywel ab Einion Llygliw (fl. c.1330–70), but instead Bingley uses two stanzas from Seward's 'Llangollen Vale' (not naming her and omitting the stanza between them). See note to p. 324.

329 *ruynous thing*: Churchyard, *The Worthines of Wales*. See note to p. 72.

330 *Cyssyllte ... time I was here*: in 1798. Thomas Telford's biographer L. T. C. Rolt (1958) described his bridges over the Menai and Conwy and the Cysyllte aqueduct as his 'greatest individual works; they are embodiments of his engineering genius'. The plan for the iron aqueduct was drawn up in 1794; Telford solved the problem of carrying a canal over the deep Dee valley by rejecting all that had been done before. The foundation stone of the first pier was laid in July 1795. A year later it was already regarded as one of the Wonders of Wales and in November 1805 the aqueduct was ceremonially opened.

331 *The Hand*: Bingley deleted here a potentially libellous remark in his 1800 edition that the innkeeper and his wife were 'oddities, as every one, who has been at the house a day or two, must know'.

Notes to pages 332–44

332 *Owen Glyndwr*: I have omitted Bingley's 'Memoranda' on Owain Glyndŵr (c.1359–c.1416), Prince of Wales, in this chapter, in which Bingley abbreviates Thomas Pennant's sympathetic discussion in his *Tour*. Bingley summarizes: 'He revolved in his mind his own genealogy, a descendant from the ancient British princes: his superstitious notions attached to himself many of the prophecies of Merlin, and other bards of former years. These, with the dreadful omens that he believed had taken place at his birth, confirmed him in the opinion that he was destined to be the redeemer of his country from the tyranny and oppression of the English throne.'

332 *Tysilio*: See note to p. 306.

333 *wild and irregular*: In Shakespeare's *King Henry IV, part I*, the Earl of Westmorland calls Glyndŵr 'irregular and wild Glendower' (Act I).

333 *Iolo Goch ... green hill*: Bingley found this in Jones, *Bardic Museum* (see note to p. 54). Iolo Goch (c.1320–c.1398) was a native of the vale of Clwyd. His patrons were largely supporters of the English crown.

333 *escuculent fish*: (esculent) eatable fish.

337 *LLYWARCH HEN*: Bingley based his summary on Owen (Pughe)'s introduction to *The Heroic Elegies and Other Pieces of Llywarç Hen, Prince of the Cumbrian Britons: with a literal translation by William Owen* (London: J. Owen and E. Williams, 1792). (For Owen (Pughe) see note to p. 43; for the publisher E. Williams see Introduction.) The book was dedicated to Thomas Pennant and Paul Panton. One suggestion today is that Llywarch Hen was a sixth-century British prince in the north of England and that a cycle of poems about him and his sons was composed in the ninth century, locating him in Powys.

340 *thro' this night*: Bingley found this verse translation of several stanzas from 'The Lamentations of Prince Llywarch Hên' in Edward Jones's new edition (1794) of *Musical and Poetical Relicks of the Welsh Bards*, dedicated to George, Prince of Wales. The translation was sent to Jones by Francis Percival Eliot (1755–1818) 'of Shenstone Moss near Lichfield'. Eliot was an English soldier and writer who lived for a few years in Lichfield before moving back to London; his father-in-law, Rev. John Breynton (d. 1799), was Welsh. Bingley made a few changes to the translation.

340 *Lyttleton ... ever beheld*: See note to p. 55.

341 *no whiting see*: Churchyard, *The Worthines of Wales*. See note to p. 72. Churchyard instead refers to the river 'Cloyd' (Clwyd).

341 *Daines Barrington*: See note to p. 158.

342 *The Burrower*: 'The Welsh word Twrch signifies a *hog*: this river, therefore, seems to derive its name from its sometimes impetuously tumbling along the stones or earth that oppose its progress.'

344 *Spencer ... Timon*: See note below.

344 *gentle roar*: Edmund Spenser, *The Faerie Queene* (1590–6), Book I, canto ix. The poet Spenser (c.1552–99) was born and died in London, but in 1580 he moved to Ireland as secretary to Lord Grey. The poem, in six books, is dedicated to Queen Elizabeth, whom it reflects in multifaceted ways, and it influenced the cult of the Virgin Queen.

346 *grass-hopper did keep*: James Thomson, 'The Castle of Indolence: An Allegorical Poem, Written in Imitation of Spenser', Canto I (1748). He began composing 'in the way of raillery on himself, and on some of his friends, who would reproach him with indolence; while he thought them, at least, as indolent as himself'; but it is a moral allegory that exhorts 'Toil, and be glad! ... Who does not act is dead.' He died a few months after it was published. See note to p. 106.

Further reading

Andrews, Malcolm, *The Search for the Picturesque: Landscape Aesthetics and Tourism in Britain, 1760–1800* (Stanford, CA: Stanford University Press, 1989). A treasury of images, research and quotations, with chapter VI on North Wales. Unfortunately he assigns *Letters from Snowdon* erroneously to Cradock, has some wrong dates, and locates Aberystwyth and Hafod in North Wales.

Bainbridge, Simon, *Mountaineering and British Romanticism: The Literary Cultures of Climbing 1770–1836* (Oxford: Oxford University Press, 2020). An insightful study by a mountaineer and academic, who sees in Bingley 'the emergence of a new conception of mountaineering as "adventure"'.

Beazley, Elisabeth, *Madocks and the Wonder of Wales: The Life of W. A. Madocks, M.P., 1773–1828: Improver, 'Chaotic', Architectural and Regional Planner, Reformer, Romantic, with Some Account of his Agent, John Williams* (London: Faber and Faber, 1967). Useful research on Madocks and his impact on North Wales.

Davies, John, *A History of Wales*, rev. edn (London: Penguin, 2007). Highly readable and informative.

Dictionary of Welsh Biography / Y Bywgraffiadur Cymreig: https://biography.wales.

Gerald of Wales (Giraldus Cambrensis), *The Journey through Wales* [1191] and *The Description of Wales* [1194], trans. Lewis Thorpe (Harmondsworth: Penguin, 1978). Bingley comments: 'Giraldus believed every thing that the inhabitants chose to impose upon him.'

Gwyn, David, *Welsh Slate: Archaeology and History of an Industry* (Aberystwyth: RCAHMW, 2015). A hefty book and admirably thorough.

Hankinson, Alan, *The Mountain Men: A History of Early Rock Climbing in North Wales – from its beginning to 1914* [1977] (Frodsham: Mara Books, 2004). Fascinating even if you are not a rock climber; he includes Lyttelton on Moel Hebog, Thomas Pennant, and the first recorded rock climb 'in Britain' (up Clogwyn Du'r Arddu) by Bingley and Peter Williams, citing what he calls 'one of the most quoted passages in British mountaineering history'.

Hernon, Paul, *Sir Watkin's Tours: Excursions to France, Italy and North Wales, 1768–71* (Wrexham: Bridge Books, 2013). Useful research on Sir Watkin Williams Wynn, 4th Baronet, especially his two-week tour of North Wales in 1771 with Paul Sandby, though unfortunately claiming Joseph Craddock [sic] as the author of *Letters from Snowdonia* [sic].

Hucks, J., *A Pedestrian Tour through North Wales, in a Series of Letters* [1795], ed. Alun R. Jones and William Tydeman (Cardiff: University of Wales Press, 1979). An important addition to the literature of tourists in Wales at this period: in 1794, Cambridge graduate Hucks walked through Wales with young Samuel Taylor Coleridge.

Hughes, W. J., *Wales and the Welsh in English Literature: From Shakespeare to Scott* (Wrexham: Hughes and Son, 1924). Particularly interesting on seventeenth-century satirists, whom some writers take too seriously and out of context, especially the endlessly quoted description of Wales as 'the fag end of Creation'. Also useful for Churchyard, Gray and quotations in travel books (though he names Craddock [sic] as the author of *Letters from Snowdon*); Bingley is quoted but not differentiated from the other travel writers.

Jenkins, Geraint H., *The Foundations of Modern Wales 1642–1780* (Oxford: Oxford University Press, 1993). Especially interesting on the revival of Welsh cultural life, and Dolgellau as 'a smoky Gomorrrah' thronging with prostitutes.

Jenkins, Simon, *Wales: Churches, Houses, Castles* (London: Penguin Books, 2011). Gorgeous colour photographs enhance this gazetteer, with Wales divided into counties (and the historic names in the Contents list). However, Lord Penrhyn did not erect the Norman-revival Penrhyn Castle that exists today; it was designed for his second cousin, Mr George Hay Dawkins, who was never ennobled.

Jones, Dewi, *The Botanists and Mountain Guides of Snowdonia*, new edn (Pwllheli: Llygad Gwalch, 2007). An important book for the history of botany (and guides) on Snowdon. He has chapters on John Ray and Edward Lhuyd, John Wynne Griffith of Garn, Hugh Davies, Bingley (using his 1804 edition) and Peter Bailey Williams. His research elucidates where Bingley climbed and names his guides and the curate (who died in his fifties), as well as changing the old Yorkshireman's name to John 'Closs', instead of Close. He is wrong about Bingley's birthdate (which we don't know) and implies that he was negligent in not recognizing Griffith's contribution more (however, Bingley named him frequently in his 1800 edition), but he is sympathetic, calling Bingley 'intrepid'.

Kendall, Alex, *Walking the Snowdonia Way* (Milnthorpe: Cicerone, 2017). A pioneering new walk from Machynlleth to Conwy. The only way to know North Wales is to walk it. I was the guinea pig for the lower route.

Kendall, Alex, *Snowdonia: North: Low-Level and Easy Walks* (Kendal: Cicerone, 2019).

Kendall, Alex, *Snowdonia: South: Low-Level and Easy Walks* (Kendal: Cicerone, 2020).

Livesey, Nick, *Photographing the Snowdonia Mountains* (n.p.: Fotovue, 2018). Brilliant photographs and guide.

Lord, Peter, *The Visual Culture of Wales: Industrial Society*; *Imaging the Nation*; *Medieval Vision* (Cardiff: University of Wales Press, 1998; 2000; 2003). The three magnificent volumes in this series are lavishly illustrated, informative and indispensable.

Morgan, Prys, *The Eighteenth Century Renaissance*, A New History of Wales (Llandybïe, Dyfed: Christopher Davies, 1981). Essential reading about the Welsh cultural revival by a great historian, which expands on the Welsh writers and scholars whom Bingley learnt about.

Morgan, Prys (ed.), *The Tempus History of Wales, 25,000 B.C. – A.D. 2000* (Stroud: Tempus Publishing, 2001). An authoritative, accessible, illustrated history.

Perrin, Jim, *Snowdon: The Story of a Welsh Mountain* (Llandysul: Gomer Press, 2012). A wonderful book that first introduced me to Bingley.

Perrin, Jim, *The Hills of Wales: Impressions, Explorations, Recollections* (Llandysul: Gomer Press, 2016). A companion volume to *Snowdon*, full of love for Welsh hills. He writes: 'Maybe Cader Idris is as close as we get to the perfected place.'

Perrin, Jim, *Rivers of Wales* (Llanrwst: Gwasg Carreg Gwalch, 2022). Part three is in

Further reading

North Wales: 'The folklore rivers: Cynfal, Dwyryd, Glaslyn'. It is horrifying to read of 'sportsmen' currently shooting Golden plover for fun on Traeth Bach. There is entrancing writing on the old routes across Traeth Mawr, of Dinas Emrys, Vortigern/Gwrtheyrn and the bride who disappeared.

Rhind, Peter, and David Evans (eds), *The Plant Life of Snowdonia: Including the Fungi and Lichens* (Llandysul: Gomer Press, 2001). Beautifully illustrated. Bingley would have been dazzled by what two hundred years of research have produced, especially knowledge of the action of glaciers and the naming of vastly ancient geological periods after Wales and Welsh tribes: the Cambrian, Ordovician and Silurian. The botanical richness of Snowdonia lies in those areas inaccessible to sheep, or unpalatable to them, such as lichens, but there was also over-collection by botanists.

Robinson, David (ed.), *The Cistercian Abbeys of Britain: Far from the Concourse of Men* (London: Batsford with English Heritage, Historic Scotland and Cadw: Welsh Historic Monuments, 1998). David Robinson of Cadw produced a superbly illustrated and informative book.

Index by Bingley

(Note: This is abridged and slightly edited, with some modern or alternative spellings within square brackets. Following Bingley's practice I have inserted only the first page for the entry when it runs to more.)

Aber 104
    castle at, now demolished 105
    ferry from, into Anglesea 105
    romantic glen near 105
    waterfall at 106
Aberconwy 87
Abergeley 85
Aber Mawr *see* Barmouth
Abermenai 225
    ferry-boat, particulars of the loss of 164
Abermule 282
Aberystwyth 274
Abren, or Sabrina, story of 280
Alleluia victory, at Maes Garmon, near Mold, account of 317
Allt Dû, slate quarry near Llanberis 136
Amlwch 175
    smelting houses, and port 179
Anecdotes
    of the removal of the body of Owen Gwynedd from Bangor cathedral 112
    of an old woman's mode of getting into her house 133
    of two gentlemen at Llanwchllyn, near Bala 343
    of the discovery of a murderer 351
    of old John Close of Llanberis, and his widow 140
Anglesea [Anglesey; Ynys Môn]
    excursion from Caernarvon into 163
    once joined to Caernarvonshire 163
    ferries into 163
    origin of name of 168
    the residence of the ancient Welsh princes 168
    copper mines 175
    marine productions of 186
Arran, a mountain near Snowdon 193

Arran Benllyn 340, 342
Arrenig mountains, near Bala 340
St. Asaph [Llanelwy] 74
    cathedral 74
    miracle said to be performed by 76
Asterias glacialis 226
Avon Vawr [Mawddach] 262

Bagillt ['little hamlet'] 64
Bala [Y Bala] 340
    lake 340
    overflowings of 341
    excursion round 342
Bangor, or Bangor Vawr, in Caernarvonshire 110
    cathedral 110
    history of 111
    castle 111
    house of friars preachers at 112
    parish church 112
Bangor ferry 112
    inn at 112
    battle near 113
Bangor Iscoed, in Flintshire [Bangor-on-Dee] 304
    monastery at 304
Bardsey, isle of [Ynys Enlli]
    voyage to 225
    account of 229
    history of 233
    monastery at 233
Barmouth [Abermaw; Bermo] 260
    inn at 260
    port at 261
Baron Hill, the seat of lord Bulkeley, in Anglesea 184
Barrows, or carnedds, ancient mode of forming 259
Basingwerk abbey 70
    chapel of knights templars at 70
    castle 71
Beaumaris [Biwmares] 182

Index by Bingley

church 182
castle 182
bay of 183
Beavers, formerly found in Wales 119
Beddgelert 197
   church 197
   tradition respecting 197
   priory 201
   inns at 201
Ben Glog, a rock in Nant Frangon 119
   waterfalls at 119
Bere castle 136
'Bermaw *see* Barmouth
Berwyn, or Ferwyn mountains 347
Bettws Garmon 194
Bettws y Coed [Betws-y-Coed] 241
Braich Dû 119
Braich y Cafn 117
Braich y Ddinas, an ancient fort on the summit of Penmaen Mawr 104
Breiddin hills, in Montgomeryshire 290
Bromfield and Yale, lordship of 312
Buccinum lapillus 225
Bwlch Cwm Brwynog 154
Bwlch Glâs 153
Bwlch Tyddiad 256

Caddy of Cwm Glâs, anecdotes of 143
Cader Ferwyn 347
Cader Fronwen 347
Cader Idris, ascent to the summit of [Cadair Idris] 271
Caunant Mawr, a cataract near Llanberis 137
Caer Custeint 364
Caer Cybi 174
Caer Gai 344
Caergwrle 314
   castle 314
Caernarvon [Caernarfon] 123
   inn at 123
   harbour 125
   castle 125
Caer Rhûn 97
Caer Segont 364
Calamine found in Flintshire 73
Cancer homarus 231
Cantref Gwaelod 257
Capel Curig, vale of 236
   inn at 236

Cardigan bay 257
Carnedds, account of 259
Carnedd Llewelyn, a high mountain in Caernarvonshire 118
   tradition respecting 118
Carreg, near Holywell 73
Carreg y Big, near Dolwyddelan 239
Carreg y Saeth 255
Castell
   Cidwm 196
   tradition respecting 196
   Corndochon 344
   Cymmer 267
   Gronw Befr o Benllyn 340
   y Craig 79
Castrum Leonis 311
Cataract *see* Waterfall
Cefyn Cicini, near Corwen 334
Cefyn y Castell 290
Char 135, 195
Chirk 298
   church 298
   castle 298
   aqueduct at 298
Cilgwyn slate quarries 215
Clawdd Coch 148, 211
Clawdd Offa *see* Offa's Dyke
Clogwyn
   du'r Arddu 146
   y Garnedd, part of Snowdon 149
Clwyd, vale of 73, 76
Clynog 220
   church 220
Cockles, modes of taking 232
Coed Euloe, in Flintshire, defeat of king Henry II at 60
Constable's Sands, near Chester, tradition respecting 71
Conwy 87
   river 85
      pearl fishery in 86
   ferry 85
      impositions at 85
   castle 87, *88*
   church of 90
   abbey 90
   Plâs Mawr at 91
   Vale of 97
   Waterfall on the river 98
Copper Mines
   in Anglesea 175

386

Index by Bingley

near Llanberis 196
of Snowdon 149
Cors y Gedol 260
Corwen 333
Crabs and lobsters, mode of taking 231
Craig Breiddin 290
Craig y Cae 272
Craig y Mwyn, lead mine at 349
Crataegus aria 103
Creigiau yr Eryri 149
Creiddin, a hundred of Caernarvonshire, near Conwy, excursion round 92
Crib Coch, part of Snowdon [Crib Goch] 132, 148
Crib y Ddysgl 148
Criccieth [Cricieth] 222
   castle 222
Cromlech
   etymology and use of the 171
   mode of erecting 172
   near Plâs Newydd in Anglesea 171
Crucis, vale of 323
Cucking stool, at Montgomery 286
Curig, a Welsh Saint 237
Cwm
   Bochlwyd 159
   Brwynog 146
   Bychan, near Harlech 255
   Dyli 209
   Glâs 144
   Idwel [Idwal] 158
      tradition respecting 158
   Llan 209
   Maentwrog 247
   Nancoll 256
   y Clo 132
Cylch Cyngrair, or Druidical Circles 255
Cynfael, waterfalls, of the 246
Cynwyd, waterfall of the 336

Daear-dor, phenomenon so called 342
Dee, river [Afon Dyfrdwy]
   source of 344
   derivation of name of 344
Dee, valley of the 332
Denbigh [Dinbych] 81
   castle 82
   White Friary at 83
Derfel Gadarn, immense wooden image of, at Llanderfel, near

Bala 336
Devil's Bridge, near Beddgelert 202
Devil's Bridge, near Havod, in Cardiganshire [Hafod, Ceredigion] 274
Diganwy 92
Dinas Brân castle 327
Dinas Dinlle 218
Dinas Emrys 206
Diserth 79
   castle 79
Dolbadarn castle *cover*, 135
Dolforwyn castle 279
Dolgelle [Dolgellau] 263
   Dr. Fuller's enigmatical description of 263
   manufactures at 264
   inn at 264
Dolmelynllyn waterfall, near Dolgelle 267
Dolwyddelan castle 237
   village 240
Downing 358
Druidical Circles 255, 257
Drws Ardudwy 256
Drws y Coed 215
Dulas Bay 181
Dwynwen, the Welsh Venus 169
Dwyryd, river 247
Dyffryn Clwyd, or Vale of Clwyd 73, 358

Edeirnion, vale of 334, 336
Eglwys Rhôs 96
Eifl or Rival Mountains 220
Eliseg, pillar of, near Valle Crucis abbey 324
Ellesmere canal and aqueducts 298, 330, 376, 379
Elwy, river 74
Erddig, the seat of Philip Yorke, esq. 307
Euloe castle [Ewloe] 60
Evionedd, an ancient Division of Caernarvonshire [Eifionydd] 219

Farndon 311
Ferry-boats from Caernarvonshire to Anglesea, lost 163
Ffestiniog 246
   vale of 247
Ffynnon Dyfnog 320

387

Index by Bingley

Ffynnon Frêch 153
Fish, monocular 158
Flint [Y Fflint] 61
   church 61
   gaol 61
   castle 62
   history of 62
Floating island 196
Friars, near Beaumaris 185
Frwd y Pennant, waterfall so called 276
Funeral, Welsh 142

Glangwna, near Caernarvon 193
Glâs Llyn 276
Gloddaeth 96
Glyder Vawr, ascent to the summit of [Glyder Fawr] 161
Glyder Bach, ascent to the summit of [Glyder Fach] 160
Glyder and Trivaen mountains, ascent to the summits of [Tryfan] 157
Glynn bridge, near Corwen 334
Glyn Dyfrdwy 332
Glynllivon, the seat of lord Newborough [Glynllifon] 220
Gorphwysfa, near Llanberis 145
Gorseddau 255
Griffith, Pierce, anecdotes of 108
Gwern Einion 256
Gwydir, near Llanrwst 242
Gwynant 206
Gwyndy 173
Gwyniadd, a species of alpine fish 341
Gyrn Goch, a mountain near Clynog 221

Harlech 252
   castle 252, *252*
   mephitic vapour near 253
   public house at 253
Hawarden 59
   castle 59
Hell's mouth, dangerous bay of [Porth Neigwl] 235
Herbert, lord of Chirbury 278, 285, 375
Herbert, Edward, esq. grandfather of lord Herbert of Chirbury, anecdote of 278
Holt 311
   castle 311
Holyhead [Caergybi] 174
   island 174
   churchyard and church 174–5
Holywell [Trefynnon] 64
   church 64
   St. Wenefred's well at 65
   mills and manufactures at 68
Hope [Yr Hôb] 315
Howell y Fwyall, and his battle-ax, anecdote of 223
Hwylfar Ceirw, tradition respecting 95

Idris, giant, tradition respecting 269

Jumpers, a singular sect of calvinistical methodists 129

Kemmer, or Y Vanner abbey, near Dolgelle [Abaty Cymer] 262, 265
Knockin [Knockin; Cnwcin; in Shropshire] 351
Kyffin [Gyffin] 97
Kynaston's cave, in Ness Cliff [in Shropshire] 352

Lavan sands 183
Lead Mines, near Holywell 73
Llanberis, vale of 131, 135
   pools 135
   slate quarry near 136
   cataract near 137
   copper mine near 137
   village 139
   public houses in 140
   church 141
   curate of 141
   well near 143
   evening scene in the vale of 161
   singular mountain pass near 144
Llanbublic church [Llanbeblig] 124
Llanddwyn abbey, in Anglesea 169
   rocks 169, 225
Llanderfel [Llandderfel] 336
Llandinam 278
Llandrillo 336
Llandudno 95
   rocks, tremendous scene at 93
Llandulas [Llanddulas] 85
Llandygai 106
   church 106
   mills at 107
Llandysilio church, on an island in the Menai [Church Island; Ynys

Index by Bingley

Tysilio] 188
Llandysilio hall [near Llangollen] 332
Llanedwen, in Anglesea 170
  tradition respecting a woman sixteen feet long, buried here 170
Llan Egwest, or Valle Crucis abbey [*medieval*: Llanegwestl] 324
Llanelian church, in Anglesea 179
  singular closet in, and superstitious practices at 180
Llanelltyd 262
Llan Elwy, or St. Asaph 74
Llanfair, in Anglesea [Llanfair-mathafarn-eithaf] 181
Llanfawr [Llanfor] 337
Llangedwen, vale of [Llangedwyn] 351
  hall 351
Llangollen 326
  bridge 326
  church 326
  Plâs Newydd, near 327
  vale of 330
  inn at 331
Llangower 342
Llangynog 347
  slate quarries at 347
  lead mines at 349
Llanhaiarn [Llanaelhaearn] 221
Llanrhaiadr, near Denbigh [Llanrhaeadr] 319
Llanrhaiadr yn Mochnant [Llanrhaeadr-ym-Mochnant] 349
Llanrwst 241
  bridge 242
  town 243
  church 243
  inn at 244
Llanvaes, in Anglesea, priory of [Llanfaes] 185
Llanwchllyn [Llanuwchllyn] 342–3
Llanydloes [Llanidloes] 276
  church 276
  manufactures at 277
Llanymynech 290
  hill 290
    cavern in 290
    view from 291
Llechog [summit in Snowdon range] 148
Llechwedd y Rè 146
Llewelyn and his dog, tradition respecting 197

Lliewedd [Y Lliwedd: mountain] 148
Lloyd, Hugh, Cynfael 247
Llugwy, waterfall of the 240
Llwyd, Humphrey, short account of 83
Llŷn, promontory of, excursion into 218
Llyn
  Bochlwyd 159
  Cadair 197
  Coch 211
  Conwy 241
  Cwellyn 195
  du'r Arddu 146
  Eigiau 98
  Ffynnon y Gwâs 154
  Glâs 211
  Gwynant 209
  Idwel [Idwal] 158
  Llwydaw 153
  Mwyngil 269
  Ogwen 121
  Tecwyn Ucha 251
  Tecwyn Isa 251
  Tegid 340
  Trigrainwyn 269
    traditions respecting 269
  y Cae 272
  y Cwm Bychan 255
  y Cwm Glâs 153
  y Cwn 157
  y Dinas 208
  y Dywarchen 196
  y Nadroedd 211
  Yr Avange 119, 276
Llyniau Nantlle 214
Llywarch Hên, the Welsh bard, memoranda of 337
Lobsters and crabs, the modes of taking 231
Lyons [Holt] 311

Machynlleth 273
Maentwrog 247, 250
  vale of 247
Maes Garmon, 'Alleluia' victory at 317
Maes Mawr Gâd, or Maes Hîr Gâd, in Anglesea 170
Margaret Uch Evan, anecdotes of 134
Marl 93
Maw, or Mawddach, river 260, 262
Mawddach, cataract of the 268
Medusa aurita 189

389

Index by Bingley

Menai, straits of 163, 187
Merlin, the enchanter, account of 206
Methodists, Jumpers, a remarkable
    sect of 129
Milltir Gerrig 347
Mochras 257
Moel Aelir, mountain, ascent to its
    summit [Moel Eilio] 193
Moel Hebog 197
Moel y Golfa 290
Moel y Don ferry 170
    battle at 170
Mold [Yr Wyddgrug] 315
    church 315
    castle 316
Môn, or Mona *see* Anglesea
Mona copper Mine 178
Montford bridge 352
Montgomery [Trefaldwyn] 282
    church 282
    castle 283
    town 286
    cucking stool at 286
Morfa Rhyddlan, battle at 78
    Welsh air so called 78
Mya margaritifera 87
Mynydd Mawr 193
Mynydd Moel 272
Myrddin Emrys [Merlin] 208
Myrddin ap Morvryn / Myrddin
    Wyllt 208

Nant
    Colwyn 197
    Frangon [Ffrancon] *16*, 118
    Gwynant 206
    Gwyrfai 193
    Hwynan [Nantgwynant] 206
    Lle [Nantlle] 214
        pools, excursion to 214
Nant mill, between Caernarvon
    and Beddgelert, cascade at 194, *195*
Nant y Bele 303
Nevin [Nefyn] 221
Ness Cliff 352
New Bridge, between Chirk and
    Ruabon, fine scene at 299
Newtown [Y Drenewydd] 279
    church 279
    cataract near 279
Northop 61

Oestrus bovis 216
Offa's dyke [Clawdd Offa] 71, 291
Ogo, a cavern in Llanymynech hill 290
Ogwen bank 118
    pool 121
    river 121
Orme's head, Great, tremendous scene
    at 93
Oswald, king of Northumberland;
    account of the death of 292
Oswaldstre 292
Oswestry [Croesoswallt; 'Soswallt] 292
    house of Industry, at 292
    castle 294
    well at, called Oswald's well 293
Overton 303
    church-yard, and Yew trees 303
Owen, Sir John, anecdote of 223
Oysters, mode of catching 232

Pabell Llywarch Hên 338
Padarn, a Welsh saint, tradition
    respecting 136
Paris mountain, in Anglesea [Parys] 175
    mine *31*, 175
Patella vulgata 226
Pearl-fishery, in the river Conwy 86
    muscle, account of [mussel] 87
Peat, mode of conveying down
    mountains 158
Penallt [Pennal] 273
Penmachno 245
Penmaen Bach 100
Penmaen Mawr 100
    accidents at 101
    road along 101
    ascent to the summit of 103
    ancient fort on 103
Penmaen Rhôs 85
Penmon priory, in Anglesea 186
Penmorfa 223
Penrhyn castle, the seat of Lord
    Penrhyn 107
    history of 107
    fine view from the grounds of 109
    baths at 109
    fishery near 110
Pentraeth, in Anglesea 181
Pen y Cader [Penygadair] 272
Pen y Llan 303

Pimblemere [Llyn Tegid] 340
Pistyll Rhaiadr *348*, 350
   whimsical painting of 298
Pistyll y Cain 268
Plants found near Diserth 79
Plâs Gwyn, in Anglesea 181
Plâs Mawr, at Conwy 91
Plâs Newydd, Anglesea, the seat of
   the earl of Uxbridge 171
   cromlech near 171
   ancient tumulus near 173
Plâs Newydd, the seat of lady Eleanor
   Butler and Miss Ponsonby, near
   Llangollen 327
Plynlimmon mountain [Pumlumon] 275
Pont Aberglâsllyn [Aberglaslyn] 202
   scenery near 202
   salmon leap at 204
   moonlight scene at 205
   tradition respecting 203
Pont Cynwyd 346
Pont y Cyssyllte, near Llangollen,
   aqueduct at 330
Pont Porthlwyd 98
Pont y Glynn, near Corwen, cataract
   at 334
Pont y Pair *48*, 240
Pont y Pandy, waterfall near 244
Pool castle, or Powis castle 289
Pool Ceris 163
Porthaethway, or Bangor Ferry 112
Porth Leidiog 166
Porthynllŷn [Porth Dinllaen] 221
Port Penrhyn 115
   inn at 115
   manufactory of writing slates
     near 116
   quay at 116
   iron rail road from, to lord
     Penrhyn's slate quarries 116
Pounderling, sir Robert, anecdote of 80
Powel, Dr. [David] 300
Powis castle 289
Priestholme island, voyage to
   [Ynys Seiriol] 187
   description of 190
   tradition respecting 191
   flight of sea-birds at 191
   puffin warren at 191
Pulpit Hugh Lloyd Cynfael near
   Ffestiniog 247

Pwllheli 222

Queen Hope 315

Red wharf bay, Anglesea 181
Rhaiadr [Rhaeadr]
   Ben Glog, in Nant Frangon 119
   Cwm Dyli 209
   Cynwyd 336
   Dû, betwixt Tanybwlch and
     Harlech 250
   Dû, near Dolgelle 267
   Mawr, betwixt Conwy and
     Llanrwst 98
   Mawr, near Aber [Aber Falls] 106
   y Craig Llwyd 244
   y Mawddach 268
   y Wenol [Swallow Falls] 240
Rhiedd, in Anglesea 170
Rhitta, a giant, tradition respecting 118
Rhiwedog 346
Rhual 317
Rhyd equestre, and *Rhyd pedestre*, two
   fords in Caernarvonshire 218
Rhyddlan [Rhuddlan] 77
   marsh 78
   castle 78
   Black friary at 79
   port of 79
   statute of 77
Rival or Eifl mountains 220
Rowlands, Henry, the Antiquarian 170
Ruabon 300
   church and monuments 300
Ruthin 320
   church 320
   castle 321

Salmon leap, near Pont Aberglâsllyn 204
Salmo lavaretus 341
Sarn Badrwyg 257
Sarn Helen 237
Sarn y Bwch 257
Segontium 127
Seiont, river 127
Setantiorum Portus, of Ptolemy 128
Seteia Portus 73
Severn, source of river [Hafren] 275
   origin of name 280
Sheep, extraordinary instance of
   activity in 230

Index by Bingley

Siamber Wen, near Diserth 80
Slate quarries
   lord Penrhyn's 117
   near Llanberis 136
   in the parish of Llanllyfni 215
   near Llangunog, and dangerous mode of conveying the slates 347
Snowdon [Yr Wyddfa]
   excursion to the summit of, from Dolbadarn castle, near Llanberis 146
   excursion to the summit of, from Llanberis 153
   excursion to the summit of, from Llyn Cwellyn 154
   excursion to the summit of, from Beddgelert 210
   height of 147
   view from 148, 212
   Copper mine on 149
Sorbus aucuparia, use of the berries in Wales 212
Star-fish, or Sea Stars 226
Studwal's islands [St Tudwal's Islands] 235
Swelly rocks [The Swellies; Pwll Ceris] 188
Sychnant 100

Tal y Moel fre, or Tal y Voel fre 167
   sea fight at 167
Tanybwlch [Tan-y-bwlch] 250
   inn at 250
Tommen y Bala 340
Tradition respecting
   Hwylfar Ceirw, on the Orme's Head 95
   Rhitta, a giant, who is said to have lived on Carnedd Llewelyn 118
   Padarn, a Welsh saint 136
   Eionion ap Gwalchmai 181
   Castell Cidwm, a rock betwixt Caernarvon and Beddgelert 196
   the erection of Pont Aberglâsllyn 203
   giant Idris, and the pool of Three Pebbles 269
   Ogo, a cavern in Llanymynech hill 290
   St. Oswald's well 293
Traethau Gwylltion 165

Traeth Mawr, and Traeth Bach 205, 224
Trefriw, near Llanrwst 244
Tre-faldwyn 283
Tre-Newydd [Newtown] 279
Trevor Hall 331
Trivaen, or Y Trivaen, mountain, ascent to the summit of [Tryfan] 157
   curious particulars respecting 120
   description of 159
Trûm y Sarn 203
Tudno and Cybi, Welsh saints, tradition respecting 95
St. Tudwal's islands 235
Tull Dû, near Llanberis 159
   amazing cataract at 159
Tuthill, a rock at Caernarvon 124
Twrch, vale of 342
   river 342
Tysilio 306

Vale of Crucis 323
Valle Crucis abbey 324
Virnwy, river [Vyrnwy; Efyrnwy] 290
Vitriol and alum work at Paris mountain, in Anglesea 179
Voryd, river 218
Vreiddin, or Breiddin hills 290

Waterfall
   betwixt Conwy and Llanrwst, called Rhaiadr Mawr 98
   called Rhaiadr Mawr, near Aber [Aber Falls] 106
   of the river Ogwen, called Rhaiadr Ben Glog 119
   near Dolbadarn castle, Llanberis, called Caunant Mawr 137
   at Tull Dû, near Llanberis 159
   at Nant mill, betwixt Caernarvon and Beddgelert 194
   a few miles from Beddgelert, called Rhaiadr y Cwm Dyli 209
   of the river Llugwy, near Llanrwst, called Rhaiadr y Wenol [Swallow Falls] 240
   of the river Conwy, near Llanrwst, called Rhaiadr y Craig Llwyd 244
   of the Cynfael, near Ffestiniog 246
   betwixt Tanybwlch and Harlech,

       called Rhaiadr Dû 250
       near Harlech 257
       at Dolmelynllyn, near Dolgelle,
          called Rhaiadr Dû 267
       of the Mawddach, near
          Dolgelle 268
       of the Cain, near Dolgelle 268
       near Cader Idris [Cadair Idris]
          271, 273
       called Llyn Pen Rhaiadr 274
       called Frwd y Pennant 276
       near Newtown 279
       at Pont y Glynn, near Corwen 334
       of the Cynwyd, betwixt Corwen
          and Bala, called Rhaiadr
          Cynwyd 336
       Pistyll Rhaiadr *348*, 350
Watt's dyke 71
Wattstay, now Wynnstay 302
Welsh Pool [Welshpool; Y Trallwng] 288
Wenefred's well and chapel, at
   Holywell [Winefride;
   Ffynnon Wenffrewi] 65
       legend of 65
Whitchurch [parish church of St
   Marcella] 83
Whitford, a Roman pharos in the
   parish of 73
Williams, archbishop 107, 108
Wrexham [Wrecsam] 307
       church and monuments 307
       fair 309
       inns at 309
Wye, source of the river [Afon Gwy] 275
Wynnstay, the seat of sir Watkin
   Williams Wynne [Wynn] 302

Y Caer Wen, near Corwen 334
Yew trees in church-yards, conjectures
   respecting 303
Ynys Enlli *see* Bardsey
Ynys Seiriol *see* Priestholme island
Yr Wyddfa, the highest point of
   Snowdon 149
Yr Wyddgrûg *see* Mold
Yspytty Evan 245
       hospital of knights of St. John of
          Jerusalem at 245

Index of people

(Note: This mainly comprises people not mentioned in Bingley's Index. Also, when he quotes verse he seldom names the author, but I have inserted the page number for the quotation. Bingley's versions of names are in parentheses. Page numbers in italics refer to illustrations.)

Addison, Joseph: *Remarks on Several Parts of Italy* (1705) 27
Aikin, Arthur: *Journal of a Tour through North Wales* (1797) 22, 57, 355
Aikin, Dr John 54, 354
Alken, Samuel (aquatint engraver) ix
Anne, Queen 372
Anon. author of *Letters from Snowdon* (1770) 21, 359, 382, 383
Austen, Jane
    Mansfield Park 359
    Northanger Abbey 24

Barrington, the Hon. Daines 158, 341, 367, 370
Bede, the Venerable 226, 305, 372
Bingley, William (c.1774–1823)
    biographical sketch and works 1–15
Borrow, George: *Wild Wales* (1862) xi, xvi
Bower, Archibald (recipient of Lyttelton's letters) 247, 354
Brontë, Charlotte 370
Browne, Sir Thomas: *Urn Burial* (1658) 303, 377
Bulkeley, Thomas James Warren, Lord 182, 184, 185, 191, 369
Burke, Edmund: *A Philosophical Enquiry into the Sublime and the Beautiful* (1757) 26, 28
Butler, Lady Eleanor 18, 327, 378, 379

Camden, William: *Britannia* (1586) 62, 128, 139, 306, 311, 314, 356, 359, 373
Caractacus 363
Carey, Henry: *The Tragedy of Chrononhotonthologos* (1734) 202–3, 370

Carte, Thomas: *History of England* (1747–55) 363
Charles I 63, 223, 242, 264, 285, 295, 372
Churchyard, Thomas: *The Worthines of Wales* (1587) 27, 71, 81, 293–4, 300, 314, 321, 329, 341, 358
Clark, Kenneth, Lord 24
Claude Gellée (called le Lorrain) 9, 23, 299, 376
Coleridge, Samuel Taylor 4, 20, 358, 360, 367, 377
Combe, William: *Tour of Doctor Syntax in Search of the Picturesque* (1812) 24
Cowper, William: *The Task* (1785) 74, 124, 142, 267, 286, 323, 359, 366
Cradock, Joseph: *An Account of Some of the Most Romantic Parts of North Wales* (1777) 21
Cunningham, John: 'An Elegy on a Pile of Ruins' (1761) 89–90, 360

Dafydd ap Gruffudd (d. 1283) (David) 62, 356
Dafydd ap Gwilym (poet; d. c.1350) xix, 39, 169, 353, 368
Davies, Hugh (botanist and clergyman) 55, 355
Dayes, Edward (artist) ix, *348*
Deighton, John (publisher) xviii, 4, 9, 11
Drayton, Michael: *Poly-olbion* (1612) 66, 206, 207, 357, 371
Dryden, John 361
    The Rival Ladies (c.1664) 101–2, 361
    translation of Virgil's *Aeneid* (1697) 176, 361, 369
Dugdale, Sir William: *Monasticon Anglicanum* (1655–73) 70, 79, 280,

394

Index of people

320, 356, 358
Dyer, John (poet and artist) 279, 375

Ednyfed Fychan (d. 1246) 31, 362
Edward I 367, 378
   Caernarvon 124, 125, 126, 127
   castles xix, 62, 183, 222–3, 274, 280, 315, 321
   Conwy 89, 91, 373
   Llewelyn ap Griffith 105
   massacre of the bards 113, 363
   Moel y Don defeat 171
   Oswestry 295, 297
   St Asaph 75, 79
   son as prince of Wales 77–8
   sons of Madoc ap Griffith 312, 315, 329
   statute of Rhyddlan 77
Edward II 77, 125, 312, 317, 329
Edward III 62, 106, 175, 317, 329
Edward, the Black Prince 315, 372
Einion ap Gwalchmai (poet; fl. 1203–23) 181, 369
Eleanor, Queen (1241–90) 89, 126, 315
Elizabeth I 82, 83, 96, 108, 223, 266, 321, 358, 363, 370, 380
Evans, Evan (Ieuan Fardd) 9, 280, 363, 367, 368, 369
   Some Specimens of the Poetry of the Antient Welsh Bards (1764) 368, 375
Evans, John (1795 map of North Wales) 353
Evans, Theophilus: *Drych y Prif Oesoedd* (1716) 21

Fabyan, Robert: *New Chronicles of England and France* (1516) 62, 356
Fox, Charles James 31
Fuller, Dr Thomas: 'The Worthies of Wales' in *The History of the Worthies of England* (1662) 67, 263, 357

Garrick, David 21, 22, 358
Geoffrey of Monmouth (Galfrid Arthur; Geoffry of Monmouth): *Historia regum Britanniae* (c.1139) 75, 306, 359, 375, 377
Gerald of Wales (Giraldus Cambrensis): *Itinerarium Cambriae* (c.1188) 22, 67, 71, 119, 158, 168, 196, 203, 301, 345, 357, 363, 364
Gibson, Bishop Edmund: edition of Camden's *Britannia* (1695) 104, 253, 358, 361, 374
Gilpin, William (Picturesque art theorist and clergyman) 23–4, 28, 370
Goldsmith, Oliver: 'The Traveller' (1764) 21, 133, 365
Gray, Thomas 358, 363, 367
   'The Bard' (1757) 29, 113, 245, 363, 377
   'The Triumphs of Owen' (1768) 167–8, 368
Griffith, Hugh Davies (antiquarian and clergyman) 97–8, 361
Griffith, John Wynne, of Garn (botanist and MP) 6, 40, 55, 354–5
Grose, Captain Francis: *Antiquities of England and Wales* (1784 edn) 65, 70, 76, 82, 181, 356–7, 379
Gwalchmai ap Meilyr (court poet; fl. 1130–80) 168, 368, 369

Hazlitt, William: 'On going a journey' (1822) 28
Henry II 60–1, 62, 65, 70, 71, 294, 334, 351, 354, 356
Henry III 75, 79, 93, 112, 266, 284, 286, 295, 312, 328, 361, 369
Henry IV (also Bolingbroke; Duke of Lancaster) 112, 185, 204
Henry V 185
Henry VII 31, 238, 313, 316, 321, 352, 372
Henry VIII 70, 186, 243, 292, 305, 313, 315, 355
Hoare, Sir Richard Colt 22, 364
Home, John: *Douglas* (1756) 206, 371
Hucks, Joseph: *A Pedestrian Tour through North Wales* (1795) 4, 28, 358, 360
Hurdis, James: *The Village Curate* (1788) 141–2, 323, 366
Hutton, William 365
   Remarks upon North Wales, being the result of sixteen tours through that part of the principality (1803) 33, 365
   'The Welsh Wedding' (1799) 134, 365

395

Index of people

Hywel ab Einion Llygliw (fl. c.1330–70) 329, 379

Iolo Goch (bard; c.1320–c.1398) 333, 380

Jenkins, D. E., *Bedd Gelert: Its Facts, Fairies, and Folklore* (1899) 370
Joan, princess (d. 1237) (Siwan; wife of Llywelyn ab Iorwerth) 185, 369
John, King 112, 185, 197
Johnson, Samuel 270, 360, 365, 372, 374, 378
Jones, Edward (Bardd y Brenin) 354, 376
   Musical and Poetical Relicks of the Welsh Bards (1784; 1794) 29, 30, 54, 354, 370, 380
   The Bardic Museum (1802) 354, 368, 380
Jones, Edward (talkative innkeeper, guide, schoolmaster) 36, 270–1, 272
Jones, Inigo 242, 243, 373
Jones, Theophilus ('Cymro'): 'Cursory remarks on Welsh tours or travels' 20–1, 22
Jones, Thomas (artist) 30
Jonson, Ben 356, 357, 371, 373

Keate, George: 'Netley Abbey: An Elegy' (1764) 70, 265, 358

'Ladies of Llangollen' *see* Butler; Ponsonby
Leland, John: *Itinerary of John Leland the Antiquary* (1710–12) 60, 82, 92, 136, 286, 292–3, 305, 328, 355–6
Lewis, Mrs (innkeeper at Barmouth) 18, 260–1
Lhuyd, Edward (Lhwyd) xi, xii, xiii, 21, 39, 146, 158, 328, 356, 366, 368
Linnaeus, Carl 4, 38, 67, 87, 103, 189, 212, 216, 225, 226, 228, 231, 341, 355, 367
Lister, Anne (Yorkshire landowner) i, 23
Livesey, Nick 1
Lloyd, Evan (botanist, poet and clergyman) 55, 355
Lloyd, William (schoolmaster and guide) xiv, xv, 19, 27, 202

Llwyd, Richard (Bard of Snowdon): 'Beaumaris Bay' (1800) 118, 364, 365, 375
Llywarch ap Llywelyn (Prydydd y Moch; court poet; fl. 1173–1220) 114, 363
Llywelyn Fawr ('the Great') ab Iorwerth (d. 1240) (Llewelyn) 28, 31, 39, 70, 90, 358, 360, 362, 369
Llywelyn y Llyw Olaf ('the Last') ap Gruffudd (d. 1282) (Llewelyn ap Griffith) 62, 93, 356, 361, 367
Longman, Thomas Norton (publisher) xviii, 12–13, 16, 21
Loutherbourg, Philippe de: *The Last Bard* 29
Lyttelton, George, Lord (Lyttleton) 20, 55, 62, 246, 247, 340, 342, 354, 362

Macfarlane, Robert 26
Macpherson, James: *The Works of Ossian* (1765) 303, 377
Madocks, William (W. A.) 28, 34, 198, 205, 265, 267, 370, 371, 372, 377
Malkin, Benjamin Heath: *The Scenery, Antiquities, and Biography of South Wales* (1804) 13
Martyn, John (Professor of Botany at Cambridge) 6–7
Martyn, Thomas (his son; Professor of Botany at Cambridge) 6–7
   The Gentleman's Guide in his Tour through Italy (1787) 7
Mason, William 23, 210, 363
   Caractacus, a Dramatic Poem (1759) 113, 363
   The English Garden: A Poem (1772–81) 210, 363
Matthew Paris (also Matthew of Westminster) (c.1200–59) 93, 128, 318, 360–1
May, Thomas: *The Old Couple, a Comedy* (1636) 136, 365
Milton, John 361, 372
   Comus (1634) 281, 375
   Paradise Lost (1667) 28, 205, 370
Mitchell, Julian 25
Morgan, Dr William (translator of

Index of people

Bible into Welsh, 1588) 350, 357
Morris, Lewis (1701–65), letters by 237, 266, 291–2, 373, 374, 376
Myddelton, Mary (monument in Wrexham by Roubiliac, 1750s) (Middleton) 308, 378

Newborough, Maria Stella, Lady 87, 232–3, 371, 372
Newborough, Thomas Wynn, Lord 220, 221, 229, 230, 232–3, 371, 372, 373
Nicholson, George: *The Cambrian Traveller's Guide, and Pocket Companion* (1808) 23

Ossian *see* Macpherson, James
Owain Glyndŵr (d. c.1416) (Owen Glyndwr) xix, 39, 53, 75, 112, 185, 197, 244, 273, 295, 311, 322, 332, 333, 334, 379, 380
Owain Gwynedd (d. 1170) (Owen Gwynedd) 60, 71, 90, 112, 158, 168, 238, 244, 317, 334, 356
Owen, Goronwy (poet; 1723–69) 181, 369
Owen, William *see* Pughe, William Owen

Panton family 181, 369, 380
Pennant, Thomas: *A Tour in Wales* (2nd edn, 1784) xi, xiv, xix, 1, 18–19, 31, 53, 54, 354, 355, 357, 358, 367, 369, 373, 380
  Barmouth 261
  Basingwerk abbey 70
  Bingley on 10, 11, 18, 54, 57
  Caernarvon castle 125
  Conwy castle 88
  date of battle mistaken 318
  Flint 61
  Glyder Bach 161
  Linnaeus 87, 357
  pollution 30
  Roman pharos 73
  St Wenefred's well 67
Penrhyn, Ann Susanna, Lady (née Warburton) 31, 107, 362
Penrhyn, Richard Pennant, Lord *16*, 17, 30–4, *32*, 107, 108, 115, 116, 117, 121–2, 215, 236, 362, 365

Perrin, Jim 1
Philips, John: *Cyder* (1708) 229, 372
Phylip, William (poet; c.1579–c.1669) 287, 375
Pocklington, Joseph, and whitewash 185, 369
Ponsonby, Sarah 18, 327, 378, 379
Pope, Alexander 362, 372
  'Windsor-Forest' (1713) 236, 372
Poussin, Nicolas *or* Gaspard Dughet 'Poussin' 23, 279, 375
Pownall, Thomas, Governor 104, 361
Pratt, Samuel Jackson: *Gleanings through Wales, Holland and Westphalia* (1795) 20–1, 37, 52–3, 353
Pugh, Edward: *Cambria Depicta* (1814) *31*
Pughe, William Owen 43, 54, 353, 363, 380

Rees, Owen (publisher) xviii, 12–13, 16
Richard II 62–3, 83, 85, 312, 315
Richards, John (guide) 36, 254, 255
Rosa, Salvator 23, 26, 159, 367, 376
Roubiliac, Louis François 300, 308, 377, 378
Rowlandson, Thomas 24

Sandby, Paul 30, 376–7
Selden, John 207, 357, 371
Seta, Cesare de 23
Seward, Anna 28, 378
  'Llangollen Vale' (1796) 28, 324, 329, 379
  'Verses on Wrexham' (1796) vi, 307–8
Shakespeare, William 22, 27, 356, 357
  King Henry IV, part I 27, 278, 333, 374, 380
  King Lear 94, 212, 361, 371
  The Merry Wives of Windsor 370
Skrine, Henry: *Two Successive Tours throughout the Whole of Wales* (1798) 57, 82, 355, 359
Smith, Dr James Edward (later Sir) 2, 4–6, *5*, 7, 10, 11, 12, 13, 14, 39, 50, 353, 355, 357, 367
Sotheby, William: 'A Tour through Parts of South and North Wales' (1790) 149, 203, 367, 370

Index of people

Southey, Robert 353, 359, 377
Speed, John (c.1551–1629) 79, 304, 320, 359
Spencer, Hon. William Robert: 'Beth Gelert or The Grave of the Greyhound' (c.1800) 28, 198–201, 370
Spenser, Edmund: *The Faerie Queene* (1590–6) 344, 380
Stowe, John: *Annales of England* (1592) 62, 63, 280, 356
Swift, Jonathan, Dean 102, 361

Taliesin xix, 361
Tanner, Thomas: *Notitia monastica* (1695) 70, 262, 358
Telford, Thomas 376, 379
Thomson, James 354, 362
  'The Castle of Indolence' (1748) 23, 346, 381
  The Seasons (1730) 106, 154, 159, 216, 246, 362
Turner, J. M. W. *cover*, 23, 25, 362

Uxbridge, Henry Bayly-Paget, Earl of 123, 171, 173, 178, 184, 187, 364

Virgil: *The Aeneid* 158, 176, 361, 367, 369
Vortigern 206, 208, 318, 371

Warner, Richard 19–20, 52–3, 57, 353, 362–3
  A Walk through Wales, in August 1797 (1798) 19, 353
  A Second Walk through Wales (1799) 19, 353
  Literary Recollections (1830) 20, 353
Webster, John, *The Duchess of Malfi* 326, 379
West, Thomas: *Guide to the Lakes* (1778) 8–9, 53, 354
William Rufus 111, 283, 316
William the Conqueror 111–12, 283, 294
Williams, Edward (Iolo Morganwg) 354, 363
Williams, Eric: *Capitalism and Slavery* (1944) 358
Williams, Evan (publisher) xviii, 9–10, 11, 14, 16, 380

Williams, Peter Bailey (mountain climber; rector of Llanberis) xi–xiv, xviii, 1, 2, *2*, 11, 17, 18, 19, 35, 36, 37, 55, 143, 146, 147, 157, 353, 354, 360, 365, 366, 367, 372
Williams, Thomas (MP; the 'copper king') 30, 68, 86, 178, 357–8, 360, 364
Wordsworth, Dorothy 20, 28
Wordsworth, William 8, 12, 20, 28, 379
Wyatt, Benjamin (Lord Penrhyn's agent and architect) 109, 110, 115, 117, 236, 362
Wyatt, Samuel (architect) 362
Wyndham, Henry Penruddocke: *A Gentleman's Tour through Monmouthshire and Wales* (1775) 22, 250, 373–4
Wynn, John, Sir (Wynne), 'History of the Gwydir Family' (early 17th century) xix, 205, 239, 242, 245, 363, 370
Wynn, Watkin Williams, Sir (4th Baronet; 1749–89) (Wynne) 300, 376–7
Wynn, Watkin Williams, Sir (5th Baronet; 1772–1840) 302, 313, 341, 351, 353, 377

Yale, Elihu (merchant and philanthropist) 309, 378
Yorke, Philip (of Erddig): *Royal Tribes of Wales* (1799) 307, 377–8

Ingram Content Group UK Ltd.
Milton Keynes UK
UKHW041840180423
420384UK00006B/204